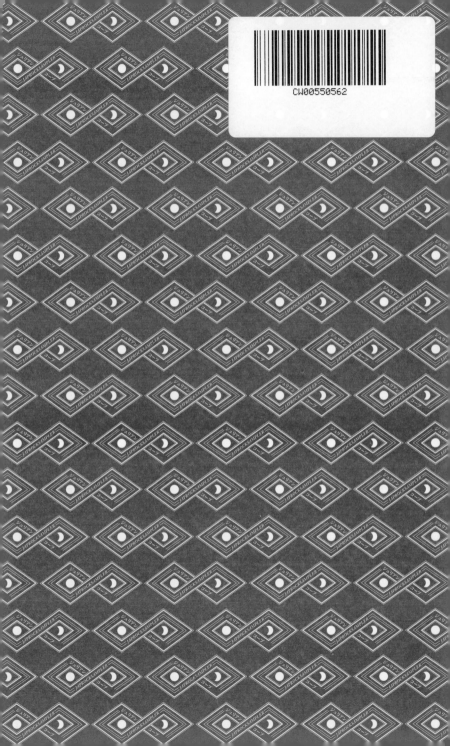

ジュリアン

JAPROCKSAMPLER

コープ゜

JAPROCKSAMPLER

HOW THE POST-WAR JAPANESE BLEW THEIR MINDS ON ROCK'N'ROLL

JULIAN COPE

BLOOMSBURY

To Dorian, as ever

First published in Great Britain 2007CE

Bloomsbury Publishing Plc, 36 Soho Square, London W1D 3QY

A CIP catalogue record for this book is available from the British Library

ISBN 9780747589457
10 9 8 7 6 5 4 3 2 1

Designed in Wiltshire, Reading and London by Will Webb
Printed in Great Britain by Clays Limited, St Ives plc

Bloomsbury Publishing, London, New York and Berlin

www.bloomsbury.com/juliancope
www.headheritage.co.uk
www.japrocksampler.co.uk

CONTENTS

ACKNOWLEDGEMENTS

Designed by
WILL WEBB

Translation by
IKUKO SHIRATORI WILSON

Commissioning Editor
MIKE JONES

Agent of Fortune
ROBERT KIRBY at PFD

Edited by
HUGO DE KLÉE & DORIAN COPE

Editorial Management by the Glamorous
MARY INSTONE

Glamorous Assistant Editor
LOUISE MILLER

Extra-terrestrial Intelligence and Foister-of-Thang
THE LATE TREVOR MANWARING

Lifeline, Sustainer-of-the-Message & Nihonese Vibemeister #1
ALAN CUMMINGS

Gatekeeper, Goader-into-Action and Supreme Cult Excavator #1
DAVID KEENAN

Metaphysical Crony and Futuristic Retro-Thinker
THE SETH MAN

JAPANESE NAMES NOTE: During the past decade, the Japanese have been returning to their old tradition of placing surnames first and given names last. And so, in the interests of cultural correctness, it would have been preferable for this *Japrocksampler* to have followed a similar path. For the purposes of this book, however, Julian Cope has considered that such a line would not be possible because of Yoko Ono's central role in the storyline; her fame is far too great, and her place in rock'n'roll myth far too established to attempt to foist the name Ono Yoko on the public at this late stage.

INTRODUCTION はじめに

The Shamanic Doorway Between

Japanese rock'n'roll music of the past decade has offered the West so much of worth that the time has now come to question how Japan's rock musicians reached this fascinating place. The long-sustained underground careers of such contemporary movers and shakers as the Boredoms, Makoto Kawabata's Acid Mothers Temple, Boris, Asahito Nanjo's High Rise, Ghost and their ilk have – while meaning doodly-squat in their own country – managed to inspire so many new musicians here in the West that I felt it was essential to investigate thoroughly the Japanese music of their childhoods and teenage years. For, just as Krautrock and the John Peel show sustained my own lost generation in those early '70s wilderness years before our own voices could be heard through punk rock, so must the musicians of the aforementioned current Japanese bands have been shown evidence from some previous (and possibly now lost) generation that a heady rock'n'roll lifestyle was still possible in Japan's notoriously anti-hard-drug culture. That these contemporary Japanese bands drank huge draughts from the same fountainhead as we British and

American rock'n'rollers is indisputable, but I knew from my own four tours of Japan that it could be barely half the picture. For those tours revealed to me just how carefully the Japanese thrust everything they discover from the outside world through their own singularly Japanese filter, mainly resulting in a peculiar copy of the original, but quite often bringing forth something magnificent and wholly better than that which had first inspired it. I figured that if Japan's rock'n'roll followed the same pattern as the rest of its culture, then there must be a high percentage of lost genius still awaiting rediscovery. For, as we have seen from some of the wonderful music recorded in the Communist Bloc and under fascist regimes, most rock'n'roll artists of any real worth will, in their quest to activate the Ur-spirit that dwells within them, inevitably cull experiences from vastly different sources.

Of course, post-war Japan was democratic, but its rules of freedom and what freedom permitted were still being set. In this way, Japanese rock artists probably share much of the same spirit of adventure and experience as their equivalent West German 'Krautrock' counterparts, only more so on account of Japan's long history of feudalism, its use of an entirely different alphabet and its geographical remove from the rock'n'roll Ur-source. Indeed, the alphabet barrier has been the main stumbling block in making any comprehensive study of Japanese music. For the poor Western author must rely on hearsay and the personal knowledge of a few elite Westerners whose experiences of Japanese culture – through their work, marriage to a Japanese, part-Japanese heritage and so forth – will see them set up as oracles of a kind purely because no one can unlock the information without first unlocking the alphabet. For our truth-seeking purposes, those 'Nipponised' Westerners are not trustworthy commentators, for they have a vested interest in keeping the mystery to themselves, enabling them to magnify the talents of their own particular favourite artists simply by not referencing those that fall outside their own personal taste. So let me make this clear from the get-go: although I don't claim to be any less subjective about the music contained within this book (having performed on stage with Acid Mothers Temple and members of Boris), readers can – through the large body of work that I have published on other subjects – trust that I am by no means a Japanophile or anything like. But while I am not setting out to whiten Japan's sepulchre, neither will I use this book as a platform to bash particular aspects of Japanese culture. There are many things about Japan that I do not enjoy or even approve of, but here is certainly not the place to snipe at or overly criticise its culture.

As with all of my books, I have written this *Japrocksampler* for several very specific reasons. The first reason (and most important for readers) is simply that Japanese rock'n'roll informs so much of the most interesting twenty-first-century music currently playing that it was abhorrent to me that so basic a problem as alphabet incompatibility was restricting our studies. Therefore, I felt duty-bound to provide some kind of key to unlock that unfairly barred door.

My second reason for writing this *Japrocksampler* is, however, a personal one and concerns my own role as an artist, and a British artist at that. In the past two decades, my commitment to fulfilling this role has grown considerably, and with it has come a dedication to understanding we Britons' place in the wider world. Indeed, I have long considered it arrogant to talk from any geographical vantage point other than my own. My personal experiences of Japan during rock'n'roll tours there throughout the 1980s and early '90s were followed soon after by over a decade of rigorous field research of my own British Isles and much of Europe for the writing of my two prehistoric tomes, *The Modern Antiquarian* and *The Megalithic European*. And what I learned through those travels was invaluable to my understanding of my own psyche and the collective psyche of the so-called British. Call it a Jungian conceit, or dismiss it entirely, but my single most overpowering discovery was of the dramatic similarity of worldviews that three island nations shared: Britain, Denmark and Japan. Each nation was comprised of a loose archipelago of islands, and each group of islands displayed the same attitudes towards its nearest continental landmass. This shared attitude is somewhat patriarchal and consists of, well, let us just call it 'Constantly Disappointed Toleration'. The British, the Danes[1] and the Japanese have, throughout their long histories, continuously acted as though everything would be fine and dandy with their continental near neighbours if only they'd take more advice from us. The British point-of-view can be best summed up by *The Times*'s legendary front-page headline in response to the dense fog that covered the English Channel in the winter of 1911: 'Fog fills the Channel – Continent Cut Off!' But I was shocked, delighted, and somewhat relieved to learn that we British were not alone in these attitudes. Like five-year-old children who, on closing their eyes, solipsistically believe that the world outside no longer exists, Japan has – throughout its long history – been just as 'guilty' of such attitudes as we British. Of course, this could all just have been down to Japan's geographical isolation from the rest of the world. But with geographical isolation comes psychological isolation, a feeling that the world outside may not really exist at all. And so I turned to a study of Japanese music initially because of these 'islander' similarities that I recognised between the British and Japanese communal psyche. But what a study it turned out to be! For the Japanese, in their physical remove from the Western world, have had time to develop a culture utterly dissimilar to anywhere else. Multiculturalism means nothing in Japan, for every outside culture must pass first through the Japanese filter, rendering it entirely Japanese in the process. And as we in Britain are currently experiencing our first major hiccups in our inelegant stumble towards a successful multicultural society, I have chosen at this important time to shine a light on Japan's unique worldview in

11

order that we all should learn something about our own worldview. Sometimes we need to step right outside our own culture in order to achieve the Gods' eye view [sic] of our own actions as seen in the greater context of the wider world.

The Rock'n'roll Shaman Demands, or 'The War against Authenticity'

In 1995, I published a short book about the effects of British and US rock music on the post-war German psyche. Entitled *Krautrocksampler*, the book dealt not with the West German music whose creators had most closely approximated the sounds of British and American rock'n'roll, but instead celebrated those whose recordings most appropriately subsumed this alien music into their own psyche and made it their own; bands such as Faust, Can, Tangerine Dream, Neu! and Amon Düül. As far as I was concerned, bands such as the Scorpions, Tiger B. Smith, Jane and Birth Control were unnecessary of investigation because they'd so successfully aped the British and American sound that there were in their songs few traces of the German culture from which they themselves had originated. These bands had been successful only insofar as they had successfully hoodwinked themselves into believing that sounding like carbon copies of British and American rockers made them more valid, somehow more 'authentic'.

But what greater oxymoron is there than the phrase 'authentic rock'n'roll'? From the mid-1950s onwards, rock'n'roll's screaming genius was its ability to pose as Saturday night entertainment for most of post-war Christendom, whilst simultaneously heathenising all and sundry with its ardent beat and screaming electric overload. But authentic? If there's anything less authentic than 'a wop bop a loobop, a lop bam boom', then I'd love to hear it. When Little Richard pulled that arbitrary sucker out of the air, you can be damn sure he wasn't about to take a jet plane to the African country of his ancestors' birth in order to authenticate the tribal provenances of its Ur-holler … HE was its provenance, motherfucker! And every rocker who conscientiously mouthed that same 'a wop bop a loobop' gobbledegook mystical formula, from John Lennon to the MC5's Rob Tyner, unconsciously affirmed what we all unconsciously knew all along … that Little Richard was a God, a divinity, a shaman blasted from the Underworld to howl his song before Hell's trapdoor swept him off his feet as the Great Goddess yanked his skinny ass back down there … C'mere you!

What could be less 'authentic' than rock'n'roll? How *could* it be authentic when rock'n'roll's inventors were the offspring of African ancestors whom pious God-fearing whitey had enslaved and uprooted to a new continent? By the mid-1960s, black Americans were so estranged from their African roots that even the visionary sax player Archie Shepp saw in his music no contemporary link to the Africa of his ancestors, when he commented that: 'Negro music and culture are intrinsically improvisational, existential. Nothing is sacred.' Of course Negro music contains umpteen sacred elements, but only when it's performed by Africans in their ancestral homeland. Archie Shepp was unable to recognise this, as he was one of those unfortunates whose ancestors had been spirited away from Africa by white slavers and denied the right to practise the religion of their homeland. Along with the rest of the lost Afro-American generations, Archie Shepp was – like the Jews in Babylon – forced to begin his culture all over again without temples, without traditions, with nothing more than oral histories and, quite literally, a New World View.

For rock'n'roll, however, its turbulent birth and lack of cultural provenance were two of the essential elements that were to ensure the form's continued survival right up to the present day. For rock'n'roll's blessed gift of spontaneity was to allow it to die and resurrect over and over in the coming years. And each new version of rock'n'roll – despite its obvious debt to previous styles and its parasitical feeding *upon* those previous styles – would manage to emerge complete and seemingly brand new to each successive generation searching for their own totems. Like the pragmatic Christians who purloined the pagan festivals while simultaneously outlaw- ing and demonising the pagan Gods, the Sex Pistols appropriated the sound of the New York Dolls wholesale whilst simultaneously disparaging Messrs Johansen, Thunders & Co. whom they'd so conscientiously pillaged. In this manner, rock'n'roll has been able to reinvent itself over and over in bizarre and unforeseeable ways. Chip 'Wild Thing' Taylor was goaded into writing his million-selling love ballad 'Any Way That You Want Me' by a fellow songwriter who'd bet that Taylor couldn't write a tender love song using his own 'Wild Thing' chords. Reggae was 'invented' by Jamaican DJs who played Sam the Sham & the Pharaohs-style R&B so loudly over their inadequate PA systems that the skanking rhythms appeared to have turned around from the 2/4 on to the One. And when Jim Morrison appropriated the Kinks' 'All Day & All of the Night' for his own 'Hello, I Love You', he could hardly have guessed that Johnny Rotten would commandeer the same melody for the Sex Pistols' own 'Sub-mission' barely a decade later. The masters of appropriation were Cleveland band Pere Ubu, whose singer Crocus Behemoth admitted to writing their finest song 'Final Solution' simply by singing new lyrics over Blue Cheer's version of 'Summertime Blues'. Soon afterwards, Pere Ubu jammed the MC5's two-chord blitzkrieg 'Looking at You' for so long that it mutated into their own barbarian classic 'Heart of Darkness', though still retaining the Five's original 'looking at you' chorus.

13

Improvisation, Free Jazz & Electronic Experiments

All of the above is the reason why a study of Japanese rock'n'roll is now so essential. For the post-war Japanese not only had the ability and the desire to take what they considered to be most attractive from Western music, they also had the motivation to marry it up to all of the Japanese musical forms that they considered might be suitable. Radical musical experiments proceeded apace, resulting in a variety of unlikely conclusions: light pop instrumentals of the Shadows variety appeared replete with chromatic scales and jarringly atonal Eastern drone notes; behind certain sober album sleeves lurked bizarre arranged marriages of big-band jazz and *musique concrète*; sugary mid-'60s Easy Listening pop hits could suddenly hit astonishing psychedelic fuzz-guitar peaks; the miserablist negative storytelling of the rokyoku traditions returned to popular audiences via the Bob Dylan-led protest-song boom, resulting in the emergence of such Japanese outsider folk figures as Kan Mikami. Combine all of these events with the Japanese love of employing 'Japanglish' phrases – strings of English words that sound 'cool' to the Japanese – and we're in for one hell of a ride, as evidenced by the singing style of Damo Suzuki, who applied precisely that principle to singing with the German '70s band Can, and who successfully inspired a whole generation of punk and post-punk singers to follow him, myself included.

14 To the insular Japanese, the West was a giant wellhead of art, experience and information from which to guzzle like punks gate-crashing a wine-tasting; a gulp of this, a wee dram of that, downing whichever had the most appealing scent. Unlike the British and American scenes, whose musicians were expected – by the press and fans alike – to keep more or less to their own musical turf, the Japanese allowed ... nay, *expected* their musicians and composers to embrace a wide variety of wildly different musical genres. This meant that much of the best and most vitally experimental of Japanese rock came not from rock'n'rollers at all, but from the underground jazz scene, from the musical ensembles of experimental theatre companies, and from progressive university musical faculties well stocked with electronic gear. Furthermore, several singular but highly successful 'experimental rock' projects came together with an actor or pop singer as its figurehead, as in the case of newly enlightened mainstreamers Yuzo Kayama, Mickey Curtis, Yuya Utchida and Akira Fuse, all of whom successfully acted as conduits or gateways between their audiences and these new mysterious underground rock sounds. Just as Italy's Franco Battiato and Germany's Achim Reichel and Udo Lindenburg temporarily waylaid their own successful pop careers in the late '60s and early '70s in order to embark on explorations of the then all-pervading psychedelic musical trends, so Japanese pop singer Akira Fuse sung songs such as the Carpenters' 'Close to You' and 'Love Story' to his teeming female fans, whilst simultaneously championing wan-

ton experimental music on his one-off King Records LP LOVE WILL MAKE A BETTER YOU, credited to the studio ensemble Love Live Life +1.

Foreign composers and musicians arriving to play shows in Japan sometimes caused cultural uproar and swayed the minds of Japan's own artists not because they were famous but because their time was right, as the German jazz pianist Wolfgang Dauner discovered when he toured Japan in March 1971 with the somewhat tackily named German All-Stars Band. In Germany, Dauner's own jazz experiments of the previous four years had ventured deep into Stockhausen territory, and his drummer Mani Neumaier had recently quit to form the experimental power trio Guru Guru. While touring Japan, however, copies of Dauner's Stockhausen-informed experimental LPs FREE ACTION, FÜR and OUTPUT began to circulate around the Tokyo jazz scene. These records, on which Dauner had channelled his piano through ring modulators and other electronic devices, caused a sensation in Tokyo and prompted an offer from jazz composer Masahiko Satoh for the pair to collaborate on a series of experimental piano duets. And although the resulting LP PIANOLOGY was positively tame by the German's standards, Masahiko Satoh successfully re-deployed Dauner's techniques in order to create such iconoclastic *kosmische* avant-garde classics as AMALGAMATION and YAMATAI-FU. The artistic success of these records was such that they were to precipitate an avalanche of similarly wild statements from within the ranks of Japan's supposedly conservative jazz community.   15

Towards a Japanese Psychedelia –
Japanese Rock'n'rollers & Drugs

Unsurprisingly, given Japanese culture's latent respect for authority and relatively recent adoption of democracy, the greatest distance between Western rock'n'roll artists and their Japanese counterparts has been revealed in respective attitudes towards drugs. Whereas we Western artists have, via religious upheavals and social revolution, had several hundred years to grow used to challenging the wisdom of authority, many of our Japanese comrades are still caught up in the overhang of feudalism and remain fearful of drug-taking. Even serious experimental Japanese artists Takehisa Kosugi and Keiji Heino maintain a resolutely anti-drug stance, while Asahito Nanjo, leader of Tokyo band Psychedelic Speed Freaks, was so fed up with having the authorities breathing down his neck that he changed the band's name to High Rise, and thereafter claimed rather disingenuously that his band's lyrical concept 'was to save the junkies … just to say if you want to take drugs, you're going to have to be prepared to die'.[2] Of course, Nanjo's Tipper Gore-like stance is entirely understandable, as it's been informed by the threat of copping heavy drug fines for possession. But such pragmatism locks and bars the very doors of perception that Jim Morrison entreated us to 'break on through'. In this, the Japanese still have a great deal to learn from we barbarian Westerners, for even the superficially nihilistic Keiji Heino will still attempt to hoodwink his audience by naively declaring his music to be as powerful as the psychedelic drugs he has never taken.[3] To claim that one's music alone, however powerful, can do the same job as LSD-25 is more than just insulting to the true psychedelic voyager; it is saying 'I know' when in fact I cannot know. For the psychic and physical effects of a twelve-hour acid trip are as different from the ecstatic oblivion of attending a three-hour show in which 10,000 watts of electric music shoot through one's body as Astral Projection is from trolling the Underworld of the Ancestral Dead. The true shaman will never make such self-deluded proclamations. For those who have been truly psychedelicised know there is nothing that they dare cross off their 'To Do' list, since enlightenment completes us when we least expect it. As I wrote in *The Megalithic European*, such states 'can be brought on by over-meditation, over-tiredness, over-amplified sound and over-medicating oneself with caffeine, alcohol, magic mushrooms, painkillers, amphetamines ...'[4]

When compared to Heino and Nanjo's puritanical attitudes, it is so much more refreshing to learn that supposedly enlightened '70s rockers Far Out were sniffing paint thinners in order to approximate at home what they'd heard took place in Britain and the West. And how much better the Japanese music of the time was because of the infiltration of such crazoid Filipino rockers as D'Swooners' drummer Eddie Fortuno and Speed Glue & Shinki's singer Joey Smith, both of whom ran riot across the Japanese mainland snorting this, inhaling that, and causing the authorities more headaches than all of the paint thinners you could ever wish to have imported. Again, the presence of these 'Western barbarians' proved essential to opening up the overly narrow Japanese mindset. So is the term 'Japanese psychedelia' an oxymoron? No, I don't believe so. Much Japanese music is truly psychedelic in the 'mind manifesting' manner that Aldous Huxley first termed it. It's just that Japan's most overtly psychedelic contributions do not lie on the surface awaiting our arrival; they have to be excavated through patient research. And so the purpose of this *Japrocksampler* is to roll up our sleeves, excavate through the sanctimonious bullshit, and reveal those hitherto unexplored shadowy basements wherein Japanese musical culture shines like a jewel. However, Japanese rock'n'roll is not the new black, and this book is not being written to create a new generation of Western neo-Japrock snobs. My four visits to Japan through the '80s and '90s were quite enough to reveal both sides of the coin, and there is a truth to be learned about ourselves from studying the Japanese ways. But this book is ultimately a quest for the truth. And, as I must restate, I have no intention of whiting the Japanese cultural sepulchre for its own sake, as the Japanese have historically proved quite capable of doing that for themselves.

A Little History of Japanese Music
1961–77, '78, '79ish

As I stated at the beginning of this Introduction, the purpose of this study was to explain to fascinated Westerners the series of historical events that contributed to giving modern Japanese rock'n'roll artists their singular worldview. However, deciding when to end the study was slightly problematic, as the great post-war Japanese musical experiment seemed not so much to have stopped as to have just petered out around the time of punk rock, subsequently lying dormant for around a decade before re-blooming in the late '80s. Looking for evidence in the LPs that I chose for my personal Top 50 would suggest that 1978 was the cut-off year. However, as this is only a preliminary investigation (and Japan is, from north to south, approximately the same distance as from Helsinki to southern Spain), I must most certainly have overlooked vast amounts of evidence. Perhaps 1978 really was the watershed year, however, because that was the time when everyone that mattered cut their hair short in response to punk and the all-pervasive robotising of Western music finally kicked in via Kraftwerk's TRANS-EUROPE EXPRESS, in Japan massively informing the direction of Ryuichi Sakamoto's hugely influential Yellow Magic Orchestra. It's clear that without out Kraftwerk's red lippy and proto-Devo dummy routine, they never could have had the same worldwide cultural impact, especially on the ever style-conscious Japanese, who dumped their long hair and progressive ways for the nihilism of the Sex Pistols only because of the bottle of hair bleach awaiting them on the other side of the cultural doorway (but that's not nearly as shallow as I make it sound, for, as we shall see in this book, Inner Transformation is essential to the Japanese only when accompanied by external evidence of that Inner Transformation). Perhaps there was no real year when the great Japanese Experiment truly hit the buffers and came off the rails; perhaps it did just peter out of its own accord. Certainly, by the 1980s, Japan's music scene would be pretty much all about Technopop, J-Pop, J-Fusion and its all-singing, all-dancing, all-colourful varieties. Of course, there would always be standard bearers of the old ways, but it had all disappeared underground by 1979. And, as we all know, brothers'n'sisters, underground is worthy of proper excavation for it's where we're all gonna spend a considerable amount of our future 'down time'. Ho hum. So, instead of being overly neurotic about locating the cut-off date, let's instead just adopt a laid-back attitude and thank the protagonists of these ensuing chapters for their hefty contribution to our music culture. For I guarantee that a detailed study of this book will have you re-thinking your attitudes to music, art, time … indeed, life itself. Yowzah!

Footnotes:

1   If current archaeological records are to be trusted, then the Danes' full islander status was
achieved only in the sixth century after Christ, when a thirty-kilometre earthen wall-and-ditch known
as the Danewerk was dug across the south of Jutland directly east–west from the mouth of the river
Schlei, at Haithabu, south of Schleswig. However, the presence of this enormous land barrier
certainly achieved its broad psychological aim, as I learned during the writing of *The Megalithic
European*. For, despite the similarities that Danish Neolithic monuments shared with those of
northern Germany and the Netherlands, no Danish archaeologist had bothered to travel south of the
Danewerk to make comparisons. To the Vikings, even an isthmus was called an island so long as a
longboat crew could drag their vessel – fully loaded and with their chieftain standing at its helm –
across its narrowest point.

2   Interview in Issue 3 of *Opprobrium* magazine, November 1996.

3   From David Keenan's own interviews with Keiji Heino (personal communication 2006).

4   Julian Cope, *The Megalithic European* (Element Books 2004), p61.

BOOK ONE

CHAPTER 1
MacARTHUR'S CHILDREN マッカーサーの子供たち

The Black Ships

When four black steam ships of the United States' navy took anchor in Tokyo Bay on 8th July 1853, they were described as 'giant dragons belching smoke' by a terrified urban coastal population who had never before witnessed steam vessels. For the Japanese government, the presence of the 'four black ships of evil mien' signalled that almost 250 years of self-imposed isolationism was about to be forced to a close, more than two centuries during which Japan's all-powerful Tokugawa Dynasty had exhibited such paranoid suspicion of *gaijin* (outsiders) that even shipwrecked foreigners washed up on Japanese beaches were summarily executed. Stuck within this deluded and solipsistic non-worldview, Japan's islanders entirely missed the enormous cultural changes that had, in much of the Western world, prepared for and permitted the Scientific and Industrial Revolutions. And thus, here in 1853, Japan found itself paying a hefty price for its withdrawal from the world, as Commodore Matthew Perry stood upon the forecastle of the largest of the four ships, USS *Powhatan*, its powerful cannon all trained on the palace of the emperor as Perry demanded of Japan's government to be permitted to create a trade treaty on behalf of the US government. That such an important empire as that of Japan could, in modern times, have been dictated to by a single determined naval officer with a fleet of just four ships is as absurd as it is astonishingly true. For such is the manner in which Japan re-entered the modern world, forced at gunpoint to sign a euphemistically titled 'Friendship & Amity' treaty in the most unashamed piece of gunboat diplomacy that the world would ever witness.

Reeling and insensible from the humiliating events that had just taken place in their own capital city, Japan's shamed Tokugawa leaders burned with resentment towards their barbarian adversary. But their isolationist stance had been in place for so long that none had ever considered the possibilities of its being challenged. Indeed, from 1630 onwards, Japan's government had even forbidden its people to leave their own islands, while the small population of Japanese Christians – baptised by Spanish and Portuguese missionaries over the previous half century – were systematically massacred in 1638 and all Bibles burned. During those two centuries of withdrawal from the wider world, Japan's only outside contact had been with certain Dutch and Chinese sailors. But even these few foreigners had been forced to maintain Japan's incredibly strict protocols, promising to remain at all times on the tiny islet of Iojima, in Nagasaki Bay, many hundreds of miles to the west of Japan's main population. Unfortunately for the Japanese, while their military might of the early 1600s had been enough to reject all incursions from outsiders, Western science and technology had, these past two centuries, advanced so far beyond Japan's crossbow, sword and musket mentality that the folly of the Tokugawa Dynasty's isolationist stance had now been revealed by a single gung-ho American naval commander. And when, one year after his coup, Commodore Perry returned to Japan with a whole slew of gifts for the government, the items he presented to the waiting dignitaries were all chosen specifically to show Japan's military leaders how important it was that they trade with the West: a small steam locomotive, the latest rifles and hand guns, modern agricultural tools, a telegraph system complete with power lines, and modern fire-fighting equipment were all notable by their absence in current Japanese culture. Throughout the following two decades, Japan embraced Western change with an unreserved gusto: Japan's first bakery appeared in 1860, by 1869 came the first telephones, thereafter the first beer brewery (1869), the first daily newspaper (1870) and the first public lavatories (1871) – all set Japan on the trail towards modernisation.

Interlocking Multiple Meanings in the Japanese Language

My great love of Japanese music is partly due to the interplay of the lyrics, and the manner in which the imagery works on multiple levels. In Japanese, the limited number of sonics involved inevitably makes a word's meaning dependent on the context in which it appears. Just as the English word 'to' is similar enough to the words 'two' and 'too' to allow the possibilities of a playful multiple meaning to creep in, so many Japanese words allow for an even more extreme form of wordplay. This playfulness is such a central part of Japanese culture that it was employed in the form of a five-line *kyoka* poem written in the early 1860s to explain the shock, terror, chaos and confusion that the Japanese suffered on the arrival of the 'Black Ships'. The poem reads:

> *Taihei no,*
> *Nemuri o samasu,*
> *Jokisen,*
> *Tatta shihai de,*
> *Yoru mo nemurezu*

This *kyoka* poem was created from a complex set of interlocking puns, pivotal words known as *kakekotoba*, which enable the Japanese reader to see multiple meanings. From a literal reading, '*Taihei*' means 'tranquil', '*Jokisen*' is an expensive brand of caffeine-laden green tea, and '*shihai*' means 'four cups'. Literally, the poem reads:

> Awoken from the sleep of a peaceful quiet world,
> By *Jokisen* tea,
> With only four cups of the stuff,
> No more possibilities of sleep tonight

There is, however, an alternative translation based on those same pivotal *kakekotoba* words, in which '*Taihei*' is 'Pacific Ocean', '*Jokisen*' means 'steam-powered ships' and '*shihai*' means 'four vessels', shifting the meaning to the far more alarming:

> The steamships break the peaceful slumber of the Pacific
> A mere four boats are enough to make us lose sleep at night

Japan's Rude Awakening – The Push to 1941

There was, however, something sinister in the manner with which Japan took its first steps away from its centuries of feudalism. For, whereas the West's Scientific and Industrial Revolutions had come hand-in-hand with new ideas such as democracy and dialogue, Japan took only the physical aspects of those revolutions and used them to shore up its rigidly hierarchical social structures. Japanese politicians happily took to the adoption of suits, ties, and top hats, but their outward appearance hid the fact that each was still appointed by the emperor himself. Indeed, every change was still overseen by the emperor, who became recast as the divine emanation of some imaginary Golden Age. Noting the power that European countries had long wielded through their armies' devotion to a single all-powerful Christian God, Japan's pragmatic leaders cleverly elevated the sun cult of Shinto to a state religion, destroying the old tribal Gods by uniting the people under the single all-powerful symbol of the emperor himself as the living embodiment of the divine: a living Jehovah, an Allah of the Far East, unquestionable, ineffable, beyond judgement. The failed Tokugawa Dynasty was replaced in 1868 by the Meiji era, whose arrival signalled a new nationalism motivated by such slogans as: 'Revere the Emperor!', 'Expel the Barbarians!' and 'Rich Country, Strong Army!'

Armed with this bizarre combination of new Western technology and fiercely singular Japanese nationalism, the next decades did not pan out in the manner that Matthew Perry had intended. The Japanese approach was best summed up by the cartoon character Mr Dooley, a creation of American satirist Finley Peter Dunne in the late 1800s: 'The trouble is when the gallant commodore kicked open the door, we didn't go in. They came out!' Hungry for some of the same colonialism that had carved up the rest of the world, but unencumbered by the same changes in social attitudes that had accompanied scientific and technological advances in the West, Japanese armies left their islands for the first time since 1630 armed with all the modern weaponry they could wish for but still retaining their viciously xenophobic hatred of the *gaijin*. The results were immediately terrifying. In 1876, in a move unnervingly similar to what Commodore Perry had forced upon Japan, the Meiji government dispatched gunboats to Korea, where its government was forced to sign a similar treaty of commerce. Over the next thirty years, Japan's warmongering gained them many colonies, mostly from China, which was compelled to cede Taiwan, parts of Manchuria, the Pescadores Islands and several ports via the humiliating Shimonoseki Treaty. But the wider world was forced to pay real attention when, after several decisive naval victories, Japan defeated Russia in 1905. The euphoria of the Japanese can be seen in the words of the nationalist historian Taiyo who, later that same year, declared ominously that Japan was 'destined to expand and govern other nations'.

The first two decades of the twentieth century were indeed like a golden age for Japan, as the world's demand for her textiles, steel and iron created the nation's first industrial moguls. The Russo-Japanese War had shown Japan the need for vehicles on the modern battlefield, and throughout 1914–17, British cars were manufactured in Tokyo as Japan fought on the side of the Allies in World War I. Indeed, the Japanese considered themselves to be honorary Westerners, little imagining that their continued expansionism could be causing long-term resentment within Russia, Great Britain and the United States. And so, by the mid-1920s, with the Ford Motor Company even having established its own factory in Yokohama City, Japan was transformed into the picture of a modern Western state.

Unfortunately for the Far East, and for China in particular, the American stock-market crash of 1929 plunged Japan into crisis, as the depression that followed reduced American sales of Japanese luxury goods to a mere dribble. Having embraced modernisation to such an extent that the country now relied on foreign nations to buy its produce, Japan was further crippled by a sudden huge rise in population. Between 1868 and 1930, Japan's increased wealth had brought down infant mortality considerably, while increasing the average adult life expectancy, causing the population to more than double in size. Now without money from foreign buyers and having limited fertile land available for agriculture, Japan had to act quickly or starve; and its leaders cast their eyes longingly at China's millions of square miles of undeveloped farmland. Throughout the 1930s, great emphasis was placed on the superiority of Japan's military in comparison to her nearest neighbours. Japan's ultra-nationalists preached expansionist ideologies as though it was the nation's destiny to rule the Far East, and China especially. Looking for any excuse to re-enter China in 1931, the Japanese military bombed a Japanese-owned railway in China's Manchuria region then claimed it as the work of Chinese saboteurs. Japan then used this excuse to seize Manchuria, wherein they installed a puppet emperor. But the extreme bloodshed that followed only succeeded in alienating the rest of the world, who condemned Japan's actions and imposed sanctions. With wounded pride and unwanted exports, Japan withdrew from the League of Nations in 1933, and set about arming itself as never before. If no *gaijin* would come to the country's aid, Japan would have to do it all itself. The military mindset quickly spread into all walks of life, as the education system grew increasingly nationalistic and robotic. Everyone became geared up for the glory of Japan and the emperor, as the hierarchical society permitted no compassion for the flaws of others. As the author Yumi Goto later wrote in her reminiscences of pre-war Japan: 'Just as our language is written vertically, so did we pay attention only to the vertical order of society without looking sideways at our fellow human beings.'[1]

By 1937, Japan's belligerence finally succeeded in goading China into a full-scale war. But it was now a war that only Japan could win, as the country's increased militarism throughout the '30s had prepared obsessively for this moment, increasing the size of its army and navy many-fold and conscientiously equipping each soldier and sailor with the best that technology could provide. Furthermore, 200 years of practised xenophobia, an education system that preached Japan's natural supremacy over her neighbours, and a devotion to a divine emperor proved to be a vicious combination. The Japanese advance into China was spectacular in its mercilessness, as vengeful soldiers raped, murdered and torched the civilian population that stood between them and victory. In Nanking, even the Nazi head of the German consulate made an official protest that hundreds of women had been raped and murdered in his consulate gardens, whilst written accounts by seasoned Japanese military journalists Imai Masatake, Yukio Omata, Kawano Hiroki and others showed experienced men at the end of their tether at what they were witnessing, one concluding: 'I stood at a total loss and did not know what to do.' Later official estimates by the International Military Tribunal of the Far East placed the murder of civilians in Nanking alone at around 260,000.

There is no need for further discussion here of Japan's role in World War II, for we all well know of the extraordinary events and how they would unfold over the next decade. But this preamble is essential in order to fix our co-ordinates on where Japan's collective mindset had been in the eighty-something brief years between discovering Western technology in 1854 and unleashing that technology on its neighbours in the late 1930s. For it is clear that the Japanese people had been taken for a ride by their leaders, used as pawns by those hierarchs and warrior overlords, all of whom had no wish to learn the sensibilities of democracy, nor any desire to free the minds of their people from their centuries of muddle-headed feudalism. And so, for the everyday Japanese man, woman and child, World War II would come to a conclusion not when Japan was beaten, but when its people had been dragged screaming into the abyss, doused in petrol and set aflame on behalf of their beloved Hirohito; when its desperate young men had ridden fuel-laden aircraft into the sides of enemy ships in some pathetic and vainglorious belief that their own deaths would save their cosseted emperor from the ignominy of surrendering – once again – to the barbarian *gaijin* hordes.

Occupied Japan 1945–51

As the mushroom clouds cleared over Nagasaki and Hiroshima, the Japanese awoke to a new and alien world. The country's redoubtable – but ultimately kamikaze – defence of Emperor Hirohito's honour had kept Japan's armies and civilian population in a state of belligerence far longer than could have been foreseen by the Allied forces. Buoyed up by an unfailing belief in the divinity of their Head of State, the Japanese had remained expectant of snatching victory over their barbarian adversary until they were way past 'the point of no return'. So far past, in fact, that without the raw materials necessary for sustaining its war machine, Japan had caved in and begun to eat itself from the inside, tearing up its infrastructure to provide materials for armaments, like a man reduced to using his own amputated leg as a weapon.

And when SCAP (Supreme Commander of Allied Powers), General Douglas MacArthur, began to assess the state of the islands in September 1945, the Japanese were found to be on the verge of starvation. Japan's once-dependable food stores in such colonies as Korea, Manchuria and Taiwan (Formosa) were now beyond its reach, as were more recent acquisitions such as the sixty-four Pescadores in the Taiwan Strait, Sakhalin to Japan's near north and the volcanic Kuriles Islands to the northeast. Japan's already crowded main island of Honshu sagged under the weight of its three million returning troops, as bad weather throughout 1945 brought the rice crop down to only 70% of its regular yield and the fishing industry reported a drop to only 60% of its normal catch. The proud but defeated Japanese found themselves with a lower per-capita rate of income than even poverty-stricken Malaya, as government attempts to boost the wartime economy had caused crippling inflation, with fourteen times more yen in circulation than there had been back in 1937.

In an effort to check immediate starvation, General MacArthur introduced official food rations of just 1,050 calories per day, and decided to concentrate his efforts on rebuilding. Cities were a nightmare of homelessness, with many conurbations entirely destroyed; indeed, firebombing had razed to the ground over 60% of Tokyo's buildings, leaving 'vast stretches of flatness, dotted with shacks made of cardboard, corrugated tin, and bits of wood for most of the way from the docks of Yokohama to downtown Tokyo'.[2] With neither customers nor the required raw materials, Japan's car manufacturers concentrated on churning out household goods such as pots and pans, and agricultural equipment; even occasionally being forced to grant 'food holidays' to allow their workers to forage for their own food. Despite their willingness to co-operate with their conquerors, the humbled Japanese were compelled, under the terms of their surrender, to raze all of their military installations to the ground and destroy all military equipment[3] before the reconstruction of their country could commence.

With Japanese *demokurashii* (democracy) as his ultimate goal, General MacArthur's administration (henceforth known as SCAP) began by making a pledge to rid the islanders of their overly feudalistic social system. In 1946, in an effort to promote the wider distribution of income, MacArthur began first by trying to break up the major *zeibatsus* – wealthy conglomerates whose many-armed octopus had for centuries held Japanese society in a stranglehold. Initially targeting such *zeibatsus* as Nissan, Nomura, Nakajima, Okura, Furukawa and Asano with an aim for their total dissolution, MacArthur was to achieve only partial success, as the US authorities gradually recognised that retaining the infrastructures of these massive combines would be essential in order to move Japan forward. Instead, the Mitsubishi and Mitsui conglomerates were chosen as guinea pigs for the new approach, being split up into 240 smaller firms,[4] while SCAP coerced the Japanese government into introducing a number of trade-union laws in a major effort to rekindle in the workforce ideas of an independent trade-union movement. Such ideas had been attempted during the 1930s, but had been constantly thwarted by the old order of *zeibatsus*. The Land Reform Act of 1946 implemented the issuing of financial loans to allow tenant farmers to buy their own land, whilst law reforms throughout 1947 provided Japanese workers with their first-ever guaranteed minimum wages, holidays and sick leaves, maximum working hours and safety conditions, accident compensation and the right to engage in collective bargaining.

In November 1948, the Japanese made another formidable break with their recent past when seven of their most well-known generals were hanged for atrocities committed during the war in the Philippines, China and Southeast Asia. This episode included the execution of Japan's highly esteemed former prime minister General Hideki Tojo, with life sentences for sixteen other Japanese generals. MacArthur also adopted a system of reparations to be paid by the Japanese to nations victimised by their rampant imperialism. However, this last idea was terminated in 1949 in favour of stabilising the Japanese economy in order to bring in a succession of strong psychological changes to the manner in which the Japanese viewed themselves and the wider world. This seemingly benevolent act on the part of the American administration was, in fact, driven by MacArthur's desire to create not a Western-style but an entirely US-style democracy within the islands.

MacArthur began by implementing a new constitution, officially drafted by the Japanese government led by Prime Minister Kijuro Shidehara, but conceived and realised in the offices of SCAP. The constitution reduced the mighty role of the emperor from that of living divinity to a mere 'symbol of the State and unity of the people', simultaneously placing the sovereignty of Japan in the hands of its people. The Japanese received a Bill of Rights and new legal guarantees that legislative bodies would in future be responsible 'to all adult citizens'. Educational reforms were also put in place to remove from schools all of Japan's pre-war rituals that promoted feelings of ultra-nationalism, while the school system was reorganised on the American lines. Ironically, SCAP was so determined to present American democracy in a positive light to the Japanese that all works criticising America were banned. Satirical cartoons that made fun of SCAP were also banned, while any mention of SCAP's censorship policies was likewise forbidden.

The first stumbling steps towards the liberation of Japanese women began in 1949, with the legalisation of abortion and the right of daughters to inherit the same property as sons. Even greater social changes came when Japanese women in bad marriages gained the right to sue for divorce. Pre-war Japanese society had always deemed marriage failure the height of social disgrace, and women were always blamed for such break-ups. Moreover, Japanese civil law did not provide women with support from former husbands. These hitherto unimaginable social changes even allowed Japanese women to become landowners, and young women over sixteen to marry without their parents' consent, as a rigorous programme of birth control also came into being.

But if many of these cultural changes appeared to be happening too quickly for some of the population, negative opinions were held in check by the exotic and attractive nature of the occupying force. Japanese society had long considered such things as eating in public, sitting on railings, and checking one's hair in a shop window to be the height of bad manners. And yet when the newly arrived Americans did such things, the Japanese found it strangely charming.[5] During these early post-war years, the urban Japanese soon grew accustomed to seeing American GIs on their streets, giving them directions and often receiving cigarettes and chewing-gum as thanks. Young Japanese women known as *pan-pan* girls began to dress in the styles of modern Hollywood in the hope of enjoying a romantic liaison with a GI.

Japanese homes situated in cities such as Tokyo, Osaka and Nagoya, or near large ports like Kobe and Yokohama began to pick up American music broadcast by the US Forces' Far East Network. Gradually, as the sounds made by Louis Armstrong and Duke Ellington became increasingly familiar to the Japanese, even black culture and jazz began to develop its own social kudos in this notoriously racist society where foreigners had long been dismissed as *gaijin*. A few Japanese musicians who hoped to earn money at the US Army and Navy bases attempted to play jazz. However, when they found it impossibly difficult, they turned instead to the blues, Country & Western and boogie-woogie. The boogie-woogie was particularly embraced by the Japanese, who adored Shizuko Kasagi's wild voodoo rendition of 'Jungle Boogie' in Akira Kurosawa's 1948 movie *Drunken Angel*. Furthermore, her impassioned performance of 'Tokyo Boogie-Woogie' later the same year gained Kasagi a new and younger GI fan base, through the song's many broadcasts on the Far East Network.

Because of the agonisingly slow manner in which both the emperor and his generals had accepted Japan's inevitable defeat, the long months before the surrender had taken its toll on a civilian population long resigned to their fate, and there was a desire among many of the young Japanese to learn English and assimilate as quickly as possible. Indeed, even though they still felt an allegiance to Hirohito, many older Japanese men and women were not slow to adopt Western styles. Nonetheless, extreme poverty among the vast majority of Japanese ensured that they were still forced to wear the loose-fitting *mompe* and *geta* footwear of the peasant classes, as crouching war veterans clogged the filthy streets hoping to hear the clink of a couple of hundred yen in their begging bowls.

The Japanese Economic 'Miracle' 1951–53

At the beginning of 1951, Japan signed the San Francisco Peace Treaty, enabling General MacArthur's SCAP administration team to pull its occupying forces out of the islands. MacArthur's policies had been so thoroughly implemented that the Japanese were already beginning to experience a massive economic recovery – a recovery that seemed to outsiders to be nothing short of miraculous. If the truth be told, however, certain obvious elements had conspired to propel Japan forwards in this extraordinary manner. Most important to their economic recovery was the outbreak of the Korean War the previous June. For, although Article 9 of Japan's new constitution had insisted that the nation renounce militarism, America was determined to utilise as many of Japan's automotive, aeronautical and munitions manufacturers as was possible against Communist Russia and China. Thus, throughout 1951, Japan's captains of industry found themselves in the midst of a 'special procurements boom' and 'special market economy' that allowed them to make huge sums of money from equipping the American military with aero engines, fuel tanks and various spare parts. Indeed, in one eighteen-month period from early 1950 to mid-'51, the fortunes of Japan's car industry swung from facing total oblivion to making profits of $340,000,000. Furthermore, these vast sums were made whilst watching not Japanese but American soldiers taking all the necessary risks to guard Southeast Asia – ironically pitted against Japan's two most dangerous historic enemies. Moreover, in spite of the two billion dollars that the US government had already pumped into the country, Japan's continued usefulness to America's war machine ensured that her conquerors exempted her from paying further war reparations. Whilst Great Britain, the USA's primary ally throughout World War II, sank to her knees and never recovered from President Roosevelt's Lend/Lease repayments, Japan's outrageous belligerence in Southeast Asia was being rewarded with million-dollar handouts.

Japan felt these effects of capitalism and democracy so immediately that it was almost impossible for them to judge Western culture as anything less than miraculous. Despite the privations of the immediate post-war years, by 1953 the Japanese economy had grown so rapidly and so visibly that the population was earning more than during any other period of Japanese history – and wages were still rising. From jobless and homeless to gadget-filled-modern-property owners in under a decade, the Japanese of the post-war age celebrated their new lives with the kind of vigour that only the newly redeemed can. And for the many Japanese who rushed out to buy Nissan's own version of the British Austin A40, when it first hit the streets in May '53, the car's appearance was symbolic of Japan at last taking her place alongside its democratic and industrialised Western peers.

Membership of Japan's Socialist Party rapidly dwindled as the LDP (Liberal Democratic Party) became the voice of Japanese business. With their desire for closer ties with the Communist nations and programmes that encouraged a more generous Welfare State, the Socialist Party could obtain no hold over a Japanese people who suddenly found themselves earning enough to pay for private health care, private insurance and their own private vehicle. For the post-war Japanese, the so-called American Dream had been shown to be a living and breathing miracle that was to be embraced, embellished and served back to the West in Japanese form in the coming years.

Car Shows, Song Contests & Televised Pro-Wrestling – Japan in 1954

Following the dramatic economic turnaround of 1953, events throughout 1954 soon proved to make this a pivotal year for the Japanese culture and self-perception. In February '54, Japan Airlines made its first scheduled international flight to San Francisco, with further scheduled flights to Brazil and the Philippines beginning later the same year. In Tokyo's Hibuya Park, over half-a-million visitors gathered at Japan's first ever International Motor Show, while the Japanese movie industry caused international tidal waves with the release of Ishiro Honda's classic monster movie Godzilla and Akiro Kurosawa's *Seven Samurai*, which won the Silver Lion Award at the Venice Film Festival.

33

To celebrate New Year 1954, NHK-TV had decided to broadcast the Kohaku Utagassen (Red & White Music) festival as their first ever TV spectacular. NHK's radio version had been broadcast at the beginning of each of the three previous years, but as the festival took the form of a song contest between two large and highly colourful teams of twenty-five singers each, 1954's festival inspired nearly half of the Japanese population to view this outrageous gala event. Like Britain, Japan would prove small enough for such TV events to take on extraordinary national meaning, and many Japanese preferred to watch the festival outside on 'street TVs', set up specially by NHK for those unable to afford their own set. The televised festival was such a hit that it became an instant Japanese tradition, one that has continued to the present day.[6] The following month NHK-TV chose to transmit a professional tag-wrestling bout between America's world champions the Sharpe Brothers, Ben and Iron Mike, and Japan's Masahiko Brothers, Rikdozan and Kimura. This international grudge match was fought over the three consecutive evenings of 17th, 18th and 19th February, each successive bout dragging in more intrigued viewers. And when the Masahiko Brothers finally defeated the world champions, the result gained them instant legend status and overnight stardom across Japan. NHK-TV was not slow to recognise that the age of the TV star was here.

Rock'n'roll Flies in on the Wings of the TV Idoru

Overnight stardom is a peculiar enough phenomenon in any country suddenly thrown into the TV age. For, via chat shows, game shows, news broadcasts and debates, it shines a spotlight on people who appear to have walked in off the street. Show business was formerly the sole domain of those who had worked long and hard at a specialist talent, often developing it for many years before they were even considered good enough to appear before a small audience. Suddenly, the TV age ushered in a culture of outrageous possibilities. A harassed businessman walking anonymously down New York's Madison Avenue could, by the 1950s, suddenly find himself 34 the victim of some spectacular ruse watched by the entire population of America's Eastern Seaboard, as a disingenuous narrator chirruped, 'Smile, you're on *Candid Camera*!' It was precisely that kind of outrageous scenario that the newly TV-ised Japanese of the mid-1950s fell in love with, as Tokyo's entrepreneurs scoured the city's coffee shops, shopping malls and jazz cafés for anyone with the kind of *je ne sais quoi* that could – when thrust under the glare of television's lights – make them appeal to millions up and down the country. A decent singing voice, a face full of character, a unique style or way of speaking; anything could be a hit in the new world of TV.

The Japanese gave their new TV stars a Japanglish name: *idoru*, literally 'idols'. And it was in this atmosphere of 'anything goes' that rock'n'roll first got its break. For, unlike classic entertainment forms such as comedy and traditional popular music, rock'n'roll was from the beginning a barbarian artform whose genius lay in its sheer novelty. Hell, even the worst singer in the world could 'have a go' at singing rock'n'roll. By the late '50s, disparagers of rock'n'roll would attempt to disarm the music of its power by writing it off first as 'children's music'[7] and then, once its appeal was enough to genuinely alarm good Christian citizens, as the 'Devil's music'. But here in good old 1955, rock'n'roll arrived in the seemingly trustworthy hands of Bill Haley, and appeared to be nothing more than a sanitised version of black R&B with a little boogie-woogie thrown in.

In Tokyo, singer Peggy Hayama obviously felt similarly when she released her own version of Bill Haley's 'Mambo Rock' in October '55, little knowing that her recording would go down in history as the first ever Japanese rock'n'roll release. At the time, Peggy was probably too busy lamenting the death of James Dean to be much bothered. For Dean's fatal accident on 30th September snuffed out one of the most potent symbols of youth rebellion. Just one month after Peggy Hayama, actress Eri Chieri released her own version of 'Rock around the Clock', again quite unaware that she was committing the Devil's music to tape. By 1955, Chieri was already five long years into her singing career, and quite past worrying about such things. She had introduced other American songs to the Japanese, including such demonic fare as Rosemary Clooney's 'Come on-a My House'. With hindsight, perhaps Chieri's seemingly innocent 1951 hit version of Les Paul & Mary Ford's 'Tennessee Waltz' contains backward messages still awaiting discovery.

However, if rock'n'roll had entered Japan by the back door, 1956 saw that door really taking a good kicking with the release of Kosaka Kazura's version of 'Heartbreak Hotel'. Known to the media as the 'Japanese Presley', 21-year-old Kosaka Kazura was a hard-knock Country & Western singer who'd formed his own backing band Wagonmasters back in 1953, then acted in macho movies with titles such as *Hoshizora no Machi* (Town with a Starry Sky) and *Jogoku Misaki no Fukushu* (The Revenge of Cape Hell). But it was Kazura's TV performances that electrified Japanese audiences and opened the door for other wild new rock singers like Keijiro Yamashita, Hiroshi Kamayatsu and Takashi Fujiki, all of whom displayed a brashness and a sneering sexuality that drove fear into the hearts of Japanese parents everywhere. It was one thing to see a *gaijin* act this way, but quite another to view it in one of our own. The torture continued throughout the following years, with the arrival of singers Yuya Utchida and the Anglo-Japanese Mickey Curtis, finally hitting the buffers in June '58 with Hirao Masaaki & His All Stars Wagon's incomparable version of Little Richard's 'Lucille'. But all was not right in the wider world of rock'n'roll, for that previous 13th October, just five dates into a two-week tour of Australia, Hirao Masaaki's hero Little Richard had been struck down by ... religion. Cough, spew, splutter, what the?

Death Rattle & Roll

Okay, you heard right. In October 1957, Little Richard got religion. Then, in March 1958, Elvis was drafted and sent to West Germany. In May '58, the world discovered through an interview with the English media that Jerry Lee Lewis was bigamously married to his thirteen-year-old cousin Myra, causing his fee to drop overnight from $10,000 to $500 per show. Somebody had stuck a knife into rock'n'roll, and it was not a well-behaved patient. Perhaps that someone was the beautiful actress Izumi Yukimura. Already five years into her singing career with hit songs like 'Till I Waltz Again with You', 'Jingle Bells Mambo', 'Que Sera Sera' and 'Love & Marriage', Ms Yukimura decided to twist the knife a little deeper into Jerry Lee with 'Hi No Tama Rock', a Japanese-language big-band version of the Killer's 'Great Balls of Fire'. No, that's too harsh. Historically, Ms Yukimura's bowdlerised version was just following a tradition in rock'n'roll that went back to Bill Haley himself, whose incomplete version of Big Joe Turner's 'Shake Rattle & Roll' had transformed it from a drunken back-alley knee-trembler to a teenage cop-a-feel. We must remember that while everyone was slagging Pat Boone for his choir-boy renditions of Little Richard songs, the composer himself was inviting Boone on stage with the announcement: 'Here's the man who made me a millionaire.' Moreover, despite her overt Doris Day tendencies, Ms Yukimura was to prove her dedication to the rock during the '60s with a version of Gene Vincent's 'Be Bop A Lula'. But I digress.

In late January 1959, Buddy Holly joined Ritchie Valens and J.P. Richardson AKA the Big Bopper on 'The Winter Dance Party' tour. On 3rd February, however, the plane in which they were travelling crashed in a storm, taking three more of rock's pioneers out of the running. Moreover, their hurried replacements at 'The Winter Dance Party' – Bobby Vee, Jimmy Clanton and Frankie Avalon – were neither frontline nor were they really even rockers. These were simply teen idols of the kind the Japanese termed *idoru*. Their connection with rock'n'roll was barely less tenuous than that of Izumi Yukimura, and the undead corpse of rock'n'roll lay in the crypt awaiting burial.

In Japan, later that month, the ultra-commercial television company Fuji-TV unveiled their brand new rock'n'roll show *The Hit Parade*, the first show of its kind entirely dedicated to youth music. It was a sensational and instant pop success, the show's millions of teenage viewers virtually guaranteeing overnight fame to all who appeared on it. And although the programme was hosted by former Elvis wannabe Mickey Curtis, he appeared here on live TV utterly de-fanged and de-clawed, clad in a smart suit with neat swept-back hair, his toothy smile and horn-rimmed spectacles reminiscent of Alex Harvey's demonic 'straight character' still fifteen years in the future. Indeed, *The Hit Parade*'s most regular guests would turn out to be not rockers at all, but the singing twins Emi and Yumi Ito, all-round entertainers and movie stars who went by the professional name the Peanuts.[8] As the conservative dress codes of its presenter signalled, rock'n'roll was over.

When Elvis Lost the Faith

When Elvis returned to civvy street in March 1960, he still looked pretty much the same Elvis. But something had changed and he was a tamer Elvis, a lobotomised Elvis, a puppet Elvis with Prince Charles's sense of rock'n'roll. While stuck in the army in distant Germany, the helpless Elvis Presley had watched as his rock'n'roll brothers-in-arms had been struck down one by one. After Little Richard's baptism into the Seventh-day Adventist Church, he himself had succumbed to the draft, followed by Jerry Lee, Buddy, Ritchie Valens and the Big Bopper. All this dying had beaten the King, and he was now the King in name alone. And the evidence? The evidence was there in the material that issued forth from Elvis like a fountain of green bile from the spinning head of Linda Blair. And the evil bunged up the arteries of rock'n'roll's undead corpse so badly that, just one month later, at the end of their British tour, rock'n'roll Gods Eddie Cochran and Sweet Gene Vincent careered off the A4 road outside Chippenham's Greenways Hospital, leaving Eddie dead and Gene for ever limping. It was 17th April 1960 and the authorities were smiling; for the sky was crying as rock'n'roll lay dying. Elvis may not have been hungry any more, but he was scared and he was lonely. In Germany, far from his mother and watching his comrades bow out one by one, Elvis sought solace in such un-rock comforts as the schnitzel and the waltz. Within the year, our man would be back at home in the comfort zone, recording 'Jesus Knows What I Need'. Henceforth, the King would never again dare venture out of that zone.

Unfortunately for the Japanese, with regard to rock'n'roll, whatever was good enough for America was good enough for them. If America was saying rock'n'roll was over, who were the Japanese to say different? However, there were right now in Japan an entirely capable group of experimental and forward-thinking musicians already at work; happy to take any leaps the USA could make, but more than happy to oblige with the fundamental research should it be required. And it is to these pioneering souls that we next turn our attention.

Footnotes:

1   Yumi Goto, *Those Days in Muramatsu* (Publication of the Center for East Asian Studies, University of Kansas).

2   Hans H. Baerwald, 'Postwar Japan – A Reminiscence' (Japan Policy Research Institute 2002).

3   Japan was also forced to guarantee that no land, sea or air forces would hereafter be maintained. However, the coming of the Cold War forced the USA to rethink this policy and allow the islands to maintain 'self-defence forces'.

4   By the 1950s, even this was considered to have been a wasted effort, as the firms reunited as soon as Allied Command left Japan.

5   Yumi Goto, *Those Days in Muramatsu* (Publication of the Center for East Asian Studies, University of Kansas).

6   As *Kohaku Utagassen* has now been transmitted for over half a century, it has taken on the kind of king-making quality that the BBC's *Top of the Pops* once held.

7   Tom Lehrer, AN EVENING WASTED WITH TOM LEHRER (Decca 1958).

8   The closest that that the Peanuts would ever get to real rock'n'roll was on their December 1960 hit 'Dans les Rues de Bahia', which was based on the Champs' instrumental hit 'Too Much Tequila'.

CHAPTER 2
EXPERIMENTAL JAPAN 日本のエクスペリメンタリズムの音楽
(1961–69)

All Hail the Omnipotent Universe

In 1960, the fortunes of Japan's experimental and classical composers were in far better shape than those of their fellow countrymen in the rock'n'roll business. For while Japanese rock'n'rollers struggled to express themselves in a foreign language that was, to a great extent, still being written by the originators themselves, the artists of experimental Japan were already some way along their own path. Unfettered by the shallow restrictions of show-business entertainment and the need to be seen to be 'up to date', Japan's experimentalists were, by 1960, already harvesting the fruits of a full decade of genuine sonic research, much of it having been realised in their own Jikken-Koubou Experimental Workshop, established back in 1951. During this fertile decade they had successfully subsumed vast amounts of Western influences into their methods, while simultaneously integrating Japanese traditional instruments and tonality into their work with the express intention of creating a uniquely Japanese worldview. Moreover, while Japanese experimental composers had avoided too much American influence by setting their sights on the world at large, Japanese patrons of the musical arts had further encouraged such attitudes with the Otaka Prize, awarded for music influenced by Japanese music and Buddhism. The long-term effects of this pro-Japanese attitude can best be summed up by the words of the 1958 Otaka Prize winner Toshiro Mayuzumi, who described his enormous and unfolding 1960 choral composition *Mandala Symphony* as an attempt 'to express a Japanese Buddhist's view of the omnipotent universe'.

In the early spring of 1960, the cultural importance of Japan's experimentalists had, in the eyes of the public, turned another significant psychological corner when composer and multi-media artist Makoto Moroi was invited to perform at the influential and prestigious new arts centre housed in Sogetsu Kaikan Hall. Situated in the Akasaka district, just west of the Imperial Palace, the square ultra-modern concrete-and-glass *kaikan*, or culture building, had been designed by architect Kenzo Tange to replace an earlier centre destroyed by Allied bombs in 1945, and had been unveiled in a grand opening ceremony just eighteen months previously. The new directors of the culture hall were a utopian bunch who prided themselves on being facilitators and patrons of the new Japanese arts, believing that it was essential 'for the artists to protect themselves and their creativity from commercialism'.[1] Enthusiastically received by the public, the Moroi shows were an immediate success both for the artist himself and for the new Sogetsu administration. Viewing Moroi's work in such a salubrious environment not only dignified this previously underground artist, but also allowed him the space to include huge abstract image projections and a special stage setting by the modern theatre designer Hiroshi Manabe. Over Moroi's dramatic mix of orchestral chamber music, spinet, disembodied chorus vocals and electronic soundscapes, a pantomime written and performed by Mamako Yoneyama inspired all who experienced it, and even nowadays comes across to the modern listener as quite as essential and mind-manifesting as the operatic works of J.A. Caesar and Christian Vander's Magma. Indeed, Moroi's work was so well received that NHK broadcast the piece later that year under the title 'Akai Mayu', with a new text written and performed by Koubou Abe.[2]

On 8th May 1960, less than a month after the death of Eddie Cochran had nailed rock'n'roll's coffin lid shut, the extraordinary improvisational ensemble Group Ongaku (music group) made their public debut at a Tokyo show entitled 'Dance & Music: Their Improvisational Conjunction'. It was an event of incredible power. For the six members of Group Ongaku, all students in the music department of Tokyo's National University of Fine Arts & Music, applied a recklessness and true rock'n'roll fervour to their performance. Opening with kitchen sounds, bottles clinked together, wild spaced-out women's voices, hoovers, insane pianos, shortwave radio, tannoy voices, etc., Group Ongaku performed their 26-minute-long 'Automatism' like the

42

speedfreak stars of a Roman Polanski movie. Indeed, the results were like a cut-up soundtrack for the mental breakdown of one of Polanski's weirdest screen characters. Group Ongaku's second piece, the seven-and-a-half minutes of 'Object', also captured on tape that same day, even featured violent assaults on the microphones themselves. Led by violinist Takehisa Kosugi and cellist Shukou Mizuno, whose experiments had begun two years previously as a duo, the pair had gradually introduced their techniques to other like-minded students, namely guitarist Genichi Tsuge, saxophonist Yasunao Tone, pianist Chieko Shiomi, cellist Mikio Tojima and tape manipulator Yumiko Tanno. The historical significance of Group Ongaku's astonishing debut would not be grasped until decades later, but is, nevertheless, further evidence that 1960 was the turning point in the fortunes of Japanese experimental music. But as 1961 would prove to be even more eventful, we must now look backwards briefly, in order to discover the order of post-war events that led to this momentous rent in the cosmic musical fabric …

Roots of Experimental Music 1949–59

Following the 1951 departure of America's MacArthur Administration from Japan, and the so-called 'economic miracle' that followed, the inexorable Westernising of the country was tempered somewhat by a new breed of tough post-war Japanese artists determined to retain the best elements of their culture. Indeed, the musicologist and critic Kuniharu Akiyama had, that same year 1951, founded the famous Jikken-Koubou experimental workshop, with his colleagues Syozo Kitadai, Hiroyoshi Suzuki and the Japanese composer Toru Takemitsu. Uniting these rudimentary electronic experiments with such timeless Japanese traditions as Buddhist *gagaku* percussion rituals yielded immediate results, bringing forth the kind of unsignposted music with neither peaks nor troughs that still sounds relevant today. Furthermore, the Buddhist traditions of improvisation were so inherent in all Japanese music that none of Japan's post-war composers would, when working closely with Japanese orchestras, be forced to navigate through the storms of hostility that greeted their Western counterparts, when relaying their ideas to the equivalent European and American classical musicians.

There was, nevertheless, an intriguing new kind of European music emerging that neither the Japanese nor the Americans had yet encountered: *musique concrète*. Its roots lay not in the work of a musician but a French recording engineer and broadcaster at RTF (Radiodiffusion-Télévision Française) named Pierre Schaeffer. In 1942, Schaeffer had persuaded RTF to initiate a new science of 'musical acoustics', which gave him access to record turntables, sound-FX records, record-cutting machines and a direct disc-cutting lathe. Armed with this equipment, Schaeffer had invented a method of locking the grooves of vinyl LPs, creating rudimentary samples. In late 1948, Schaeffer had concluded his first composition 'Etude aux Chemins de Fer' (Study of Locomotives), which comprised six steam locomotives in various actions. On 5th October, RTF broadcast Schaeffer's work 'Etude au Piano 1&2', which employed the piano-playing of his friend, the composer Pierre Boulez. Public reaction was divided but positive enough to justify RTF sending Schaeffer abroad on a symposium tour, with composer Pierre Henry as his assistant.

In 1949, the pair created 'Symphonie pour un Homme Seul' (Symphony for a Man Alone), a piece of *musique concrète* utilising vocal sounds (breathing, chatter, shouting), pianos, orchestral sounds, footsteps and sound FX, while 1950 saw Shaeffer's first public performances of *musique concrète* utilising record decks, mixers, vinyl LPs and a large PA system. Standing at his turntables like some primitive DJ, Pierre Schaeffer gave concerts that caused such outrage that they caught the ear of the world's music critics. Schaeffer's next composition 'Orphee', a collaborative piece of so-called '*opera concrète*' composed with Pierre Henry, created an even more ferocious press reaction, and the fascinated world was up in arms.[3] Did this unearthly noise signal the end of real musicians?

The German executives and engineers at WDR Cologne Radio quickly recognised the significance of Schaeffer's new artform and, on 18th October 1951, agreed to the building of their own electronic studio so as not to be left behind. That same evening WDR broadcast a programme entitled 'The Sound World of Electronic Music', presented by physicist Werner Meyer Eppler, whose wartime experiences had led him to explore the role of chance and random luck in musical composition. For Meyer Eppler, *musique concrète* and electronic music summed up best what he termed 'aleatory music' ('alea' means dice) which celebrated the seemingly random nature of fate.

With the Americans for once temporarily out of the loop, the Japanese found themselves ahead of the experimental game via composer Toshiro Mayuzumi, who was – seemingly by chance – engaged in post-graduate studies in Paris. Gaining access to Pierre Schaeffer's recording studio Club D'Essaie in early 1952, Mayuzumi found himself in the enviable position of the true pioneer, creating his first *musique concrète* around the same time as such legendary composers as Stockhausen and Pierre Boulez. Fate's roll of the dice would, over the next few years, add considerable weight to Mayuzumi's place at the heart of Japan's experimental scene.

It's quite impossible nowadays to imagine the shock that musicians would have experienced when first hearing the dissonance of experimental music in those post-war years. Karlheinz Stockhausen's 'totally organised' music of this period, even when played upon traditional instruments, often elicited fits of giggles from his audiences, whilst the premiere of his 'Kreuzspeil', with its a-rhythmical, themeless single notes and a particularly loud bass clarinet, was greeted with such howls of derision that the composer fled the auditorium. In May '52, at Columbia University, Otto Luening and Vladimir Ussachevsky's suggestion of 'enhancing' classical instruments with the aid of reverb, echo and distortion was greeted with equal hostility by students. In comparison, the premiere of American composer John Cage's first *musique concrète*, 'Imaginary Landscape No. 5', was a killer success. Like Werner Meyer Eppler, Cage delighted in music resulting from chance, this four-minute work having been created from forty different vinyl records selected randomly by the composer.

In 1953, Toshiro Mayuzumi returned to Tokyo, where he formed a 'composer group' Sannin no Kai ('Group of Three') with the opera composer Ikuma Dan and the Russian-influenced Yasushi Akutagawa. In the daring spirit of the day, Akutagawa spent the best part of 1953 planning a secret visit to the Soviet Union in order to meet his heroes Stravinsky, Prokofiev and Shostakovich. Akutagawa went ahead with his plan the following year, entering the USSR illegally, though only managing to meet Shostako-vich and Khatchaturian.

Toshiro Mayuzumi remained in Tokyo throughout 1954, however, where he created his first unaided piece of *musique concrète*, entitled 'X, Y, Z', thereafter experimenting with prepared pianos (affixed with various implements) and also cre- 45 ating Japan's first electronic work 'Shusaku I'. This was proving to be yet another year of musical 'firsts'. As Japanese electronic composer Joji Yuasa fumbled his way to his first *musique concrète*, so Werner Meyer Eppler's dice-throwing was starting to intrude into and erode Stockhausen's methodology of total organisation. The bizarre result of Stockhausen's about-turn was his 'Song of the Youths', an anarchic elec-tronic piece written for five groups of loudspeakers, whose elements seemed out of control from the moment the piece kicked off.

And so it was in late October '54, on a trip to New York, that Stockhausen finally came to meet composer John Cage, experimental music's Lord of Chance. Having shocked American sensibilities since the early 1940s with his doctored pianos and bizarre percussion compositions, the early '50s had seen Cage's cult grow consider-ably, as he attracted new young devotees including composers Earle Brown, Christian Wolff, Morton Feldman and pianist David Tudor. Like Stockhausen, however, John Cage had suffered huge post-war depression, at times seeing 'no useful function for music any more'.[4] In the early '50s, Cage had sought answers in the I Ching, thereafter attending three years of New York lectures by Japan's Zen philosopher Daisetsu T. Suzuki as a substitute for psychoanalysis. Cage's protracted encounter with Zen philosophy had gradually relocated his own relationship with time (and Western linear time especially), influencing the composer to such an extent that his 1952 composition '4'33"' had been a four-and-a-half-minute piece of performed silence, in which nothing was heard but the audience awaiting the performer's next move. It was, therefore, a far more confident and mentally healthy John Cage whom Stockhausen encountered that October in 1954, so much so that Stockhausen wrote of their time together: 'Cage is the craziest spirit of combination I have ever come across; he is not so much an inventor … as a finder; in addition, he has that indifference towards everything known and experienced that is necessary for an explorer.'[5]

Enter Toshi Ichiyanagi … Pursued by Yoko Ono

It was into this highly charged atmosphere of cultural cross-pollination between Japanese Zen and Western post-war anarchy that the green and unworldly Japanese composer Toshi Ichiyanagi was thrust at the beginning of 1954's academic year, when he entered New York's Juilliard Conservatory to study composition under John Cage. Born in 1933, in the overcrowded seaport of Kobe, on Osaka Bay's northwestern shore, Ichiyanagi's early mastery of the piano had made him the star of his run-down inner-city high school, endless evenings spent as a cocktail pianist in Kobe's tough harbour bars bringing in essential cash for Toshi's impoverished parents. The young composer had, furthermore, reached New York only through nonstop hard work, winning Juilliard's prestigious Elizabeth A. Coolidge Prize and the hefty scholarship that accompanied it. Determined to extract every last drop of inspiration from his time as Cage's student, Toshi Ichiyanagi immediately set himself the mighty task of researching everything available about his mentor. Reading of Cage's own student days under Arnold Schoenberg, Ichiyanagi was initially overwhelmed to learn that the great Schoenberg himself had called the young Cage: 'not a composer – but an inventor of genius'. Thereafter, Ichiyanagi burned with the desire to create works to rival those of Cage himself, afire with the notion of becoming 'an inventor of genius'.

Halfway through his first year, Toshi Ichiyanagi began to date the young Yoko Ono, three months older and a student at the nearby Sarah Lawrence College. Although Yoko and her family had arrived in the USA only two years before Ichiyanagi, her family wealth and cultural connections had presented Yoko with an open door into New York's avant-garde, and she was already gaining a reputation in the art community, not as a great artist but as one who made things happen. Yoko's ideas on performance art were highly influenced by the radical Japanese Gutai Art Association, which had formed the previous year and whose ideas took the form of a journal named simply *Gutai*. In the journals, performance-art works such as Saburo Murakami's 'Work Painted by Throwing a Ball' were described in detail, as was Kazuo

Shiraga's 1955 piece, 'Challenging Mud', in which the artist himself crawled through a muddy field, his limbs leaving chaotic marks similar to Jackson Pollock's wild action paintings.

For Yoko, artists existed only in context with their audience, and she had long agreed with the words of Arch Dadaist Marcel Duchamp: 'I attach even more importance to the spectator than to the artist.' Yoko's later assertion that 'you don't need talent to be an artist'[6] would be exemplified in such Dadaist works as her 'Light Piece', which involved sitting at a piano and lighting a cigarette, and her 'Kitchen Piece', whose sole written instruction that 'the artist should chuck the day's leftovers at a canvas' unintentionally betrayed her rich-girl roots in those austere post-war days. Leftovers? Who had enough for leftovers?

Despite their great financial losses during World War II, Yoko's still-wealthy and highly cultured parents were not at all impressed with Toshi's somewhat servile manner while around them, and begged her to find someone else. This, of course, only drew Yoko closer to Ichiyanagi, and the couple thereafter attended Cage's Greenwich Village lectures together, often accompanied by Yoko's future Fluxus artist friend George Maciunas and former jazz musician LaMonte Young. Yoko soon became intoxicated by Cage's lectures and often wrote even more notes than the fastidious Ichiyanagi.

Ichiyanagi's second year at Juilliard ended spectacularly, however, when he won the 1956 Serge Koussevitsky Prize, and the couple celebrated by getting married with the prize money. When Yoko's parents threw a sumptuous party for the couple but refused to attend themselves, the affronted bride insisted that the couple declare their independence by relocating to an unheated fifth-floor loft conversion on Chamber Street, in Manhattan's Lower West Side. But whilst Toshi agonised for months over 'Trio', an eight-minute-long work for harp, flute and Japanese *nokan* (bamboo flute), Yoko was soon forced to take a job as a waitress to make ends meet, at which point her overly romantic notions of young love were harshly tested.

Throughout 1957, Toshi's epic 23-minute 'String Quartet' presented many problems for his friends in the Juilliard Student Quartet, and seemingly endless rewrites had been necessary to make the piece playable to all. With perfectly bad timing, John Cage chose to unveil his 'Winter Music' just as Toshi's 'String Quartet' premiered. Hailed as Cage's masterpiece, the success of 'Winter Music' pitched Ichiyanagi into a deep depression that his wife could not snap him out of. Throughout 1958–59, Yoko Ono continued to accompany Ichiyanagi to his John Cage lectures, but the marriage had groaned to a standstill by the end of the decade. The couple struggled on throughout 1960, with Yoko's performance art gaining little ground despite her appearance at George Maciunas's gallery. However, Yoko's parents had mysteriously taken a late shine to their proletarian son-in-law, and the older Onos even offered the young couple use of their eleventh-floor Tokyo apartment, should they ever wish to visit Japan.

With the offer of his in-laws' Tokyo apartment ringing in his head, Toshi Ichiyanagi entered New Year 1961 with renewed vigour, as the news came through that Mr Hidekazu Yoshida of Tokyo's 20th Century Institute had organised an international festival celebrating experimental and avant-garde music for the coming August. Even more important was the news that only Ichiyanagi himself had been invited to represent the music of such avant-garde luminaries as John Cage, Morton Feldman, Earle Brown and Christian Wolff. In his dreams, Ichiyanagi had always imagined himself as the poor Kobe boy returning as the Culture Hero, clutching scrolls of magnetic tape under each arm as evidence of his time in the Underworld. And now he intended to return home as the Herald of the Coming Future, as John Cage's musical Emissary of Chance …

Yuji Takahashi & the Continuing Story of Group Ongaku

Unbeknownst to Ichiyanagi, however, Japan's home-grown experimentalists had already started 1961 with something of a bang. In January, the incendiary young pianist Yuji Takahashi had caused a sensation at Nippon Broadcasting's 'Tokyo Gendai Ongakusai' (modern music festival), when his last-minute substitution for the scheduled soloist inspired within him an unparalleled performance of Bo Nilsson's 'Quantitaten'. Watching this masterful recital in the audience was the renowned Greek experimental composer Iannis Xenakis, whose acclamations pitched Takahashi headlong into a long and sustained international career. From now on viewed as a 'leading exponent of the new piano music', Takahashi quickly took his place beside David Tudor and Alfons Kontarsky as the only other pianist truly able to navigate his way through the weight of difficult modern music that was emerging throughout the postwar period.

On the other side of the city, the extrovert members of Tokyo's improvisational ensemble Group Ongaku pressed on with their sonic-research programme. First, leader Takehisa Kosugi had recorded a mesmerizing violin piece composed by Group Ongaku's Yasunao Tone. Accompanied by New York violinist Malcolm Goldstein, Kosugi's interpretation of Tone's hypnotic 'Anagram for Strings' was a bilious ever-descending spiral ski slope into the Underworld.[7] Soon after, Kosugi and Tone corralled the talents of cellist Shukou Mizuno and pianist Chieko Shiomi for the 'Anti-Music and Anti-Dance' symposium at dance teacher Miki Wakamatsu's house in Tokyo. In early summer, Kosugi revealed his own fizzing and explosive experimental electronic work 'Micro 1', whilst later that summer, at Sogetsu Kaikan Hall, the full Group Ongaku ensemble performed at the dance concert entitled 'Miki Wakamatsu's Recent Works'.

Joji Yuasa, Icon of White Noise

In the meantime, important clandestine activities were taking place in the basement of the Sogetsu Kaikan (culture hall). Throughout the late winter and far into the spring of '61, electronics expert and composer Joji Yuasa had been holed up in the *kaikan's* sound studio, slowly putting together his ambitious 'Aoi No Ue', his full half-hour *musique concrète* soundtrack composed in celebration of a Noh play of the same name. Yuasa had by now been engaged in the creation of *musique concrète* since 1954, having joined the Jikken-Koubou workshop as fifth member in late 1951. With his rich cultural background, Keio University education and friendship with composer Toru Takemitsu, Joji Yuasa's music was singular and uniquely visionary. Indeed, his artful 1959 piece 'Mittsu No Sekai' (Three Worlds), which had been composed for the Tokubei Hanayagi Dance Troupe, had cleverly and wholly successfully utilised Messaien-styled orchestration to add coherence to the otherwise jarring and disorientating sounds. Now, here in the *kaikan's* basement studio, surrounded by spools of half-inch tape and often sitting up until midnight, Yuasa and engineer Junosuke Okuyama slowly, sometimes painfully slowly, built up Yuasa's epic from numerous disparate sources. As the *Aoi No Ue* play had long been Joji Yuasa's favourite piece of Noh theatre, he invited his friend, the Noh actor Hideo Kanze, to create the fundamental vocal chant from the original text. *Aoi No Ue* told the story of the imperilled Princess Aoi, and had been written by the famous fifteenth-century playwright Ze-Ami, who had based his work on a much earlier eleventh-century work called *The Tales of Genji* by Murasaki Shikibu.

49

In order to add weight and authenticity to the Noh chant, actor Hideo enlisted the help of his two brothers Hisao and Shizuo, their performance creating the evocative and eerie fundament on which Yuasa subsequently added sounds. Over the next months, electronic FX, stroked wine glasses and manipulated vibraphones were mixed into the performance, which was then fed through multiple speakers and re-recorded. Slowly dripping water was added, with huge spring reverbs creating the feeling of some death ritual being enacted with unparalleled slowness on the granite floor of a gigantic Cretan antron. Birdsong and backwards birdsong were also added to lend comfort and alienation to the final mix, which was then radically edited and extended. By the time Yuasa and Okuyama stumbled out of Sogetsu with a finished master tape, they had been working for nearly six months. But the piece was so masterful and utterly unlike anything else that it, even today, sounds fresh and timelessly exhilarating.[8] Long after the event, the hermit-like Yuasa would learn that 'Aoi No Ue' had won him the Jury's Special Prize at the 1961 Berlin Film Festival.

Mr Yoko Ono Emerges from the Shadows – the Toshi Ichiyanagi Recital

And so we arrive in August 1961, at the moment when Toshi Ichiyanagi, the poor boy from Kobe, returned to his homeland from America after six long years away – returned for the glorious musical recital of which he had long dreamed. Armed with all of our prior knowledge of Japan's already healthy experimental scene, it's nigh on impossible to entirely accept Toshi Ichiyanagi's highly personalised recent claim that 'the fall of 1961 marked the dawn of Japan's era of experimental music'.[9] But there's little doubt that the composer's August performances at the Sogetsu Kaikan Hall were anything less than sensational. And although the Ichiyanagi Recital, as it has come to be known, was the first encounter by Japanese audiences with John Cage's concept of accidental or indeterminate music, the most important aspect of the shows appears to have been Ichiyanagi's own place in the greater scheme of things. For the Japanese accepted the validity of Cage's peculiar music far more readily, safe in the knowledge that their man Ichiyanagi was not only in direct contact with Cage, Earle Brown and Morton Feldman, but was considered by them all to be their peer and worthy representative.

The huge success of the Ichiyanagi Recital ignited a series of similar concerts that autumn, first on 15th September, when Group Ongaku returned to Sogetsu Kaikan Hall for their 'Concert for Musical Improvisation & Sound Objects'. Four of the ensemble returned to the hall the following month to open the proceedings at the Yuji Takahashi recital, on 30th October. With his typical flair and moody performance style, the young master pianist delivered an outstanding performance of John Cage's 1957 masterpiece 'Winter Music' in a ninety-minute recital that held the audience spellbound. Continuing the momentum, Ichiyanagi returned to the Sogetsu Kaikan on 30th November, to deliver a startling first performance of Cage's electronic music. The results were so well received that Ichiyanagi was, in December, invited by Yuji Takahashi to form the New Directions Music Ensemble with himself, experimental violinist Kenji Kobayashi and the forward-thinking musicologist Kuniharu Akiyama, most famous as founder of the Jikken-Koubou Experimental Workshop back in 1951.

With the spectacular success of the previous autumn behind him, Toshi Ichiyanagi spent Christmas '61 entertaining his new colleagues in the sumptuous surroundings of his in-laws' eleventh-floor Tokyo apartment. Yuji Takahashi was by far the most talented young pianist that Ichiyanagi had ever encountered, and the composer took careful note of Takahashi's commitment to setting everything down on tape for posterity while its composer's original intentions were still fresh in everyone's mind. Back in New York, eighteen months previously, one of Ichiyanagi's most difficult compositions, the fifteen-minute 'Music for Metronomes' – an abstract piece employing massed electric metronomes 'in addition to other sound-making objects and instruments' – had caused such head-scratching by the prospective musicians that Ichiyanagi had, out of frustration and misguided compassion, dropped the piece entirely.[10] Feeling far more confident now that he was back in the bosom of his own culture, Ichiyanagi was determined that such things should no longer happen. In New York, his mentor was more than delighted with the reports coming out of Tokyo; hell, Cage's ideas were receiving more coverage in Japan than here in New York. The elated Cage readily agreed to appear in Japan that coming February in a series of shows, to be billed, appropriately enough, as 'John Cage Shock'.

'John Cage Shock', the Return of Yoko Ono, the Sinking of Yoko Ono

When Yoko Ono heard of Cage's impending trip to Tokyo, she took matters into her own hands and contacted Cage, asking permission to open his Japanese shows with some of her own performance art. Cage was more than happy to oblige her. He had a soft spot for this turbulent troublesome imp of the perverse, and had been dismayed to learn of the break-up of her marriage to Ichiyanagi. Furthermore, while her estranged husband had been doing such a fine job as Cage's Japanese ambassador to Tokyo, Yoko had sought to prove herself with several more of her singular performance actions. And while none of the shows had succeeded in anything more than raising the psychic hackles of New York's art critics, Cage was percipient enough to recognise that few so-called artists other than Yoko herself would have dared celebrate their debut performance at Carnegie Recital Hall by miking up the flushing toilet in the ladies' room. Indeed, it was the contrary and unexplainable nature of Yoko's shows that would later inspire her friend George Maciunas to describe this new art movement as 'Fluxus' – forever changing, being forever in a state of flux.

Stepping off the plane into the freezing February air at Tokyo's Haneda Airport, both John Cage and Yoko Ono were giddy with the possibilities that this Japanese trip had in store for them. Cage was thirty-seven years old, yet beginning to recognise that his singularly Zen attitude to time and the manner in which he projected his music into time was slowly making more and more sense to more and more people. Yoko Ono, on the other hand, was, at twenty-nine years old, struggling to convince herself that her art was really her future, and hoping for a reconciliation with a husband whom she'd been more than happy to wave goodbye to twelve months previously.

The reunion between the estranged Ichiyanagis was not as Yoko had planned, however. Indeed, Yoko's feet had barely alighted on Japanese soil when she recognised in her former husband an entirely new and indomitable spirit that she had never experienced back in New York. Toshi greeted Cage not as a mentor, but with the muscular virility of an excited collaborator, and the pair talked almost incessantly all the way into Tokyo. That cold February night in 1962, the crowds that gathered in Sogetsu Kaikan Hall gave Yoko's performance short shrift, yet greeted her husband enthusiastically when he walked out after her performance to announce John Cage. For Yoko, the entire tour was a disaster as Cage's engaging performances and easy style captivated the Japanese press; Yoko's own performances were never more than a footnote to Cage's rave reviews, and mostly even less than that. Lonely and depressed and feeling foolish for having returned to her homeland with such high hopes, the erstwhile Mrs Ichiyanagi took an overdose of sleeping pills and woke up in a mental institution under extreme sedation.

52 'Dinner Party on the Anniversary of the Defeat of World War II'

Underground art in the wake of Cage's visit was, however, raging. And although emphatically the least musical of the hefty New Directions Music Ensemble, art critic and musicologist Kuniharu Akayima had taken Tokyo's post-'John Cage Shock' world by storm with his extraordinary 'Noh-Miso', a 24-minute *musique concrète* composition which Akiyama had created as an accompaniment for four February '62 performances at the Sogetsu Kaikan Hall, by the experimental puppet-theatre group Hitomi-za. Akayima had modulated the sound of Yuji Takahashi's piano as the virtuoso reached inside the instrument's belly to scrape the strings, as well as employing what later came to be standard *musique concrète* techniques: rough-cutting together all manner of disembodied voices, descending bowed-string instruments, snatches of seemingly famous tunes, repeated reversed human coughs, stutters, burps, and other arbitrary sounds in order to create a sinister unease that permeated throughout. Unfortunately for composer Joji Yuasa, whose contribution to the puppet show 'Moment Grand-Guignolesques' featured an accompaniment by Group Ongaku, the recording engineer failed to engage the 'record' button across certain machines, so most of the performance was lost.[11]

Later that spring, Yuji Takahashi debuted a radical and seethingly amorphous piano piece 'Herma' that Takahashi himself had commissioned from Greek composer Iannis Xenakis, who had been lecturing in Japan throughout 1961. After several friends had admonished him for writing something 'unplayable', the Greek composer had phoned the young pianist to apologise for the difficulty of the piano piece. With typical aplomb, Takahashi brushed aside Xenakis's apology, admitting that, yes, it had been a little difficult to play at first, but he could now play the entire piece from memory. At the same Tokyo premiere, Takahashi had unveiled a new piano piece by Toru Takemitsu, entitled 'Corona', plus one of his own compositions, a long untitled piece for electronics and twelve instruments. All were rapturously received by audience and press alike.

Buoyed up by the success of his fellow members of the New Directions Music Ensemble, Ichiyanagi completed his 'Parallel Music', a nine-minute-long electronic piece that was premiered as a radio broadcast by NHK, in October '62. As a sop to his beleaguered ex-wife, Ichiyanagi even arranged for Yoko to record the soundtrack for *Ai* (Love) a movie by his friend Takahiko Iimura. Yoko achieved her contribution to the movie by hanging a microphone out of the window of the Ono family apartment and combining the results with white noise. But the reasons for her still-fragile mental state were revealed through some detective work by her new beau, an English drummer fluent in Japanese named Tony Cox. Checking her prescription one day, Cox discovered that the dosage prescribed for Yoko was considerably higher than the legal limit, and he proceeded to take charge of her affairs.

The success of John Cage's Japanese visit had, meanwhile, also added spectacularly to the manner in which the members of the Group Ongaku ensemble were treated. Although the Sogetsu Kaikan Hall had continued to be a kind of home fixture for all of them, art galleries and museums throughout Tokyo now threw open their doors to the young musicians. At Tokyo's Minami Gallery, Group Ongaku performed Yasunao Tone's 'One Man Show', whilst an evening performance at the prestigious Fugetsudo Hall was billed 'Toshi Ichiyanagi & Group Ongaku'. Next came performances at Tokyo Municipal Museum's spectacular 'Yomiuri Independent Exhibition', while Takehisa Kosugi and Yasunao Tone appeared as an improvisational duo at several actions and happenings, including the defiantly anarchic 'Dinner Party on the Anniversary of the Defeat of World War II'. Taking place at Tokyo's Kunitachi Public Hall, this event caused outright anger among many war veterans and many of the performers were intimidated and threatened by members of right-wing groups. There was, however, no turning back for Japan's new wave of performance artists, and the 'Dinner Party' was just a taste of the anarchy that was to come. In gratitude for freeing up so many Japanese minds throughout 1962, the final event of the year was a special celebration at Tokyo's Asbestos Hall, entitled 'Concert in Honour of John Cage and David Tudor'.

Actions, Happenings & the Birth of Hi-Red Center

If 1962 had been the year of the recital, then '63 turned out to be the year of the action group, as the outrageous performance-art trio Hi-Red Center was blasted into being at the behest of Group Ongaku's Yasunao Tone. Hi-Red Center's members were three young Fluxus artists Jiro Takamatsu, Genpei Akasegawa and Natsuyuki Nakanishi, all of whom were intent on creating 'live action happenings', amorphous events whose only hard evidence of their having taken place at all would be in photographs and newspaper reports. Influenced by Yoko Ono's solo 'toilet flushing' actions at Carnegie Recital Hall, Hi-Red Center had actually commenced their cultural assault the previous November at the so-called 'Waseda University Event', in which the three protagonists had painted all the seats of the public toilets bright red. But now urged on by Yasunao Tone, the three enlisted the aid of other like-minded 'auxiliary members' in order to enlarge the scope of their statements.

The year of action commenced with Genpei Akasegawa's show at the Shinjuku Daiichi art gallery, in early February. Aided by several Fluxus members, Hi-Red Center printed out counterfeit 1,000-yen notes with Hi-Red Center invitations concealed within Akasegawa's subtle design. These were then mailed out in money envelopes. In March 1963, at Tokyo's Ueno Museum, Hi-Red Center staged the 'Yomiuri Andi-pandan Show', in which 10,000 clothes pegs handmade by Natsuyuki Nakanishi were attached to visitors by the artist himself, and more counterfeit 1,000-yen bills were given away. A miniature dinner comprising five grammes of curried rice or seven grammes of spaghetti was served to those visitors willing to pay 100 yen. Throughout the proceedings, Fluxus associate M. Kazakura danced naked to the music of Group Ongaku founder Takehisa Kosugi, who 'performed his Anima 2 by entering a bag and playing an Indian drum inside'.

Accompanied by Group Ongaku's cellist Shukou Mizuno, Kosugi and Tone continued to pursue their musical actions, first at the 'Dance Action 2' at Tokyo's Toshi-center Hall, thereafter returning to the Sogetsu Kaikan Hall for the performance-art festival 'Sweet 16'. However, Tone and the rest of Group Ongaku were highly shocked when, in spring '63, Takehisa Kosugi announced his decision to quit the ensemble. The others petitioned Kosugi to stay, but the composer, having long ago completed his university studies, was adamant that he should turn his considerable experimental-music research into a sustainable career. Kosugi had received an offer of employment from soundtrack composer Matsuo Ohno, who'd just been commissioned by NHK-TV to write and record the music for a brand-new futuristic TV cartoon series entitled 'Tetsuwan Atom' (Atom Boy). With a decent recording budget, access to state-of-the-art technology and guaranteed income for a full year, Kosugi had jumped at the chance to be involved.

Reeling from the loss of his best friend to a TV series, Yasunao Tone now poured his energies into becoming Hi-Red Center's spiritual mentor, suggesting happenings, co-ordinating events and adding his considerable imagination to wreaking further havoc on the Tokyo streets. On 7th May, Hi-Red Center returned to the Shinjuku Daiichi gallery for their '3rd Mixer Plan' happening, closely followed by their so-called 'Promotional Event' at Shinbashi Station Square on 10th May. Much of the late spring and early summer was spent in the organisation of special events and commissioning auxiliary members for special performances. On 15th August, inspired by the previous year's antagonistic 'Dinner Party on the Anniversary of the Defeat of World War II', Hi-Red Center celebrated the similarly argumentative 'Dinner Party on the Anniversary of Non-Victory Day', in which performers visited Tokyo's Citizens' Hall, where 'a great and delicious meal [was] eaten energetically by the performers while the audience observed'. Across the city, on the roof of the Bijitu-Shuttupan Corporation Building, an absurd dance was enacted entitled 'Ror-Rogy', whilst the dinner party came to its ritual conclusion at midnight, as Fluxus associate M. Kazakura branded his chest with a hot iron.

While many of Japan's main underground composers found themselves caught up in these exhilarating street actions, deep in the basement studio of Sogetsu Kaikan, experimental composer Joji Yuasa quietly completed another of his extraordinarily evocative theatre works entitled 'Oen' (A Woman Named 'En'). Yuasa once again summoned up a full half hour of his mind-manifestingly voluminous and fragmented combination of *musique concrète*, Noh theatre and ambient orchestration to tell the tragic tale of Oen, a woman who was imprisoned for forty years during the Edo era. Around the same time as Yuasa was emerging from his months of self-imposed hermitdom – November '63 – Takehisa Kosugi was at the NHK-TV studio on the other side of Tokyo, having taken the evening off from his 'Atom Boy' recording schedule in order to participate in Hi-Red Center's first TV appearance. And as Kosugi once more lay inside his bag performing the solo drum piece 'Anima 2', Fluxus associate M. Kazakura danced and blew up balloons for the TV cameras.

Tokyo Olympics, the Government Sues Hi-Red Center, but Yoko Gets Her Life Back

While the wider world would be fixing its gaze on Japan's forthcoming 1964 Tokyo Olympics, the microcosmic Japanese underground clanged with the deafening news that the Tokyo Metropolitan Police had, on 8th January, arrested Hi-Red Center's Genpei Akasegawa in connection with his production of counterfeit 1,000-yen notes. But when the 27th January edition of the Asaki newspaper accused Akasegawa outright of being a forger, Hi-Red Center inaugurated a protest action against the publication. Writing in the Japanese daily *Nippon Dokusho* two weeks later, Akasegawa explained his actions in a piece headlined: 'My Counterfeit 1000Y As a Problem to Capitalist Realism'. But while Akasegawa's problems appeared too absurd to the outside world to have any possible serious outcome, the ramifications of the artist's actions were becoming increasingly worrying to Yasunao Tone, himself almost a generation older than the members of Hi-Red Center and cognisant of the bigger picture. Mindful of Akasegawa's refusal to take his situation seriously, Tone began to compile a coherent testimony of all Hi-Red Center's previous activities in order to explain the alleged counterfeiting within the original context of the group's overall spirit of intentions. Tone's contemporary in experimental music, Toshiro Mayuzumi, had in the meantime just won himself the prestigious Mainichi Music Prize with his electronic-music soundtrack for the forthcoming movie *Tokyo Olympic*.[12] Its extremely high profile virtually handed Mayuzumi an international career, for within the month the composer had been commissioned by American director John Huston to write the soundtrack music for his impending movie epic *The Bible*.

Also in America, a devotee of John Cage named Terry Riley had just released his insidious orchestral drone-a-thon IN C to universal acclaim, whilst Stockhausen had made the momentous decision to bring his electronic music to the concert hall with a reduced-in-size ensemble modishly named the Stockhausen Group, 'the members of which performed on volume knobs, ring modulators, shortwave radios, and a few acoustic instruments. Instead of creating traditional scores, Stockhausen drew symbolic charts with descriptions of the processes to be realized.'[13] Back in Tokyo, Toshi Ichiyanagi completed his experimental piece for orchestra and tape recorder, entitled 'Life Music',[14] and the convalescing Yoko Ono contributed vocals to her ex-husband's soundtrack for the movie *AOS*, by director Yoji Kuri. Yoko was by this time married to her temporary saviour, the young drummer Tony Cox, and the couple planned that she should soon resume her performance-art career in New York.

The fortunes of Hi-Red Center, however, remained in the balance throughout 1964, as Yasunao Tone petitioned the three members to keep their actions somewhat toned down. Taking Tone's pleas as literally as they could, Hi-Red Center immediately announced that their forthcoming event 'The Great Panorama Show' would take place at the Naiqua Gallery between 12th and 17th June. Lines of puzzled visitors remained shut out of the locked gallery for the entire five days, while, in the final hour of the final day, the beleaguered Akasegawa released a single cockroach on to the gallery floor as a symbolic gesture of his new restrictions.

Yasunao Tone was also feeling the walls closing in now that his erstwhile cohort Takehisa Kosugi was ensconced in the NHK-TV recording studio twenty hours per day. As nursemaid of Hi-Red Center, Tone felt the loss of Group Ongaku more acutely than anyone else in the ensemble. For, although Kosugi had been around for several of the early Hi-Red Center actions, it was becoming increasingly clear to Tone that Kosugi's cartoon-series project was going to be a long and protracted affair. And so, as the whole of Japan geared up for the 10th October opening ceremony of the Tokyo Olympics, Hi-Red Center – urged on by an ever more belligerent Yasunao Tone – geared up for their next action, also to be held on opening-ceremony day.

As the first Asian nation to win the honour of hosting the Olympic games, Japan's Olympic committee had chosen a highly symbolic (and highly controversial) athlete to light the Olympic flame. For Yoshinori Sakai was neither old enough nor good enough to be a part of Japan's Olympic team, having been selected for the honour of lighting the flame purely because he'd been born in Hiroshima, on 6th August 1945, the very day that the Allies had dropped the atomic bomb. Shortly after the opening ceremony, Hi-Red Center performed their spectacular 'Roof Event' aka 'The Ochanomizu Drop' in which the three protagonists stood on the flat roof of Tokyo's Ikenobo Building and threw caution to the wind, along with several pairs of trousers, shirts, umpteen shoes and a full trunk of books, all of which bombarded bewildered passersby as they went quietly about their business several storeys below. Thereafter, the debris was collected, labelled and stored in the baggage room of Ochanomizu railway station, while Tone breathed a sigh of relief that no innocent had been injured by the fusillade of random laundry.

Six days later, on 16th October, Hi-Red Center concluded their yearly list of actions with what would become one of the Fluxus movement's most famous art pieces: 'The Cleaning Event' aka 'Be Clean!' Waking early, they dressed in white coats, white gloves, surgical masks, blind-man's spectacles and armbands printed with Hi-Red Center insignia. At 9.30 a.m., everyone gathered at one end of Namiki Street, in Tokyo's frantic Ginza district, where (according to the action group's original printed directions) 'Performers used dusters, floor brooms, house-cloths, scrubbing brushes … cleaning fluid, soap, deodorizer, alcohol, etc. to clean the streets which they did very gently as they would their own rooms'. The action complete, Namiki Street was then marked with posters that announced: 'this place already cleaned'.

A Cultural Exchange of Sorts (1965–66)

While the Japanese pop music of 1965 still remained in thrall to the West, the singular nature of Japan's experimental culture was increasingly gaining interest in Europe and the USA, where Hi-Red Center was receiving plaudits from New York's Fluxus artists, and several improvisational ensembles were at last picking up where the now-defunct Group Ongaku had left off. However, whilst Messrs Tone, Kosugi and the rest of the Group Ongaku ensemble had taken their inspiration from such Japanese institutions as Buddhist *gagaku* percussion ceremonies and the rituals of Noh theatre, those Western musicians at the forefront of improvised music were mostly jazz guys who had been around to experience the pioneering late '50s work of Cecil Taylor, Ornette Coleman and Sun Ra. However, as jazz had its roots in the performance of popular songs of the day, these players tended to associate improvisation mostly with having the confidence to stray from an original melody, an essential element entirely absent in Japanese improvisation. And so, when drummer John Stevens formed his Spontaneous Music Ensemble in 1965, the Londoner's choice of musical cohorts ensured that whatever first burst forth from the ensemble would always be rooted in jazz before devolving into the kind of abstract and buzzing atonal soundscapes that the players themselves affectionately termed 'insect improv'.[15] The same could be said of other free ensembles of the '65 generation, especially Rome's Musica Elettronica Viva, formed by seven American ex-pats, London's AMM, who played 'Spontaneous Underground' sessions at the Marquee Club; and Chicago's portentously named Association for the Advancement of Creative Musicians, formed by Anthony Braxton, Famoudou Don Moye and future Miles Davis drummer Jack DeJohnette. The most notable example of this 'devolved jazz' approach occurred –

58   again in '65 – on side two of Patty Waters's debut LP for ESP-Disk PATTY WATERS SINGS, on which the young jazz singer abstractedly repeated the traditional tune 'Black Is the Colour of My True Love's Hair' for thirteen avant-garde minutes of apoplexy. So extreme was Waters's inconsolable and demented femaelstrom that it gained instant legend status within underground art communities across the world, and would become the blueprint for Yoko Ono's subsequent 'singing' style.

But still these improvisational ensembles of the West required time for their musical pieces to descend into the primal murk of abstraction. Rarely if ever did they commence with the same emphatic amphibian confidence that Group Ongaku had always appeared proud to exhibit. Ironically, however, Japan's own jazz community was so rooted in Western culture that its musicians exhibited no desire whatsoever to follow Group Ongaku's improvisational lead, at least, that is, not until the Spontaneous Music Ensemble and their ilk had validated such free actions. Indeed, most of the Japanese jazz scene was currently following the lead of their most popular player, saxophonist Sadao Watanabe, whose versions of such Top 40 hits as Jimmy Smith's 'The Cat' and Peter, Paul & Mary's 'Trains and Boats and Planes' had made him into a big star. Jazz was by now a huge business in Japan, and such top players as Watanabe and trumpeter Terumasa Hino had also become popular TV personalities, having long before eschewed the more radical free-jazz approach in favour of the guaranteed chart smashes that Watanabe in particular had scored with his massive LP SADAO WATANABE PLAYS BACHARACH & THE BEATLES. That Miles Davis himself had rejected the free-jazz route was a guarantee of its experiments receiving short shrift, at least initially, in a country where the sharply dressed trumpeter was considered to be the ultimate icon of existentialist cool.

By 1965, however, the free-jazz experiments of Sun Ra, John Coltrane and Albert Ayler had caused enough of a schism to develop among Japan's jazz community for the arrival of scratchy meltdown outfits such as AMM and the Spontaneous Music Ensemble to have a considerable knock-on effect even among Japan's most seasoned jazz veterans. Spurred on not so much by the music but by the wayward attitudes of these Occidental broadsiders, Tokyo jazzer Toshiyuki Miyami of the New Herd Orchestra brought together the Modern Jazz Trio Club in late 1965. Inspired by the idea of consciously and intellectually moving jazz forward out of its cosy post-'50s night-club-entertainment cul de sac, Miyami envisioned the Modern Jazz Trio Club not as a band, but as a kind of 'Free Thinkers' Union' in which the most visionary and open-minded of jazz composers could write together, discussing arrangement methods and conceptualising generally about the route forwards. Completed by heavyweight jazz composers Keitaro Miho, Norio Maeda and Kiyoshi Yamaya, the Modern Jazz Trio Club would come to exert considerable influence, not only on the Japanese jazz community, but also on the country's entire experimental-music scene of the late '60s and early '70s. However, like the 'composer group' Sannin no Kai (Group of Three) that composers Toshiro Mayuzumi, Ikuma Dan and Yasushi Akutagawa had formed back in 1953, Miyami's Modern Jazz Trio Club would remain for ever a back-room project, a sonic Masonic lodge of movers and hip shakers.

i) Ichiyanagi in N.Y. for the Bell Armoury Show meets Tadanori Yoko'o

By the mid-'60s, certain Japanese ideas were slowly penetrating the West's superiority complex. And, as Toshi Ichiyanagi's erstwhile colleague Yuji Takahashi jetted from his Berlin post with Xenakis to a new scholarship in San Francisco, Ichiyanagi himself flew to New York for the first time since he'd returned to Japan as John Cage's emissary half a decade before. Ichiyanagi had much to be happy about. Tokyo's Victor Records had recently dedicated an entire side of vinyl to the composer's new untitled seventeen-minute electro-acoustic work on the double-LP ORCHESTRAL SPACE, a project that also celebrated the work of Toru Takemitsu, Joji Yuasa and Takahashi himself. Furthermore, new Ichiyanagi music now appeared on a sumptuous New York vanity project shared with Yoji Kuri and ex-wife Yoko Ono. This limited edition of 300 red vinyl 7" EPs (with an accompanying book) was released on the tiny Greenwich Village imprint Salon de Coco, whose wealthy owner had now graciously invited Ichiyanagi over to New York for the EP's promotion. Quickly sucked back into the New York street life that he'd fled over five years before, Ichiyanagi attended 'Nine Evenings of Art in the Armoury', a cultural experiment sponsored by the Bell Laboratories and co-ordinated by an exciting new company E.A.T. (Experiments in Art & Technology). E.A.T. was run by Bell engineer Bill Kluver, a Ph.D. in electrical engineering, long-time devotee of William Burroughs and cohort of Andy Warhol. Kluver believed that heavy technology should be turned over to the art community in order to investigate its potential artistic purposes. And so, with the class of the true cultural visionary, Kluver rented out the New York armoury for nine evenings during the summer of '66, during which time hundreds of New York artists, Andy Warhol and Jasper Johns among them, came to see for themselves where heavy technology could take them.

Ichiyanagi was still reeling from the after-effects of the Armoury Show when the Rockefeller Trust invited him to the Museum of Modern Art for an exhibition by the young Japanese artist Tadanori Yoko'o. Unlike the majority of modern artists, Yoko'o had eschewed pop art in favour of a kind of radical traditionalism, and Ichiyanagi was amazed at the manner in which Yoko'o had integrated famous photos into cartoon settings, juxtaposing icons such as Yukio Mishima next to lactating women, and America's President Lyndon Johnson bestriding mountains – the world in one hand and a fighter plane in the other. Furthermore, Yoko'o's highly original psychedelic style had turned him into a kind of hippie godfather figure among many young Japanese. When Ichiyanagi met the artist later that evening, the two got along so well that Yoko'o's wife invited the composer to stay at their New York apartment. And for the next couple of weeks, Mr and Mrs Yoko'o watched their houseguest bloom into a psychedelicised hippie. The previously stuffy Ichiyanagi dumped his conservative suits in favour of rococo gear, adopted circular shades in place of his horn rims and spent hours every day mesmerised by the endless rotations of a clockwork carousel in the guest room. Every day, he returned from his Manhattan wanderings with a new psychedelic tie, while his hosts became convinced that the composer was tripping for the entire duration of his stay with them. Indeed, these effects on Ichiyanagi were so notable that they were to precipitate in him an artistic change such that many of his oldest friends, John Cage and ex-wife Yoko Ono included, felt that they hardly knew him any more.

ii) NHK invites Stockhausen to Japan

Continuing the game of metaphysical musical chairs, NHK Broadcasting, with typical aplomb, chose to celebrate their fiftieth anniversary by commissioning Karlheinz Stockhausen to spend February to April '66 in their Tokyo studio creating two new electronic works. Like many Western artists, Stockhausen found Japanese culture so entirely overwhelming that he initially felt as though he had fetched up on a different planet. The jet lag alone cost him a week's work, and, for a workaholic such as Stockhausen, this was emotionally disastrous. Thereafter, the composer found himself so drawn to this alien land that he became, in his own words, 'more Japanese than the Japanese'. Just as John Cage's encounter with Zen philosophy had entirely altered the composer's relationship with time, so Stockhausen's months in Japan re-orientated his own response to time and the manner in which we pass through it. Attending one of Japan's slowly unfolding Buddhist rituals, a day-long event, Stock-hausen was forced to stop fidgeting and allow the drama of the sky above him to take hold. This was a revelation to the uptight composer. Stockhausen immediately recog-nised that the seemingly endless Japanese tea ceremonies were not for the drinking, but for the process of the ritual itself. Thereafter, he devoted much of his time in Japan to exploring traditional Noh dramas, intrigued by their sudden tempo shifts and bizarre time transitions; he watched spellbound as *gagaku* percussionists performed their highly stylised but mainly rhythmless ceremonial music, these Japanese con-ventions challenging his most basic ideas on the uses of percussion. Overwhelmed by all of this and humming with the possibilities, Stockhausen was inspired to create a new kind of music, what he would come to call 'Telemusick', which the composer described as 'a music of the whole world, of all countries and races'.[16]

Stockhausen quit Japan in late April 1966, just eight weeks before the Beatles hit Tokyo. But before he left, the composer made a point of paying a visit to that same Japanese Zen philosopher who had, over a decade before, radically altered John Cage's worldview. Now over ninety years old, Daisetsu T. Suzuki was fascinated by Stockhausen's deep concerns about the manner in which his own music was made. Stockhausen confessed to Suzuki that new technology and his own fascination with it forced the composer to create sound in 'a very artificial way'. Suzuki, however, would have none of it, accusing Stockhausen of creating his own problems by draw-ing too many arbitrary Western lines between electronic technology and traditional acoustic ways of composing. From the Zen philosopher's point of view, Stockhausen was still on course and staying absolutely true to his artistic convictions: 'I cannot understand why you say this is artificial and this is natural ... It would only be artificial if you went against your inner conviction. You're being completely natural in the way you do it.'

iii) George Maciunas invites Hi-Red Center to New York

In New York, during 1965, several Fluxus artists acknowledged their debt to Hi-Red Center's punk ethos by re-enacting the trio's 'Cleaning Event', while George Maciunas issued a highly detailed and annotated Tokyo Street Map of Hi-Red Center's various activities from his influential Fluxus Publishing Company. This high-level recognition from the cultural mothership came none too soon for the beleaguered Genpei Akasegawa, whose status as a probable professional counterfeiter increased with each new article that appeared in Japan's press. For while the art world was happy to turn Akasegawa's predicament into an artistic *cause célèbre*, the Tokyo District Court was preparing its case for his prosecution. The case was, furthermore, so singular that Yasunao Tone was forced to become the co-author of Akasegawa's opening defence statement, as the artist's chief defence lawyer readily admitted to having extreme difficulties in recognising the subtleties involved. Feeling the eyes of the popular press upon them at all times, the three members of Hi-Red Center were, therefore, highly delighted to accept George Maciunas' invitation to New York. And on 4th June 1966, they performed their 'Hi-Red Center Fluxclinic' at Manhattan's Waldorf-Astoria Hotel, in which arbitrary details were taken from a pre-planned list of Fluxus patrons and integrated into a fake health report for which Maciunas himself designed a chart of 'pseudo-medical records' as part of the presentation piece.

Most peculiarly for these anti-traditionalist street punks of Hi-Red Center, the three found themselves, at the height of a scorching Manhattan summer, engaged in a bizarre piece of traditionalism. At the behest of grand master Maciunas, Hi-Red Center re-enacted their now legendary 'Street Cleaning Event' at Grand Army Plaza, between 58th Street and 8th Avenue. Like the punks they undoubtedly were, however, this refusenik trio re-drew their original brief somewhat by painting an area of the plaza in their trademark red, although this was rather poorly represented in the single commemorative photograph taken by Maciunas himself. Yasunao Tone, meanwhile, was delighted by the international press response to Hi-Red Center's New York actions, and believed it was essential to capitalise on this increased level of interest. And so, in the autumn of 1966, Tone organised the 'Biogode Process Music Festival', the world's first computer-arts festival. Tone then used the event as a platform on which to showcase his new computer-art group Team Random, a musical collective brought together to perform Tone's compositions on programmed Univac mainframes.

The Coalescing of Cultures Begins

The overwhelming result of such important 1966 events as the Bell Armoury Show, the Hi-Red Center actions, Tone's computer-arts festival and both the Beatles' and Stockhausen's high-visibility presence in Japan, was that the invisible barriers that had previously existed between technology, popular culture, serious art and abstract action art all began to break down. If the Bell Laboratories were courting Andy Warhol's opinion, who was anyone else to doubt his cultural credentials? If it was possible in New York to buy a highly detailed Hi-Red Center street map of fleeting moments enacted thousands of miles away in Tokyo, then the map itself (and the effort that went into plotting it) was evidence enough of the validity of those events. The artist, the performer, the poet and the storyteller, the singer and musician, the magician, the illusionist: all shared their beginnings as the shaman/priest of the tribe. Far back in humanity's nomadic days, when rituals were conceived on the hoof as it were, the temple had rarely needed to be anything more than a particularly significant and time-honoured tribal location: a great tree where great-grandfather had had a meaningful dream; a natural gorge where the echo seemed to repeat everything spoken by the shaman's voice; an isthmus of land bisected by two fast-flowing rivers; anywhere the shaman could contain the family band or tribe long enough to show them the illusion that they were being addressed by the Gods.

In the latter part of the mid-'60s, as Western secular culture increasingly turned its back on organised religion, this breaking-down of cultural barriers not only prepared the minds of the general population to receive this information from new and unexpected sources such as entertainers and adventurers, but it also opened up the minds of the artists themselves, allowing the greatest among them to glimpse just what could be achieved were they only to let themselves fly unfettered. For Westerners, the priests were no longer in churches – almost anywhere but. The priests were now folk singers, they were rock singers, they were moulders of the new technologies, they were sci-fi writers, they were beat poets, they were Olympic athletes, they were hanging in space on the end of a rope. While Buzz Aldrin space-walked behind his Gemini craft, the Russian cosmonauts even made heroes of humanity's oldest ally, as Laika the German shepherd returned in good health from her Soyuz mission. Furthermore, the swinging doors between cultures almost came off their hinges that summer of '66, as the World Cup brought on to the world's stage such dazzling mythical beings as Portugal's Eusebio and Brazil's Pele. And as 1966 tumbled to its juddering conclusion, the most symbolic meeting of the entire period took place on 9th November 1966, when Beatle John visited Yoko Ono's exhibition 'Unfinished Paintings and Objects' at London's Indica Gallery.

Standing on the Verge of Getting It On

While the result of this mighty cultural cross-pollination created a slamming, humping, bucking bronco of action and chaotic creativity in such cities as Swinging London, New York, Los Angeles and San Francisco, 1967 remained something of a cosmic in-between time in Tokyo and much of the rest of the world. And so, while Yoko Ono was appearing alongside Pink Floyd, the Move, AMM, John's Children, Syn and the Soft Machine on the bill of 'The 14-Hour Technicolour Dream' at London's Alexandra Palace, performing her 'Cut Piece', in which members of the audience were invited to remove her clothes with scissors, her ex-husband Toshi Ichiyanagi was delivering the first musical evidence of his psychedelically informed New York experiences with a voice-and-computer piece entitled 'Extended Voices'. However, without the wherewithal to act upon the new psychedelic era, drug-free Japan could only imagine what an acid trip would be like. And without psychedelic drugs, truly psychedelic music just couldn't be made. The only Japanese then on acid were those abroad in the West. Moreover, despite the Beatles' Japanese tour of the previous year having set the nation alight, the fallout was disappointingly far short of artistic expectations, being little more than a field day for entrepreneurs, as hundreds of groups had formed with the sole intention of aping their heroes (see Book One, Chapter Four).

Japanese pop in '67 was in stasis; three years behind the times with a chart filled to the brim with Herman's Hermits wannabes, Animals-alikes and bands with bad cases of the Beatles. And yet Beatle John was looking to the underground and the experimental for his own inspiration. Indeed, Lennon was constantly on the phone to Karlheinz Stockhausen throughout '67, according to the composer himself.[17] The circle was completed, however, when, as the Visiting Professor of Composition at San Francisco's University of Davis, even Stockhausen became enamoured of the burgeoning psychedelic scene when he heard Frank Zappa & the Mothers and Jefferson Airplane, and met the Grateful Dead in summer 1967, famously remarking of psychedelic music: 'It really blows my mind.'[18] In November '67, the first fruits of Stockhausen's Japanese vision of 'a music of the whole world, of all countries and races' could be experienced at the premiere of his incredible 'Hymnen', a rich musique-concrète-cum-sample-montage of the world's most famous national anthems as filtered through radio sets and various other receivers.

Also in 1967, Group Ongaku's Takehisa Kosugi emerged at last from his three years of creating electronic TV scores, hungry for the rumbling activism that his erstwhile colleague Yasunao Tone had engaged upon with Hi-Red Center. On an even more positive note, Hi-Red Center's Genpei Akasegawa, although found guilty of conspiracy to counterfeit money, was released back into the community on 24th June, having been sentenced to serve just one year's probation.[19] This was an outstanding result for Akasegawa, who was by now recognised as a culture hero among both the underground art community and the disillusioned young longhairs who had begun to congregate in Tokyo's Shinjuku area. If the anarchic actions of Hi-Red Center were being taken seriously in the art-houses of New York, then they were of even more vital importance to Japan's new wandering futen generation, whose own parents had been the brainwashed footfolk of Emperor Hirohito's war machine. And while the saccharine clamour of umpteen mop-headed Group Sounds bands ducked and dived, preened and sashayed, did anything their managers asked of them in ever more desperate attempts to reach the cherished number-one spot on Japan's Oricon Top 40, droves of disenfranchised teenagers quit their rural homes and made their way towards Tokyo and the other cities within the congested conurbation that strung out east–west across the bulging midriff of the main island of Honshu.

The Release of TWO VIRGINS

Rock'n'roll music and the experimental scene collided head-on in May 1968 with the release of John & Yoko's terrible LP UNFINISHED MUSIC NO. 1: TWO VIRGINS, the front sleeve of which showed them both totally naked, a notion so disturbing to the public that it quite obscured the fact that the shrieking avant-garde birdsong contained within moaning-minnied at its audience from as far left of field as the thorniest of hedges would allow. But if viewing a Beatle's wedding tackle wasn't heart-stopping enough for the Western media, journalists were soon required to respond to the Beatles' 'Revolution Number 9', a derivative slab of *musique concrète* that occupied the penultimate slot on side four of THE BEATLES, the fabulous four's brand new double-LP. Out of context, 'Revolution Number 9' sounded just like a radio edit of side three of Stockhausen's epic HYMNEN double-LP, and wouldn't have sounded out of place on Frank Zappa's LUMPY GRAVY, released twelve months earlier. However, sandwiched between the sub-'I Am The Walrus' cod/plod of 'Cry Baby Cry' and the Spanish-galleon over-arrangement of Macca's mawkish 'Goodnight', John and Yoko's avant-garde statement outstayed its welcome within the first minute then hung around to disastrous effect as listeners kicked their heels urging the damn thing to hurry up and finish. The press, discovering that neither Macca nor Ringo had even played on 'Revolution Number 9', compared its bizarre racket to the equally bizarre racket caught within the grooves of TWO VIRGINS, and laid the blame firmly at the door of Lennon's new bed partner. Not content with hoodwinking poor sap John, the Ono influence had even spilled over into the Beatles' output. And as a twice-divorced older Japanese woman was not at all what the king-makers of Fleet Street and its American counterparts had had in mind as a worthy consort for Beatle John, the xenophobic press unleashed a torrent of sustained racist (and even ageist) abuse at Yoko that finally reached its nadir in an American *Esquire* magazine article bearing the execrable headline 'John Rennon's Excrusive Gloupie'. In Japan, naturally, Ono's new relationship was rapturously received across the whole of society, and among Japanese women in particular, for Japanese women had traditionally always remained in the background. For a powerful man such as John Lennon to have consciously chosen a Japanese woman as his partner, this was indeed hard evidence of the diminishing gap between these once-radically estranged cultures.

The Freeing of Japanese Jazz & the Uniting of Cultures

Among Japan's jazz community, the influence of pop music (and the Beatles especially) was, by 1968, redefining jazz musicians' attitudes through their sheer proximity to pop culture. Indeed, the lack of heavyweight rock musicians in Japan had ensured that, by the late '60s, many seasoned jazz rhythm sections were in high demand playing on the pop hits of the day, ensuring that these players remained adaptable and open-minded to the continuous change that the music scene demanded. For example, drummer/arranger Akira Ishikawa had been a professional since way back in the early 1950s and had scored late '50s hits of his own with such LPs as MOOD IN IMMORTAL CLASSIC OF JAPANESE SONGS [sic]. But, despite this, and his long service throughout the early '60s as musical director for Helen Merrill – Tokyo's own Doris Day – it was still to Ishikawa that most producers turned when they required a killer dance beat. Similarly adaptable and even more successful was trumpeter Terumasa Hino, who'd been professional since the mid-'50s by mode lling himself on Miles Davis and Freddie Hubbard, but who had even jumped temporarily (and successfully) aboard the early '60s *eleki* scene with his hit LP TRUMPETS IN BLUE JEANS.

The contributions of such jazz players to Japanese '60s pop music had serious repercussions within their own jazz scene, musicians becoming increasingly aware of the seemingly opposing styles uniting in current pop and digging what they heard. In the two long years since Brian Jones had added his exotic and alien marimba to the Rolling Stones' single 'Under My Thumb', Japanese teenagers had – via the Beatles, the Yardbirds and their own musical genius Terry Terauchi (see Book One, Chapter Three) – become so used to hearing such unlikely instruments as sitars, balalaikas, oboes, shawms and bassoons that the hip young French gypsy violinist Jean-Luc Ponty scored an unlikely hit in Japan with his instrumental LP MORE THAN MEETS THE EAR and its attendant single, a version of the Beatles' 'With a Little Help from My Friends'. Wild and dashingly good-looking, Jean-Luc Ponty was little less than a pop star in Japan, where his more extreme experiments with Germany's Wolfgang Dauner Septet on the LP FREE ACTION, released in summer '67, had soon caught the approving ears of Japanese jazz musicians.

Stuttgart-based Dauner had been inspired in equal measures by the electronic experiments of fellow countryman Karlheinz Stockhausen, the gypsy violin of Stephane Grappelli, and the exotically dissonant Turkish pop of Mavi Isiklar, Cahit Oben and others, whom Dauner heard playing continuously in Stuttgart's large Turkish area. By early November 1966, Dauner had begun to Stockhausen-ise his piano by putting it through ring modulators and other electronic devices to bizarre and sensational effect. Next, Dauner and fellow Stuttgart musician Eberhard Weber began to investigate the Turks' use of quarter- and half-tones in their music, again with excellent results. Indeed, by early '67, Dauner had jettisoned his traditional jazz-trio format, opting instead to build an incredible seven-piece free-jazz ensemble around the hitherto non-jazz instruments violin and cello, now played by Jean-Luc Ponty and Eberhard Weber respectively. Dauner's new septet was completed by bassist Jurgen Karg, percussionist Fred Braceful and the wild free-drumming of the young Mani Neumaier, future leader of Krautrockers Guru Guru. This turn of events, therefore, put Dauner in possession of the kind of heavy bass section unheard even in the later John Coltrane sojourns.

By the end of 1968, Wolfgang Dauner's bold experiments had gained many fans among the Japanese jazz community, including pianists Masahiko Satoh and Masabumi Kikuchi, guitarist Masayuki Takayanagi, trumpeters Takehisa Suzuki and Tetsu Fushimi, drummers Akira Ishikawa and Hiro Tsunoda, and countless others who saw Dauner's moves as a way of reconciling their own experiments with the prevailing 'progressive' moods of the day. By this time, Frank Zappa's fourth release – the bizarre orchestral LP LUMPY GRAVY – had also started to work its curious magic, its vicious combination of *musique concrète*, redundant surf-guitar themes, bozo spoken word and jarring percussion-fest all conspiring to confirm to the insular Japanese jazz community what Dauner's FREE ACTION had anticipated one year earlier: that there could be a place for all of them in the coming pop free-for-all.

By early 1969, the effects of this unlikely Japanese-German jazz connection united both cultures in their love for the kind of exotic Asian sounds that could never hope to penetrate the overbearing British and American scenes. Japanese traditional instruments such as the three-string *shamisen* and the *sanshin* (Japanese banjo) began to be integrated into jazz experiments, just as such instruments as the *biwa*, *koto*, and the bamboo *sho* had, by this time, long informed Japan's post-war classical and experimental music. In the meantime, pianist Masahiko Satoh hooked up with Wolfgang Dauner himself and prepared to record an LP of electrified piano duets, whilst drummer Akira Ishikawa made plans for his first real field trip abroad to record an adventurous percussion-only LP.

For many in the jazz community, however, the biggest shock of '69 came when master guitarist Masayuki Takayanagi made the momentous decision to take the free-jazz route, a resolution that would see his art catapulted into stellar regions whilst his social position would plummet. For Takayanagi it was to whom other jazz musicians had long turned when they couldn't read a chart, a guitar hero whose name had, seemingly for ever, graced the number-one spot in the annual polls of Japan's jazz bible *The Swing Journal*, whose face was well known from his regular TV performances on the late show *11pm*, whose New Artist Organization had been formed specifically to encourage young jazz players and whose published musical theories had made him a universally trusted brother figure. But here in the upheaval of 1969, Takayanagi now dumped his bossa-nova band and struck out with all the abandon of Albert Ayler's fiercest experiments. Within months, even Takayanagi's free-jazz ensemble was haemorrhaging members at the rate of one a week, as the guitarist strove to locate new musicians vital enough to replicate what he heard in his newly mushed brain … feedback, feedback and more feedback … And which of the great free-jazzers had precipitated this sea change within our stalwart veteran of the jazz community? 'Trane? Ayler? Why, none of the above actually. Takayanagi's change of heart had come about whilst putting on side three of the new double-LP CHICAGO TRANSIT AUTHORITY, by future AOR kings Chicago. It sounds positively daft now, but the late '60s electronic jazz-based experiments of the Electric Flag begat Chicago and Blood, Sweat & Tears too. On hearing Chicago guitarist Terry Kath's seven freak-out minutes of 'Free Form Guitar', Masayuki Takayanagi saw the future and the future was both distorted and extremely a-rhythmical.

Cross-Disciplinary Principles at the Crossroads of 'Crosstalk' & Hair

It's fair to say, however, that guitar feedback was a standard rock'n'roll obsession in the spring of 1969. Indeed, the May release of John & Yoko's UNFINISHED MUSIC NUMBER 2: LIFE WITH THE LIONS superseded the ugliness of the loving couple's first collaboration by bringing forth a stunning and unyielding blitz of free-rock feedback guitar and accompanying holler. Furthermore, the harsh levels of Chicago-ian guitar feedback that Masayuki Takayanagi had sought out so specifically also lay right at the rock'n'roll heart of Toshi Ichiyanagi's newest composition – an experimental opera no less – as the work inspired by his New York revelations at the home of Tadanori Yoko'o and at the Bell Armoury Show, two years previously, finally came to fruition that spring. Ichiyanagi's meeting with Yoko'o had forced the composer to 'update his music and stop hiding in the abstract', as Yoko'o himself would later describe it. In order to free himself from the classical sound system, Ichiyanagi had first composed a piece entitled 'Orchestral Space', which he performed at Tokyo's Second Modern Music Festival with the aid of Yuya Utchida's maverick new psychedelic rock'n'roll group the Flowers. Propelled by a caterwauling barrage of whooping stratospheric feedback courtesy of steel-guitarist Katsuhiko Kobayashi, the Flowers' sound summoned up the same wayward spirits as Californian band the Misunderstood, led by Glenn Ross Campbell. Together with Tadanori Yoko'o himself and soundtrack composer Toru Takemitsu, Ichiyanagi also created a bizarre TV work entitled 'The

Third Trend', in which clowns, circus carnies and samurai all appeared together in a veritable spoof of psychedelic culture. But Ichiyanagi's real *pièce de résistance* was a vast multi-disciplinary work that he had been labouring over since the halcyon hallucinations back in the New York apartment of Tadanori Yoko'o. Now entitled OPERA INSPIRED BY THE WORKS OF TADANORI YOKO'O, Ichiyanagi's new work combined orchestral scores, spoken-word pieces, *musique concrète* and free-form suites of heavy rock'n'roll. Housed in an art-house twelve-inch-square box printed with the most famous examples of Yoko'o artwork, the so-called opera was pressed on to two incredible picture discs, and came with accompanying playing cards bearing further Yoko'o designs.

Still on a considerable high, Ichiyanagi next instigated the 'Crosstalk/Intermedia' show at Tokyo's Yoyogi Gymnasium, an event he had long dreamed of curating. Determined to bring to Japan some of the same visionary spirit that Ichiyanagi had witnessed at Bill Kluver's Bell Armoury Show, two years previously, the composer's 'Crosstalk/Intermedia' event was another of 1969's cultural highs, being both a place for performance art by old friends such as Group Ongaku's Takehisa Kosugi, and also an opportunity to allow 'artists to interact and co-operate with technology-related people to put on all-inclusive performances of modern art'.[20]

And so, in a bizarre turn of fate, 1969 saw in Japan the coming-together of umpteen unlikely strands of popular culture, as the Far East finally met the West via John and Yoko, via John Cage, via Toshi Ichiyanagi and Yuya Utchida, via Karlheinz Stockhausen ... oh, and via the unlikely 'tribal love musical' *Hair*! For, in the midst of this flurry of underground, experimental and jazz activity and visionary conceptualising, the news came through of the imminent arrival in Japan of the hippie musical. By early 1969, *Hair* had already become a worldwide phenomenon, upsetting the straight community with its nudity and drug references, and even getting itself banned in such places as New Zealand and Mexico. The musical's influence on Japanese culture was felt even more immediately, however. For *Hair*'s Japanese producers made it quite clear that it was from the jazz community that they were going to make their first choices for the heavyweight musical ensemble that would, every night, perform *Hair*'s hit soundtrack. While Masahiko Satoh was adamant that his experiments with Wolfgang Dauner should remain in place, most others buckled. That *Hair* – the epitome of pop culture – should get to be played by a mainly jazz band was like a dream come true. And so it was that, of *Hair*'s nine-piece ensemble, seven were invited from the jazz community and the leader was to be none other than drummer Akira Ishikawa himself. His free-jazz experimental percussion LP would have to wait!

Footnotes:

1   'Sogetsu Arts Center: History of the Four Iemotos' at:
     http://www.sogetsu.or.jp/english/ie_history/index_04.html

2   NHK's broadcast version was released in 2006 by Omega Point, as part three of their series
     'Obscure Tape Music of Japan'.

3   Pierre Schaeffer wrote his ideas and visions of future music in his book *A la recherche d'une musique
     concrète*.

4   Niksa Gligo, *Ich traf John Cage in Bremen* (Melos 1973).

5   Karlheinz Stockhausen, 'Texte Zu Eigenen Werken – Zur Kunst Anderer, Aktuelles, vol. ii'
     (Cologne 1964), quoted in Michael Kurtz, *Stockhausen: A Biography* (Faber & Faber 1992).

6   Taken from the inaugural speech for Yoko Ono's exhibition at Everson Museum of Art.

7   Yasunao Tone's 'Anagram for Strings' was released on clear vinyl LP, in 2005, by Slowscan Editions
     in the Netherlands. On side two was Tone's 1979 piece 'Geography & Music', featuring John Cage,
     Takehisa Kosugi and David Tudor.

8   Joji Yuasa's 'Aoi No Ue' lay unreleased until 2004, when it was issued by Omega Point, as part one of
     their series 'Obscure Tape Music of Japan': see http://homepage2.nifty.com/paganmusik/omega/top.html

9   Toshi Ichiyanagi, 'Japanese Experimental Music of the 1960s:
     "Where Are We Going?" and "What Art We Doing?"' (Internet essay, 1997).

10   'Music for Metronomes' was finally recorded in 1998, in a performance by the quintet Ensemble
     Nomad, at the Kimitsu Shimin Bunka Hall, at Chiba, Japan.

11   Along with Akiyama's 'Noh-Miso', the lost performance was later released 2004, in its ghost form as
     MUSIC FOR PUPPET THEATRE OF HITOMI-ZA, credited to Joji Yuasa and Kuniharu Akiyama, on
     Edition Omega Point.

12 Mayuzumi's award-winning theme music was not the first to have been commissioned for a Japanese Olympic event. Back in 1956, the director of Japan's Olympic gymnastics team commissioned an electronic soundtrack from Isao Tomita, who went on to gain fame in the '70s for his SNOWFLAKES ARE DANCING.

13 Michael Kurtz, *Stockhausen: A Biography* (Faber & Faber 1988).

14 This 16-minute-45-second piece was released in 1968 on the Victor Records LP ORCHESTRAL SPACE VOLUME 1.

15 Tellingly, the ensemble's guitarist Derek Bailey would gain most approval in Japan, whilst Miles Davis soon snapped up the services of bass player Dave Holland.

16 Michael Kurtz, *Stockhausen: A Biography* (Faber & Faber 1988).

17 Karlheinz Stockhausen, 'Texte zur Musik 1963–1970' Volume 3, (Cologne 1971, privately published).

18 Jay Marks, 'Conversation with Stockhausen', *Saturday Review* (30th September 1967).

19 Over the next few decades, Akasegawa would become a celebrated author and cultural commentator with a series of books, including *Sen no Rikyu – Mugon no Zenei* (The Silent Avant-Garde of Sen no Rikyu), *Raika Domei* (The Laika Alliance) and *Han-geijutsu Anpan* (A Mocking Critique of the Andepandan Art Institute).

20 Toshi Ichiyanagi, 'Japanese Experimental Music of the 1960s: "Where Are We Going?" and "What Art We Doing?"' (Internet essay, 1997).

CHAPTER 3
THE ELEKI
STORY エレキ ブーム

Beloved Invaders

In the meantime, back in the world of show business, 1961 was anything but a forward-thinking place to be. The plane crashes, car accidents, deaths, divorces, humiliations and public exposés that had beset rock'n'roll's first wave of pioneers of the late '50s had now all conspired to return popular culture to that same world of light entertainment that had so transfixed society in the early post-war years. For the true rocker, 1961 was a lonesome world where the all-rounder was king, and where the King was a puppet who sung 'Wooden Heart' to a bunch of wooden puppets. What hope was there for natural wetniks like the Everly Brothers and Cliff Richard but to follow their leader with their own dreadful equivalents of January '61's 'Are You Lonesome Tonight?'? Placing themselves firmly in the middle of the road just as the title of Elvis's current LP SOMETHING FOR EVERYONE instructed, Cliff and the Everlys dutifully filled up the charts with such stillborn fare as 'Walk Right Back', 'Theme From a Dream' and 'Gee Whizz, It's You', while new boy Adam Faith out-blanded them all with his shameless 'Easy Going Me'. That September, bad boys across the globe felt their world getting ever more claustrophobic when the last of the greats to fall, Chuck Berry himself, was sent down for three years for 'violating the Mann Act' when he unwittingly transported a fourteen-year-old girl across state lines. In Japan, that same month, the opportunist schmaltzmeister Fritz Friedel rubbed salt into rock'n'roll's open wound by topping Japan's chart with a German-language version of 'Wooden Heart'. Faced with such an MOR onslaught of songs about nothing at all, the only way to remain cool was to listen to music with absolutely no words at all. And as Fritz slid down the Japanese charts, so the Tokyo hep cats pushed Jimmie Tokita & His Mountain Playboys up the charts, as Tokita's version of the Shadows' 'Apache' ushered in the new Japanese musical obsession … *eleki*!

Ah, the *Eleki Buumu*, or 'Electric Guitar Boom'. Always up for a new craze with a new name, the Japanese-in-the-know had followed the exploits of foreign instrumental groups since the late '50s, via radio shows on the American military's Far East Network. In 1960, Johnny & the Hurricanes' 'Red River Rock' had been a worldwide killer that sax player Johnny Paris had re-arranged from an old traditional song 'Red River Valley'. Hoping to appeal to American GIs across the world, Paris had done a similar job with the far less successful follow-up 'Reveille Rock', but the braying jazzy alto sax was by now altogether too archaic and too monolithic a lead instrument to sustain interest, especially in comparison to the mysterious-looking solid-bodied electric guitars that America's Fender and Gibson companies were selling by the truckload. And if the Japanese were to embrace the West and its Future Dream, then that dream needed to be propelled not by pre-war acoustic horns, but by polished futuristic machines in whose gleaming modernity was a declaration that they were worthy of this new Space Age.

First, the musicians of the early '60s Japanese scene turned for inspiration to Britain's the Shadows. And, right here in October '61, it was Tokyo Country-&-Western star Jimmie Tokita who was reaping the rewards with his remake of Hank Marvin & Co's 'Apache', the original itself already over a year old. Or rather, Jimmie Tokita was reaping the benefits of having such a fine musician in his band. For it was the Mountain Playboys' guitarist Takeshi Terauchi to whom the plaudits should rightfully have been directed. In the year since 'Apache', the Shadows had scored more worldwide successes with 'FBI', 'Frightened City', 'Kon-Tiki' and 'Wonderful Land', further increasing the hip credentials of the guitar instrumental and raising its profile to the level of genuine phenomenon. Of course, Tyneside's Hank B. Marvin was not the first to have scattered spangly guitar solos across 7" plastic. That honour probably goes to back to 1957 with Duane Eddy's grungy debut 'Ramrod' and the following year's 'Rebel Rouser'. But Duane's music – achieved on a big old fat-bellied Gretsch semi-acoustic – belonged to an earlier time that had more in common with such post-big-band hits as the Champs' 'Tequila'. And, besides, the Eddy approach was not nearly fastidious or fetishistic enough for the Japanese. Where were the suits? Where was the automotive gleam of the Fender Stratocaster? Where was the synchronised kicking? Heck, the guys in Duane's band all stood about all casual like. And, on hits such as 'Shazam', Duane had even let some sax player smear outdated Benny Hill themes all across the groove. Nasty.

But if the Shadows had honed down Duane Eddy's miscreant muse to a clearly defined and tightly self-contained metaphor, then the Ventures from Tacoma, high up on the northwest coast of America, were a whole other world. For the Ventures, there could be no time for smiling at their audience, nor even at each other. No, where the Shadows still inhabited a good-natured Keltic half-world where fun for the group was important too, the Ventures were cold, scientific and focused, four radical Germanic technicians, studious alchemists for whom nothing could sway their singular goal. And, unlike the vast majority of their contemporaries, the Ventures used their singles releases merely as an advert for the more expensive albums that they offloaded on to their fans with style and real panache. Indeed, three or more thoughtfully pack-aged LPs per year guaranteed that Japan's obsessive *eleki* fans would buy their entire oeuvre, their main sequence of early albums being WALK, DON'T RUN (December 1960), THE VENTURES (July 1961), ANOTHER SMASH (September 1961), THE COLORFUL VENTURES (October 1961), TWIST WITH THE VENTURES (January 1962), TWIST PARTY VOLUME 2 (May 1962), MASHED POTATOES & GRAVY (August 1962) and GOING TO THE VENTURES' DANCE PARTY (November 1963). What's more, these practitioners each played ice-white Mosrite guitars with black scratch plates, each axe bearing 'The Ventures' logo upon their headstocks. Furthermore, each album by the Ventures was carefully themed, as every subsequent release distilled their metaphor ever more tightly. THE COLORFUL VENTURES, for example, included the songs entitled 'Yellow Jacket', 'Red Top' and 'Orange Fire', plus several of the more obvious 'blues'. This quasi-military precision combined with the financing of Semie Moseley's great guitar corporation said these Ventures were no punks; indeed these gentlemen had the authorities on their side. For the efficiency-worshipping Japanese, nothing could have reached their pleasure centres more easily or with greater accuracy. And when the Ventures played an all-too-brief support set on Bobby Vee's 1962 tour of Japan, it was not with Vee but with the Ventures that the Japanese began an everlasting love affair, truly an affection that has not died out even to this day. And so, in the absence of any likely future Ventures tour of Japan, a home-grown version known as the Adventures began to make *eleki* records for the huge Toshiba company, while musical members of the mysterious Buddhist sect Sokka Gakkai formed their own Tokyo Ventures, pumping out spirited morale-boosting *eleki* versions of traditional Japanese army songs.

In the free-for-all that followed, Japanese musicians from all walks of life hopped on to the *eleki* gravy train. A disparate bunch of dropouts from two late '50s Country & Western bands – the Wagonmasters and the Chuck Wagon Boys – had been working together on and off since the 1959 album sessions for rockabilly singer Masaaki Hirao's LP MACHAN OINI UTAU. But now in the *eleki* boom of summer '62, the six musicians united loosely around the guitar virtuoso Hiroshi Tsutsumi. In rapid succession, this cynically shifting alliance metamorphosed briefly into a twist band, before turning inexorably *eleki* as Hiroshi Tsutsumi & All Stars Wagon. In 1962, they released three successful albums, first their twist cash-in LP LET'S TWIST, next their album of simpering love ballads done *eleki* style entitled FROM 'DIANA' TO 'YOU'RE EVERYTHING', concluding with the YOUR HIT PARADE LP, in which hits of the previous year were refashioned into the current *eleki* style. Obviously inspired by this radical turn of events from such seasoned session hacks, their erstwhile C&W compadres the Caravan suddenly became known as the Van-Dogs, thereafter issuing twangy instrumentals of their own on 7" sonosheets, the overly flexible soon-to-become-obsolete Betamax format of their day. With the *eleki* craze now in full swing, the incredible international success of Britain's Joe Meek-produced 'Telstar' was such that even the Ventures themselves felt it necessary to cover the song. Moreover, its protagonists the Tornados remained at number one on the American Billboard chart for sixteen consecutive weeks, both reinforcing the power of the instrumental and –

76   powered as 'Telstar' was by a stellar-sounding miniature *eleki* keyboard known as the Selmer Clavioline – inadvertently opening the way for other instruments to take a lead role once more. Opportunistic Japanese jazz trumpeter Terumasa Hino[1] charted immediately with his *eleki* cash-in LP TRUMPET IN BLUE JEANS, whilst Osaka's own Smiley O'Hara & His Skyliners revamped even the Champs' hoary 'Tequila' in November '63. The Daiei Film Company had accidental success with the Sounds Ace, an ensemble originally formed merely in order to give the company sufficient control of its own soundtracks, whilst the lauded LP ROMANTIC ELEKI MOOD by Toshio Kawamura & Eleki Sound was actually the cynical studio creation of a bored jazz guitarist and his mates. Other studio bands, such as RCA Records' outfit the King's Road, offered chaotic rhythmic assaults quite at odds with the Western notion of rhythm & blues, whilst Teichiku Records unleashed their jazz-flavoured two-volume LPs BITO GITA NO SUBETE (All About Beat Guitar), and BITA GITA SEKAI O IKU (Beat Guitar Goes out to the World) under the guise of another studio outfit by the wonderful name of Dynamic Echoes. The anonymous and unknown Sammy picked up on the Japanese love of car songs with his two instrumental singles 'Wild Datsun' and 'Ace of Toyota', inspiring four American servicemen who, as the Hondells, cashed in with their vocal single 'Little Honda'. But it was the total absence of vocals and words that inadvertently opened up the Japanese *eleki* market to all comers from around the world, as many otherwise failed combos scored big successes on the coat-tails of

this purely Japanese obsession. And with their massive single 'Bombora', Australia's surf kings the Atlantics were geographically well suited to a Japanese career, as were Thailand's the Galaxies, whose LP ELEKI MOOD IN JAPAN featured cover versions of popular contemporary Japanese songs played in the style of Sweden's Tornados copyists the Spotnicks. The term 'Euro-surf' sounds like an oxymoron, but there were several such bands worthy of Japanese obsessions, not least Belgium's red-velvet-suited Jokers, who struck gold with unlikely singles such as 'Football Boogie' and 'Spanish Hully Gully' before topping the charts with their LP BEAT ON CHRISTMAS, which was also successful in South Africa! But, then again, the Japanese were entirely on their own in celebrating Finland's unlikely surf combos the Quiets and the quartet the Sounds, whose matching honey maple Fender guitars and royal-blue suits gave them a ghoulish glow somewhat akin to the Shadows lost in the Nordic underworld. A surfing version of Rimsky-Korsakov's 'Troika Chase' anyone? Japan's Philips label certainly felt that it was worth a shot! The Sounds' big Japanese hit 'Mandschurian Beat' would, three years later, be covered by their heroes the Ventures, who would ironically only get to hear it for the first time on their own Japanese tour in 1965. Also successful nowhere but in Japan were Denmark's soberly dressed and even more strangely named Cliffters, who scored big with their jazzy surf song 'Django'. Throughout all of this, the Ventures themselves maintained such a masterful grip on Japanese heartstrings that, between 1960 and '63, their hit singles included 'Walk, Don't Run', 'Perfidia', 'Ram-Bunk-Shush', 'Lullaby of the Leaves', 'Yellow Jacket', 'Instant Guitars', 'Lolita-Ya-Ya', 'The 2000 Pound Bee', 'The Ninth Wave' and 'The Savage'. Even the Hollywood movie-world now had to sit up and take notice of guitar instrumentals. Ironically, however, when MGM's producers stalled in their search for a sufficiently groovy opening theme for *Doctor No*, their forthcoming James Bond movie debut, it was not to the Ventures that they turned for help, but to the man who'd put his own version of the Ventures' 'Walk, Don't Run' into the UK charts … John Barry. And if Japan's *eleki* scene had been thriving throughout the early '60s, then the May '63 release of *Doctor No* sent the whole phenomenon stellar.

Here Comes Terry

After the James Bond theme, everything was spies and low-slung guitar twang. The Cold War may well have been happening since the 1950s, but it was right here right now in 1963 that the Cold War was suddenly a Happening! But if these early years of Japan's *eleki* scene were to be validated by the twang of spy-theme music and dominated by chancers, opportunists and foreigners, at least this strange turn of events was to enrich and nourish the culture, enabling it to sustain itself for several more years, and furthermore allowing Japanese musicians to develop their own very specific take on the music. And it should here be made absolutely clear that *eleki* was an entirely Japanese phenomenon, even if many of the original protagonists hailed from overseas. For, just as reggae had initially emerged from Kingston DJs' overuse of bass filters when playing American R&B, so it was the Japanese collective mindset that first located the particular thrill that those islanders came to call 'the *eleki* sound'. And as the Japanese guitarists' study of Western techniques increased, so new instrumental stars emerged from the ranks of backing bands who nightly accompanied famous singers on their national tours; instrumental stars discovering their own true timbre, a sound that was informed almost as much by jazz, big-band and traditional Japanese instruments as by the rock'n'roll of the day. As the hits kept coming, who knows whether the all-vocal Sharp Hawks were put out when their own backing band the Sharp Five emerged temporarily from the shadows to score their own big *eleki* hit with the single 'Golden Guitar'. Did English singers Chad & Jeremy care when, in the middle of a Japanese set, Hiroshi 'Monsieur' Kamayatsu, lead guitarist for their own Japanese backing band the Spiders, stepped into the spotlight to offer his own spectacular take on the Ventures' 'Wipe Out'? And pity poor Jimmie Tokita, the Country & Western singer who'd first shone the spotlight on his young guitarist Takeshi Terauchi in order to have a hit with 'Apache', only to find that he'd created a major star. Within twelve months of 'Apache''s success, the young guitarist had Anglicised his name to the catchier Terry, and started his own hugely successful *eleki* band the Bluejeans. Terry Terauchi's hits came thick and fast as he thundered out such dizzying and urgent tracks as 'West Side Guitar' and 'Terry's Theme' on a Ventures-style Mosrite guitar; performing in a stinging and overtly whammy bar-heavy manner his Orientalised takes on Western instrumentals. And although Terauchi's Bluejeans had a major album with 1964's KOREZO SURFING (This Is Surfing), the guitarist transcribed virtually all popular genres into *eleki*; not just garage, frat rock and surf-guitar instrumentals, but sentimental ballads, popular classics such as 'The Blue Danube', 'Flight of the Bumblebee' and 'Swan Lake', and even Japanese folk song. This last idea was surely Terauchi's masterstroke, for the 1965 album SEICHO TERA UCHI BUSHI contained a version of the timeless Japanese song 'Kanjuncho/Genroku Hanami Odiri', which was so popular with young and old alike that the record became the biggest-selling *eleki* album of all time, picking up over 100,000 sales. Ever the hustler, Terauchi was even opportunistic enough to intercept the major moves of other opportunists. One spectacular example was Terauchi's gazumping of an idea by Sunset Strip hustler Mike Curb, whose own skiing vacations had just inspired an unlikely double-A-side hit 'Ski Jump' b/w 'Ski City USA' for his LA surf band the Buddies. Following Curb's lead, the percipient Terry & the Bluejeans unleashed a whole EP of such stuff entitled LET'S GO SKI SURF, containing the

The Rise of the Japanese Eleki Guitar

Despite Japan's love of rock'n'roll, early Japanese attempts at manufacturing solid-bodied guitars yielded such crude results that young musicians armed with these late '50s instruments had little chance of success. Instead, Japanese rock'n'rollers imported USA-built guitars at huge expense, or returned from trips abroad armed with the Fenders and Mosrites that their heroes played. However, when the Ventures toured Japan in 1965, Nokie Edwards & Co allowed Japanese craftsmen to study their Mosrites first-hand, after which Japan's guitar industry took off almost overnight. The new Japanese guitar companies all studiedly avoided Gibson's more traditional electrics, concentrating their efforts instead on building futuristic machines in the Fender and Mosrite mould. They also developed an obsession with the rocket-shaped EKO Rokes, built in Italy for the Rokes, Italy's answer to the Monkees. Several Japanese companies replicated the Rokes, the best efforts being manufactured by Kingston and Honey (pictured here and on the cover). Much to the chagrin of Mosrite boss Semie Moseley, one Tokyo company even named themselves Mosrite. When Moseley challenged this, the boss stated calmly: 'But you are Mosrite of California ... we are only Mosrite!'

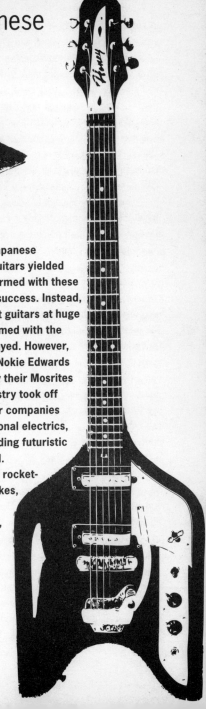

unlikely rock'n'roll titles 'Ski a Go Go', 'O My Darling Clementine', 'Ich Bin der Cluck-lickste Mensch auf der Welt' and 'Die Schlittschuhlaufer'. This Japanese propensity for mix'n'matching Western metaphors to suit themselves probably hit its apogee in 1965, with the release of the LP CHRISTMAS WITH ELECTRIC GUITARS by the super-smooth Blue Comets, led by drummer Jackey Yoshikawa. Contained within its grooves were fiery guitar- and flute-led versions of 'Jingle Bells', 'Blue Christmas', 'I Saw Mommy Kissing Santa Claus' and 'Here Comes Santa Claus', all of which owed a debt of inspiration to the earlier BEAT ON CHRISTMAS by Belgian surf band the Jokers. Perhaps it could here be suggested that – despite the Coca-Cola, rock'n'roll and baseball – what really defined the Westernisation of Japan was the Japanese acceptance of the jolly fat red guy into this essentially Buddhist country.

Contemporary themes of space, spies and the Cold War continued to dominate the later *eleki* scene, as Japanese outfits such as the Goldfingers, the Launchers and the Spacemen appeared on the scene,[2] the latter bunch thereafter leaving behind Yukuio Hashi, their famous leader, pop star and heartthrob, in order to score three big album hits 1965 with ELEKI GITA DE MINYO O and HAWAIIAN SURF GUITAR for Victor Records, and ELEKI GITA BANZAI for Toshiba. But this was an unusual move for the time, as 1965 saw the beginnings of a change in the Japanese pop scene, espe-cially evidenced by the sudden appearance of the strangely named *eleki* band the Tokyo Beatles. Well-established *eleki* dudes the Spiders were possibly the first to recognise the implications of the distant rumblings coming from British beat groups, when drummer/manager Shochi Tanabe had, the previous year, employed the much younger Eurasian singer Jun Inoue alongside the Spiders' original flautist and occa-sional vocalist Masaaki Sakai. And now, *eleki* veterans the Blue Comets appeared on live TV backing the charming Akira Fuse on his new single 'Let's Go Swim'. Blue Com-ets' leader/drummer Jackey Yoshikawa was an outgoing media-savvy businessman, somewhat akin to British drummer Dave Clark; and Yoshikawa had no intention of appearing behind the times. Unlike most Japanese, Yoshikawa had paid close atten-tion to what was going down on the American rock'n'roll scene. Moreover, he'd observed that, from that moment in February 1964 when Beatle John and his cohorts had first stepped off the plane at New York's Kennedy Airport, the British beat-group assault on American and Americanised culture had built and built and did not appear to be letting up. Indeed, by April '64, the Beatles famously held all five places at the summit of the American Top 40, with the singles 'Can't Buy Me Love', 'Twist & Shout', 'She Loves You', 'I Wanna Hold Your Hand' and 'Please Please Me', while a second wave of be-suited British groups had mopped up the US charts throughout '64 with such classics as the Animals' 'House of the Rising Sun' (number one in July), Manfred Mann's 'Doo Wah Diddy Diddy' (number one in August), the Kinks' two garage burn-up Top 10's 'All Day and All of the Night' and 'You Really Got Me' and the Dave Clark Five's four proto-Strangeloves Top-10 beltathons, including 'Glad All Over' and 'Bits & Pieces'. Weirdly, such was the intense competition for US chart positions that even the Rolling Stones (themselves billed on the 1964 cover of their first Stateside LP as ENGLAND'S NEWEST HITMAKERS) would be forced to wait until 1965 to score their first three US number ones. And Jackey Yoshikawa well knew that, as America fell to the English beat groups, so would all the other bastions of US culture themselves fall – Australia, New Zealand, West Germany and, inevitably … Japan, where strategic army, navy and air-force bases blasted American radio's Top 40 loud and long into the night, via their Far East Network.

The Ventures Tour Japan

All that, however, was still several months away. And as seven days in the life of a pop star can make or break a career, worrying about the British Invasion was temporarily deferred whilst everyone anticipated the long-awaited first headlining tour by their all-time heroes the Ventures. At last! The arrival of Messrs Bogle, Edwards, Wilson and Taylor provoked the fastidious Japanese media to fetishistic levels of behaviour – indeed every move the Ventures made was set down in writing and caught on video, 35mm and Super 8. On stage, the band's famous three-guitars-in-a-line was rendered starker than ever against the ultra-modern backgrounds of the culture halls in which they played. Behind each guitarist stood their futuristic Fender Twin Reverb amplifiers, and all would turn ninety degrees to the right to address drummer Mel Taylor's furious pounding tom-tom interludes, before each simultaneously resumed their characteristic stance facing out to the audience. It's been suggested that much of the nation's fascination for the Ventures' music was because of its relationship with the melancholic minor-key ballad form known as *enka* that has for so long transfixed Japanese culture. Perhaps, but unlikely, I feel. *Enka* has always belonged to the older more experienced generations, its defeated sound invoking emotions more akin to the Southern States' Country & Western music. For me, even in the cold light of this early twenty-first century, the Ventures' black-and-white-movie performances on that starkly lit 1965 tour still seem both futuristically Kafkaesque and somehow prehistorically ancient. No cosiness, no jokiness, nothing undermines the honed-down perfection of their performance; yet there is a spectacularly industrious warmth in the glowing face of each concentrating member of the band.

Supporting the Ventures throughout their '65 tour was the most unlikely *eleki* star of all, the dashingly handsome actor Yuzo Kayama and his guitar band the Launchers. Kayama had first become a star in 1961, when he played the title role in *Wakadaisho* (Young General) in the first of a series of highly successful teen movies. But the actor had become besotted with *eleki* music after that brief Ventures support slot back in '62, and had brushed up on his rudimentary guitar skills with quite spectacular success. Unlike other *eleki* outfits, however, the Launchers had been unable to remain entirely instrumental because of Kayama's presence. For it was a well-known fact that the actor/guitarist was also in possession of the kind of sweet baritone that would drive the teenagers wild. And so, interspersed between the wild surf burn-ups were slightly cringe-worthy love ballads that had the ladies biting their sodden hankies in grief and frustration. Throughout the tour, however, the Ventures took all this good-naturedly because Kayama the guitarist was just so damn good. Indeed, at the finale of the Tokyo show, they presented him with one of their signature ice-white Mosrites (and later recorded their own versions of his 'Black Sand Beach' and 'Yozora No Hoshi').

The Death of Eleki

When the Ventures' tour was finally done, Kayama was expected to fulfil his contract and film the sequel to his first Young General movie. His producers had allowed the actor to postpone the movie shoot temporarily due to his sudden change of career direction. But now, inspired by the frankly ridiculous plots of current Elvis movies, the producers cleverly brought together these two radically disparate elements – rock'n'roll and historical hero – in a bizarre mixing of metaphors. Entitled *Eleki no Wakadaisho* (The Young General's Electric Guitar), the film featured a guitar duel between Kayama and his arch *eleki* rival Terry Terauchi. The movie was a frightening success, causing Kayama's star to shine even more brightly. He was asked to present his own early-evening chat show, which he duly did with his customary charm. However, when Kayama chose to invite Blue Comets leader Jackey Yoshikawa on to his show, the drummer – himself a well-known media personality – was less than happy with Kayama's line of questioning. For while the arrival of rock'n'roll had stormed Japanese culture in the late 1950s, the name of the genre with its difficult-to-pronounce combination of multiple 'r' and 'l' sounds had long been a thorn in Japanese pride. Furthermore, many Japanese movers and shakers had been searching around for a more easily pronounced equivalent. The term '*eleki*' had been a highly useful substitute, but only for the instrumental genre that it so accurately described. And with the British Invasion imminent, Yuzo Kayama – right there on live TV – demanded of his guest how could any of them possibly become true to their chosen art form if they couldn't even manage to pronounce 'lock'n'lorr'! Placing great emphasis on this mispronunciation in order to get a rise out of the drummer, the media-savvy Yuzo Kayama was surprised when Yoshikawa admitted his difficulty.

But instead of merely sweating and looking foolish, Jackey turned the tables on his debonair adversary and challenged his TV host to come up with something more appropriate. Raising his eyes heavenwards and blowing out several lungfuls of hot air, Kayama fell silent briefly before asking: 'Why don't we call the music "The Group Sounds"?'

By the end of the month, the Japanese media and rock fans alike had taken to this easily pronounced catchall and so it was … Group Sounds was born.

Footnotes:

1   From the late '60s onwards, Terumasa Hino turned out some fabulous Miles Davis-informed jazz.
While Hino's hectic full-tilt 1975 LP SPEAK TO LONELINESS showed him at the peak of late-'60s Miles
obsession, the trumpeter once again struck gold in 1981 with DOUBLE RAINBOW, an album whose
sounds were a homage to Miles's 1975 funkathons DARK MAGUS, AGARTHA and PANGAEA. On such long
grooves as the quarter-of-an-hour 'Merry-Go-Round' and the twelve minutes of 'Aboriginal', Hino employed
the same multiple percussion, wah guitars and atonal soul organ that Miles favoured during the AGARTHA
period, as well as the sinking-proto-dub mix effects that producer Teo Macero deployed throughout GET
UP WITH IT and AGARTHA itself, but which Macero had first contextualised within the confines of the
disorganised punk R&B of 'Right Off' from A TRIBUTE TO JACK JOHNSON.

2   When the producers of the James Bond films opted to follow up John Barry's 'Theme from James Bond'
not with another similar instrumental but with a Shirley Bassey vocal for their *Goldfinger* movie, Japanese
organist Munetake Inoue & His Sharp Five seized their opportunity for a hit with their own outré
instrumental take. Inoue's bizarre version of 'The Theme from Goldfinger' first requisitioned the
pedestrian-pumping organ and slacker drums of Sam the Sham & the Pharaohs, utilising this backing
track as a vehicle for Hank Marvin's 'Apache'-period guitar style, with some added Joe Meek-in-space
sound FX.

CHAPTER 4
THE
GROUP SOUNDS
STORY グループ　サウンズの時代

The Beatles' Japanese Tour & the Second Coming

On 29th June 1966, Japanese music, nay, the whole of Japanese culture changed for ever with the arrival of the Beatles. Taking the arduous polar route north via Anchorage, where they were grounded overnight to avoid a typhoon in the China Sea, it's fair to state that when the exhausted and irritable John, Paul, George and Ringo stepped off the plane at dawn into the oppressive summer heat of Haneda Airport, everyone was delighted to see these four young Gods, with the possible exception of certain militant nationalist student groups and the Tokyo Beatles themselves. Indeed, rock'n'roll singer Yuya Utchida had gone out of his way to honour the band with his specially recorded ballad 'Welcome Beatles'. Unfortunately, it was the malevolent attitude of the student fanatics that provided the real backdrop to the Beatles' stay, and Tokyo's police commissioner greeted Beatles manager Brian Epstein with the news that death threats had been made against the fabulous four. Already unhappy with the ever increasing Westernisation of Japan, the students were outraged at the authorities' decision to stage the Beatles' shows at Tokyo's legendary Budokan culture centre, which contained a shrine for Japan's dead war heroes. The Japanese authorities, painfully obsessed with maintaining their national honour whilst playing host to such international stars, would not kowtow to the students' demands by relocating the shows, and chose instead to guard the Beatles and their entourage with several thousand police and soldiers for the entire duration of their stay. And so it was as part of a military motorcade that the Beatles' touring party made their way along the Tokyo road from Haneda Airport, as armed motorcycle outriders announced the group's arrival to the tens of thousands who struggled to break through the police cordon to hurl themselves delightedly at the Beatles' vast white 1950s limousine[1] as it crawled through the early-morning chaos. The four Liverpud-lians holed up in the 24-room Presidential Suite in the penthouse of Tokyo's Capitol Tokyu Hotel, where the lifts had been programmed to terminate at the floor below. Here, guests of the touring party would be greeted by an entire platoon of military guards, who allowed ascent into the penthouse only via one single rear staircase. Brian Epstein was informed that none of the Beatles' party must leave for fear of assassination. Instead, seemingly endless supplies of fine jewellery, garments, trinkets and the like were brought up for their inspection, as an overawed gaggle of star-struck celebrities crowded the expansive lobby, awaiting an audience with these alien lords. Spurred on by the overwhelming success of the Ventures' 1965 Japanese tour, Japanese guitar companies had built over 760,000 guitars up to year's end. But if the *eleki buumu* of the previous four years had looked like being the pinnacle of rock'n'roll in Japan, it was only because the Beatles had not yet been factored into the equation; and many of the exotic wares now being paraded through the Beatles' penthouse, especially such technological triumphs as cameras and recording equipment, were accompanied by the enthusiastic managing directors of the companies which had made them.

Preparations for the tour had been fastidious at the Japanese end, and all the major music production companies had battled hard to secure their artists a support slot on the five controversial Budokan shows, scheduled to take place in Tokyo's Kitanomaru Park. All except the Spiders, that is, who already ran their own Spiduction management company and whose five-year climb to the top of the Japanese music scene was considered far too important to risk being dismissed by weepy teens with eyes only for Beatle John and his cohorts. No, the Budokan support slot was an honour to be shared between Terry & the Bluejeans and the humorous pop troupe the Drifters[2] – both outfits led by former sidemen of *eleki* pioneer Jimmie Tokita – as the Beatles laid upon the Japanese an eleven-song live set that was more dutiful than inspired. Indeed, over those five consecutive shows, rigorously policed by 3,000 armed cops, John, Paul, George and Ringo played just eleven songs to their 9,000 delirious fans before high-tailing it south to Manila, where they would be unwittingly plunged into an even bigger diplomatic spat with Imelda, wife of Filipino dictator Ferdinand Marcos. It's now common knowledge that, by the time the Beatles hit Japan, they'd just about had it up to here with touring, and were about to call it a day. But it's still something of a shock to peruse the Beatles' Japanese setlist and see nothing more than a catchall of their previous four years' work. Who could believe that Lennon, McCartney, Harrison or Starr (then arguably at their artistic height with RUBBER SOUL and REVOLVER) could have gained one iota of satisfaction from churning out, night after night, Chuck Berry's 'Rock'n'roll Music', 'She's a Woman', 'If I Needed Someone', 'Day Tripper', 'Baby's in Black', 'I Feel Fine', 'Yesterday', 'I Wanna Be Your Man', 'Nowhere Man', 'Paperback Writer' and 'I'm Down' (and always in that order)? But, with only two current tunes in their set, that was precisely what the Beatles chose to unleash, as armed military sharp-shooters hidden in the orchestra pit and placed high in the eaves of Budokan scanned the exits for evidence of extremist reprisals. However, the Japanese audiences in attendance that summer were not at Budokan to applaud the quality of their heroes' respective performances so much as to honour and worship the Beatles themselves. Thus waving goodbye to the Beatles at Haneda Airport, on 3rd July 1966, was – to the newly Westernised and still-insular Japanese – somewhat akin to watching four divinities departing Earth; so much so that damn near everyone in Japanese popular culture was, for the next half decade at least, consumed with following 'The Way of the Beatles'.

Careful with That Mosrite, Masayuki!

If early July 1966 was a cool time to be English in Japan, then late July '66 was even better, as the England football team won the World Cup by beating Germany 4–2 at Wembley Stadium. Carnaby Street threads, Union Jack prints, Swinging London and the fabulous four were all the Japanese could think about, as scores of new groups formed in the wake of the Beatles' visit. The media resounded with the new term Group Sounds, as Yuzo Kayama's clever catchall description was applied wholesale to any and all of the British-Invasion- and Beatles-inspired ensembles that had been cropping up across Japan throughout late '66; groups with names such as the Free Lancers, the Dimensions, the Carnabeats, the Fingers, the Darts, the Glories, the Black Stones and the Napoleon [sic]. Of the first wave of these all-new post-Beatles-Tour bands, however, those who were first to make a real impression were certainly the Mops, the Golden Cups, the Tempters, the Jaguars and the Tigers.

The Mops were a Tokyo quintet led by drummer Mikiharu Suzuki, who had actually begun as an instrumental Ventures-styled four-man combo in the spring of '66. However, the band was completed with the arrival of Suzuki's older brother Hiromitu, a lead vocalist with an Eric Burdon obsession. Suzuki added hugely to the Mops' fuzzy garage soul, and Victor Records soon snapped up the band. Despite their redundant Merseybeat-homage name, the Mops were a dedicated closely knit family whose love of garage rock and the burgeoning psychedelia would, in the coming years, help them to create some of the most urgently deranged and euphorically disruptive music of the entire Group Sounds era. Moreover, it was the Mops' love of rock'n'roll excess in all things – lighting rigs, huge PA systems, FX pedals, etc. – that was to goad other contemporary Japanese bands into making real sonic statements.

Similarly screwy, and in collective possession of a delinquent gene hitherto unknown in the overly polite Japanese society, were the fabulous Golden Cups. This young quintet hailed from the cosmopolitan port of Yokohama City, whose nearby docks and US Army base guaranteed that every local hipster who bothered could get their hands on the newest sounds from the West months in advance of the rest of Japan. Moreover, the Golden Cups were a truly international bunch, whose lead vocalist Tokimune 'Dave' Hirao and lead guitarist Eddie Ban had both (separately) made rock'n'roll pilgrimages to the United States in 1965. Indeed, when Eddie had returned with the first fuzz box to arrive on Japanese soil, a local guitar manufacturer had copped a look at its contents and was soon selling knock-offs around the islands. Rhythm guitarist Kenneth Ito was actually an English-speaking Hawaiian, giving the Cups an easy entry into authentic rock'n'roll lyrics, and Ito claimed to be the first in Japan with a genuine Fender guitar; whilst the Cups' 6'1"-tall bass player, who went by the stage name of Louis Louis Kabe, was a beautifully lean Franco-Japanese druggie from the local international school, who – in the absence of marijuana and LSD – turned the rest of the Golden Cups on to sniffing paint thinner and Marusan Pro Bond glue. Compared to other Japanese bands, the Golden Cups were sociopathic renegades from the wrong side of the world, and their career was to be one of multiple highs, lows and total disasters. But dammit they were (mainly) forward-thinking motherfuckers whose attitudes (if not always their music) dragged Japan's reluctant ass out of its sobriety like none before or after them.

Also of immense importance to the fashioning of the early Group Sounds scene was the six-piece known as the Jaguars, led by drummer Yukio Miya. The Jaguars, or 'jaggerz' as the Japanese referred to them, straddled the hinterland between pure pop music and garage rock, turning out versions of the Blues Magoos' arrangement of 'Tobacco Road' and Mitch Ryder's 'See See Rider', but taking their shorter-haired image from those overly smiley British muckers Dave Dee, Dozy, Beaky, Mick & Tich. Indeed, the Jaguars recorded their own version of that band's 45 'Zabadak' and scored another Top-20 hit with Dave Dee's cod-Spaghetti-Western epic 'Legend of Xanadu', transplanted into a Greek context with balalaikas and the whole band done out as Greek-peasant fashion victims.

Far heavier and more garagey were the Tempters, a smart-looking five-piece from Saitama led by sixteen-year-old soul singer Kennichi Hagiwara. The Tempters prided themselves on their Shadows-of-Knight-style dedication to the Rolling Stones and Them, and the band's earliest singles have long appeared on Western *Nuggets*-style garage compilations. And although the Tempters' roots as a Ventures-styled instrumental act were given away somewhat by their two guitarists' use of ice-white Mosrites, the overall effect was of something brand new and refreshingly free of artifice.

Not so the Tigers, however, whose lead singer Julie Sawada was a pouting effeminate prima donna whom everyone adored and loathed in equal measure, but whose presence made his band the biggest of all these brand-new Group Sounds outfits. The ultra-poppy Tigers had begun in the ancient city of Kyoto, in 1965, as the comparatively raunchy and rebellious Sally & the Playboys. Led by bass player Osami Kishibe, who went under the name 'Sally' to wind up the locals, Sally & the Playboys had one night found themselves upstaged by the antics of the lead singer of their support band the Thunders. This singer, Kenji Sawada, joined Sally & the Playboys, who changed their name first to the Funnies, then to the Tigers, as new boy Sawada – inspired by bass player Sally – adopted the stage name Julie after his beloved heroine Julie Andrews. Thereafter, the band came under the temporary influence of the ever aspirational Yuya Utchida, who secretly wished to dump Julie and become lead singer himself. However, when Utchida signed the band to a management contract at the powerful Watanabe Pro., the Tigers fell under the spell of 23-year-old Watanabe staff songwriter Koichi Sugiyama, who told them of Utchida's plans and derided him as an old failed rocker from the '50s. Unfortunately, while the Tigers' story is of great historical importance to our Group Sounds tale, their post-Utchida music was so diluted and compromised by Watanabe that it was to contribute about as much to rock'n'roll as the Pope has given feminism. So while the Tigers became arguably the biggest pop stars of the new Group Sounds scene, Yuya Utchida was so outraged at being ousted that he quit Japan and headed for the heart of the action ... Swinging London.

Catch Us If You Can

Besieged by this abrupt influx of famished skinny young pups on to their scene, pre-Group-Sounds-era bands such as Jimmie Takeuchi & the Exciters and Jackey

Yoshikawa's Blue Comets rightly felt pressured to drop their suddenly dated *eleki* sound in favour of English-language songs. The Spiders had cleverly anticipated just such a musical change by adding, two years previously, a much younger singer to their line-up in the form of Jun Inoue, the band themselves gradually adding songs by the Animals, the Kinks, Them and the Yardbirds to their repertoire. But certain groups really struggled with the new orthodoxy, especially the specific Group Sounds demand for be-suited young males bearing guitars. This Beatle Age certainly improved the lot of the Sharp Hawks' aptly named singer Jimmy Lennon. But this once-exotic four-boys/one-girl soul-revue band found it difficult to learn to play their own instruments to the level demanded by their heavyweight managers. Moreover, the presence of female singer Yuji Nozawa was now deemed inappropriate for the Sharp Hawks' essential new Group Sounds direction, so she was unceremoniously dumped. It was not quite such a drag for everyone, however. In Yokohama City, the Robin Hoods' sixteen-year-old leader Ai Takano simply renamed his band the Carnabeats and cultivated a friendship with the Walker Brothers to imply links to the British Invasion bands; whilst the Outlaws, a sextet from Tokyo in existence since 1964 and led by future '70s guitar star Hideki Ishima, changed their name to the Beavers for their first Spiders support show, giving everyone the impression that they had blasted out of nowhere as fully formed as Athena appearing from the head of Zeus. From the Philippines, the wild quintet D'Swooners were spotted supporting Manfred Mann and the Kinks in Hong Kong by a holidaying Yuzo Kayama, who invited the band to Japan where they were immediately adopted as an honorary Group Sounds act. Refusing to become anybody's has-been, the ever opportunist *eleki* legend Terry Terauchi left his Bluejeans to fender for themselves, and commenced a new vocal career backed by a younger ensemble whom he named the Bunnys. Meanwhile, intuitively understanding the Group Sounds trend for younger and younger ensembles, and increasingly stimulated by the new electric FX coming out of Western rock'n'roll, Terauchi also percipiently started his own stable of Group Sounds bands with whom he could conduct further sonic studio experiments in the style of Joe Meek. First, Terry hooked up with a very young six-piece ensemble who had long worshipped his *eleki* sound, and whose members included Mitsuharu Yamada, who played the mysterious-sounding new Yamaha Electone keyboard. Naming them the Phoenix, Terry signed the band to the King record company and produced their debut single 'Koisuru La La La' (La La La in Love), adding a mysterious early Electric Prunes atmosphere to the song with his clever use of Yamaha Electone and sending Tadashi Kutiyama's lead guitar through a wah-wah pedal. It was the first use of such an effect on a Japanese record, and the reaction was sensational. Other groups clamoured to join Terry's stable, which soon included the Edwards,[3] the Crack Nuts, 491 (Four Nine Ace)[4] and the confusingly named the Terrys. It was a business trend soon to be followed by production companies all over the big cities, as Group Sounds (or GS as it was quickly becoming known) became the only pop scene in which to be seen.

Watanabe, Asuka Pro, Spiduction & the Rise of the Management Companies

With 20/20 hindsight, it's easier nowadays to explain the Group Sounds period as a business phenomenon rather than as a musical movement, for the power was forever to remain in the hands of heavyweight management companies such as Watanabe Pro. and Asuka Pro. These big management companies paid their stylists to spot potential *idoru*, or lead-singer material, to overly dress and colour-code their young charges, to coiffure and manicure, paint and powder them, until many groups who had been signed up as wildly unpredictable longhairs found themselves so battered and brutalised by their arduous journey through the Group Sounds management blender that their record and TV debuts bore little or no resemblance to the refusenik bedroom ensemble they had started in the first place. Inconsistency became the order of the day, as GS outfits such as the Golden Cups – who played live shows full of screaming feedback and delivered blazing B-sides of Leaves/Love/Blues Magoos-informed punk rock – were still forced, through razor-sharp management contracts, to appear on TV performing creepy ballads that made them sound like whingeing ninnies. The Cups' light and breathy version of the Classics IV's 'Spooky' epitomises this approach, the original's tough chiming guitar and desperate vocals here replaced with a string section straight out of 'A Walk in the Black Forest' and zippy and overly loud apeman snare-drum fills.

93

The once rowdy Tigers eventually became absolute lords of the GS scene, but only through playing their management company's game absolutely to the letter. This included changing their image to suit each new single release and recording what-ever the staff writers churned out for them, plus going along with whatever scam their PR team at Watanabe Pro. dreamed up. For example, as success abroad had always been the ultimate seal of approval to Japanese pop fans, the Tigers' manage-ment team sent the band to film a Japanese TV commercial in the USA, where they also appeared as part of the studio audience on the legendary *Ed Sullivan Show*. When, on the band's return home, their PR team announced 'direct from their appear-ance on *Ed Sullivan*', none of the Tigers dared admit that it had been only as members of the audience. And although the Tigers were soon generating over $1,000,000 per year, it's said that Watanabe never increased each band member's salary beyond $300 per month.

Right at the top echelon of the GS scene, staff songwriters working for the management companies guarded their territory so fiercely that, even with two self-penned hits under their belt, the Tempters were forced to record a sickly ballad as their third single. What chance was there, then, for saccharine choirboys such as the Genova, the Floral or Ox? Such was the iron fist of the GS management style that bands were even banned from hanging out with other bands for fear of giving away secrets; the Carnabeats' drummer Ai Takano later admitted to donning disguise in order to visit his good friend Sin Okamoto, vocalist with the Jaguars. Luckily, long-term careerists the Spiders had managed to avoid falling under the spell of any heavy-handed management team by forming their own Spiduction management company long before the Group Sounds phenomenon had arisen. So when the Tempters found themselves being forced to record songs they had no interest in by their bullying management, the musicians jumped ship to Spiduction because of its artist-led approach.

Early on in the GS era, producers constantly thwarted GS musicians' attempts to infuse their sound with the tough new soul-based noise that spewed from the mouths of Eric Burdon, Steve Winwood, James Brown, Wilson Pickett and Barrett Strong. Luckily, however, the tough rampaging sound of the Philippines' D'Swooners were already big hits in Japan, providing leverage for the musicians' arguments that Japanese audiences had already shown their need for hard R&B. In this way, the Voltage got to release Otis Redding's 'In the Midnight Hour', the Tempters got hold of Howlin' Wolf's 'Boom Boom' and the soul standard 'Everybody Needs Somebody', and even the Tigers couldn't ruin the Rolling Stones' 'Time Is on My Side'. Zoo Nee Voo released a pretty fine version of Sam & Dave's 'Hold on, I'm Comin'', but no one was ready for their cover of Booker T's 'Green Onions', which featured an obstinate organist who ran riot across the blue notes of the melody like a Bavarian lederhosen band, but achieved a sound so dry and extremely stereo that it comes across like an early dub mix.[5]

'But What Is Group Sounds?'

By the middle of 1967, the Japanese propensity for formalising artistic and cultural phenomena was beginning to take its toll on the GS scene, as movers and shakers within the biz went further and further out of their way to define and distil the Group Sounds metaphor. And as Group Sounds had ultimately become a 'product' created not by the musicians themselves, but by young hip managers, stylists, Hairdressers, record producers and musical entrepreneurs (all of whom had shared a mutual love for such scams as the Monkees and *A Hard Day's Night*), then it was probably only to be expected that these music-business insiders would have taken increasing pleasure in creating the ultimate Group Sounds act. So what was their estimation of the ultimate GS configuration? Well, although the Tigers were right at the top of the Group Sounds order and wore all the correct garb, there was still something too fey, too precious, too feminine about their lead singer Julie Sawada for him to be worthy of consideration as an ultimate Group Sounds archetype. The Spiders were surely wild enough, but they'd been around since the early *eleki buumu* and were just too old. The Mops on the other hand were too weird, too punk, too real, too ugly! The Golden Cups? Too fumed up on paint thinners and glue and too capricious to play the game; hell, the Cups wouldn't even wear the outfits their stylists brought to promo sessions! This left the Tempters and the Jaguars as the main contenders, both bands featuring handsome Eurasian lead singers, and both sharing a thirst for immaculate King's Road-style mod uniforms, a dedication to collective haircuts à la Monkees' Davy Jones and Peter Tork, and ne'er a dork amongst them! Add a dash of Paul Revere & the Raiders' rebel costumerie and the Japanese love of chintzy minor-chord string-laden ballad weepies, and you've entered the Group Sounds' pleasure zone.

It's my assertion, however, that the Jaguars ultimately won the day and forged the uber-GS archetype with their six-piece ensemble of vocalist, two guitars, organist, bass player and drummer. For it was this precise configuration that, at the height of the GS phenomenon, cropped up again and again and again, in such sextets as the Cougars, the Rangers, the Gullivers, the Phoenix, the Lions, the Swing West and the Terrys, all of whom obeyed every GS rule to the letter, and never appeared without their uniforms. Also conforming to the Jaguarine archetype were the Lind & Linders, an exuberant all-winking, all-smiling Nehru-suit-wearing sextet who recorded their wonderful version of Otis Redding's 'Ha Ha Ha' for Philips Records, as did the Youngers, who'd been cobbled together by Philips Records stylists from GS wannabes from all across Japan.

Then there was the Out Cast, led by future guitar star Jun 'Kimio' Mizutani, who'd clearly believed that his band fitted the Jaguarine sextet archetype perfectly, only to discover that their managers Watanabe Pro. were quite happy to replace any or all of them whenever they stepped out of line … which of course they did, and then some. By the end of the Out Cast's two-year career, only one original Out Cast member survived. Then, of course, there was Mustang … ah yes, Mustang. What the hell would Watanabe have done with Mustang? Still, despite hanging out with the rest of the underground Commie sociopaths in Kyoto University, and despite looking like genuine renegades from Australia's Pretty Things-styled garage-rock scene (yeti such as the Creatures, Missing Links and Running Jumping Standing Still immediately come to mind), somehow Mustang fitted in with the rest of London Records' GS roster just long enough to fulfil their Jaguarine GS metaphor AND have a hit with their sexy garage classic 'Mustang Baby'. Oo yeah!

Marianne & the Folk Rock Boom

As the Group Sounds scene became increasingly commercialised by huge management companies, many artists and musicians seeking a genuine alternative turned to playing folk music or folk rock. And so, throughout 1967–8, acoustic songs such as 'Just One More Time' by the Wild Ones, 'Memories of Bouquet' by the Darts, 'Lili' by the Route Five, 'When You Love Me' by the Black Stones and 'Kazeyo Kazeyo' by the Savage provided a genuine alternative soundtrack to the schlock served up by the Tigers and their ilk. Indeed, future Faces/Free bassist Tetsu Yamauchi began his career in the folk-rock band the Mikes, whose single 'Ramblin' Man' gained considerable attention. However, the real leaders of the folk rock boom were the dark and radicalised quartet the Jacks, whose black clothes, existentialist angst and refusal to kowtow even to the underground made them instant stars. Starting out in 1966 as the drummerless trio Nightingale, the Jacks were led by the ultra longhaired and perpetually be-Rayban'd singer Yoshio Hayakawa, whose surly interviews caused a sensation:

'We are not underground. That's just an idea created by the media. We became outsiders from the folk jamboree [as] we don't have the goal to be famous, so it's difficult for people to understand and define us ... it's a dirty world, you gotta go in there yourself and find out.'

The Jacks' choice of jazz drummer Takasuke Kida gave their music an off-kilter sound, especially as they set the poems of singer Hayakawa and his girlfriend Yasuko Aizawa to music.

The band went stellar after the 1968 release of their debut LP VACANT WORLD and its nihilistic single 'Marianne'. Written by Yasuko Aizawa, this was an incredible minor-key death dirge about the undead Marianne, who emerges from the stormy seas to seize the unsuspecting singer and drag him to his doom.

Other sextets ignored the Jaguars' archetype and opted instead for the Spiders' proto-Sam & Dave/Righteous Brothers twin-vocalist soul-revue approach. The Beavers may have been the best artistic example of this approach, but it was the Jet Brothers & the Fighters who did it with the most aplomb – and that convoluted name was certainly the best GS mouthful yet. It all came about when Toshiba's subsidiary Express Records signed two young mop-topped singers the Jet Brothers, but decided that the duo needed a fierce-looking backing group to pep up their image, at which point the Fighters were born. And how about the Free Lancers, who took both the look and the sound of Merseybeat into a strange almost Maoist retro-folk area with button-fronted serge land-army outfits, Salvation Army wide-eyed exuberance and Seeds-like 'Pushin' Too Hard' repeated choruses, all executed in a highly driven Beatlesesque acoustic yammer. In the 1966 movie *Seishun A Go Go*, the Free Lancers' wonderfully Japanglish-titled 'I Know You Love Nuts about Him' was performed by a drummer and six front men, three of whom were playing no instrument, and all this at a time when the guitar-slinging male was at its zenith as a sexual archetype. How free is that? In the same movie, big stars the Spiders were co-opted by Lulu-style singer Judy Onng as she howled out a vile big-band number 'Say Mama' like a Lena Zavaroni brat with a melting lollipop. By the end of said big show toon, Ms Onng's phizog was extended – mouth agape – across the whole cinema screen, leaving the Spiders themselves as anonymous as contenders for the Liberal Democrats' leadership. But the Spiders were, nevertheless, involved in the first of their many successful teen movies. And where the Spiders dared to tread, so the other GS bands were destined to follow …

Feature Films of the GS Era

Teen movies had taken the post-war world by storm as early as 1956, when such fare as *Blackboard Jungle* and *The Girl Can't Help It* had captured the spirits of cinema-seat-slashing Teddy Boys. But not even the post-army Elvis movies had captured the Zeitgeist of its generation like Richard Lester's depiction of the Beatles in *A Hard Day's Night* and *Help!*. The Japanese, with their love of monster movies like *Godzilla*, *Ghidorah*, and (most especially) director Ishira Honda's *Mothra* trilogy, were well used to ludicrous themes that mixed the sublime with the ridiculous. The entire Japanese population appears to have embraced the female singing duo the Peanuts almost as mythical beings when the two had played the faerie guardians of the giant insect goddess Mothra. This Japanese acceptance of the entertainment industry as a mythical hinterland wherein almost any opposing ideas could meet head-on had made Yuzo Kayama's transition from film star to lead guitarist comparatively smooth.

Indeed, his fans had not even complained when the erstwhile 'Young General' had combined both elements in the 1965 movie *Eleki no Wakadaisho* (The Young General's Electric Guitar). And so it was with a sense of inevitability that the biggest of the Group Sounds bands found themselves embarking on a movie career.

For the Spiders, their aforementioned guest appearance in Judy Onng's *Seishun A Go Go* had been an essential reminder that they were still the Godfathers of the scene. So when the similarly titled *Wild Scheme A Go Go* was sent to the Spiders in script form, the band jumped at the opportunity to be the first Japanese band to star in their own movie. That the plot and camera techniques plagiarised every Beatles'n'Monkees movie thus far invented was of no matter to the Spiders, who were seasoned enough to make any rip-off entirely their own. By '67, each of the seven members had his own personal fan club and occupied a place in the hearts of both teenage girls and boys, similar to Madness's role in the early '80s. Like Chas Smash and Suggsy, no amount of goofing around on Saturday morning TV shows, presenting prizes with old-timer celebrities or doing the occasional sappy ballad was going to convince their fans that they'd gone soft. And so long as singers Masaaki Sakai and Jun Inoue could be seen doing their James Brown-inspired 'Monkey Dance' up on the big screen, all was still right with the world. Moreover, even their film producers insisted that the wild Monks-like 'furi furi furi furi' garage chanting of 'O Monki De Odoro' (Let's Dance Monkey) be included in *Wild Scheme A Go Go*. 99

The movie was, however, a far bigger hit than any of the band had anticipated and immediately elevated them above the rest of the Group Sounds scene. There were, therefore, no surprises when the Spiders were offered a fake spy movie entitled *Go Forward* the following year. With their proto-Devo chant ('Are We Not Crazy Cats? No, We Are Spiders!') and stomping whooping self-referential rebel yell 'Here Come Spiders', the Spiders were in their element as sinister types engaged in airport brief-case mix-ups while dead guys fell out of guitar speaker cabs; the movie makers successfully followed 'The Way of Richard Lester' to the letter.

Feeling themselves being upstaged by the old guys, the Jaguars were the first to respond later in '68 with their movie *Tekizen Youriko* (Hey You, Go!). Again, the blue-print never veered off the Beatles map for a moment, but, with an evil Blofeld type manipulating the Underworld one minute, and guitarist Hisayuki Okitu soloing wildly whilst surrounded by suggestive models sucking, nay, giving head to ice lollies the next, no one was really complaining … except, of course, the Tigers, who prided themselves on being the biggest on the GS scene. Unfortunately for Julie'n'Sally'n'Co, however, disaster had struck in November 1967 when several fans had been injured in a stampede at a Tigers show. NHK-TV had thereafter pulled the group from all of their proposed television appearances as a sop to the parents' groups, teachers' unions and other authority figures who had long been questioning the acceptability of the Group Sounds scene. In short, the Tigers were temporarily used as scape-goats and, in honour-obsessed Japan, there were (and still are) protocols to be followed if a media figure falls from grace through some *perceived* indiscretion. Furthermore, the Tigers' mighty Watanabe Pro. management were determined – as Japan's industry standard – to be seen to have acted with utmost professionalism. In summer 1968, Watanabe cannily rushed their boys into filming their first full-length movie, allowing the Tigers temporary respite from media overexposure. Watanabe then organised *The Tigers' Charity Show*, so that the band was seen to have publicly atoned for its somewhat ghostly wrongdoings.

So where were the Spiders? They were still working hard at it, in fact totally flat-out. Our leaders had managed a second movie for 1968, in the rather Bob Hope/Bing Crosby-titled *Road to Bali*, again featuring secret-agent men, plutonium-smuggling and atom bombs; then without even a break, the seven launched into the filming of their psychedelic flick *Big Commotion*, in which chaotic scenes full of groovy nude painted chicks, mod boutiques and ultra-disorientating rock sounds conflated together to create a generic overview of the period. In comparison to the Spiders' formidable output of this period, however, the Tigers' ill-named movie *Sekai Wa Bokura O Matte Iru* (The World Waits for Us) was just too little too late. And, by autumn '68, the Tigers' days at the top were slipping away as the Group Sounds era began slowly to unravel and fail.

The GS scene may have reached enormous numbers of teenagers inside Japan, but it had gained remarkably little success outside the islands. Even the Spiders had made no progress towards a successful Western career, despite having appeared on BBC-TV's top pop show *Ready Steady Go!* and having seen several of their 7" singles released in Britain, Australia, America, Brazil and the Netherlands.[6] Moreover, only in its death throes was the GS scene considered worthy of a real article in America's *Rolling Stone* magazine, finally appearing in the 1st March 1969 edition.[7] But for Western rock'n'roll fans engaged in necking vast quantities of psychedelics and, throughout 1968–69, participating in street and campus protests against racism, social injustices and the Vietnam War, Group Sounds was never going to be perceived as anything more than a charming anachronism at best.

Back home in Japan, the scene's movers and shakers had – in their attempts to define the GS phenomenon too rigidly – shut the door on anyone trying to break the mould. Groups offering Western-style heavy guitar music were not accepted into the GS camp, and these outfits – Helpful Soul, Apryl Fool, Powerhouse among them – all complained that they were being given no opportunities to play concerts. So whilst Western music had by this time already been through its folk-rock phase, its psych-edelic phase and its heavy phase, the success of the Tigers, the Tempters and the

Jaguars had given Japanese talent scouts such tunnel vision that their quest was only for Eurasian pretty-boy singers. These half-baked missions resulted in manufactured latecomers the Lead, three of whom were European, and the shamelessly named the Half Breed, a quintet comprised of three Japanese, one Hispanic and one European. Even the mighty Watanabe Pro. had gained only minimum headway when they'd attempted to change the GS formula in order to capitalise on the success of Procul Harum's 'A Whiter Shade of Pale' with Kuni Kawachi's organ-dominated Happenings Four. 'B... b... but where are the guitarists?' spluttered everyone. 'It just ain't Group Sounds!'

Mercifully, there was still one particularly straight-talking *agent provocateur* unwilling to toe the official GS line. In mid-1968, the ever belligerent Yuya Utchida had returned from his self-imposed exile in Britain, where he had bided his time experimenting with psychedelics and formulating a dramatic return to his homeland. All the while watching the rise of hard psychedelic rock via the Who, the Yardbirds, Pink Floyd, Cream and Jimi Hendrix, Utchida was more determined than ever to create a Japanese outfit capable of such sonic outrage. Starting with the Beavers' disillusioned star guitarist Hideki Ishima, Utchida cherry-picked the best Group Sounds musicians he could find and named his new band the Flowers. Next, lap steel guitarist Katsuhiko Kobayashi was invited to join in order to capture the stratospheric tone of Glenn Ross Campbell, from John Peel's Californian protégés the Misunderstood, 101 whom Utchida had seen perform several times at London's UFO club. Furthermore, inspired by Grace Slick and Janis Joplin, Utchida smashed the GS mould to smithereens by asking the beautiful female singer Remi Aso to front this wild new artrock ensemble, whom he assured his colleagues were also going to play Japanese-styled instrumentals of a kind never before experienced. The new ensemble made their debut performance at the end of '68, performing their instrumental 'Sohshiju' over the opening credits of the movie *Ah Himeyuri-no-Tou*, and the Flowers' live shows began soon after. With their debut LP, appropriately entitled CHALLENGE!, the Flowers blasted the GS scene out of its stasis in mid-1969. For the album not only contained hard versions of Big Brother, Cream and Jefferson Airplane songs, but also entirely re-wrote the rock'n'roll map by featuring all of the band members – Miss Aso included – naked in a cornfield.

The Death of Group Sounds, the Rise of Futen & the Coming of Hair

Inspired by the hippies of San Francisco's Haight-Ashbury district, disaffected teenagers from across Japan had, from mid-1968 onwards, begun to congregate in the Shinjuku area of Tokyo, around the Village Gate jazz club and two coffee shops, Ogi and the Go-Go-Café. And, just as acid guru Timothy Leary's mantra 'Turn on, tune in, drop out' had become a rallying cry for alienated Western youth, so Japan's runaways had lately become infatuated with the romantic dropout 'Futen' character, a crazy cartoon hobo whose restless lifestyle had first become popular in the April '67 edition of *Com* magazine. Like America's hippie cartoonist R. Crumb, the 'Futen' cartoon's creator Shinji Nagashima had become an underground hero in Japan, and teenagers had – in the past eighteen months – rushed out to buy each latest edition of *Com* in order to keep up with the exploits of their proto-slacker hero, whose every thought process was antagonistic to their parents' generation.[8] The archaic pop-idol values of Group Sounds were diminishing with every long-haired hippie who arrived on the streets of Tokyo's Shinjuku area, and the ultimate celebration of the new values arrived at the beginning of 1969 with the announcement that America's hippie 'Tribal Love Rock Musical' had been translated into Japanese for a forthcoming season in a major Tokyo theatre. Yes, *Hair* was about to hit Japan!

From our twenty-first-century vantage point, it's quite impossible to explain the levels of worldwide hostility and adulation that greeted *Hair* when it first appeared in the late '60s, or, moreover, the grand kudos that rockers and entertainers received from having appeared in it. To we moderns, the songs are dismally twee playground singalongs, the so-called choreography is anarchy, the nudity is obligatory, and the script and plot are as out of reach as heat haze on a summer road. For contemporary audiences brought up on *Oliver!*, *West Side Story* and *Porgy & Bess*, however, it was precisely this lack of structure that held them all spellbound. From its small beginnings in a New York discothèque in October '67, *Hair* had – by the time it hit Japan – come by way of successful performances in Los Angeles, San Francisco and Chicago, thereafter crossing the Atlantic to stages in England, France, Germany, Portugal and the Netherlands. So seriously was *Hair* taken by the rock business that many would use it as a springboard to major '70s careers, the London cast alone yielding Alex Harvey, Elaine Paige, Melba Moore and *The Rocky Horror Picture Show*'s future stars Tim Curry and Richard O'Brien. The Sisyphus theatre ensemble that accompanied the London performances used their position to help launch a long international career as the progressive band Curved Air, as did their Amsterdam equivalent, who became Focus, best known for their international hit 'Hocus Pocus'. Furthermore, this controversial show was further validated for Middle England's *Daily Mail* readership when Queen Elizabeth's eighteen-year-old daughter Princess Anne joined the cast on stage at London's Shaftesbury Avenue. However, in Australia and New Zealand, even the LP itself was banned because of the song lyrics of 'Sodomy', 'Hashish' and 'Ain't Got No Grass', while the Mexican stage version in Acapulco was shut down by the authorities after just one performance, and its cast detained overnight then expelled from the city.

With *Hair*'s reputation for shock and social upheaval already preceding it, both the Japanese authorities and the country's music business prepared for the storm. At Watanabe Pro. and all the other big management companies, the news of *Hair*'s impending arrival was received with outright dismay, as umpteen musicians from the already haemorrhaging GS scene handed in their notice and immediately got in the queue to audition for parts in this uber-hip musical. Indeed, by the time auditions had begun, over 4,000 applicants had put forward their names to fill the places of the 28-strong cast. But while every GS musician dreamed of scoring a major role in *Hair*, when jazz drummer Akira Ishikawa was chosen as leader of the theatre band, it became immediately clear that the producers intended to rely on seasoned veterans. Ishikawa had been a successful career musician since the mid-'50s, releasing his own records in a variety of guises as well as under his own name. The *Hair* producers' intentions became even more clear when not only the brass section and rhythm section was taken from Japan's jazz scene, but so was rhythm guitarist Kiyoshi Sugimoto. However, Group Sounds was at least represented when Apryl Fool's organist Hiro Yanagida and Out Cast's lead guitarist Kimio Mizutani were invited into the ensemble. Furthermore, Tigers lead guitarist Katsumi 'Kato' Takahashi finally found his opportunity to step out of the shadows of Julie and Sally, when he was given the lead role of 'Claud'. That, however, was as far as the GS contingent was going to get in the upper echelons of *Hair*'s cast. Still, the rest would be content to take parts in the so-called 'Boy Tribe', a male chorus that soon became populated with ex-Group Sounds stars. From the Carnabeats came bass player Paul Okada, from the Glories came singer Fumio Miyashita, from the Dimensions came lead guitarist Shi Yu Chen, from 491 came singer Akira 'Joe' Yamanaka, from Apryl Fool came singer 'Chu' Kosaka; each taking a severe drop in salary and social cachet, but all happy to have jumped off the drifting ship that the foundering GS scene had become. For *Hair* was Right Now, and, compared to their obsolete GS scene, now seemed like the future.

Footnotes:

1   The Japanese promoters hired a special pink limousine to carry Brian Epstein, causing him enormous embarrassment as a gay man still in the closet and struggling to accept his own predicament in those homophobic times.

2   The Japanese Drifters were a cross between the Baron Knights and Freddie & the Dreamers, seaside-resort/pantomime fare from the days when being a pop musician was seen only as a useful springboard into the world of popular entertainment. The Drifters were a quintet led by Jimmie Tokita's former bass player Choichi Ikariya, whose intentionally gormless expressions endeared him to TV audiences.

3   The Edwards combined excellent fuzz-guitar riffs with Latin rhythms and minor chords, their Capitol Records 45 'Cry Cry Cry' coming on like American bands such as the E-Types and the Jaguars. But they also exhibited that horrible string-laden Spanish-galleon sound, all overblown weepy self-destruction that makes the Love Affair's 'Everlasting Love' sound Presbyterian.

4   491 was the kind of band no one would remember if not for the vocal presence of Akira 'Joe' Yamanaka, who later joined Flower Travellin' Band. This blue-suited quintet was a cringe-worthy proposition, their single for Seven Seas Records even including a straight '50s-styled spoken-word bit ('You're a pretty girl, like a white little shell'), whilst bland weak-as-shit harmonies further undermined the song's ersatz provenance like a powdery film of coffee complement around the rim of an instant caffé latte.

5   Tatsuya Ogino & the Bunnys' bizarre eleven-minute 'Lento Fantasy' aced even Zoo Nee Voo! Like some percipient prequel to Creedence Clearwater Revival's massively weird instrumental 'Rude Awakening', still some four years in the future, 'Lento Fantasy' was a hostile and atonal sea of guitars and sound FX that permeated an otherwise accommodating landscape of samba rhythms and Swingle Singers-by-the-sea, whilst generic Hammond organ was daubed arbitrarily over the entire track.

6   The front cover of their EP 'The Spiders in Europe' may have featured seven delighted band members
    euphoric with the excitement of having gained approval in the culture that had first inspired them. But
    however much kudos it gave them back home, the Spiders' career in the West was a non-starter. Few
    other Group Sounds acts even received foreign single releases, Mickey Curtis's Samurais (Britain,
    Italy, Germany) and Jackey Yoshikawa's Blue Comets (Mexico, Brazil, Argentina, Chile) being the only
    two I know of. Stranger still, Takeshi Terauchi & the Bunnys had their album LET'S GO CLASSICS
    released in Germany! Perhaps its bizarre sleeve, which depicted the band as a kind of Wagnerian
    Boney M, swayed the Deutsche record company.

7   However, even this *Rolling Stone* piece, entitled 'Rockin' in the Land of the Rising Sun' included the
    inanely patronising caption: 'Lock music is very popular ... Like Rady Jane and Yerroh Submaline ...
    But Japanese people cannot pronounce Lock'n'Lorr, so we call it Group Sounds.'

8   Japanese dictionaries formerly described the Futen as a crazy man with neither home nor family ties.
    However, through the upheavals of the late '60s, the dictionary nowadays offers this far wider
    definition: 'someone who runs away, has no fixed job, sometimes unusual (sometimes provocative)
    garb, which can be frowned upon. Futens tend to hang around the Shinjuku area, sometimes called
    Shinjuku Beggars. But some among them are dropouts from Tokyo University, even company
    managing directors who have left their homes after experiencing self-doubt, all sorts of people.'

BOOK TWO

CHAPTER 5
COME TOGETHER
1969 カム　トゥギャザー　'69
THE BIRTH OF UNDERGROUND JAPAN

Only barbarians are able to rejuvenate a world in
the throes of collapsing civilisation.
Frederick Engels
The Origins of the Family, Private Property and the State (1884)

Heralds of Astonishing Change

Book Two of our musical odyssey commences in 1969, when the cultural barriers that had long separated Japan's many artists and entertainers were – through the arduous process described in Book One – finally removed, allowing rock'n'rollers to work with classical composers, poets with easy-listening entertainers, experimental musicians with free-jazz fanatics, or any permutation of the above. The results of these experiments brought forth incredibly highly charged works, many of which defied attempts at categorisation, having been created during this unique period's mass celebratory orgy of grand holistic statements and hitherto unheard-of cultural unions. In the chapters of Book One, we learned of the post-war routes navigated by each of Japan's many and disparate artistic and musical factions, and of those characters involved in successfully bringing them all together in 1969's bizarre but cosmically righteous marriage of creative ideas. The history contained in Book One should, therefore, have equipped us to sit here in 1969 and enjoy the swift unravelling of Japan's most intensely fertile musical period, that is, the years 1969–75. But before we embark on a chapter-by-chapter study of the careers of my favourite artists, we should first remember to view all of these happenings in a worldwide context.

Stomp 'em! Stop 'em! Get 'em under Control!

In 1969, the world outside Japan's still-conservative society was undergoing astonishing changes. Indeed, 1968 had seen civil disobedience in Paris, Warsaw, Rome, Beijing, Prague, Mexico City and nearly every major US city with a large black population. If radicalised student youth culture had finally mobilised itself against the stasis of the ruling classes, then it was only because they had been spurred on by alienated racial minorities and the overworked underprivileged classes. Here in 1968, everything about the current social and political order was wide open to question. The Vietnam War and the segregation policies of America's openly racist southern states were making a mockery of the USA's claim to be at the heart of world democracy. No one was free from this time of extreme change, and even the previously self-serving Rolling Stones found themselves goaded into singing songs to 'The Salt of the Earth' and the 'Factory Girl', while Jim Morrison – with typical braggadocio – claimed to be all for slugging it out with the Man on the Doors' brazen anthem 'Five to One'.

For other rock'n'rollers, however, evidence of civil insurrection had been brewing on their doorsteps for three long years. In the USA, despite the Nobel Peace Prize that Martin Luther King had won in 1964 for his deeply moving 'I Have a Dream' speech and sustained policy of non-violent protest, Frank Zappa had, in August '65, witnessed the fallout from the riots in nearby Watts, where anger boiled over at the federal government's cynical decision to block the fair-housing section of the Civil Rights Act with its insertion of the controversial 'Proposition 14'. Holed up in his LA studio working on the Mothers of Invention's debut album FREAK OUT, Zappa poured out his feelings in the song 'Trouble Every Day', his lyrical portents of gloom accompanied by Dylan-alike protest-song harmonica. 'I'm not black, but there's a lot of times I wish I could say I'm not white,' he concluded.

But the injustices were not just about colour of skin. Some of this shit was tribal too. In March 1966, three black Muslims from America's Nation of Islam were sentenced to life imprisonment for the murder of black activist Malcolm X, whose defection from the party had incensed its leader Elijah Muhammad. That same spring, it was also tribalism that lay at the heart of Chairman Mao's desperate and misguided attempt to regain power from rivals Liu Shauqi and Deng Xiaoping via his so-called 'Cultural Revolution'. The move caused a national calamity, as Mao's Red Guard youth-militia movement had sought to prove its dedication to the cause by turning in neighbours, even their own families, killing millions of Chinese between '66 and '69. In Hong Kong, between May and October 1967, while the Monterey Pop Festival was showcasing performances by Jimi Hendrix, the Who, Otis Redding, Janis Joplin and Jefferson Airplane, Communist extremists sympathetic to the chaos of mainland China had embarked on a policy of randomly bombing capitalist institutions and murdering all media figures who dared speak out against them. In January 1968, Czechoslovakia's brave President Alexander Dubcek instigated a period of liberal reforms that were in direct opposition to the wishes of his Moscow bosses. But whilst the Czech reforms appeared to be holding, further antagonism towards the Soviet Union occurred in mid-March when 3,000 Polish students demonstrated on the streets of Warsaw. Over 200 were injured in the riots that ensued, as eleven university faculties were temporarily shut down.

On 6th April, further US race riots exploded in Baltimore, Washington DC, Cincinnati, Chicago and Los Angeles, when black Americans learned that Martin Luther King had been assassinated. Less than one week later, German students took to the streets to protest at the attempted assassination of their leader Rudi Dutschke, whose would-be assassin had been provoked into shooting the activist in the head by a particularly inflammatory right-wing-press headline that declared 'Stop Dutschke Now!' The following month, over-zealous riot-policing by the French authorities caused such outraged protests from student activists that General de Gaulle felt compelled to seek refuge in neighbouring Germany as a national strike by sympathetic workers brought the country to a standstill. That same May, in New York, on the third anniversary of the murder of Malcolm X, the Last Poets came together to tell the plight of black Americans in song. Inspired by Huey Newton and Bobby Seale's Black Panther Party, whose formation eighteen months previously had included a programme that called for 'Land, Bread, Housing, Education, Justice and Peace', the Last Poets set about politicising their brothers and sisters with such cultural broadsides as 'Wake Up, Niggers', 'When the Revolution Comes', 'Run Nigger' and 'Niggers Are Scared of Revolution'. Also acutely aware that Malcolm X had taken up the same Muslim religion as the Arab slavers who had sold his ancestors to whitey, and that Martin Luther King had preached the Christian gospel as taught to his family by the same white plantation owners who had imprisoned them, the Last Poets attempted to break this vicious cycle of oppression by choosing also to celebrate the Yoruba nature religion of their Nigerian ancestors.

But whilst the world's underprivileged were up against it that summer of '68, neither the Beatles nor the Rolling Stones appeared committed enough to describe through their art the extraordinary events taking place around them, preferring instead to deliver songs with pretentious titles that suggested unity and brotherhood – 'Revolution' and 'Street Fighting Man' – but which were in reality all mouth and no trousers. And in a righteous double blow against their pop-star political fence-sitting, the Stones' single 'Street Fighting Man' failed to hit the Top 40, and John Lennon failed to get 'Revolution' released as the first Beatles single on their new Apple label, losing out to McCartney's rousing but la-de-da anthem 'Hey Jude'. However, as the cringe-worthy chorus of 'Revolution' ('Don't you know it's gonna be all right?') stood in direct opposition to all current evidence, perhaps it was best that Lennon was offered more time to adjust his political position.

And, thus, the torture and chaos continued unabated. On 21st August, Soviet tanks invaded Czechoslovakia, bringing to a bloody end the country's brief period of liberalisation that would become known as 'The Prague Spring'. On 2nd October, just weeks before the Mexico City Olympics, thousands of Mexican students in Tlatelolco gathered in La Plaza de las Tres Culturas to protest against social injustices. With 112 many women and children in their throng, the protesters had planned to march peacefully through a suburb of their city, but found by early evening that the square had been surrounded by the military. The ninety-minute massacre that followed killed over 200 people, and was later shown to have been instigated by the CIA who, nervous of the protest's proximity to the athletes in the Olympic Village, had sent extra weapons, ammunition and riot-control materials to the Mexican authorities. Two days later, on 5th October, a civil-rights march through Londonderry, Northern Ireland, was brought to a violent conclusion when police from the Royal Ulster Constabulary used water cannon against the Catholic protesters and beat with batons those at the head of the march, including two MPs. Eleven days later, on 16th October, seven people were killed in riots that erupted in Kingston, Jamaica, in protest against the white government's treatment of Guyanese lecturer Walter Rodney. The African-history lecturer had been banned from returning to his position at the University of the West Indies for having attended a black writers' convention in Montreal, Canada. Rodney was an avowed socialist and had travelled to Cuba and the USSR in the past, but his dismissal caused severe rioting among Jamaican university students, who marched on the prime minister's home. In Mexico City the following day, in a 'silent protest' against black oppression, America's Olympic 200-metres sprint champion Tommie Smith and bronze medallist John Carlos raised their black gloved right fists in a Black Power salute, as they stood on the podium at the medal ceremony. It was against this burning backdrop of almost worldwide lunacy that the Japanese underground was formed.

Barricades-a-Go-Go – Enter Les Rallizes Denudés

By the beginning of 1969, the Tokyo streets around Shinjuku had filled up close to bursting point, as other cities also reported huge rises in the numbers of long-haired teenage *futens* arriving from across rural Japan. Despite the Tokyo authorities' natural tendency to attempt to disperse all of these unwanted itinerants, the Japanese government's recent implementation of a programme known as 'Understanding among Youth' forced the authorities to accommodate them all by opening up a disused US Army camp at Fukuzumi, where a commune began in earnest. This hazing of the rules had caused much hesitation and head-scratching among council officials, enabling other *futens* to set up their own communes in Tokyo's Kokubunji district without hindrance. Moreover, certain educational establishments – acutely aware of the rioting on European and American university campuses – had decided to enter wholeheartedly into the spirit of the 'Understanding among Youth' programme. And so, despite being apprehensive about this decidedly non-Japanese way of behaving, lecturers were encouraged to allow students to speak their minds in order to forestall any unnecessary outbreaks of *Gakuen funso*, as the Japanese press termed campus riots.

113

At the forefront of this liberal attitude was Doshishi University, in the ancient city of Kyoto. As one of Japan's first universities, Doshishi had long enjoyed a rich and deserved reputation as a place of free-thinking and idealism, and many of Japan's greatest minds had completed their educations there. On 12th April 1969, the university authorities even organised their own rock'n'roll festival, playfully entitled 'Barricades-a-Go-Go', in the basement of Doshishi's anonymously named Building A. The festival was sponsored by a local Kyoto newspaper and featured four Kyoto bands, Mustapha, Wax, Mustang and a mysterious headlining act known as Les Rallizes Denudés, whose members attended the university. Playing to a packed house of 500, the festival was a huge success for all of the musicians involved.

But while the first three bands mentioned had roots in something approaching standard rock'n'roll (the ultra long-haired sextet Mustang having even enjoyed an Oricon Top-40 hit the previous year), Les Rallizes Denudés was an entirely different kettle of piranha. They were smart, they were idealistic, and they were Communist sympathisers out to overthrow the established order. Dressed all in black and led by songwriter and guitarist Takeshi Mizutani, all four band members considered themselves to be true revolutionaries. On stage, rhythm guitarist Takeshi Nakamura played bar chords high up the fretboard, his hands a blur, as drummer Takashi Kato hammered his floor- and side-toms, with no thought for a snare or cymbal crash. On bass was the uber-refusenik Moriyasu Wakabayashi, whose mind always appeared elsewhere as he stood motionless, from time to time delivering painfully slow epic blasts of sub bass then staring out into the audience making no sound at all. Rallizes's most famous song of the time, the near-twenty-minutes 'Smokin' Cigarette Blues', had been known to empty concert halls, but for their hardcore following it was an orgasmic experience.

Billing themselves as 'The Radical Music Black Gypsy Band', Les Rallizes Denudés believed in 'total sensory assault of the culture' in the dark style of Andy Warhol's *Exploding Plastic Inevitable* and the unfathomably dense ramalama of early Blue Cheer, the so-called 'loudest band in the world' (and by whom leader Mizutani was obsessed). Indeed, by deploying incessant strobe lights and excruciatingly high volumes the previous year, Les Rallizes Denudés had even managed to alienate their own revolutionary theatre troupe Gendai Gekijo (Modern Arts Society), whose seven members had accompanied the band's songs with radical dances and theatrical moves until the feedback had driven them all up the wall. Despite their refusal to appear on stage any longer, however, the idealistic members of Gendai Gekijo had continued to bring their lighting rigs and smoke machines to all the shows in order to facilitate Rallizes's belief in 'total cultural assault'.

114

Dr Acid Seven, Futen Tora, ○△□ & the Folk Guerrillas

Talking of total cultural assault, the whole long-haired lifestyle received a further credibility boost in mid-1969, when Shinji Nagashima's *Futen* cartoon was made into a full-length feature film entitled *Otoko Wa Tsuraiyo* (It's Hard to Be a Man). Starring the well-loved actor Kiyoshi Atsumi as 'Futen Tora', the movie was a huge success across Japan, sending even more young disillusioned Japanese kids on the road in search of some of that same footloose freedom they'd just seen propelling *Futen* Tora from adventure to adventure.

But in this acutely competitive and hierarchical Japanese society where status was everything, there was still, even among the Shinjuku *futens*, a perceived pecking order, and the fascinated media soon homed in on four particularly controversial and long-haired *futens* who went by the mythological names of Gurriba (Gulliver), Kiristo (Christ), Barbara (the Barbarian) and Julius Caesar. And when Japan's own *Playboy* magazine ran an extended piece about the four, the article's author hit upon the idea of calling them 'The Four Longhaired Brothers of Japan', declaring that the *futen* lifestyle was the last word in cool among the burgeoning hippie population, and intimating that there had even been turf wars between the four.

On the teeming Shinjuku streets, meanwhile, refusenik singers and musicians played their songs of rebellion and idealism, whilst it became commonplace for improvised theatre and revolutionary dance to occur right there on the pavements in front of the coffee houses of Ogi and the Go-Go-Café. The first band to stage street concerts appears to have been the improvisational freak-out ensemble Jigen, whose name meant 'zero dimension'. Jigen had originally formed in late '67 and were a loose aggregation of that same first wave of Shinjuku *futens* that had spawned the Four Longhaired Brothers. But although Jigen swiftly became the other Shinjuku *futens'* rave of choice, their itinerant lifestyle and tendency to hop between Tokyo and Kyoto ensured that the ensemble made no records, though it is claimed that later recordings were made in Kyoto by several of the original members, who had by that time adopted the splendid name Sakenomido (Drunken Kid).

Of the other commune bands, probably the most legendary was ○△□ , a freaked-out quintet led by the drummer Sakuro 'Kant' Watanabe, who'd attended many of the mid-'60s actions by Hi-Red Center. Taking his name from Germany's eighteenth-century rationalist philosopher Immanuel Kant, the drummer and his bizarrely named cohorts – Tôhchan, Reck, Chiko-Hige and Juno – always appeared in face paint and wild clown outfits. Although the band also admitted to the name Maru Sankaku Shikaku (Circle Triangle Square), Shinjuku *futens* always learned of any impending street concert by the band via their simple advertising tactic of spraying ○△□ upon the walls with a date next to it. Like Germany's commune group Amon Düül, ○△□ were to avoid the historical oblivion suffered by most of these Shinjuku street groups through the legacy of three homemade freak-out LPs, all recorded at the height of the *futen* scene.

On 7th August 1969, however, the honeymoon period between the *futens* and the government came to an abrupt end with the passing of Law No. 70 (Daigaku no Un'ei ni Kansuru Rinjisochihou), which defined 'urgent measures to normalise management of universities disordered by student activism'. Throughout the hot summer of '69, TV footage of seemingly endless university-campus protests and hairy hippies frolicking in city-centre water fountains had, for most of Japan's government and other authority figures, been evidence enough that their softly-softly approach was not working. Within the *futen* scene, a tough new activist type had started to appear on the streets. They called themselves *Foku Gerira* (Folk Guerrilla) and modelled themselves on America's Black Panthers, the German militant student factions and Tokyo's situationist action groups of the mid-1960s, such as Team Random and Hi-Red Center (see Book One, Chapter Two). And when, two days after the passing of Law No. 70, the actress Sharon Tate was murdered by loopy hippies in the Hollywood Hills, it appeared to the authorities that the legislation had been passed in the nick of time. To the Japanese media, who were themselves simultaneously repelled and fascinated by the unfolding story of this increasingly lawless underground, the most infamous and subversive of Japan's activists was Dr Acid Seven, a camo-clad longhair who organised underground events and dispensed psychedelics openly throughout this previously drug-free society. Dr Seven's radical freak-out ensemble Acid Seven Group was not a street group but a burning electric free-rock band whose riffless barrages of chromatic distortion were suffused with Seven's own shamanic proclamations and fist-raised pleas, nay demands, for unity.

The Revolutionary War Manifesto of 3rd September 1969

Between 15th and 18th August, outside a small town in upstate New York, the Woodstock festival passed off entirely peacefully despite attracting crowds of close to half a million kids. But here in Japan, the authorities' inclination towards paranoia and suspicion of their own teenagers was beginning to cause big problems. While most of the Shinjuku street groups had always had sympathies for the *Foku Gerira*, many now chose intentionally bizarre names to reflect the times in which they were living, consciously aiming to alienate all members of straight society with their Communist manifesto-style chanting and stomping.

Among the media, the most infamous of these bands was the Communist duo Zuno Keisatsu (Brain Police), whose songs bore such ominous titles as 'Sekigun Heishi No Uta' (Song of the Red Army), 'Ju o Tore' (Pick up Your Gun), 'Kanojo Wa Kakumeika' (She's a Revolutionary), 'Senso Shinka Shiranai Kodomotachi' (Children Who Know Only War) and 'Iiwake Nanka Iraneyo' (We Don't Need Your Bloody Excuses). Taking their name from Frank Zappa's song 'Who Are the Brain Police?' Zuno Keisatsu's minimalist chants were similar in style to New York's street activists David Peel & the Lower East Side but delivered with a threatening darkness more akin to Notting Hill revolutionaries Third World War; always the same driving acoustic guitar of songwriter Haruo 'Panta' Nakamura, whose yelping and barked vocals were urged along by the congas, bongos and equally yelping vocals of sidekick Toshi Ishizuka.

But, on 3rd September, the whole underground scene climbed up a couple of rungs on the ladder of notoriety when the so-called Communist Allied Red Brigade Committee delivered their thirteen-point manifesto to the Japanese press. The manifesto – aimed primarily at the bourgeoisie of Japan, then Asia and the whole world – was a public declaration of the organisation's intention 'to throw you into a revolutionary war and wipe out all of you all over the world'. Aware that they should be taking all this stuff seriously, but not sure quite how seriously, the authorities began to send undercover agents to observe these so-called street bands, as Panta and Toshi quickly added the entire manifesto (word for word) to Zuno Keisatsu's song repertoire, renaming it 'Sekai Kakumei Senso Segen' (World Revolution War Declaration).

Having successfully upped the ante by inducing paranoia across all strata of Japanese society, the *Foku Gerira* movement so inspired the street bands that many even increased their efforts to show contempt for accepted social mores. And in this society where honour and social position is everything, a couple of bands even chose names that suggested diminished social status. For example, Miyako-ochi took their name from a very specific type of Japanese job demotion, in which a businessman who was considered to be failing his employer's expectations was not sacked outright, but was instead removed to head a distant local branch in some forlorn part of Japan, to live out the rest of his workdays in ignominy and despair.[1] Then, there was Murahatchibu, whose name means literally 'social ostracism', cut off from the community, sent to Coventry, utterly ignored. Two hundred years ago and more, to be the victim of *murahatchibu* in Japan was to face ruinous disaster, and nobody dared stray out of line for fear of its being implemented. The name comes from *mura* or village, and *hatchibu*, which means 8-out-of-10. According to ancient Japanese farming laws, people in a rural community came together in ten different ways to help each other. Victims of *murahatchibu* lost eight of those ten social privileges. A funeral was still guaranteed, and your community would come to your aid if your house was burning down, but even that was only to prevent the fire from spreading to everyone else's houses. For the other eight things, victims were entirely on their own: 1) nobody could attend your family's weddings, 2) no one acknowledged your growing children at coming-of-age ceremonies, 3) no one helped if your family was struck down by illness, 4) there was no help in the building of a new house, 5) no aid if the house flooded, 6) you were not allowed in the local temple during the anniversaries of loved ones, 7) no help was given to those moving house, 8) and no help was given to women of your family when giving birth. In naming their band Murahatchibu, these guys were not taking the easy way out. But, then again, their other choice for a band name had been Nanashi No Gonbe (The Nobodies without a Name)…

Murahatchibu as a Metaphor for the Underground

It's essential at this juncture in the narrative that we examine in some detail the so-called career of Murahatchibu, not because they were musically important to our story (they weren't!), but because the vibrant and inflamed personalities in

Murahatchibu have ensured that, as movers and scene-shakers at least, the band are deserving of an important place in Japanese rock history. For, in spite of their music being mainly monotonous crap, Murahatchibu hung around with so many other street musicians and important underground rock bands that their story is to a great extent the story of the Japanese underground.

Murahatchibu looked like utter rock'n'roll stars, and with reason ... For, while four of the band had been living the *futen* lifestyle, lead guitarist Fujio *Yamagauchi* had been enjoying chart success with Group Sounds stars the Dynamites. But if ever there was a band destined to live the rock'n'roll lifestyle and get nothing out of it except for the simple reward of having played, then it has to have been Murahatchibu. For, despite their having appeared on the same festival stages as all the bands excellent enough to have demanded their own chapter in this book, long-playing records or 45rpm singles bearing the Murahatchibu name were rarely released, as line-up changes, cancelled shows and drug busts followed them everywhere. This was because their two main songwriters – Fujio *Yamagauchi* and lead singer Chahbo – were too out of it to bother writing much material, and just too obsessed with living the rock'n'roll life, so their set-list was to remain the same for years on end. But rock'n'roll has always loved a loser, and at least these gentlemen did it with disgrace ...

Murahatchibu's story really begins on 6th December 1969, at the Rolling Stones' infamous Altamont Speedway festival, for this is where singer Chahbo had the life-changing experience that was to turn him from a rock'n'roll wanna-be to a rock'n'roll gonna-be. In truth, Chahbo had always acted like a rock'n'roll singer, but he'd done precious little about achieving any of it. Born Kasushi Shibata, in 1950, it had always been enough for Chahbo to swan through life being treated differently, for he was an exquisitely exotic longhair whose muse, ultimately, would always be his beautiful self. But when Chahbo's American model girlfriend Stephanie lost her Japanese visa in May '69 and was forced to return to the States, Chahbo followed her to the Japanese quarter of San Francisco, where the gorgeous one found himself surrounded by other Japanese rock'n'roll wannabes all doing as little as he. However, when fellow Japanese *futen* and prospective drummer Shigeto Murase turned Chahbo on to LSD just before he experienced the Stones' death-trip fiasco at Altamont, Chahbo was never the same again. The '60s were coming to a close and so was Chahbo's former self. Thereafter, so friends say, his entire body language changed, his refusenik elements sharpened, his attitude amplified 2,000-fold, and from this time onwards Chahbo wanted only 'to dance like Mick' ...

Meanwhile, back in Japan, Dynamites guitarist Fujio Yamagauchi symbolically quit his Group Sounds outfit on the last day of the '60s. While the Dynamites had been considered outrageous in 1967 for their Blue Cheer version of 'Summertime Blues', they were by now as anachronistic and obsolete as the surf bands had been when the GS groups had taken over. Many of the less career-minded Group Sounds guys had reached Fujio's conclusion earlier than he, running to audition for a place in *Hair* in the absence of anything better to do. Fujio, however, had far bigger plans – and swapping one guaranteed gig for another almost the same was hardly his idea of a rock'n'roll lifestyle. Like his good friend guitarist Shinki Chen, who had just quit the Yardbirds-inspired Powerhouse, Fujio had not got into guitar-playing for the guarantees that it offered. He wanted the glory, the drugs, the women and the same accolades as his all-time hero Chuck Berry. Er, don't hold your breath, mate …

The Birth of Foodbrain, Blues Creation Wows 'Too Much', so the Helpful Soul Become Too Much

By January 1970, a large percentage of Tokyo's rock'n'roll musicians – Fujio included – had become obsessed with America's so-called super-sessions LPs, two of which had been released during the previous eighteen months by guitarists Stephen Stills, Mike Bloomfield and organist Al Kooper, producer of the Blues Project. In August '69, an English equivalent featuring Steve Winwood, Eric Clapton, Ginger Baker and Family's Rick Gretsch had been released under the name Blind Faith, and the Japanese record companies were by now desperate for their own home-grown version.[2] Fujio decided to form his own super-session outfit in January 1970, and invited ex-Golden Cups drummer Mamoru Manu, keyboard player Shigero Narumo and bass player Shinishi Aoki to join his projected super group, to be named Fujio Dynamite. Completing the band with jazz drummer Hiro Tsunoda on lead vocals, Fujio was hugely disappointed when he learned from Tsunoda that the drummer had also been chosen to work on a Polydor Records 'super session' that was to be called Foodbrain. Named by Fujio's mad guitarist mate Shinki Chen and commissioned by Polydor's label boss Ikuzo Orita, the Foodbrain[3] project was going to be a wild affair precisely along the lines that Fujio had envisaged. Foodbrain's star-studded line-up was to include ex-Golden Cups superstar and paint-thinner fiend Louis Louis Kabe (now going by his real mame of Masayoshi Kabe) on bass. With Polydor's financing, hefty production by Mr Orita himself, and the promise of a full gatefold sleeve with a pop-art design, Foodbrain was the underground project on which all envious eyes were to focus.

At the end of January, however, Fujio's disappointment was slightly cushioned when his new band was asked to play at the forthcoming 'Too Much' concert at Kyoto's 2nd Kaikan Hall, on 28th February. Still billed as Fujio Dynamite, his super-session quintet shared the stage with an amazing new heavy band called Blues Creation – whom ex-Bickies guitarist Kazuo Takeda had formed after hearing Black Sabbath and Led Zeppelin – and the Helpful Soul, a really cosmopolitan and bluesy late GS band from the ultra-hip port city of Kobe. Although the Helpful Soul could in places devolve into a fairly pedestrian blues wank, they were nevertheless in possession of one truly superlative piece of gonzo genius that felled skyscrapers with its snotty nihilism. Hidden at the end of side one of their sole LP for Victor Records, 'Peace for Fools' was an eleven-minute drunken clodhop across the Doors' 'Five to One' as played by the inept Josephus during their 'Dead Man' phase. Crappy, autistic, strung out and loserish, 'Peace for Fools' was like Kim Fowley's OUTRAGEOUS LP played at 16rpm by farm punks with electric pitchforks and a gasoline habit. Unfortunately, Blues Creation's sheer professionalism and savagery totally destroyed everyone else who played at 'Too Much', as lead guitarist Kazuo Takeda copped whole passages of Tony Iommi riffs from Black Sabbath's then still-brand-new 'Behind the Wall of Sleep', interspersing each section between his own songs to create one continuous barrage of guitar assault. Although still young, Takeda was a past master of rock showmanship whose long experience in Europe and the USA enabled him to pass off many Jeff Beck and Jimmy Page rock moves as his own. Moreover, with a dedication to rehearsal, dynamics and arrangements that few Western bands could muster, Blues Creation always sounded incredibly powerful, as evidenced from the countless amazing bootlegs available from that period. No one in Japan had ever heard anything remotely like it before, and everyone thereafter considered this to be the new way ahead. Indeed, watching from the side of the stage, the Helpful Soul's rhythm guitarist and lead vocalist Junio Nakahara was so utterly freaked out (and simultaneously inspired) that he split up his band right after their performance at 'Too Much'. The next time anyone heard from Nakahara, he'd switched to lead guitar, changed his name to Tstomu Ogawa and formed a heavy band called ... Too Much! The Japanese media soon caught on to this new rock coming from the underground and, with incredible inventiveness, hit upon a name for this unusual form ... let's call it 'New Rock'!

The Hair Debacle

In Tokyo's Toyoko Gekijo Theatre, rehearsals for the Japanese production of *Hair* had been progressing rapidly throughout the latter half of '69. As we saw at the end of Book One's Chapter Two, the producers' decision to pick musicians from the jazz community was an enlightened one, for those involved were both professional enough to deliver what was required of them, free-thinking enough to infuse the proceedings with a uniquely Japanese approach rather than merely following the New York original. Moreover, the addition of the two much younger ex-Group Sounds musicians, former Apryl Fool organist Hiro Yanagida and former Out Cast lead guitarist Jun

'Kimio' Mizutani, to the otherwise all-jazz ensemble had been a stroke of genius. For the leader of the ensemble, drummer Akira Ishikawa, was so smitten by the open-minded attitudes of Yanagida and Mizutani that he had soon introduced both of them to his closest friends in the jazz community.

Before long, the corridors of the Toyoko Gekijo Theatre were heavy with the sweet stickiness of marijuana smoke, as cast, crew and musicians were visited by an endless stream of music-industry heavyweights, Shinjuku *futens*, jazz musicians and folk guerrillas at this counter-cultural rallying point. Romances soon flourished between the young hippie-looking women in the so-called 'Girl Tribe' chorus and the many ex-Group Sounds musicians in the 'Boy Tribe'. Dr Acid Seven could be seen dispensing free samples of powdered happiness to all and sundry, while the members of Zuno Keisatsu (Brain Police) preached violent revolution to anyone who would listen. Former rock'n'roll singer Yuya Utchida explained the bizarre manner in which his new psychedelic ensemble the Flowers had been allowed to contribute an entire twenty-minute-long track of guitar freak-outs to the experimental opera currently being recorded by Yoko Ono's ex-husband, composer Toshi Ichiyanagi (see Book One, Chapter Two). *Hair*'s drummer/leader Akira Ishikawa became fast friends with the two ex-Group Sounds guys of the ensemble – Kimio Mizutani and Hiro Yanagida – telling them of his plans to make an all-percussion LP based on field research that he intended to make in Africa. The drummer introduced the two to his old friend Masahiko Satoh, a pianist whose recent move into free jazz via German connection Wolfgang Dauner had made him determined to unite Stockhausen electronica with Hendrix-style apocalyptic guitar-playing.

121

Watching all of this with fascination and the money to facilitate it was Foodbrain producer and Polydor Records' label boss Ikuzo Orita, whose own dream had long been to create a uniquely Japanese underground culture, run with neither commercial restraint nor even expectations, just for the sheer pleasure of what could tumble forth. So inspired by his place in *Hair*'s cast was former 491 singer Joe Yamanaka that he had recently jettisoned all remnants of his former Group Sounds past by transforming into a living, breathing representative of the *Hair* poster itself, his massive Afro dyed in rainbow colours. Smoking pot together every night and listening to each other's radically different influences, unlikely sets of musicians and artists from entirely different age groups and backgrounds enjoyed the *Hair* rehearsals as a glorious and intense period of bonding.

It was, therefore, a highly irritated Fujio Yamagauchi who overheard his drummer Hiro Tsunoda telling a friend about how well the Foodbrain 'super sessions' were going. Having missed out on *Hair*, Fujio was now also missing the super-session event of the season. However, when Fujio also heard ex-Apryl Fool organist Hiro Yanagida's name being mentioned in the same conversation, the annoyed guitarist questioned

Tsunoda – how come Yanagida can find the time to do Foodbrain if he's so busy working on *Hair* as well?

Haven't you heard? said Hiro Tsunoda. The whole cast was busted for marijuana last night … the whole show's been cancelled! It sounded unbelievable but it was true. After six months of exhausting rehearsals, endless auditions and endless heart-breaking rejections, the show, which had only just opened in late November '69 to standing ovations every night, was already over within its second month of performances. The cast, the chorus, the technicians, the musicians had all thought they would have guaranteed employment for at least the next two years. But with the authorities in their current ruthless and anti-youth-culture mindset, suspicious undercover police had been monitoring the presence of Dr Acid Seven and Zuno Keisatsu at the theatre. Now, the whole *Hair* production had been thrown away when just a few joints had been discovered in the theatre during that unexpected police raid. The '70s were apparently well under way, and Fujio Yamagauchi was not about to be left behind…

The Return of Chahbo

122 Approximately two weeks later, in late March, Fujio was in Tokyo's uber-funky Roppongi district rehearsing for another outdoor festival, when he spied the most amazing long-haired guy dancing and laughing, surrounded by a gaggle of enthralled young *futen* women. Presuming from this guy's outrageous demeanour that here was some foreign rockstar crash-landed in Tokyo, Fujio strolled over and struck up a conversation. But no, this spaced alien was just the newly re-made Chahbo back on his own home turf. Despite all his rock'n'roll experience, Fujio felt out of his depth with this worldly androgyne, as Chahbo regaled the former Dynamites guitarist with incredible tales of LSD, cannabis, amphetamines, San Francisco all-nighters, Mick Jagger's dancing and the Altamont Speedway's infamous murder in the afternoon courtesy of armed Hell's Angels. But when the two extended their hang over at Chahbo's crash pad, a borrowed apartment belonging to his mate Kant from ○△□ , they forged an intense friendship over mucho pot and multiple plays of the Stones' BEGGARS' BANQUET LP. Through a green haze, Chahbo informed Fujio that Takaya Shiomi, the founding father of Japan's infamous Red Army Faction, had been arrested the previous day, and that rumours on the street said the authorities were gunning for any longhair with a reputation for preaching violence. Panta and Toshi from Zuno Keisatsu (Brain Police) had temporarily split from Tokyo, and Dr Acid Seven was getting so much grief that he was thinking of changing his name to just Dr Seven … like that would have made a difference. And so the pair crashed out late that night, little

guessing that sunrise the following morning would herald incredible changes for Japan's underground culture …

In the very late morning of 1st April 1970, Chahbo came around gently from his evening of planning world domination through rock'n'roll and switched on the radio to find out the time. What he heard on the radio news, however, hardened even this stoner pixie. For in the early hours of the previous day, nine members of the self-styled Japanese Red Army had hijacked a Japan Airlines Boeing 727 and fled to North Korea. Events were still unclear – in Chahbo's borrowed apartment even less so – but rumours on the Tokyo streets later that day intimated that one of their own had been involved in this world event. They were not to be disappointed …

The Yodo-go Hijack Incident

The truth emerged piecemeal over the next few days, but all of it was utterly shocking. In the early morning of 31st March, nine members of the Japanese Red Army Faction, all aged between nineteen and twenty-one years old, had boarded a Japan Airlines Boeing 727 at Tokyo's Haneda Airport, on an internal flight bound for Fukuoka. At 7.33 a.m., soon after the aircraft had reached its cruising height, the nine terrorists had stormed the cockpit armed with pipe bombs and samurai swords, and 123 screaming the fearful words: 'We are Ashitano Jeo!' From this first moment of the hijacking, many of the 129 passengers aboard, still bleary-eyed and expecting a 45-minute flight, had become hysterical with fear because their assailants were screaming longhairs who were aligning themselves with a famous Manga outsider TV hero who'd striven to win a boxing championship in a cartoon series of the same name. Like the Manson Family's daubing of phrases such as 'Political Piggy' and 'Helter Skelter' around their crime scenes, the Yodo-go hijackers decision to invoke the 'divine' power of cartoon hero Ashitano Jeo was way too far outside all frames of reference for the stricken passengers.

Demanding that the pilot take them all to Cuba, the hijackers were furious to discover that the Yodo-go had only enough fuel for its original destination, and they reluctantly agreed to land at Fukuoka's Itatsuki Airport. For three long days, the Yodo-go sat on the tarmac as negotiations took place. Eventually, a compromise was reached. The authorities agreed that the airliner should be allowed to fly instead to Pyongyang, in Communist North Korea, if twenty-three women and children were allowed to leave the airline in return for a total refuelling and the substitution of the Japanese transport minister Shinjuru Yamamura as hostage. The aeroplane set off westwards, but the Yodo-go's pilot Shinki Iashida hoodwinked the hijackers into landing at South Korea's Gimpo Airport, at 3 p.m. Believing that the runway was a part of

North Korea's Pyongyang Airport, the hijackers sought to confirm this by asking a member of the ground crew for a photo of dictator Kim II Sung as proof of their northerly position. Denied this proof, the nervous hijackers then panicked and refused all food and drink. However, they eventually accepted that all the passengers – including many US nationals – should be allowed to leave the aircraft, in return for permission to fly to North Korea. The plane left Gimpo Airport and headed north, landing at the disused Minimu Airport, where the North Korean authorities hailed the nine as cultural heroes, granted them political asylum, and insisted that they remain in North Korea, where they received military medals and were given 'luxury accommodation' at the Village of the Revolution.

In Japan, the ramifications were massive, for the hijacking was both humiliating for the Japanese authorities, and disturbing to the wider world, which was then still reeling from the bombing of Milan's Piazza Fontana by right-wing extremists the previous December. Furthermore, the presence of so many US nationals aboard the Yodo-go had brought the CIA to Japan and the names of the nine hijackers only emerged via the media in dribs and drabs. Slowly, the Japanese underground realised that this hijack had indeed been the work of their own people, many having been students from Osaka University or Kyoto's forward-thinking Doshishi University. But for Japan's burgeoning underground rock'n'roll scene, the strangest presence of all among the hijackers was that of Moriyasu Wakabayashi,[4] bass player with 'The Radical Music Black Gypsy Band' Les Rallizes Denudés.

Aftershock of the New & the Birth of Flower Travellin' Band

In the mixed-up, messed-up, shook-up world that was now Japan, two things were gradually dawning on both the authorities and the media. Firstly, the world was in chaos and, like it or not, post-war Japan was a part of that chaos. Secondly, some of the long-haired rock'n'roll children whose ways they'd tried to accommodate were, after all, as weird and as dangerous as they'd appeared on the surface. Furthermore, while many of those involved in the airliner hijack had given no clues to friends and relatives of their criminal intentions, many had blabbed long and hard about it to anyone who'd listen but just not been taken seriously. Like the murder of Sharon Tate and her friends the previous August, the uniqueness of the hijacking lay so far outside the imagination of even the most paranoid that the events could only be judged clearly with real hindsight.

Gradually, as the unfolding drama took on a life of its own quite separate from facts, Tokyo rock'n'rollers were disturbed but secretly delighted to discover that the bass player from Les Rallizes Denudés was now hiding out in Communist North Korea as an international outlaw. As a long-time friend of Rallizes's singer Takeshi Mizutani, Fujio Yamagauchi had met Moriyasu Wakabayashi several times, but had always suspected that beneath the whole Communist activist thing was a very posh guy from old money who might just have been play-acting. Now, however, in this post-hijacking world, to be a long-haired rock'n'roll musician was to arouse suspicion from the authorities. And Fujio's friendship with Les Rallizes Denudés ensured that, henceforth, undercover police followed him everywhere.

Chahbo's return to Japan now took on an air of greater significance to Fujio. It was as though this all-dancing/all-drugging Altamont renegade'n'friend of the outlaws had arrived as a herald of the burgeoning chaos. Now viewing Chahbo as a powerful totem, Fujio invited the beautiful one to become lead singer in the band. But as soon as Fujio mentioned this idea to the professionally minded Hiro Tsunoda and organist Shigero Narumo, both winced at it – wasn't that Chahbo guy just a bad'un destined to send Fujio down the hijacking route? With Hiro Tsunoda's connections in the music industry, the drummer and organist felt quite rightly that they didn't need Chahbo's weirdness, and drifted away to form their own dreadful power trio named Strawberry Path.

Forming bands was all the rage now that the *Hair* production had collapsed. Indeed, once cast and crew realised the implications of the drug bust, *Hair*'s spirit of universal love and peace had imploded overnight into tantrums, finger-pointing and recriminations, whilst friendships forged over surreptitious toking in the theatre dressing rooms became hastily firmed up into future plans for rock'n'roll careers. Drummer Akira Ishikawa was immediately courted by his jazz friend Masahiko Satoh, who insisted that now was their perfect opportunity to unite free jazz with pop just as Satoh's German friend Wolfgang Dauner had done with the FREE ACTION LP. Commandeering the services of *Hair*'s rhythm guitarist Kiyoshi Sugimoto, the sextet Akira Ishikawa & Count Buffaloes was born within the week. Ex-Glories singer Fumio Miyashita was so inspired by the promise of the impending so-called Age of Aquarius during his brief period in the chorus of *Hair* that he formed his own hippie troupe Far Out, inviting the new Brain Police lead guitarist Eiichi Sayu to join him. Masumi Ono and Mamoru Hoiuchi – the two *Hair* actors who'd shared the lead role of 'Wolf' – formed the acoustic band Garo, who quickly signed with the mighty Watanabe management team. Garo's immediate future career was to spawn several huge chart hits.

Ever the opportunist, Flowers manager Yuya Utchida invited the rainbow-Afro'd Joe Yamanaka to sing Led Zeppelin's 'You Shook Me' with the Flowers at the band's forthcoming concert 'Rock'n'roll Jam '70'. Starring older Group Sounds acts such as the Happenings Four, the Mops and the Golden Cups, the Flowers were the only

125

contemporary thing on the bill. For, while all of those bands still plied their mid-'60s trade with versions of songs by the Animals, Ray Charles, Dionne Warwick and the like, the Flowers' confident delivery of experimental material by blind saxophonist Moondog and heavy Led Zeppelin riffage only proved to Yuya Utchida how wide was the chasm between those already looking to the '70s and those stuck firmly in the beat era. Indeed, Utchida disbanded the Flowers immediately after the 'Rock'n'roll Jam '70', and invited Joe Yamanaka to join the re-styled band, now slimmed down to quartet and known henceforth as Flower Travellin' Band.

Mizutani's Rallizes? Chahbo Rallizes!

Back in the land of Murahatchibu, Fujio and Chahbo had been left to cobble together an entirely new ensemble in time for Kyoto's impending 'Floating In' festival just four weeks away on 30th June. But when festival time came around, all conversations would return inevitably to the single subject of the aeroplane hijacking. Kyoto is a small ancient city with no place to hide, and Rallizes's leader Mizutani had been compelled to run to the protective anonymity of Tokyo. The hijack – which was now popularly termed the 'Yodo-go Incident' after the nickname of the aeroplane itself –

had been such an embarrassment to Japanese authorities that all longhairs were under suspicion. In early July, out of the blue, Rallizes's leader Mizutani phoned Fujio from his hideout in Tokyo. He was paranoid, depressed as hell and he had no band *any more*; they'd all quit when that lunatic Wakabayashi had stolen the plane. Rallizes had been booked to play the forthcoming 'Rock in Highland' festival, with the Mops and Yuya Utchida's brand-new Flower Travellin' Band – a huge event that was being billed as Japan's 'Woodstock'. But without a band, the aggrieved Mizutani was nowhere. As Fujio's band was still fronted by a guy who would only dance, the guitarist suggested to Mizutani that they become his new Rallizes for the festival. There were only a couple of weeks until the performance, but Fumio knew the Rallizes songs were even easier than his own, and now was a perfect time for an act of solidarity, especially as the Nobodies would be getting to play such a prestigious show. Mizutani was relieved and delightedly agreed. And so, on 26th July 1970, in the true anarchic spirit of the time, the Nobodies without a Name aka Murahatchibu played the 'Rock in Highland' festival billed as Les Rallizes Denudés and fronted by Mizutani. According to one local underground free newspaper of the time, Mizutani interspersed his songs with performances of the Stones' 'Midnight Rambler' and 'Gimme Shelter', whilst 'accompanying the Rallizes was the beautiful and mysterious man/woman Chahbo, who sung the same phrase over and over again'.

The 'Rock in Highland' festival was, however, a disaster for all concerned. The promoters were bankrupted when barely one hundred people attended, most absentees still reeling from the fallout of the Yodo-go Incident and scared by Rallizes's presence on the advertising posters. In an effort to vibe up the sparse audience, Chahbo had – without consulting Mizutani – invited the members of local band Haruophone-Biburasuton on stage. These actions, coupled with Chahbo's Yoko Ono-like screaming throughout Mizutani's performance, drove the Rallizes singer to distraction, and he took off back to his temporary Tokyo home straight after the show. With further Rallizes shows booked around Kyoto that summer, Chahbo and Fumio found themselves perceived by local Kyoto freaks as full members of the new Rallizes Denudés. They were, therefore, expected to fulfil these obligations. The two saw it as an opportunity to have some fun at Mizutani's expense. At Kyoto Sangyo University Festival, Kyoto Silk Hall, and a Kyoto disco called 'Catseye', Rallizes stalwarts were surprised to observe this bunch of out-of-towners posing as their hero's band. That summer, a despondent Mizutani told his old friend bass player Makoto Kubota that he was seriously considering making Rallizes into an acoustic band[5] after he'd even found himself on the same bill as the 'other' Rallizes, now billing themselves shamelessly as 'Chahbo Rallizes'! A temporary respite in the Mizutani/Chahbo vendetta took place in late summer, and the bizarre ensemble was booked for a performance alongside Too Much at Kyoto's 'Maruyama Odyssey' festival, on 30th September. However, when at the last minute the freaked-out Mizutani once again failed to show, Fumio this time insisted that it was immoral to play under the Rallizes name now that the disagreement had been patched up. At the end of that month, Chahbo was picked up by police on the streets of Kanuma City and thrown in jail for possession of drugs.

By now, no one else wanted to touch Chahbo and Fumio even with a long barge-pole. In a country that prides itself on punctuality, these punks had their own fiscal year. In a country that adjudges heroin, marijuana, LSD and amphetamines to be all the same, they were drug punks. All the favours that Fujio could have begged from his former GS colleagues had long ago been used up. Hell, these ne'er-do-wells had even tried to rustle poor Mizutani's band from under him. Furthermore, six Murahatchibu songs recorded at Osaka Studios during that time really captured the distilled essence of Chahbo and Fujio's characters – and it was not pretty. Over a generic backdrop of Fumio's punky Chuck-Berryized Everystones riffs, Chahbo barked out his arid world-weary comments in a forty-ciggies-a-day Yoko Ono voice. Never had a rock'n'roll band been so appropriately named as the social outcasts of Murahatchibu.

New Rock Emerges – Foodbrain & Flower Travellin' Band's ANYWHERE

By mid-1970, the decaying corpse of the Group Sounds scene was still refusing to be buried with dignity, as former scene leaders the Golden Cups struggled on in their umpteenth incarnation. With heartthrob bass player Masayoshi Kabe now ensconced in Foodbrain and lead guitarist Eddie Ban fronting his own heavy band, the rest of the Cups were by now reduced to playing songs by Three Dog Night and Randy Newman. At least the Spiders had had the good grace to bow out in '69 while still at the top of their game, but the Jaguars and the Mops had made misguided attempts to incorporate the New Rock sound while still hedging their bets by continuing to pad LPs with sub-GS ballads and soft rock. The Happenings Four attempted to update and modernise their keyboard-dominated sound by opting for a Procul Harum/Greenslade-like twin-keyboard-player attack, while Julie Sawada and Hiroshi Oguchi of the Tigers created the cynical 'heavy' band PYG, joined by ex-members of the Spiders and the Tempters. The Tigers' five years at the top of the GS scene had, however, only been sustained through Sawada's ruthless dedication to the sell-out, and this was by now the only route he knew. Most music fans were, therefore, too appalled by the Tigers' recent past to pay much attention to his cynical new PYG set-list comprising songs by contemporary heavies Deep Purple ('Speed King', 'Black Night'), Mountain ('Travelling in the Dark'), Traffic ('Every Mother's Son'), Led Zeppelin ('Babe, I'm Gonna Leave You'), and Free ('Walk in My Shadow').

In the meantime, truly enlightened souls like Flower Travellin' Band's manager Yuya Utchida and Polydor Records boss Ikuzo Orita tried their best to bring credibility to the so-called 'New Rock' scene. Unfortunately, the inventiveness of new Western bands such as King Crimson, Black Sabbath and Led Zeppelin was causing immense problems for Japanese musicians physically ill equipped to achieve such heavy statements. The Foodbrain project had foundered initially because of the lack of a suitable vocalist to tackle the kind of barbarian spew currently emanating from white fiends like Ian Gillan and Robert Plant. Japanese drummers, too, were renowned for the lightness of their touch, and Foodbrain's producer soon discovered that only seasoned jazz drummers like Akira Ishikawa and Hiro Tsunoda could approximate the levels of energy required to achieve the effects of a Keith Moon or a Mitch Mitchell. And John Bonham's primal thud? Forget about it!

It was for this precise reason that while the Foodbrain debut LP A SOCIAL GATHERING was to achieve legendary status in Japan, it would mean bugger-all to the rest of the world. On its release, the Japanese media hailed the record as a masterpiece of free-flowing excursions into brand-new territory. In Western terms, however, it was nothing more than a jaunty mild'n'boogie posing as the real deal. Encased in a gatefold sleeve depicting a bull elephant in a pop-art style, A SOCIAL GATHERING was, nevertheless, a genuine break with the Group Sounds past and was, therefore, a first for Japanese rock musicians.

Far less experimental and all the better for that was ANYWHERE, the brilliant debut LP by Yuya Utchida's re-styled Flowers, now billed as Flower Travellin' Band. Never one to mince metaphors, Utchida's protégés delivered a mammoth driving album chock full o'riffs and hell rides, devilish screams and divine utterances, and all delivered in the all-time greatest album cover (see book jacket). For even Utchida surpassed himself this time with a sleeve photo depicting five butt-naked Japanese longhairs sitting astride Honda low-riders doing their *Easy Rider* thing. Where are we heading? ANYWHERE!

Ostensibly a covers album that included versions of such behemoths as '21st Century Schizoid Man', 'Black Sabbath' and 'House of the Rising Sun', ANYWHERE was actually a hugely inventive record. The Sabbath title track was reduced to a proto-Doom crawl more reminiscent of modern bands such as Boris or Reverend Bizarre than the original by Ozzy'n'Co. Flower's version of '21st Century Schizoid Man' lost its braying King Crimson sax, its prissy snare-led drumming and its la-de-da Greg Lake-in-a-washing-machine vocal, all replaced by a proto-metal power trio with a demented and shrieking ork on lead vocals. 'House of the Rising Sun' became an entirely different song with new chords and an arrangement that placed it firmly on LED ZEPPELIN III. Even better was Flower Travellin' Band's own sixteen-minute-long 'Louisiana Blues', a stunning epic in the tradition of the Doors at their most driving (MORRISON HOTEL meets LA WOMAN), complete with bottleneck guitars and wailing blue harp courtesy of singer Joe Yamanaka. Here at last was evidence that the Japanese could indeed do the hard-rock thing!

129

'Third World Head Rock' & the Rise of the Festivals

The spirit of intense musical experiment throughout this early 1970 period created bizarre festival configurations, as ex-Group Sounds musicians jostled with free-jazzers and underground street musicians for a place on the festival stages. Superstars like the Tigers' Julie Sawada found themselves sharing dressing rooms with street urchins and experimentalists as all factions attempted to claim a place in the new hip underground. During that 1970 summer of rock festivals, tight-assed heavy-rock bands like Dew, Blind Bird and Slash would often be followed by the newly emerged Takehisa Kosugi and his wild new ambulant ensemble Taj Mahal Travellers, whose simmering stew of bowed cello and violin, rudimentary electronics and

Gedo & the Rise of
the Festival Bands

Hideto Kano of Gedo

As Japan's rock festival era was inextricably linked to the '60s *futen* scene, so, even by the late '70s, the majority of the festival bands still held fast to the belief that they were – like Hawkwind and the Pink Fairies in the UK – itinerant upholders of anti-capitalist values and keepers of the old traditions of pre-Westernised Japan, even providing new traditions where nothing suitable could be appropriated from the past. Nowhere was this more apparent than in the music and lifestyle of Gedo, a power trio formed by ex-members of festival stalwarts Too Much and the M. Led by singer/ guitarist Hideto Kano, Gedo's success in the late '70s came only after years of endless festivals, live albums and courting Japan's biker fraternity, who turned each Gedo show into a hootenanny. Gedo LPs are full of in-jokes, mysterious crowd chants, and sudden bursts of sentimental balladry right there amidst the 'Born to Be Wild'-style guitar burn-ups. Indeed, to the outsider, the innate power of Gedo's bludgeoning music is somewhat undermined by the constant feeling that we're eavesdropping on a sacred gathering. Gedo's sense of cultural guardianship developed from the chaotic events of the so-called 'Sanrizuka Conflict' of August 1971, more commonly known as the 'Genya Concert' (see main text), which had attempted to reconcile the new rock traditions with the ancient past by holding the festival during Shinto's sacred period of *Bon-odori*, allowing the ancestor worship and archaic dancing of local rural people to mingle with the electric music of young political idealists. Thereafter, the format of the 'Sanrizuka Conflict' was adopted as a blueprint for future festivals by the ubiquitous counter-culture guru Dr Acid Seven, whose own reputation among the prime movers of the underground had begun on Tokyo's Shinjuku *futen* scene back in 1968. In 1973, Acid Seven organised the now-legendary 'Oz Days' three-day festival, which included Taj Mahal Travellers, Les Rallizes Denudés and his own Acid Seven Group, and which gained mythical status via a bootleg LP that was widely distributed in the West. Acid Seven was the organiser of such '70s festivals as the 'All Night Rainbow Show' series, the 'Rainbow 2000' shows, and 'The Festival of Life', the last of which attempted to continue Japan's traditional 'Yuyake Matsuri' (celebration of the ancestors) in an updated form. These festivals starred Les Rallizes Denudés, as well as such forgotten names as Mentampin, Weeping Herp Seno'o & His Rollercoaster, Masaki Ueda & South to South, Sentimental City Romans, Makoto Kubota, Yuyake Gakudan (Sunset Band) and Orange County Brothers. Also in 1975, Acid Seven contributed music to the soundtrack of the snappily titled 1975 hippie documentary *Dokko Nigenbushi-Kotobukijiyu Rodosha No Machi* (Heave Ho Human Song & the Town of Free Labourers). Nowadays, Acid Seven performs poetry readings, and recently contributed sleevenotes to the UNDERGROUND series of historical CDs.

131

abstract woodwind would evoke the feelings of being not at some crummy urban festival site, but ecstatically out of it in some primeval oak forest.

Following the success of the Japanese-only 'Floating In' and 'Mojowest' rock festivals, promoters of the 'Hokone Aphrodite' festival that June asked Pink Floyd to play at the hot-spring resort of Hokone, near Tokyo. The promoters were astounded at the amount of PA equipment demanded by the Floyd, but when their trancelike workouts resounded around the spa town at previously unimaginable volumes, every Japanese rock musician in attendance took special notice.

The next big summer rock extravaganza of 1970 was 'The Third World Head Rock', which took place in Tokyo on 23rd July 1970. The three bands that closed the festival – Blues Creation, Zuno Keisatsu and Foodbrain – are typical of the diverse approaches then emanating from the underground. As has been described earlier, Blues Creation shows were an incredible live proposition, as guitar maestro Kazuo Takeda's heavy and highly organised hard-rock band methodically destroyed the rest of the opposition with the same thoroughness as Terry Knight's brutal protégés Grand Funk Railroad. Foodbrain, on the other hand, were an ever shifting unit whose erratic live performances bore no resemblance to the restrained weak-sounding jams that had passed for their recent LP A SOCIAL GATHERING. Ex-Golden Cups bass player Masayoshi Kabe had such a laissez-faire attitude towards Foodbrain that he didn't even own a bass. While this freaked out Foodbrain's ever professional jazz drummer Hiro Tsunoda, now also of Strawberry Path, at least all of Foodbrain's band members were united in their recognition of their absolute freedom to play just what they wanted. However, such concepts of absolute freedom were still so alien to the Japanese psyche that it was impossible to realise that freedom without taking the piss somewhat. Shinki Chen had proved this once and for all with his incredibly patchy solo Polydor LP SHINKI CHEN & FRIENDS recorded that same summer. With no songs written and no particular musical direction in mind, Shinki had taken up Ikuzo Orita's offer of a solo album and begun recording straight away. With a band cobbled together from anyone who was around, the sessions had unfolded in such a haphazard manner that most songs, most ideas, even most of the lead vocals had been provided by George Yanagi, the bass player from the Powerhouse ensemble that Shinki had only recently left. Rather than take any control, Shinki had simply adopted the same casual attitude as he had for the Foodbrain project. A genius guitarist Shinki might have been, but there was precious little evidence of it on his own recordings. Indeed, even on the festival stage with Foodbrain, Shinki was always a punk of the highest order, sloping off for a spliff mid-song and sitting down mid-solo.[6]

Ironically, despite having had their first two LPs banned by the authorities, it was the controversial acoustic duo Zuno Keisatsu (Brain Police) who most regularly headlined the outdoor festivals throughout this period. Panta's simple two-chord protest mantras may have preached anarchy and insurrection, but the duo always showed a disconcerting ability to unite all the disparate factions of the festival audiences against 'The Man'. Furthermore, the unavailability of Zuno Keisatsu records further legitimised the band as genuine underground heroes, as Brain Police bootleg cassettes many generations removed from their original source were passed from *futen* to *futen*.

Three Classics Emerge from the 'Super Sessions' of 1970

Back in the studio world, the concept of the so-called 'super session' continued to obsess Japan's New Rock elite throughout the middle of 1970. Despite the many artistic failures of Ikuzo Orita's Foodbrain and Shinki Chen projects, so much had been learned from those sessions that the two LPs prepared the way for several similar and extraordinary projects during the latter half of 1970. Indeed, Orita was already planning similar solo album projects for his 'super session' stalwarts Kimio Mizutani and organist Hiro Yanagida. Moreover, former Happenings Four leader Kuni Kawachi had shocked everyone that summer with his amazing new LP KIRIKYOGEN, a song-orientated 'super session' that featured various members of the Flower Travellin' Band, which appeared to have come out of nowhere. True to past form, the horribly obsolete Golden Cups now jumped aboard the bandwagon with their unambiguously titled LP SUPER SESSION.

But the inconsistency of the Foodbrain and Shinki projects served also as a salutary warning to producer Ikuzo Orita that, however talented the musicians in the studio, no producer or engineer could merely stand aside and let them get on with it. There had to be a focus, a precise metaphor to be worked towards, as Frank Zappa had shown with the release of his own 'super session' HOT RATS the previous February. HOT RATS had upped the 'super session' ante considerably by introducing the jazz-rock violins of Jean-Luc Ponty and Sugar Cane Harris to stunning effect, something that Hiro Yanagida would hope to emulate on his own Orita-produced 'super session' MILK TIME. Combined with his Utopian belief in creating singularly Japanese rock statements, Ikuzo Orita's access to large studios, big budgets and the best session musicians would ensure that the period between the end of '69 and the middle of '71 would become the most iconoclastic period in Japanese rock history.

I shall now describe three of my favourite 'super session' LPs from this period. For each one united so many seemingly disparate (and apparently irreconcilable) elements into their sonic stew that these works extended the Japanese rock experiments forwards in a manner entirely outside the realms of the West:

i) Love Live Life +1

In the late summer of 1970, producer Ikuzo Orita began to bring together musicians for another 'super session' that he wished to name 'Love Live Life'. Inspired by the songs of sax player Kei Ichihara, Orita seemed to be obsessed with the idea of uniting free jazz Sun Ra style with stomping soul and heavy-guitar chaos, somewhere along the lines of Steve Katz's Blood, Sweat & Tears, but more rhythmically out there. Orita decided to retain ex-Out Cast lead guitarist Kimio Mizutani and ex-Apryl Fool organist Hiro Yanagida from the Foodbrain sessions, but the producer was looking for a tight-knit unit with a brass section to emulate some of the elements in Sly & the Family Stone's most recent LP STAND. Named after his favourite Ichihara's songs, LOVE WILL MAKE A BETTER YOU was at first forced to remain an interminably long time on the backburner as no suitable musicians were forthcoming. But when Ikuzo Orita turned up at a theatre show by his old friend and national pop star Akira Fuse, Fuse enthusiastically suggested that Orita employ Fuse's own backing band as the basis of the ensemble. Fuse's band contained a hefty brass section that featured a couple of old-school jazz players just ripe for this kind of music. Ever open-minded and eager to kick the project off, Orita watched Fuse's show that night and agreed with his friend's judgement. Behind Fuse's endless MOR versions of Dusty Springfield's 'You Don't Have to Say You Love Me', Stevie Wonder's 'For Once in My Life' and Spencer Davis Group's 'Keep on Running', it was clear that the Fuse ensemble would be able to deliver tight-assed soul and raggedy-assed free jazz with equal aplomb. Next, Orita summoned the services of jazz guitarist Takao Naoi, who'd spent most of his adult life jamming in New York, but who'd recently returned to Tokyo at the behest of Japanese jazzers Sharps & Flats. Over a series of thrilling rehearsals, Ikuzo Orita brought Kei Ichihara's songs to the Love Live Life ensemble and adored what he was hearing. One problem remained, however. There was no Japanese rock vocalist remotely equipped to deliver this kind of confident-but-searching style of song. The members of Fuse's band immediately suggested their boss take the role, but Orita was nervous about the public's reaction to a heavy LP fronted by a household name and Japanese icon along the lines of Britain's Tom Jones. However, when no other singers emerged from subsequent searches, Fuse was finally asked with immediate results – the LP an instant classic. Four of Ichihara's most carefully crafted songs were recorded in one day, the scorching title song coming over like a cosmic version of Sly's 'I Wanna Take You Higher'. In true Orita fashion, side one was then reserved for 'The Question Mark', an incredible eighteen minutes of free-rock blitzout that took themes from each of Ichihara's songs and augmented them with wild distorted guitars, chaotic free-form rock, and the questioning childlike vocals of Fuse at his most delicate. All of the blips and hiccups of the Foodbrain project were here banished to the outlands, as LOVE WILL MAKE A BETTER YOU raised the bar higher than even Orita had imagined was possible. In gratitude to Akira Fuse's contribution, Orita added '+1' to the band name. Delighted by his own good fortune, and quite unaware of the historical gravity of the moment, Fuse still dutifully delivered two further career LPs during 1971, AKIRA FUSE LIVE AT SANKEI HALL and FUSE LIVE IN NISSEI THEATRE, both of which were chock-full of such songs as Barbara Streisand's 'The Way We Were', the Carpenters' 'They Long to Be Close to You' and Perry Como's 'It's Impossible'. Fuse would continue to sing the 'Love Will Make a Better You' long into his MOR career. To this day, no popular artist has so successfully straddled (nor wished to straddle) such cultural chasms.

ii) Masahiko Satoh's AMALGAMATION

In autumn 1970, jazz pianist Masahiko Satoh embarked on the most remarkable and confounding project of his long career, the bizarre experimental LP AMALGAMATION. Celebrating the true spirit of the time, this record sounded (and still sounds) like nothing achieved before or afterwards. For AMALGAMATION was the wildest hybrid of them all, a truly mind-boggling synthesis of Stockhausen-influenced radio static and *musique concrète*, highly arranged brass sections, extrovert guitar noise, and all propelled by the incredible Detroit hard-bop drumming of Louis Hayes. For all of its jazz roots, AMALGAMATION is one of the greatest acid-rock albums ever made, containing the radically distorted guitar of Kimio Mizutani, violins, violas and cellos courtesy of the Wehnne Strings Consort, and rising and falling brass sections that enter and leave the mix in the manner of Teo Macero's late '60s and early '70s work with Miles Davis. 135 Throughout all of this, here at the centre of the AMALGAMATION sessions, Louis Hayes's drumming remains the bubbling ever unfolding fundament on which the whole trip proceeds, as though the rhythm section is a magic carpet constantly being pulled out from under the feet of the other performers.

What else concerns us here is that something so considered, so carefully constructed and yet so breathtakingly inappropriate could have burst forth from the mind of Satoh, an artist not at the beginning of his career but over a decade into it. However, the real reason for AMALGAMATION's existence is far too prosaic to imagine, so I'll allow the composer himself to take up the story: 'The music magazine *Guts* asked readers to send in an essay about the kind of music I should create. None of the readers' ideas impressed me much, so we dropped the idea and instead agreed to pick from two essays and adapt from both. So this album that seems so conceptual and futuristic actually came from a magazine idea.'

Despite Satoh's attempts to defuse the lofty heights reached by AMALGAMATION, even this explanation does little to soften the cultural impact that the record contains. Indeed, Satoh was by this period of his career so experimental that, as a matter of course, he purchased three Minimoogs for the recording sessions and had Roland build him ring modulators for his piano and electric harpsichord. Combine all of this information and it soon becomes clear that Satoh's attempt to reduce such a visionary work to being merely 'from a magazine idea' is disingenuous to say the least. Indeed, AMALGAMATION remains one of the greatest experimental records of its time.

iii) People's CEREMONY – BUDDHA MEETS ROCK

In early 1971, inspired by the artistic success and high visibility of Ikuzo Orita's projects, Hideki Sakamoto, a director of the big independent label Teichiku Records, decided to create his own and so set out to find writers who might help him achieve this. Sakamoto was particularly impressed by the work of two men, keyboard player Yusuke Hoguchi and Buddhist poet and songwriter Naoki Tachikawa. The two agreed to create an inspirational rock album for Teichiku Records based on turning hip young Japanese rock kids back on to Japan's own version of Zen Buddhism, by making great play of its being similar to Western rockers' then current obsession with anything Hindu, Buddhist or Maoist. Being by now the king of the weird projects, as it were, Kimio Mizutani was immediately summoned to daub his enormous vibe all over it, and make it sound authentically Orita-esque. In fact, Mizutani's electric, slide and acoustic guitar entirely inform the whole sound of the album, not to mention his electric sitar. Thereafter, four female vocalists injected a holiness to the eight tracks, whose names screamed spiritual and meaningful: 'Prologue', 'Gatha', Shomyo', 'Prayer Part One', 'Prayer Part Two' and 'Prologue'. Unfortunately, Teichiku's budget ran out before the project was completed, so producer/poet Tachikawa cleverly created a final track by asking his musicians to jam over David Axelrod's 'Holy Thursday' from his 1968 masterpiece SONG OF INNOCENCE. The results were startlingly beautiful, and came across like a collision of the Chocolate Watchband's most extreme extended orchestral instrumental songs, the more elegant passage of John Cale's THE ACADEMY IN PERIL and the marching stentorian orchestral themes from Frank Zappa's LUMPY GRAVY.

136

A PATH THROUGH HAZE & Other Stories

While all three of the albums discussed above contained the incredible guitar-playing of ex-Out Cast leader Kimio Mizutani, the guitarist himself ironically never managed to make that same kind of monumental statement under his own name, despite being given every opportunity by label boss Ikuzo Orita and having at his disposal the same hefty set of musicians who'd contributed to those aforementioned classics. I think this was mainly down to the weird choice of material that Mizutani chose to record for his own solo album. Not being a writer of any particular merit, the guitarist chose to showcase his talent by picking 'classy' and quite conservative material written by ex-Happenings Four keyboard player Kuni Kawachi and jazz pianist Masahiko Satoh, who also contributed the title track 'A Path through Haze'. Listeners were in for a dreadful disappointment if they'd bought Mizutani's mid-1971 LP A PATH THROUGH HAZE hoping for a display of the same kind of bile that he'd contributed to the records of Masahiko Satoh's AMALGAMATION, Love Live Life +1's LOVE WILL MAKE A BETTER YOU and People's BUDDHA MEETS ROCK. Instead, by choosing to record material written by particularly fine keyboardists, Mizutani forced himself to play the material with the utmost restraint, never moving outside the confines of the themes themselves. And so, despite being quite clearly intoxicated by Frank Zappa's own 'super session' album HOT RATS, Kimio Mizutani has – like Shinki Chen – gone down in Japanese rock history as an incredible session guitarist with one highly average solo LP to his credit. Indeed, Mizutani's performance of Satoh's beautiful title track so underwhelmed the track's composer that Masahiko Satoh recorded his own version just five months later, for his collaborative album of the same name with German guitarist Attila Zoller. Unlike Mizutani's tightly wound six-minute version, the piece as played by Satoh and Attila Zoller was a majestic and hauntingly beautiful work that lasted almost a quarter of an hour.[7]

The Sanrizuka Conflict & the Making of the Underground

One particularly significant event in Japan's 1971 rock'n'roll social calendar serves to bring this chapter to a conclusion. For it was during August's three-day-long 'Genya Rock Festival', an event which took place in the paddy fields outside Sanrizuka, a small town near Tokyo, that the concept of a refusenik consciousness was at last truly ignited among the wider Japanese intelligensia. Here, over three days of performances by Zuno Keisatsu, Blues Creation, Dew, Masayuki Takayanagi's New Directions for the Arts and several local folk groups were used to shine a spotlight on the plight of scores of poor farmers who were in grievous danger of losing their land and their livelihoods because of a proposed runway extension to nearby Haneda Airport. The runway project was especially controversial in those anti-US times because it shamelessly set the interests of the internationally minded capitalist community far above the interests of locals.

The brilliant decision to use a rock festival as a platform for the farmers' protest was made by the anti-establishment 'Seine Kodotai', a wing of the Communist Youth Action Committee. The committee cleverly chose to hold the festival directly in the middle of August's *Bon-odori*, a traditionally divine period when, according to Shinto, the ancestors return temporarily and the Japanese dance to celebrate and entertain these ancient spirits with traditional tunes known as *Takeda-bushi*. This decision allowed the committee to invite hundreds of Sanrizuka residents to perform their traditional dances at the rock festival, imbuing the occasion with a genuinely local flavour. The organisers next contacted Hi-Red Center's Genpei Akasegawa, whose controversial '1000 Yen' art statement of five years before had made the artist legendary among Japanese youth. Akasegawa was asked to design a special celebratory poster that the organisers could then use to promote the festival and subsidise their scheme by selling for 1,000 yen.

The festival was organised with such thoroughness that, even before it had begun, Communist activists from all across Japan descended on Sanrizuka to show unity with the farmers. But while the protesting farmers were surprised and delighted by this unexpected show of strength, the arrival of the hippies caused outrage among local Sanrizuka businessmen, who'd long aimed to gain considerably from the building of the runway. These disgruntled businessmen in turn summoned the strong arm of the local *yakuza* (mafia), whose bullyboy tactics only strengthened the resolve of the protesters to stand firm.

On the first of the three days, scores of members of Japanese TV's powerful Terebiman Union descended on the event, bringing with them broadcast-quality film cameras and tape recorders, in order to capture the atmosphere of this unique event and to provide evidence should the *yakuza*'s tactics get out of hand. For the first two days of the festival, however, everything passed off peacefully, as Blues Creation delivered their typically brilliant and bombastic proto-metal set, followed by superb performances by the Toshi Ochiai Trio, free bass player Mototeru Tagaki, and the scruffy belligerent hard rock of Dew, led by ex-Blues Creation singer Fumio Nunoya. These sets were interspersed with various political speakers and performances of the aforementioned *Bon-odori* dances.

On the final evening, however, the festival organisers made their single (and almost fatal) error, by asking Zuno Keisatsu not to headline but to play as the penultimate act, therefore allowing people to begin to wend their weary way home while the final, less famous, band wound the event down. Of course, Panta and Toshi's revolutionary songs were received ecstatically by the entire crowd, especially such crowd-pleasing statements as 'Ju o Tore' (Pick up Your Gun), 'Kurayami no Jinsei' (Life in the Dark) and the emotive 'Senso Shinka Shiranai Kodomotachi' (Children Who Know Only War). Those in attendance claim that Zuno Keisatsu's set was a righteous thing to behold, as farmers, hippies, locals and union men came together in one single stand against the grey face of capitalism.

Unfortunately, everyone had reckoned without the new festival 'headliners', a bunch of inexperienced free-jazzers doing only their second ever show. Led by drummer Hiroyuki Takahashi, this band, Lost Aaraaff, hit the stage with all the nihilistic attitude of the Stooges' infamous METALLIC KO show. Nineteen-year-old singer Keiji

Heino told the blissed-out audience that he wanted to kill them, and proceeded to scream obscenities into the mike. The festival erupted as protesters, farmers, *yakuza* hard men, *Bon-odori* performers, organisers and union men attempted to avoid the vile noise emanating from the PA by killing those guilty of creating it. As the festival was taking place in a paddy field, huge rocks below the feet of the festival crowd were suddenly utilised as ammunition, which rained down on Lost Aaraaff and sent them scurrying for cover. The festival erupted into violence and the police, having hovered at the fringes of the festival throughout the past three peaceful days, finally found an excuse to break some hippie heads.

Genya Concert thereafter came to be known as 'The Sanrizuka Conflict', and the members of Lost Aaraaff were to spend much of the '70s as social outcasts for their reckless and selfish behaviour. Eventually, however, a transcription of the days' events was released, first on a heavily edited live LP, and thereafter as an unedited piece of *cinéma verité* in which was included all the 'speech, debate, confusion and chaos of the place, also boldly including the objections of the farmers, optimism of the activitists, and ultimate disappointment', making the whole GENYA CONCERT LP document essential, enlightening, 'more realistic, and not easy listening'. The actions of Lost Aaraaff were never forgotten, although their music certainly was. For the Japanese underground, however, their movement came of age during 'The Sanrizuka Conflict'.

139

Footnotes:

1   The Roman Empire used the idea of social disgrace in a highly similar way. One Roman general who
    lost a battle he was expected to win easily was removed from his position and made governor of the
    Isles of Scilly, twenty-five miles off the coast of Cornwall.

2   The Japanese became so enthralled by the 'super session' phenomenon that the Rolling Stones'
    Japanese record label London/King Records invented and released a special 'Japan only' EP entitled
    SUPER SESSION, which featured the three songs 'We Love You', 'Live with Me' and 'You Can't Always
    Get What You Want'.

3   According to producer Ikuzo Orita, guitarist Shinki Chen mistakenly entitled the project Foodbrain
    when he intended to say 'brain food'.

4   The eight other hijackers were Takamaro Tamiya, Takeshi Okamoto, Takahiro Konishi, Shiro Akagi,
    Yasuhiro Shibata, Kintaro Yoshida, Yoshimi Tanaka and Kimihiro Uomoto aka Kimihiro Abe. Of the nine
    who boarded the Yodo-go, four of the group – including Wakabayashi – remain in Pyongyang. Two are
    in jail in Japan, and three are dead. The hijack was part of a series of worldwide abductions that
    continued right into the late 1980s, and it's believed that thirteen Japanese nationals are still stuck in
    North Korea. Red Army Faction leader Takaya Shiomi was jailed for twenty years for his part in the
    plot.

5   Interview with Makoto Kubota in *Mondo Music* magazine, 2001.

6   According to journalist Toreno Kobayashi's 2004 interview with Ikuzo Orita, the source of Shinki
    Chen's outward indifference lay in his Yokohama City punk attitude, which allowed no outward
    displays of emotion.

7   A PATH THROUGH HAZE by Attila Zoller & Masahiko Satoh was released on the
    German label MPS Records.

CHAPTER 6
FLOWER TRAVELLIN' BAND

フラワー　トラベリン　バンド

Determined Am I Now to Live All in Flame

Bare-butt riding across the front sleeve of their 1970 debut LP ANYWHERE, the biker gang known as Flower Travellin' Band enslaved the collective mind of Japan's rock'n'roll audience without a single warning power chord having to be fired. But then, who needs to hear a note when you're in the presence of five such audacious refuseniks? And in the world of rock'n'roll, where symbolism means everything, Flower Travellin' Band has come to be regarded as Japan's ultimate '70s hard-rock band, a quintet whose main sequence of albums managed to distil all the best moves of their Western counterparts – Led Zeppelin, Alice Cooper, Black Sabbath, the Who – without once sounding like copyists. Instead, like peak period Amon Düül 2, Flower Travellin' Band successfully relocated all the New-Boss-Same-as-the-Old-Boss disap-pointments of those aforementioned bands on to an obliterated post-war landscape wherein even a Failed Democracy was infinitely preferable to the petulant diktats of their so-called divine former leaders. Moreover, each album delivered by Flower's dervishes was wrapped up in a highly contrived art-statement sleeve every bit as *Hipgnosis*tically packaged as Townshend & Co – fake newspaper covers, expensively tooled'n'stamped leatherette outer coveralls: you name it, they tried it. Unite all of this with Flower Travellin' Band's wilfully Jap-o-centric post-war worldview, axe hero Hideki Ishima's singularly Far Eastern guitar explorations, and their manager Yuya Utchida's painstakingly thorough attitude to the concept of each new record, and from behind the mountains of evidence emerges Japan's brightest rock'n'roll sun.

Flower Travellin' Band were lean, they were loose, and they were forward-thinking enough to pick an Afro-headed punk like Joe as their singer. Skinny-hipped and howling like a banshee, Akira 'Joe' Yamanaka was both an Iggy Stooge and Percy Plant of epic proportions, confident enough to do his vocal bit and then sod off for ten or more minutes at a time: 'This is my stage so fuck you.' Riffs would build and build, then build some more even now without vocal interruption; song rhythms could change with the deft organic touch of a Zeppelin song or with Sabbath's first-ciggie-of-the-morning abruptness, but still Joe would only sing when absolutely necessary. Yup, Flower Travellin' Band was a true otherworldly force, an amazingly concentrated ensemble with the kind of vast cosmic sense of musical space that made them into 144   the Can of heavy rock.

And yet all of this was achieved not by a single visionary within their ranks, but by the collective hard work of the four musicians involved, all of whom were urged on by their mentor, their instigator, their manager and Gurdjieff-in-residence Yuya Utchida. For Utchida it was who pulled Flower Travellin' Band together in the first place, yet Utchida whom we should applaud for having had the confidence to allow his charges artistic space in which to breathe. Like Uwe Nettelbeck's role within Faust, and like Terry Knight's role within Grand Funk Railroad, Yuya Utchida was Flower Travellin' Band's field marshal, map maker, chief cook and bottle washer, providing his troops with the uniforms, ground support and wherewithal to achieve their greater aims. That Flower Travellin' Band were far less successful than the Japanese music business at first predicted should in no way reflect badly on Yuya Utchida. Indeed, he kept them supplied with enough ideas and projects to fill ten albums. Unfortunately, however, Flower Travellin' Band suffered because of the Japanese rock audience's capricious decision to abandon so-called New Rock in favour of the earnest MOR-styled sub-Carole King soft ballad rock currently being served up by the likes of Happy End, Garo and other singer-songwriter-led outfits of the time. Flower Travellin' Band's lack of recognition would eventually compromise their place at home to such an extent that they felt forced to travel abroad to seek their fortune. Worse still, their continued lack of success would ultimately compromise their place at Atlantic Records to such an extent that, by 1974, singer Joe would be singled out for the solo star treatment. But at least by that time, Flower Travellin' Band had been given ample opportunity to show what they could deliver – and deliver they most certainly did. The first three of their four albums – ANYWHERE, SATORI and MADE IN JAPAN – are undisputed hard-rock classics, while even their posthumous double live LP MAKE UP contains many extraordinary highs of its own. Before we enquire as to how the band's best music was created, however, let us first return to the pre-Flower Travellin' Band days in order to discover what moved them all to make their incredible hard-rock statements.

The Tale of Yuya Utchida

Note: Those of you who are feeling light-headed from the sheer weight of uncommon Japanese names flying out from within the pages of this Japrocksampler may not yet have noticed that the name Yuya Utchida has appeared again and again over the past chapters. Indeed, Utchida first appeared in the latter stages of Book One, Chapter One as a young rock'n'roller then enthralled by Elvis Presley. And so it is to this point that we return briefly to shore up Utchida's place in the Japanese Rock Pantheon.

Like a large proportion of rock'n'rollers, Yuya Utchida's formative years were spent in earnest industry preparing for an entirely straight adult life. Born in 1939, in the port city of Kobe, Utchida was the sixteen-year-old Deputy Head Boy of his local high school when his worldview was torn to pieces one Saturday afternoon, after visiting his local cinema to see two youth exploitation movies, *Seasons of the Sun* and *Violent Classroom*. By his own admission, Utchida thereafter went off the rails and spent his entire time 'posing with a broom in the mirror, miming to Elvis [Presley] records'.[1] Falling behind in his studies, Utchida was forced to go to a local *Yakan Koko* (evening high school), where he found himself surrounded by similar refusenik types, all far more interested in cultivating their sneers than their careers. In 1957, Utchida left education behind to begin work as a 'band boy', and formed the Blue Caps with his friend Mitsuo Sagawa. Determined to make a success of rock'n'roll, Utchida spent the next few years hopscotching from one humorous-sounding band to the next before settling in as vocalist for George Tagawa & the Double Beats in 1960. In spite of the early '60s pop boom, Utchida remained faithful to the pre-army Elvis and sung nothing but rock'n'roll, considerably limiting his career possibilities. However, Utchida's fundamentalist stance eventually paid off when, in mid-1962, he was invited to join the hugely successful Takeshi Terauchi & the Bluejeans, who allowed him to record several Japanese-language versions of Elvis songs. After two highly success-ful TV appearances on *The Hit Parade* and *Pant Pop Show*, Yuya made his movie debut in *Subarashiki Akujo* (Femme Fatale), thereafter continuing to ply his trade as a singer of rock'n'roll.

In 1964, however, Utchida's mind was blown when a friend played him the Beatles. According to Utchida's autobiography, the singer realised after hearing a single Beatles song that the entire rock'n'roll genre had now been rendered obsolete. With Utchida continuing to act in movies, his current band the Bluejeans supported international stars such as the Spotnicks and the Astronauts on their Japanese tours. But, in early '66, the news of the Beatles' forthcoming Japanese tour inspired Utchida to write the cheesy 'Welcome Beatles' in the hope of having a hit. In the Japanese Beatlemania that followed their tour, Utchida discovered a young Kyoto group called the Funnies, whom he felt could be his backing band once their singer had been sacked. However, when the singer, Kenji 'Julie' Sawada, refused to be ousted, it was Utchida who was given his marching orders, while the Funnies went on to immediate fame and fortune as the Tigers.

'Fretting, agonised and full of disgust, I went to Europe,' says Utchida in his autobiography. Throughout 1967, the singer lived 'like a hippie', first in London then Paris, witnessing shows by Jimi Hendrix, the Who, Led Zeppelin, the Misunderstood, and countless other underground bands, whose vocal sound convinced Utchida that the only way forward in rock'n'roll continued to be through the use of English. Determined to replicate these wild happenings back in Japan, Utchida left Paris in early '68 and headed for home, his new psychedelic project already alive in his head and named Yuya Utchida & the Flowers.

Yuya Utchida & His Naked Septet

Almost from the moment that Yuya set foot on the tarmac at Tokyo's Haneda Airport, this gruff iconoclast knew that he had his work cut out. The Group Sounds scene that had begun so auspiciously two years previously was already drifting rudderless, as the artists, musicians and singers involved had long before chosen to kowtow to management consultants, stylists, hairdressers and the like, in an all-out offensive to earn mucho dollar. By mid-1968, Group Sounds had become so narrowly defined that few charted their songs without a Eurasian pretty boy in the spotlight, a hefty sweetener of string-section overload and a lame saccharine lyrical allusion of the kind that the Floral churned out on their embarrassingly twee late GS single 'Tears Are Flower Petals'. Indeed, the staff writers inside the Tokyo hit factories turned out this stuff so routinely that any outfit whose line-up strayed outside the 'official' GS mould was deemed unsaleable.

Much to Utchida's chagrin, the chief culprit in all of this was his own arch-nemesis, that fey MOR clown Julie Sawada, whose career had risen higher with every cynical step he'd taken away from his rock'n'roll roots. Utopian as ever, and with plenty of heavyweight friends in the business, Utchida decided to bust the bloated guts of the GS scene wide open with as spirited and arty a broadside as he could muster. The Flowers would be, he declared to anyone who'd listen, a transcendental one-time affair, whose 'multi-media actions would make [their] statements across many different fronts'.[2] To his long-time record-producer buddy and chief of Polydor Records, Ikuzo Orita, Utchida explained his determination to reconcile high art with disposable pop, experimental composition with film scores, and all contained within record sleeves of the kind yet to be encountered in Japan. To Orita, then knee-deep in the problems of returning some credibility to the ailing career of Julie Sawada's dreadful Tigers, Utchida's words were pure poetry. Indeed, he personally knew of many disenchanted GS musicians just waiting to bail out of their obsolete pop groups, and immediately suggested a few names to this ornery visionary who, every day, drank Orita's coffee machine dry and dictated incessant notes to the label boss's perplexed secretary.

And so it was that the Flowers came into being with alarming speed and alacrity. Indeed, even before the band's personnel had been confirmed, Yuya had secured a deal with the producers of the forthcoming *yakuza* movie *Ah Himeyuri-no-Tou* to run one of Utchida's own instrumentals 'Sohshiju' over the opening sequence, with full credits going to the Flowers, whomsoever they should turn out to be. Next, auditions for this visionary outfit began in earnest. Disgusted by the manner in which women had so cynically been erased from any group purporting to be part of the patriarchal GS scene, and awed by the tough new breed of rock ladies like Big Brother's Janis Joplin and Jefferson Airplane's Signe Anderson and Grace Slick, Utchida immediately contacted the beautiful Remi Aso to sing alongside him in the new ensemble. Having been sidelined by the male-orientated Group Sounds scene, Remi had actually given up singing and was on the point of getting married when she received Yuya's phone call.[3] But the indomitable Utchida was having none of it ('Just gimme nine months!') and eventually Remi agreed.

Having successfully injected a bit of Grace'n'Marty Airplane's yin'n'yang into the proceedings, Utchida – with Ikuzo Orita's help – next set about cherry-picking the best instrumentalists from the drifting GS scene. First, he lured away the Beavers' disillusioned star guitarist Hideki Ishima with promises that the Flowers would play instrumentals of the kind that no Japanese audience had yet witnessed. With Ishima on board, Yuya was then able to command the services of musicologist and pedal steel guitarist Katsuhiko Kobayashi, whom Yuya had heard playing in an Osaka jazz *kissa* (coffee shop). While Kobayashi's masterful control of his instrument enabled him to capture the stratospheric tone of Glenn Ross Campbell – the seventeen-year-old boy wonder from John Peel's Californian protégés the Misunderstood, whom Utchida had seen perform several times at London's UFO club – Yuya himself restricted his own contributions to what he termed 'lead tambourine'. Uh, look out!

Swiftly, the Flowers' line-up fell into place as Utchida's propensity for talking up projects set the collapsing Group Sounds scene alight. As his Flowers project had, from the very beginning, so openly declared itself capable of presumptuously straddling the rock scene, experimental music scene and art world simultaneously, so Utchida himself became a lightning rod for all of Tokyo's most extraordinary visionaries, seers, hustlers and chancers. And in the Tokyo scene of late '68, where there were furry freaks by the Freudian couch-load, Utchida soon found himself introduced to the newly psychedelicised Toshi Ichiyanagi, whose own visionary multi-media OPERA INSPIRED BY THE WORKS OF TADANORI YOKO'O was itself progressing at an extraordinary pace. Formerly of sober demeanour and an even more sober appearance, Toshi Ichiyanagi was, by the time of his meeting with Yuya, so outwardly changed that even Yoko Ono had had a problem recognising her ex-husband when she encountered him by chance early in the year. But Toshi Ichiyanagi was so electrified by Yuya's maverick confidence and determination that the composer's carefully laid plans of recording a loud electric rock band with a symphony orchestra were soon cast aside in favour of letting the Flowers lay down precisely what they fancied. Indeed, Ichiyanagi's only stipulation was that the Flowers' track should be entitled 'I'm Dead' after one of Tadanori Yoko'o's most famous paintings, and must be no less than twenty minutes in duration.

'I'm Dead' & the 10,000 Years of Freak-out with T. Ichiyanagi

Late October '68, with Yuya Utchida and Toshi Ichiyanagi sitting at the mixing console of Tokyo's enormous NHK Radio studio, the Flowers' five instrumentalists summoned up their courage with black coffee and Santori whisky. Ahead of them lay a full half hour of emptiness, the time which NHK's studio engineer had made available to them by setting the great Toshiba sixteen-track tape machine to half speed. With the machine running at 15-inches-per-second rather than at the regular 30ips, the Flowers could now immerse themselves in the past 10,000 years of freak-out, as composer Ichiyanagi had termed it.[4] And so they began, cagily at first, each awaiting the others' moves. A few rudimentary riffs had been surreptitiously worked upon in secrecy, for neither Utchida nor Ichiyanagi could be allowed to find out, everything supposedly having to well up directly from the Ur-spring of the Right Now. Bang, splash, crash, a few oozing bluesy bottleneck riffs from rhythm guitarist Susumu Oku, a suppressed and distant buzzing from Ishima's overloaded Les Paul ... then the track began in earnest, the five crouched over their instruments determined to summon up all of the spirit and experience that had scored them the gig in the first place. Inevitably, the pedal steel guitar of Katsuhiko Kobayashi dominated the proceedings, his stratospheric tones hanging over the rest of the ensemble like a restless ghost observing its own funeral.

In truth, the twenty-seven minutes of 'I'm Dead' is neither the earth-rending violation of sound that the Flowers promised, nor the schizophrenic stalemate that so many sidelong pieces from the same psychedelic period tend to fall into. Instead, 'I'm Dead' was a uniquely Japanese ritual piece that sat righteously alongside the *gagaku* percussion of its time, and Japan's experimental *musique concrète* of the previous eighteen years; a stop/start ever-breathing workout that reached into obliteration without ever achieving oblivion, a searching, stumbling struggle for the single candle lighting the musicians' way out of their torture chamber. But for the Flowers, for Yuya Utchida, for Toshi Ichiyanagi, and for the entire Japanese rock'n'roll underground scene, 'I'm Dead' was nothing short of R E V E L A T I O N!

At the end of the session, the five relieved musicians laid into bass player Ken Hashimoto's bubbling elliptical bass line, and out of the ether they grabbed a hold of a cosmic Hawaiian-styled instrumental, later to be titled 'Hidariashi No Otoko'. Again propelled along by the furious and masterful lap steel of Katsuhiko Kobayashi, this churning and insensible masterpiece bustled along like some Joe Meek-produced psychedelic space flight from San Francisco to Tahiti, a greased rotund behemoth whose groove would not be out of place on any West Coast psychedelic classic album from Country Joe's ELECTRIC MUSIC FOR MIND & BODY to the Kaleidoscope's SIDE TRIPS. Mercifully, the delighted and grateful Ichiyanagi handed Utchida the master tape of this final jam for his own use, and Yuya knew he had the makings of an excellent Flowers debut LP. Using the results of his band's sessions with Ichiyanagi, Yuya next scored a record deal with the big independent Synton label, allowing the Flowers to commence recording of the band's first album.

Ironically, the Flowers one week later began their first series of club dates in the basement of a Tokyo jazz café, hitting the stage at precisely the same time as Julie and Sally's Tigers were schmaltzing the floor above them. But the news of the Flowers' arrival had hit the disenchanted GS scene head-on, reminding many of just how sidelined their art had become on the mainline to pop success. For the Tigers especially, the previous year had been a nightmare from which they were still waiting to emerge, as TV commercials for chocolate bars and increasingly vapid singles releases had led to a total media hammering for their most recent 'mature' LP HUMAN RENASCENCE [sic]. Other GS bands travelling a similarly commercial route to the top now realised that they too risked media wrath should they follow the hapless Tigers into the world of deodorant and candy endorsements.

In truth, however, even the visionary Yuya Utchida had chosen a dreadful time to launch his spectacular commodity, as other equally disenchanted rock musicians flailed about on the lookout for an entirely new sound. By the time he had put every plan into place, even Utchida was at least a year behind his contemporaries in the West, with the result that the Flowers' debut LP CHALLENGE was another schizophrenic stalemate of the kind released by similarly heavy-styled bands such as Apryl Fool, the Helpful Soul, Shinki Chen's Powerhouse and Kuni Kawachi's organ-dominated Happenings Four+1. Yet again, despite the exhilarating performances of both band and singers, this excellent concept had been marred by its eclecticism and lack of truly great new songs. Forced once again to rely on well-known cover versions, the Flowers' inclusion of such other average post-Group Sounds stock covers as Cream's 'White Room' and 'I'm So Glad', Jimi Hendrix's 'Hey Joe' and 'Stone Free', and Big Brother's 'Piece of My Heart' made the brilliant Japanese-styled psychedelic instrumentals sound anachronistic and merely token gestures, ultimately dragging the CHALLENGE LP out of any Real Contender territory.[5] Perhaps, in the same way that Alex Harvey's Soul Band of the mid-'60s made up for in nihilistic spirit what it lacked in Detroit professionalism, so the Flowers, conversely, made up for in soul review professionalism what it lacked in sheer Western Will-to-Power individualistic change-the-worldness. But even Utchida's astute decision to release the album in a controversial cover that featured all seven members naked in a cornfield, Ms Aso included, was not enough to make the record a success, and Utchida began to lose interest.

Forced to bide his time with money-making gigs that would earn enough to pay seven musicians, Utchida was aghast to find the Flowers sharing festival bills with precisely those acts he'd returned to Japan to destroy: the Mops, the Tigers, the Golden Cups in their umpteenth incarnation. On stage, however, the Flowers were able to deploy their full arsenal to devastating effect, as the three guitarists regularly overpowered all comers with their wailing Far Eastern-styled instrumental psyche-outs 'I'm Dead' and 'Hidariashi No Otoko', whilst their sitar'n'tabla version of Moondog's classic 'All Is Loneliness' proto-drone meditation revealed just how out-on-a-limb this ensemble really was. After such bombast, the band would unleash extraordinarily dynamic arrangements of 'River Deep, Mountain High', Jefferson Airplane's 'Greasy Heart' and such Janis Joplin songs as 'Summertime', 'Kosmic Blues', 'Combination of the Two' and 'Piece of My Heart', not forgetting Remi's undy-wetting prostrate-pummelling-the-dust take on Led Zeppelin's 'How Many More Times?' whose freight-train ramalama served to remind listeners of that song's roots in the Count Five's 'Psychotic Reaction'.[6]

Joe's Afro

Over the coming months, Utchida's renewed friendships with old music-business mates saw him regularly hanging out at Tokyo's Toyoko Gekijo Theatre, in the Shibuya theatre district, where rehearsals for the forthcoming Japanese-language version of *Hair* had made it a focal point for all the renegades and forward-thinkers in Tokyo. Now thirty years old and increasingly agitated at his own lack of commercial success, Utchida surveyed the young hippie cast as he sat drinking with his old friend and Polydor Records boss Ikuzo Orita. The two shared a mutual hatred of the GS scene and Orita declared his wish to overthrow its commercial-mindedness with a series of uniquely Japanese heavy-rock statements.[7] Plotting together in the fertile and symbolically revolutionary atmosphere of the *Hair* scene, the two promised to work together to realise these ambitions as soon as possible. Utchida was particularly taken with the young cast member Joe Yamanaka, who'd become so intoxicated by *Hair* that he had grown out his own tight curls into the same magnificent wild Afro as that depicted on the show's original poster. Although Yamanaka had formerly been lead singer with the GS band Four Nine Ace, his frizzy hair had been something of a GS liability in those days of mop tops and bowl cuts. But now, Joe was a super-skinny hippie with an Afro to rival Sly Stone and a gaggle of giggling *futen* girls in tow as evidence of his transformation.

Utchida invited Joe to sing guest lead vocals for the Flowers at their next show, ironically a vile old-timer affair entitled 'Rock'n'roll Jam '70', to be recorded for a Toshiba Express Records double-LP, in which the Flowers had been invited to compete in a 'Battle of the Bands'-style competition with former GS glory boys the Mops, Happenings Four and the Golden Cups. The Mops opened the show with a hoary set of Animals covers ('I'm Crying', 'Don't Bring Me Down') that sent everyone straight back to 1965. Next up, the latest beleaguered incarnation of the Golden Cups worked out their current obsessions with a ridiculously eclectic set that included songs by Ray Charles, Patsy Cline, the Beatles, Blood Sweat & Tears and the especially ill-chosen Dionne Warwick classic 'I Say a Little Prayer', during which singer Dave Hirao happily sang 'the moment I wake up – before I put on my make-up'. After a brief set of keyboard-dominated chintz from Kuni Kawachi's Happenings Four, the Flowers took to the stage and pummelled their audience into submission with their regular show of Big Brother standards and tumultuous guitar workouts. However, when Joe Yamanaka walked out on stage to perform Led Zeppelin's arrangement of Willie Dixon's 'You Shook Me', Utchida was so thrilled at the audience's delighted response that he sensed right away that a vital new career discovery had been made. Ironically, the Flowers concluded their set that night with the greatest performance of their short career, Remi's distraught vocals on Zeppelin's 'How Many More Times' caught for ever as the final track of that double live album. Truly, it remains one of the greatest moments of late '60s rock music – East or West – easily transcending Zeppelin's own version by several leagues, and encapsulating in its seven minutes all of the weeping proto-metal blue-eyed soul-driven garage frenzy that Grand Funk, the MC5 and Blue Cheer would come to symbolise down the decades. For the Flowers, however, it was all over. Yuya Utchida had glimpsed nirvana and the naked septet was history. From here on in, power trios fronted by golden Rock Gods were to be his preferred mode of expression. And, in an act of righteous self-pruning, Yuya dismissed his entire band (himself included), retaining only drummer Joji Wada and axe hero Hideki Ishima. Steel guitarist Katsuhiko Kobayashi and singer Remi Aso sailed to America, while Yuya adopted the producer/manager role à la Grand Funk's Terry Knight. The '70s were here and, having missed the boat in the '50s and '60s, Yuya was not going to get left behind this time.

KIRIKYOGEN & the Flowering of Flower Travellin' Band

In the early spring of 1970, Yuya's new Flowers took over a large rehearsal space in a Tokyo basement where drummer Joji Wada set about the task of de-learning much of what he'd long been playing. In Utchida's desire to start with a clean slate, the new manager had seriously considered replacing Wada in the new band. But Yuya's many conversations with Polydor's Ikuzo Orita had convinced him that good drummers were particularly difficult to locate in Japan. And so it was now Joji Wada's task to empty his playing of all unnecessary jazzy fills, replacing it instead with the kind of heavy rock action employed by Westerners such as Led Zeppelin's John Bonham and Black Sabbath's Bill Ward. Still without a bass player at this point, Yuya's new Flowers were invited by Capitol Records to act as the backing group on the debut solo album by his old friend Kuni Kawachi of Happening Four+1, whose Procul Harum-styled twin-keyboard line-up and classical stylings had been given a wide berth by Japanese audiences. Kawachi had subsequently written for theatre troupes such as Tokyo Kid Brothers, but he was now determined to record a 'heavy' album with the help of Yuya's new Flowers. Yuya decided that the Kawachi recording sessions would be a perfect opportunity for the musicians to test their musical ideas out, and the keyboard player was delighted by the results. Entitled KIRIKYOGEN, Kawachi's solo album was by far the best music he'd ever released and featured both Joe Yamanaka's lead vocal and Hideki Ishima's slashing guitar throughout. It is on this record that we begin to see the sheer breadth of guitar-playing which Hideki Ishima was capable of. For his masterful acoustic performances within the grooves of KIRIKYOGEN equal any Western player, whilst his electrifying lead breaks run from mental lowbrow gut-churners to the kind of screaming bottleneck only seen in the playing of the Misunderstood's Glenn Ross Campbell. Gone too were Kawachi's previously ostentatious licks, replaced here by long empty chords and a rolling funk that sounded unlike anything before or after. Elsewhere, songs such as 'The Scientific Investigation' and 'Classroom' echoed the more acoustic later side of the Velvet Underground. Ironically, this album that was recorded in just a few days and treated like a recording demonstration by most of those musicians involved turned out to be a genuine classic of Japanese rock.

Yuya Utchida himself was not so convinced, however, believing instead that the organ and piano that Kawachi contributed to his own solo record had unnecessarily filled up too many spaces. On listening to KIRIKYOGEN, Yuya became even more certain that emptiness and bombast must be the key to his new ensemble. Gone were the days of supportive rhythm guitarists and organists filling every available space, the new riffing approach considerably broadening the range of heavy music's brooding dynamics. Yuya had originally poached guitarist Hideki Ishima from the Beavers because of their shared passion for Indian musical scales. But it was only in the early rehearsal days after the dissolution of the Flowers that Yuya realised how perfectly suited to power-trio playing was Ishima's guitar style, especially as Joe Yamanaka was in possession of a scream from the bowels of Hell itself. Hidden behind two vocalists and two other rhythm guitarists, Hideki Ishima could never have hoped to provide more than an extra flavour to the Flowers' music. Within the emptiness of a trio, however, Ishima's guitar would become the sole provider of chords, even able to kick the music entirely free of chords should he so wish.

While the three musicians adopted the techniques of heavy music by learning songs from the debut LPs of Black Sabbath and Led Zeppelin, the irrepressible Yuya soon scored a one-album deal with Philips Records and delivered to rehearsals a young long-haired bass player by the name of Jun Kosuki, who'd formerly played with an obscure late GS band called Taxman. Now determined to build on the Flowers' excellent live reputation, but wishing to imbue the new outfit with some of the free-wheeling spirit of current road movies such as *Zabriskie Point* and *Easy Rider*, Yuya decided to name the new quartet Flower Travellin' Band. Flowers? Sure, we're still Flowers but now we're a travellin' band like the Creedence man sang.

Naked Proto-Metallers on the Hard-Rock Road to ANYWHERE

Fearful of losing the momentum and justifiably terrified of being gazumped by hard-rock interlopers, the ever paranoid Yuya Utchida rushed his new charges into the studio to record their debut album even before the quartet had had time to write any material. Friends and enemies alike predicted another disaster in the making, but the October 1970 release of Flower Travellin' Band's debut LP ANYWHERE was a massive change of musical style and a hugely listenable record. From the off, the driving near-sixteen minutes of 'Louisiana Blues' defined Flower Travellin' Band's direction. Coming on like the Doors' 'Roadhouse Blues' in a James Dean collision with the Chocolate Watchband's 'Expo 2000' as played by the power trio CONTINENTAL CIRCUS-period Gong, 'Louisiana Blues' was one brutally rock behemoth that explored guitar theme after guitar theme. Bucking slide guitar and fierce trucking rhythms allowed space for only brief vocal performances from Joe Yamanaka. But his singing was wild and this guitar music was h-e-a-v-y! Side two closed with a nine-minute ambient version of 'Black Sabbath' so heavy that its extraordinarily a-rhythmical take on Tony Iommi's Satanic chords sagged and creaked like the doom metal of the Melvins and Earth still almost twenty years in the future. Side two opened with another strung-out cover, this time the Animals' hoary 'House of the Rising Sun' was entirely restructured, given 'Stairway to Heaven' chords and extended to the kind of full-on eight minutes that Traffic delivered on their self-titled second album. As though such iconic rock songs were not enough for Utchida's new project to take on, Flower now concluded their LP debut with a thirteen-and-a-half minute power-trio blitz of King Crimson's venerable steed '21st Century Schizoid Man', here Black Sabbathised to the point of no return, the prissy jazz sax and stentorian snare drum of the original replaced by pure shock-rock metal mayhem. And all of this was captured for the delectation of the Japanese listening public and delivered on a gatefold sleeve that depicted Utchida and his four cohorts righteously and defiantly cruising butt-nekkid down the deserted highways of uptight Japan. Destination? Anywhere!

By the beginning of 1971, as the initial rush created by ANYWHERE's release had given the band the opportunity to play at the better Japanese festivals alongside such refuseniks as Les Rallizes Denudés and Murahatchibu, many were at last beginning to appreciate the singular guitar tones of Hideki Ishima. Free from the restraints of a rhythm guitarist and utterly in synch with drummer Joji Wada, Ishima began to take the stage apart with his combination of scything dervish dance and gleaming Far Eastern take on Western hard rock. Still unused to merely standing by and watching his boys from the side of the stage, Yuya occasionally laid some of his 'lead tambourine' on the unsuspecting audience and even barked out the occasional rock'n'roll standard in his own inimitable style.

Yuya Utchida & Ikuzo Orita in Search of SATORI

By now, the general public perception of Flower was that of an entirely new band. And so, in the spring of '71, Yuya was delighted to learn that his great friend and facilitator Ikuzo Orita was about to leave Polydor Records for Atlantic, where he wished to make Flower Travellin' Band his first signing. While at Polydor, Orita's winning combination of unabashed enthusiasm for hard rock and determination to locate a singularly Japanese rock sound had helped give rise to many of the most imaginative (though occasionally failed) experiments thus far achieved; Love Live Life +1, Foodbrain, Shinki Chen & Friends, you name it and Orita had probably had a hand in it. Now in control of Atlantic Records' entire Japanese budget, no one was more aware of the company's hefty worldwide musical mythology (both past and present) than Orita himself, and he put the weight of the company behind Yuya's band. Immediately thereafter, Orita brought his Polydor protégé Shinki Chen into the Atlantic fold and formed a supergroup named Speed, Glue & Shinki around this whizzkid guitarist whom many rated as Japan's answer to Jimi Hendrix.

While Flower Travellin' Band wowed audiences across Japan, Yuya and Orita conspired in the Atlantic offices, determined to create fabulous rock artefacts to rival Atlantic's biggest progressive bands Led Zeppelin and Yes, whose albums were housed in fabulously arty and multi-levelled packages. Orita secured guaranteed releases for the band in America, Canada and the UK, while Yuya commissioned fine artist Shinoba Ishimaru to work up some ideas based on Buddhism, Hinduism and psychedelia for Flower's forthcoming second LP.

When Yuya and Orita took the band into the rehearsal studio to routine the new material, however, both were staggered at its outrageous confidence and uniqueness. The endless shows and summer festivals had given Hideki Ishima boundless opportunity to work up each riff idea into an ever unfolding Far Eastern monster, which the band unleashed upon their mentors with note-perfect precision. Even more astonishing was the freedom that Joe had given the rest of the band, often singing no more than four or so lines of verse before opting out and letting the band rip it to shreds. Through Ishima's continued fascination for Eastern enlightenment, three of the tracks had acquired the simple working titles of 'Satori I', 'Satori II' and 'Satori III'. Fantastic, said Yuya. Let's keep the entire album just as mysterious and give nothing away. And so it was that Flower Travellin' Band's second LP became known as SATORI, with each of the five long tracks becoming known only as 'Satori I–V'.

With Yuya Utchida and Ikuzo Orita sharing production, SATORI was for ever to remain Flower's most singular and demented work, coming over like some super-fit combination of Led Zeppelin's 'The Immigrant Song' and the Yardbirds' 'Happenings Ten Years Time Ago' as played by a non-blues guitarist such as Michael Schenker, or perhaps Uli John Roth's power trio Electric Sun. However, even these descriptions cannot come close to doing justice to Hideki Ishima's extraordinarily inflammatory playing on SATORI, and although the past decade and a half (1990–2006) has brought so-called heavy metal to entirely new heights, the succinctness of SATORI's arrangements and its economy of playing are still somewhat depressingly unique. Clad in its sumptuous gatefold package, the front page announcing 'Flower Trip Band'[8] sitting atop a psychedelicised Eastern world contained within Shinobu Ishimaru's enormous Buddha, SATORI wowed the Japanese audience and even climbed into the Canadian Top Ten album chart.[9]

Exiles on Vancouver Island:
The Story of MADE IN JAPAN

Despite the huge artistic success of SATORI, both Orita and Utchida were highly disappointed with Flower's commercial progress at home in Japan. Sure, they continued to play large concert halls, but compared to musically tame Japanese-language bands such as Garo and Happy End, Flower was nowhere at all. In hindsight, the so-called New Rock phenomenon had been nothing more than a brief afterglow of the death throes of the Group Sounds scene, and Japan's capricious hippie audience was by now more enthralled by the wishy-washy singer-songwriters thrown up in the wake of international stars such as James Taylor, Carole King, Carly Simon and Neil Young. Even Julie Sawada's cynical New Rock supergroup Pyg had failed on account of their hard-rock stance and dedication to Stones, Mountain and Deep Purple covers, and no one understood their own market better than the ex-Tigers vocalist.

Yuya Utchida decided that his band should tour where its audience was most enthusiastic, and accepted an offer to support the Canadian band Lighthouse on their forthcoming home tour. Led by keyboard player Paul Hoffert, Lighthouse was a jazzy Blood Sweat & Tears-styled outfit with a brass section and a large Canadian audience. At the end of the tour, the band agreed that Paul Hoffert should produce their third LP, and they played before a Toronto audience of 30,000 as support to Emerson, Lake & Palmer and Bob Seger.

In the Canadian studio, however, Hideki Ishima found himself entirely compromised by the producer. As a songwriter and jazz-orientated keyboard player, Hoffert felt no particular affinity for loud rock guitar and appeared determined only to explore Joe Yamanaka's ballad side. Worse still, Hoffert commissioned Yoko Nomura – wife of Flower's road manager – to write a whole set of lyrics for the new Canadian-recorded album, to be titled (with no little irony) MADE IN JAPAN. Thousands of miles adrift from the safe lunacy of Utchida and Orita, and worried about paying the rent, the band set about reconciling their music with Hoffert's decidedly conservative vision. Then, with the album completed by early spring 1972, the four broke and pissed-off band members fled back to Tokyo where the folk revival was burning even more blandly than before they'd left.

Back in Tokyo, this new album that had sounded so abject in Vancouver was actually well received by Utchida and Orita, who recognised that Hoffert's decision to trim back Ishima's guitar chaos at least allowed the record its place in the current Japanese scene, and even agreed to release the song 'Kamikaze' as a single. The acoustic minor-chord blues of the opening song, 'Unaware', sounded like Arthur Lee's classic Love song 'Signed DC', while Ishima's clever acoustic implementation of Black Sabbath's so-called Satanic chords throughout rendered the record unlike anything they'd heard before. For 'Hiroshima', Hideki Ishima had cleverly set Yoko Nomura's beautiful death lyrics to the same music as 'Satori Part 3', here rendered both on acoustic and electric guitars, evoking the same transcendental raga effects as YETI-period Amon Düül 2. Indeed, of the eight tracks, only the facile lyrical Crosstianity of 'Heaven and Hell' stood out as being poorly translated C.S. Lewis fare; Joe's bizarre genius for running long syllables right across the metre managing to render even these dubious sentiments palatably mysterious. Utchida gathered all of the Canadian reviews and promotional material together and pasted up the MADE IN JAPAN cover to look as though it had arrived in a heavy brown reinforced cardboard case. Ikuzo Orita agreed to release the album in a heavy cardboard box, and the band set about promoting the record.

From MAKE UP to Break-up

With all the moves of a P.T. Barnum, Yuya Utchida now pulled out all the stops to hoodwink the Japanese media into believing that Flower Travellin' Band had become enormous in America. Press shots of them backstage with ELP in Toronto helped to create this façade, scoring the band the prestigious support slot on the Rolling Stones' forthcoming Japanese tour. But their joy soon evaporated when the paranoid Japanese authorities denied Mick Jagger a work permit on account of an ancient drug conviction, and Flower – still reeling from their Canadian disaster – felt their inner fire coming close to extinction. Gone now was Hideki Ishima's valiant axe-wielding militancy, his Tony Iommi-like ability to descend into the Underworld and return with Riffs from Hell, replaced instead by a sidelined soul bereft of licks adrift and unplugged from rock's third rail. In an effort to shake the band out of its stupor, Orita and Utchida decided to take the reins once more and book the band into Tokyo's Mouri Studios, where they routined any and all material the musicians could lob their way. Nothing. Not a sausage, not a riff nor a lick emanated from Ishima's direction. Instead, it was the previously acquiescent Joe Yamanaka who delivered the bulk of the new songs, and on whose shoulders the bulk of writing was to fall, co-writing material with his girlfriend Patti and drummer Joji Wada. Utchida and Orita scratched their heads and wondered what to do. There was clearly not enough material to commence the recording of Flower's fourth LP, yet the concert offers coming in were hardly sufficient to keep such a large concern afloat. Finally, the producers took Joe and Joji Wada's slight 6/8 minor-key ballad 'Shadows of Lost Days' and attempted to arrange it into a single. Although the song was a depressing retreat into the Percy Sledge of late '60s soulified Flowers, its retro charm was at least somewhat catchy, especially when Utchida summoned the aid of Nobuyuki Shinohara, Kuni Kawachi's cohort and second organist in Happening Four+1. But when 'Shadows of Lost Days' failed to chart, the band that limped on into the summer was indeed a shadow of its lost days, buoyed up only by its producers' spiky enthusiasm and endless entreaties for more songs, more songs. Nevertheless, the sidelined Hideki Ishima remained a spent force despite the efforts of the rest of the band; even bass player Jun Kosuki managing to bring forth the bizarre ballad 'Broken Strings', a homage to all of the broken guitar strings he'd so casually dumped in dressing-room waste baskets around the globe(!).

158   In order to pep the band up and reinstate some kind of vigour and occasion into the unit, Utchida now resorted to releasing a live LP and, with that plan in mind, booked Flower to perform at Yokosuka Bunkakaikan, a huge culture hall high up in the mountains, on the Miura Peninsula, one hour's drive south of Tokyo. But when the mobile studio arrived at the hall in a downpour on the dreary morning of 16th September 1972, radio reports of flash flooding throughout the region and landslides suggested they cut their losses and cancel the show. 'There was a typhoon … tons of rain … The wind was so strong we thought of cancelling,' remarked Ikuzo Orita years later. 'But about a thousand people had already showed up so we decided to do it.' And thus, high up in the mountains far from anywhere, Flower Travellin' Band played their last great concert, aided and abetted by '50s rocker Yuya Utchida on occasional lead vocals and a Hammond organist from '60s stalwarts Happening Four+1. And as Utchida barked out his infamous version of Carl Perkins' 'Blue Suede Shoes', no song could have seemed further from Flower's auspicious and bold beginnings just thirty-six months previously.

       Sorting through the recordings back in Tokyo, Utchida discovered that much of the concert had been ruined by the mobile-studio engineer's failure to earth the truck properly, resulting in crackles throughout many of the performances. With the live album already scheduled for release as a double-LP by Atlantic, Utchida was now forced to comb through the wretched fourth-album demo tapes for filler material.

The completed album was a disastrous hotchpotch, completed by Utchida's own 'Blue Suede Shoes' and a ridiculous and interminable 24-minute-long 'Hiroshima' dragged out by Joji Wada's seemingly endless sub-'TNUC', sub-'The Mule', sub-'Toad' drum solo. In true Utchida fashion, however, the packaging was one of the greatest of double-albums of the entire 1970s. Titled MAKE UP, the record's gatefold sleeve came housed in an incredible 12"x12" stitched brown leatherette case, worthy of Andy Warhol himself.

The spectacular artwork deflected much of the criticism away from the useless contents within, but everyone knew Flower's days were done. Struggling on into early 1973, the band split as soon as Joe Yamanaka let it be known that he wished to embark on a solo career. Whilst in Japan the so-called New Rock had stalled almost before it had even begun, by 1973, even hugely successful international 'heavy' acts had returned to do battle with acoustic'n'Mellotron progressive-styled new albums quite at odds with their former displays of dark bombastic proto-metal overkill, as evidenced by Black Sabbath's SABBATH BLOODY SABBATH and Led Zeppelin's HOUSES OF THE HOLY. Just as in the UK, the Japanese rock scene of '73 was split between an overly serious semi-intellectual progressive rock scene full of keyboard-dominated dribble and an overly-dumb pop scene led by Vodka Collins, whose micro-cephalous take on rock'n'roll claimed inspiration from David Bowie but really aped the compressed Skinhead Moonstomp of Gazza Glitter, Mud, Sweet and Quatro. Ever the Kim Fowleyan chameleon, the opportunistic Yuya Utchida hopped aboard this temporary revival with the appalling album Y.U.Y.A. 1815KC ROCK'N ROLL BROAD-CASTING STATION, whose avant-garbage yielded such gems as 'Heartbreak Hotel', 'Tutti Frutti', 'Long Tall Sally' and (natch) 'Blue Suede Shoes'.

159

Dead Flowers in Joe Yamanaka's Yard

By 1975, Flower Travellin' Band's career had become nothing more than an append-age to Joe's burgeoning Moon-in-June croon-a-thon. Like Roger Daltrey, Rod Stewart and other non-writing lead singers of heavy bands, Joe's decision to call in the profes-sionals at least ensured a place in the charts. A Flower Travellin' Band compilation entitled THE TIMES was released in 1975, and discourteously credited to 'Joe, featur-ing Flower Travellin' Band'; one god-awful ballad tacked on at the end of side two to force devotees to shell out. Yuya Utchida headed underground once more and forgot to resurface until 1991, when – now aged fify-one – he ran for the governorship of Tokyo Prefecture. Ever the iconoclast, his unorthodox campaigning techniques in-cluded singing an unaccompanied version of John Lennon's 'Power to the People', concluding with the claim that he was born in 1999. In 2002, the failed MAKE UP concert was re-enacted, not in Yokosuka but in the more convenient location of Yokohama City. True to the ersatz spirit of the occasion, the only original band members involved were singer Joe Yamanaka and drummer Joji Wada. In 2004, the ever be-shaded and still-long-haired Utchida was awarded the Golden Outlaw Award for his role as a tattooist in the suicide movie *Akame 48 Taki Shinju* (48 Waterfalls). True to himself as ever, nothing more has been heard of guitar maestro Hideki Ishima, whose extraordinary virtuosity and unique take on Western heavy rock continues to inform the heavy-metal bands of this early twenty-first century. Indeed, in metal mags across the world, SATORI is regularly voted up there with BLACK SABBATH, PARANOID, MASTER OF REALITY, LED ZEPPELIN 2, Blue Cheer's VINCEBUS ERUPTUM and OUTSIDEINSIDE and the MC5's KICK OUT THE JAMS. Perhaps it's best that Hideki Ishima has kept away from the limelight, keeping his dignity and mythology intact while others embarrass themselves. For, as Ikuzo Orita remarked so percipiently in a recent interview about that period: 'We wanted to be underground, we itched to be that way.'

160

Footnotes:

1   Yuya Utchida's online autobiography is at: www.uchidayuya.com

2   *Big Globe* magazine interview with Utchida, 1997.

3   Taken from the sleeve notes of Remi Aso's debut solo LP OWN LINES.

4   The incredible rarity of Ichiyanagi's opera was such that most Japanese rock fans (myself included) were first introduced to this material via Apex Records' immaculately named vinyl bootleg FROM PUSSYS TO DEATH IN 10,000 YEARS OF FREAK-OUT, credited to Flower Travellin' Band.

5   During this in-between time of late '68/early '69, every Japanese musical visionary suffered from the same GS stasis. Former Out Cast members Jun 'Kimio' Mizutani and Kenji Todoroki formed the Adams, a symphonic rock band replete with choir and orchestra. They soon discovered, however, that there was no audience for such music and their debut LP KYUYAKU SEISHO (Old Testament) was such a disaster that their record company CBS/Sony incinerated all of the unsold records.

6   How's that for an ex-Yardbird paying back those Michigan punks for stealing Beck & Co's 'I'm A Man'?

7   Toreno Kobayashi. 'Ikuzo Orita Interview' in *Black Shapes of Doom* magazine (2004).

8   As continued evidence of the confusion that the Japanese suffer from concerning 'l' and 'r', artist Ishimaru credited the band on the inner gatefold as 'Frower Travellin' Band'.

9   Despite rigorous research, I've located neither American nor UK versions of SATORI, suggesting that Utchida's claims of foreign success were no more than bragging. I do, however, have a British 7' Atlantic single of 'Satori Part 2' b/w 'Satori Part 1'. As it's not a promo item, it can only be assumed that the band did enjoy some kind of release here in Britain, albeit on a highly limited level.

Album Discography

CHALLENGE (by the Flowers) (Synton 1969)
ANYWHERE (Philips 1970)
SATORI (Atlantic 1971)
MADE IN JAPAN (Atlantic 1972)
MAKE UP (Atlantic 1973)
THE TIMES (compilation) (Atlantic 1975)
FROM PUSSYS TO DEATH IN 10,000 YEARS OF FREAK-OUT (Apex 1995)
MUSIC COMPOSED MAINLY BY HUMANS (Ain't Group Sounds 2002)

Singles Discography

'Satori Part 1' b/w 'Satori Part 2' (Atlantic 1971)
'Map' (Atlantic 1971)
'Kamikaze' (Atlantic 1972)
'Shadows of Lost Days' b/w 'Satori Part 2' (Atlantic 1972)
'Make Up' b/w 'Shadows of Lost Days' (Atlantic 1977)

CHAPTER 7
LES RALLIZES DENUDÉS 裸のラリーズ
OR
'I WILL FOLLOW HIM'

Note: Their career has been down in the dumps ever since bass player Moriyasu Wakabayashi helped hijack a JAL Boeing 737 back in 1970 (see Book Two, Chapter Five). Their last official release was a double live LP recorded back in 1977. And nobody even knows quite what the official name of their band is, or even what its most popular French form means because there are no such things as 'rallizes' in the French language. And yet the cult that surrounds Les Rallizes Denudés increases in size year after year. This is because, in a world where the sacrilegious reunions of former punks like the Velvet Underground and the Stooges have destroyed utterly the myth of their legendary non-conformity, devotees of Les Rallizes's Takeshi Mizutani and his black-clad cohorts can relax safe in the knowledge that their erstwhile heroes would rather commit collective hara kiri than sell out their gruelling 37-year-long self-imposed isolation up in the wildernesses of northern Japan by doing anything remotely as gauche as releasing a new record. Combine all of this attitude with leader Mizutani's intense devotion to re-recording the same small canon of material over and over again, and you have the blueprint for a rock'n'roll cult that transcends all others. When French movie maker Ethan Mousike trekked across the globe to make a documentary about the Rallizes (and at his own expense I hasten to add), Mizutani refused to allow him to film the band close-up, insisting instead that Mousike set up his tripod in the dressing room, thereby allowing the camera lens to focus on less than one-third of the stage. When, after twenty minutes of this suffocatingly boring footage had elapsed, Mizutani contemptuously jumped off stage and kicked the door shut, our heroic French director chose not to remonstrate with the churlish Mizutani, preferring instead to allow the film stock to conclude naturally, thereby allowing Les Rallizes Denudés's errant metaphor its full reign.

When, in November 2003, I showed the complete Mousike movie at my two-day festival Rome Wasn't Burned in a Day, at London's Lyric Theatre, the theatre's tiny cinema was rammed with Rallizes freaks for over an hour before the movie was due to be shown. Sociopaths to a man, these fundamentalists stared straight ahead, fidgeting occasionally, but barely communicating with one another. When the movie concluded, nearly every one of these Rallizes buffs headed straight for the theatre's exit, having no interest in any of the other many underground feasts that I had prepared to unleash. Taj Mahal Travellers? SunnO)))? Van der Graaf Generator? Vibracathedral Orchestra? Forget about it! I like to imagine that each one then returned to his (there are no female Rallizes fans) home, where each carefully surveyed then carefully counted his large collection of Rallizes bootlegs before scurrying bedwards. While I'm sure this imagined reality of mine bears little resemblance to the truth, it does, however, fit in well with the overall mythology of Les Rallizes Denudés and their devoted horde, and in that sense my vision is probably accurate enough. For, like the lives of the Keltic saints, the best way to tell the story of Les Rallizes Denudés is through a bizarre combination of fact, hearsay and outright hagiography. Right, we're gonna go back …

'The Radical Music Black Gypsy Band'

Imagine a high-school band playing the bass-heavy stentorian outro of Television's 'Marquee Moon' title track in 25-minute bursts, while a Blue Cheer-informed (Leigh Stephens period, natch) be-shaded guitar moron with waist-length black hair unloads over the track the kind of pent-up white-noise sonic fury that entirely buries said backing track under an avalanche of mung. Imagine that, from time to time, that same skinny moron temporarily interrupts his invasion-of-Manchuria guitar techniques in order to bring focus to the chords of this so-called song via a series of charmingly unpleasant croons, hiccups, yelps and whooping sub-sub-Buddy Hollyisms in an Alan Vega stylee. Next, imagine a second song just as long as the first that takes its form and sound from the same Ur-spring whence the first was drawn, but which is propelled by a curiously catchy soul-standard bass riff lifted directly from Little Peggy March's 1963 hit single 'I Will Follow Him'. Imagine that this music is being played by a quartet of musicians, each of whom is a carbon copy of the singer/guitarist, each be-shaded, each tall and lanky, each black-clad and sullen, and you're close to approaching the world of Les Rallizes Denudés. For the scene that I have described above could have taken place at any time between 1969 and 1990, and none of us would have been any the wiser. For so strong is the fundamentalist aesthetic stance that Rallizes's leader Takeshi Mizutani adopted back in 1969, that all future members of Les Rallizes Denudés – all 600,000 of them – have happily complied with their leader's rules just to get near him long enough to stand downwind of that auto-panned guitar maelstrom that he so effortlessly unleashes. And such is the fundamentalist nature of Takeshi Mizutani's recording art that the other members of the band rarely make a difference to Rallizes's sound; they can't because Mizutani limits their playing by imposing extraordinarily tight restrictions, both to players and recording engineers. And in this paranoid adherence to Mizutani's secret formula lies the greatness of Les Rallizes Denudés. For it has ensured that no one has been able to judge a Rallizes song by any other standards than the band's own. Indeed, they could do a note-for-note copy of another band's song and it could only sound like Les Rallizes Denudés. Okay, now I've got you intrigued about Mizutani's formula, I shall slightly deflate you all by revealing its incredible simplicity:

1 Never record in a studio.
2 Play only with musicians for whom even the slightest deviation
   from the riff will most certainly be calamitous.
3 Never release records (never ever).
4 Persist for three decades until the outside world catches on.

So how do we actually know of Les Rallizes Denudés if they don't even release records? Through bootlegs, bootlegs and more bootlegs. Indeed, Les Rallizes Denudés has operated in this manner for so long now that both musicians and fans know so far in advance what to expect from each other that there's even a caste system within that world of bootlegs. Yup, while certain Rallizes LPs are considered so much less bootleggy than others that they've almost become official in the minds of fans, others are just dismissed as cash-ins, re-runs and … well, just plain bootlegs. If all this sounds a little cretinous, then you'd better turn your attention to another part of this book and come back when you're feeling less tense. For Les Rallizes Denudés operate only at this level, at that unlikely meeting point between total nihilism and utter blandness, a doorway you'd never guess would even need to exist until you discover it. But be in no doubt whatsoever that Les Rallizes Denudés is a rock'n'roll band of world importance. For, unlike many so-called legendary rock acts, this band has, down the years, delivered umpteen classic songs to our door, songs that our children's children will no doubt still be hiccupping, yelping and crooning in fifty years. For while the sonic delivery of Les Rallizes Denudés owes its sound to the avant-garde, Mizutani's songs are themselves as focused and folk-based as those of Lou Reed. Indeed, a solo acoustic Mizutani show would be a rather excellent proposition full of catchy choruses and 'he's playing our song' moments. But, in this final stage of my opening gambit, and before I take you all on a historical trawl through Rallizesville, I should make this plea to newcomers to their mighty canon of work. The music of Les Rallizes Denudés demands total attention, and without that attention this band is nothing. Put their records on as background music and they fail utterly. But play albums such as HEAVIER THAN A DEATH IN THE FAMILY, LIVE '77, BLIND BABY HAS ITS MOTHERS EYES, FUCKED UP & NAKED in the darkness of your lonely room, and you will experience yourself being sucked up into the ether with ne'er a stain left as evidence of your former presence here.

A Refusenik Named Neesima Facilitates a Refusenik Named Mizutani

The story of Les Rallizes Denudés begins on the campus of Kyoto's highly respected Doshishi University, one of Japan's oldest teaching establishments and notable throughout its islands as 'a living testament to the courage of the human spirit'.[1] Built in 1875 as Doshishi Eigakko (Doshishi Academy), the university was founded by a former samurai, Joseph Hardy Neesima, who'd stowed away aboard an American ship eleven years previously when such an act was, under Japanese law, still punishable by death. Returning to Japan with American university degrees and a profound love of Western freedom, Neesima founded Doshishi on precisely those democratic values of questioning authority and demanding change where necessary.

It was into this atmosphere of learning and liberal ideas that nineteen-year-old Takeshi Mizutani stepped in October 1967 to commence his degree studies in sociology and French literature. The young Mizutani was typical of many post-war Japanese intellectuals, having rejected the all-pervasive American popular culture presently Coca-Cola-ising his country in favour of French culture. Similar to the USA in its revolutionary beginnings, French democracy offered a far deeper well of literature and political thought from which to draw. Besides, there was an added existentialist nihilism running through post-war French society that was particularly appealing to these young urban Japanese whose own childhoods had been filled with ghastly experiences of picking their way through the devastation of their local neighbourhoods.

At Doshishi, Takeshi Mizutani soon joined the university's 'light music group', where the more intellectual students were currently obsessed with Japan's burgeoning folk scene. This obsession had initially grown out of an irritation with the ultra-commercialism of Japan's Group Sounds bands, who took their musical cues only from Britain and America. For Kyoto's anti-American intellectuals, folk music was the sound of refusal, of protest, of determination to change society's status quo. And in Kyoto's jazz and folk *kissa* (coffee shop) scene, the impressionable young Mizutani instantly fell in love with the older black-clad existentialists who smoked only French cigarettes, read French-language copies of works by Jean-Paul Sartre, Antonin Artaud and Jacques Derrida, and spun French gypsy violinist Stephane Grappelli's dark minor-chord folk jazz endlessly on the huge chrome jukeboxes. The sounds, the smells, the darkness of the scene all appealed to Mizutani's own dark soul and, in November '67, the singer formed his first folk-based band with four likeminded university friends: bass player Moriyasu Wakabayashi, drummer Takashi Kato and rhythm guitarist Takeshi Nakamura.

Their initial blueprint for the band was Tokyo's existentialist folk quartet the Jacks, whose notoriety had grown throughout 1967 through its band members' vociferous rejection of all things commercial. Indeed, throughout '67, Japan's left-wing press had hailed the Jacks as the absolute antidote to all things Group Sounds. For, unlike media whores such as the Tigers' Julie Sawada who would dress and act in any manner that their management requested, the Jacks' sullen lead singer Yoshio Hayakawa wore his black hair as long as possible, hid behind perpetual Ray-Ban sunglasses, and refused even to be interviewed, fascinating journalists with such defiant comments as: 'We don't have any goal to be famous' and 'It's a dirty world'. The Jacks surrounded themselves with highly intelligent women, referred to these women as their muses and even wrote songs around the words of the female poet Yazuko Aisawa. Double-bass player Hitoshi Tanino claimed the Jacks' severe attitudes had caused them to be ostracised even from their own local clubs, and the band called themselves 'outsiders at the folk jamboree', a concept that resonated powerfully in the mind of the young Mizutani.

Determined to be even more 'outsider' and anti-American than the Jacks, Mizutani composed several songs with French titles such as 'Les Bulles de Savon' (soap bubbles) and 'La Mal Rouge', after a kind of alcoholic sickness that he'd recently experienced. Then his as-yet-unnamed young band began their first stumbling rehearsals over Christmas 1967. One evening at the jazz *kissa*, however, Mizutani and bass player Wakabayashi were introduced to Yoko Nakamura and

Tatsuo Komatsu, two founding members of Kyoto's Gendai Gekijo (Modern Arts Society),[2] Kyoto's legendary underground theatre company. Formed six years previously, in 1962, by seven Doshishi graduates, Gendai Gekijo were a defiant bunch of radicals in their late twenties whose portentous and highfalutin aim was, according to their company's manifesto, 'to deny all existing theatre styles'. With their French affectations and tendency to speak in a lazy Franco-Japanese pseudo patois, the company's members had an immediate impact on the intrigued Mizutani gang, who quickly began to adopt the theatre troupe's manner of speech. Then, as a further declaration of unity, Mizutani decided to name his band 'Les Rallizes Denudés', one of the Gendai Gekijo's favourite fake-French slang terms for a stupid person (anyone who was a 'valise denudé' (empty suitcase) was an airhead not worthy of consideration). Encouraged by the interest being shown by these much older beatnik types, Les Rallizes Denudés honed down their sound and gratefully accepted the help of Gendai Gekijo's lighting designer Tatsuo Komatsu, who believed that the band could be hugely successful. At the end of May 1968, a demo recording was made with Komatsu featuring Mizutani's own compositions, 'La Mal Rouge', 'Otherwise My Conviction' and 'Les Bulles de Savon'. But the band's lack of experience, Komatsu's negligible input and the unsympathetic studio sound yielded embarrassing results. With Mizutani's strained and highly tuneless singing voice exposed so high in the mix, the Rallizes sounded not like their heroes the Jacks, but like some weak American garage band whose fuzz guitarist had deserted them. Mentally scarred by this abject failure, Mizutani vowed to keep away from studios in future and keep his warblings strictly within the concert hall.

The 'Summertime Blues' Volte-Face

For the kind of Commie Francophiles that Rallizes claimed to be, music should hardly have been the sole major concern in the summer of '68, what with the rather more satisfying news that the Paris student riots had caused the terrified General de Gaulle to seek sanctuary in neighbouring West Germany. For Mizutani, however, two events during July 1968 drew a line under the guitarist's entire past, and created within him a genuine feeling that this was Year Zero. For it was now, just two months after the whole Rallizes recording debacle, that Mizutani received a musical revelation on hearing Blue Cheer's debut LP VINCEBUS ERUPTUM and the Velvet Underground's second album WHITE LIGHT/WHITE HEAT. Already a fan of the Velvets' first LP and of Lou Reed's harsh criticisms of the American flower-power movement, Mizutani was so overwhelmed by the seventeen-minute brain death of 'Sister Ray' and the free-form guitar chaos of 'I Heard Her Call My Name', that the singer believed that he had just been handed a psychic mind map with which to plot his entire future. Furthermore, Blue Cheer's debut album, also released in July '68, contained more of that same bile, as feedback and ineptitude issued forth from the speakers and engulfed the room. The guitarist summoned the members of Gendai Gekijo and explained his new strategy.

With the technical help of Gendai Gekijo, Les Rallizes Denudés played their first show in August '68 like a low-budget, more primitive form of Andy Warhol's *Exploding Plastic Inevitable*. The company's lighting whiz Tatsuo Komatsu operated strobes and mirror balls throughout the show, while the others danced Gerard Malanga/Mary Woronov-like at the front of the stage. Ecstatic with the effects created by Gendai Gekijo, Mizutani decided that this multi-media approach was his way forward, and the new term 'total sensory assault' became his modus operandi. In the short space of two highly effective gigs, the band became a genuine force to be reckoned with, as evidenced by a live recording of the amazing nineteen minutes of 'Smokin' Cigarette Blues', which revealed the Rallizes to be an atonal free-rock blitz of hollow tom-toms and 'I Heard Her Call My Name' guitar mayhem. Unfortunately, all the members of Gendai Gekijo freaked out, complaining that the band played at a volume too loud for them to perform comfortably. The nihilistic Mizutani was delighted. No one in Japan had ever accused a rock'n'roll band of being too loud before; quite the opposite, in fact. Historically, Japanese entertainers wished only to please and impress their paying audience enough for them to return next time. Sensing that he was on to something special, Mizutani refused to budge on the question of volume; this was 'total sensory assault', doncha know? So the idealistic members of Gendai Gekijo adopted a temporary policy of wearing earplugs while they operated the light show and special FX, and dutifully grooved as the feedback rearranged their molecules.

Between September '68 and April 1969, the Rallizes practised their stagecraft as Mizutani built upon his own mythology by printing up a series of dark moody press flyers for forthcoming Rallizes shows, with photos that cast him as the nihilistic God of Phaseshifter Guitar. Emblazoned across Mizutani's sullen and pouting mush was this alienated message writ large: 'For those young people – including you – who live this modern agonising adolescence and who are wanting the true radical music, I sincerely wish the dialogue accompanied by piercing pain will be born and fill this recital hall'. From the words of this flyer, it becomes evident that Mizutani had, even at this early stage, already surrendered the poetic side of his character to that nihilistic Bringer of Oblivion that manifested whenever he wielded a solid-bodied electric guitar. Moreover, as the band gradually received pressure from associates and promoters to take a name with more meaning, so the ever cantankerous Mizutani adopted the entirely meaningless Hadaka no Rallizes (The Naked Rallizes) as an occasional substitute for the equally mysterious Les Rallizes Denudés. If Japanese

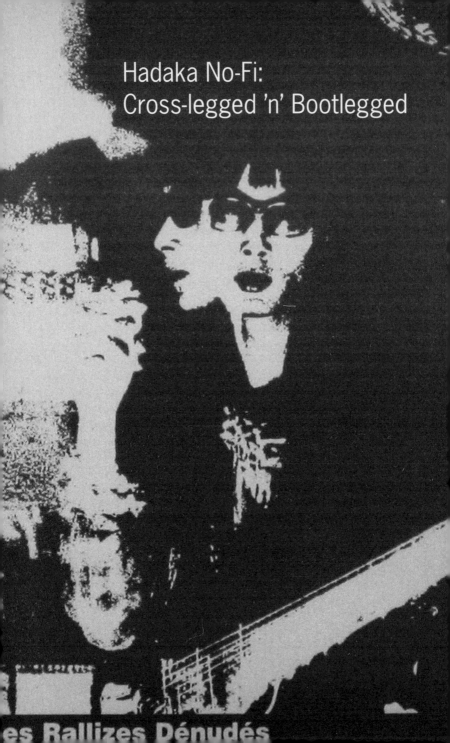

A MONOCHROME SELECTION OF MIZUTANI'S MORE OBSCURE VINYL AND CD RELEASES

DEEPER THAN NIGHT (LP)

DOWN & OUT IN TOKYO (CD)

ENCYCLOPEDIA VOLUME 2 (CD)

FRANCE DEMO TAPE (CD)

FUCKED UP & NAKED (LP)

HIGH OR DIE (LP)

ENTER THE MIRROR (LP)

OZ DAYS (LP)

was the perfect language in which to hide multiple meanings, then Mizutani would become a Prince of the Opaque via his ingenious use of regular Japanese, Franco-Japanese beatnik slang and that wonderfully hideous Japanglish, so beloved by Japanese ad men and media types.

'Unexpected Events' in Building A

In the typically patronising spirit of the times, 1969 had seen the commencement of an international programme known as 'Understanding among Youth', a well-meaning but ultimately shallow attempt by the Western adult world to understand the problems faced by teenagers. As Japan's urban authorities were already being overwhelmed by the everyday arrival in Tokyo, Osaka, Hiroshima and Nagoya of thousands of teenage *futens*, however, no attention was being paid to implementing that youth programme. No attention, that is, except on the ultra-liberal campus of Doshishi University, where the authorities now chose to honour the spirit of the 'Understanding among Youth' scheme by organising their own 'Barricades-a-Go-Go' rock festival in the university's Building A. And so, on 12th April 1969, unaware of Les Rallizes Denudés's recent rejection of folk, jazz and French gypsy music, the university authorities booked the band as its headline act, to be supported by two local bands, Mustapha and Mustang. Little is remembered of Mustapha, but the six-piece Mustang tore the place down with their high-energy garage rock and extremely long hair. Indeed, Mustang was a real paradox, for they looked like a much longer-haired version of the Rolling Stones, but wore the clichéd uniforms of some dutiful Group Sounds act. Furthermore, having scored a big hit in the Oricon Top 40 the previous year with their single 'Mustang Baby', Mustang had recently become the talk of Kyoto when the band's singer Ringo Yamamoto had interviewed Mick Jagger for *Music Life* magazine.

For the 500 people in the audience of Building A, however, no one was in any doubt as to who the headliner was, as the Rallizes obliterated the audience with their avalanche of sound and lights. In the audience were the owners of Kyoto's highly respected Gallery Sagittarius, who came backstage after the show and invited Mizutani to headline their forthcoming festival portentously entitled 'Menzaifu to Shiteno Risaitru' (Recital As Pardoner). Still reeling from the thrill of hearing the live version of 'Smokin' Cigarette Blues', Mizutani chose to record the gallery show with the intention of releasing it on vinyl.

During the summer of '69, however, Rallizes came right off the rails, as Mizutani's decision to avoid studios garnered mounting hostility from bass player Wakabayashi and rhythm guitarist Nakamura. And when, on a whim, Nakamura threatened to quit,

Mizutani blandly accepted his resignation. In August, several new members were auditioned and invited to join only to be jettisoned even before a show was played. Drummer Takashi Kato remained firm, but even Wakabayashi absconded briefly before returning once more. And then, on 18th October, a flyer appeared casting Mizutani as 'Nippon Gypsy '69'. Describing the band as 'the much talked about Radical Music Black Gypsy Band' the Rallizes were back with 'new members – new style' as the flyer proclaimed. Gone were the seven members of Gendai Genkijo, replaced instead by a new highly confident noise band dressed in exotic stage gear designed by Kyoto's pop-art designer Kazuko Ryoke.

By now, so much was expected of Les Rallizes Denudés that Gendai Gekijo's Tatsuo Komatsu had taken over as manager. But interviewers found Mizutani's bland, stylised answers boring and few pieces were ever printed about the band. One journalist, interviewing Mizutani in January 1970, declared that he missed the multimedia action that Gendai Genkijo had injected into the shows, and demanded to know what had become of them. Eventually, manager Komatsu grew so tired of Mizutani's refusal to answer even this simple question that he snapped, claiming the band no longer needed the support of actors and dancers for their 'guerrilla performances'. Komatsu's rant concluded with a very peculiar and prescient comment: 'Sometimes you have a guitar, sometimes you arm yourself … protest songs are boring.'

Never Mind the Feedback, Here's the Hijack

In the early morning of 31st March 1970, Takeshi Mizutani's life changed for ever when Rallizes Denudés's bass player Moriyasu Wakabayashi took part in the infamous Yodo-go aeroplane hijacking (please turn to Book Two, Chapter Five, for a detailed account of these bizarre events). Unfortunately for Mizutani and Les Rallizes Denudés, Wakabayashi's actions guaranteed that the band would thereafter be reduced to no more than a footnote in an international scandal. Following the hijacking, the other members of Rallizes disappeared from sight as Mizutani found himself pursued by Japanese federal agents, who never arrested him but observed his actions from a distance. However, the presence of many US nationals aboard the Yodo-go inevitably brought the CIA to Japan, and these gentlemen were far from casual in their observations of Mizutani. Finally, the Rallizes leader went into hiding, moving into a friend's Tokyo apartment in the highly exclusive Aoyama district. He talked of embarking on a solo career, or of re-forming the Rallizes as an acoustic band, but ultimately his mind was fried from the hijack fallout. As member after new band member came and went, Mizutani invited his friends Chahbo and Fujio from Murahatchibu to become his backing band, only to have them temporarily steal the name and do Rallizes shows without him! On being added to the highly important 'Rock in Highland' festival, a huge and prestigious event featuring such massive bands as the Mops and Flower Travellin' Band, Mizutani it was who got the blame when only one hundred people turned up. Everyone stayed away because of the presence of the Rallizes, said the promoters to themselves, and they were most probably correct. This 'radical existentialist gypsy' was swiftly becoming a figure of fun, a forlorn failure whom the Japanese rock'n'roll scene needed to pass by.

In August 1970, when Mizutani bumped into the singer/songwriter Masato Minami, whilst out walking in Tokyo's Shibuya district, the two decided to jam together and even discussed forming a band as they set up their equipment. But as soon as Mizutani's colossal phaseshifter and guitar feedback kicked the walls down, the stunned Minami 'realised such an idea was impossible'.[3] Determined to let his depressed friend down as lightly as was possible, Minami invited Mizutani to contribute guitar to his new LP KAIKISEN (Tropic of Capricorn). But when Minami's album went on to be the highly successful beginning of a high-profile career, the embittered Mizutani felt even more rejected, and continued to remain unrecorded and unreleased throughout 1970.

For most of 1971, Mizutani remained holed up in the Tokyo apartment, venturing out only to buy milk and other essentials. Paranoid and deluded, he was by now convinced that the world was against him. Four years of playing rock'n'roll had got him nothing but a CIA tail, and all kinds of lesser talents were by now headlining tours across Japan. Worse still, by late April '71, even Mizutani's most reliably unreliable friends Fujio and Chahbo from Murahatchibu had successfully navigated through the perils of studio recording and had the promise of a record deal. Occasionally, a much-reduced Rallizes would play at the Oz club in Tokyo, but no one came because the world had really moved on. Solo shows sandwiched between such class acts as the Mops, Blues Creation, Zuno Keisatsu and Speed, Glue & Shinki only further reduced the spirit of this great nihilist, this sonic executioner. And slowly Mizutani faded away. His only champion was Oz's sound technician Doronco (Covered in Mud), but even he was preoccupied with publishing his own Communist free newspaper. Once, Mizutani's acolyte Keiji Heino tried to revive Mizutani's career by forming with him a power trio that played only early Blue Cheer songs, but even this idea died before show-time and the tapes went missing. By 1973, even the Oz club had gone bankrupt and Les Rallizes Denudés, now managed by Doronco – himself now the bass player – found themselves with nowhere left to play in Tokyo.

The Underground Goes Underground

And so Takeshi Mizutani took the path of all unsung rock'n'roll genii. He went underground, retired from the world, and – in the minds of the general public – disappeared for ever into the abyss. He walked out into the Wilderness and stayed there. He rode off into the sunset and over the horizon. He sailed to the edge of the world and was consumed by Midgardsorm. He walked northwards to the foot of Mt Osorezan, where his followers built for him a stone chamber in the lee of that sacred mountain, where so many of Japan's ancestors' spirits reside. Suffice it to say that Mizutani thereafter eked out a livelihood through stealth, courage of his convictions, the goodwill of his followers led by Doronco, and that intuitive genius shared by all truly Gnostic visionaries that know their world exists only in a future world, in a time 'Yet to Come'. Intuitively, Mizutani grasped that only once the world had been through several chaotic decades could his sonic clamour be judged as anything less than horrible noise, for the static hiss that pervaded every Rallizes recording to become understood and accepted as integral to Mizutani's trip.

For most of the '70s, Mizutani occupied a place of suspended animation, where – like Von LMO and Sun Ra – he resided in an incubation chamber outside time and space, waiting, forever waiting. At times, opportunities presented themselves for a show of strength and value to take place. But even when joined on bass by his old Kyoto cohort and former Zuno Keisatsu member Hiroshi Nar for a magical show entitled 'Sunset Glow' at a highland ski resort, such was the bad luck of the Rallizes that the festival took place during a typhoon. The organisers, fearful of an avalanche, insisted the band turn down the volume. When Mizutani refused, the terrified crowd fled to the safety of the funicular railway.[4]

In 1977, Mizutani was brought word that English punk rock was ushering in a new dawn, and his acolytes spoke in hushed tones of this being Mizutani's time. The artist himself, however, did not hold his breath, for he had also heard that these supposedly radical audiences were nothing more than weekenders out on the carouse, part-timers who 'for the sake of appearances take on the superficial aspects of the quest'.[5] If Rallizes's day had really dawned, thought Mizutani, then why am I also hearing reports that Suicide were attacked while supporting the Clash, that Nico was bottled off while supporting Siouxsie & the Banshees? Occasionally, a small new crowd of black-clad existentialists would lure the guitarist out of his isolation chamber and drive him to some location where, surrounded by beautiful young things, the God of the Phaseshifter would once more re-awaken the lost spirits of the Ancient Days Before Yodo-go as the eager new be-shaded backing band dutifully tore off yet another twenty-five minutes of Little Peggy March's 'I Will Follow Him'. And every single appearance Mizutani made was gathered together and collected on tape, then edited and presented on slabs of label-less 12" vinyl, which were passed around between believers. Mizutani's friend Fujio, being by now without Murahatchibu and being also of a similar mental persuasion, contacted Mizutani and even briefly joined him for shows in August 1980, creating a twin-guitar eruption that sent the vinyl hoarders mental with rapture. But the believers within the band[6] could not accept Fujio as Mizutani's sacred Twin, and, by March 1981, the experiment had blown up and Mizutani had returned to his chamber in the lee of Mt Osorezan. Mizutani, this great nihilistic spirit, this sonic executioner, bided his time as humanity – having had their ears syringed by post-punk and No Wave – gradually became more used to sonic imbalance. And some called it Lo-Fi, and celebrated it. And others called it No-Fi and worshipped it. And all the Rallizes acolytes declared that Mizutani's time was finally here. But their hero had slipped quietly away to France, remaining there for five years to play with free sax player Arthur Doyle. And no one knew his precise whereabouts. And his inaccessibility made them yearn for their lost hero and his cult grew and grew. And Tokyo underground record stores began to sell more and more vinyl bootlegs than ever before, and still Mizutani's legend grew. And by the early twenty-first century, websites had emerged dedicated only to Les Rallizes Denudés, websites whose webmasters traced each arduous step of their hero, and would not accept that Mizutani spent his days in suspended animation. Several

obsessives drove up to Mt Osorezan and searched out Mizutani's chamber, determined to bring their hero back to civilisation, in chains if necessary, until the rehabilitation of their hero became the mission of every Rallizes fanatic. But despite the appearance of bizarre new records with exotic and frightening names, nothing could lure Mizutani out of hiding, for he knew that his time had not yet arrived.

Footnotes:

1   Doshishi University profile.

2   In 1968, Modern Arts Society was comprised of Eiko 'Hideko' Kubota, Tatsuya Shimizu,
    Yoko Nakamura, Kenichi Hikawa, Tatsuo Komatsu and two others now unknown.

3   Quote from Minami's website at: http://apia-net.com/minami

4   Thereafter, Hiroshi Nar became destitute, fetching up in the '80s owning no more than a futon
    and a single Amon Düül 2 cassette (personal communication from Alan Cummings).

5   Tommy Hall's sleevenotes for THE PSYCHEDELIC SOUNDS OF THE 13TH FLOOR ELEVATORS.

6   'All the members of the band just worshipped Mizutani' (Fujio Yamagauchi).

CHAPTER 8
SPEED, GLUE
& SHINKI スピード、グルー&シンキ

The edge? The only people who
really know where it is are the ones
who've gone over.
Hunter S. Thompson

Who's Nicked My Paint Thinners?

Speed, Glue & Shinki … now, there's a name to conjure with. Talk about wearing
your influences on your sleeve, this lot named their band after their drug habits. Put
crudely and succinctly, which is the only way to talk about anything to do with this
bunch, Speed, Glue & Shinki were a drug-addled early-'70s Japanese free-blues power
trio whose eulogies to snorting speed, shooting heroin, toking marijuana and sniffing
paint thinners and Marusan Pro Bond glue manifested in such songs as 'Sniffing &
Snorting', 'Stoned out of My Mind' and their debut single 'Mr Walking Drugstore Man',
which concluded with the unaccompanied voice of the singer hissing at his audience:
'Hey, d'you wanna buy some speed? I mean … d'you wanna buy some speed?' Starting as they meant to go on, or what? Indeed, with just a few notable exceptions

(degraded sex, glimpses of nirvana, alcoholic oblivion) there are only three recurring song themes that emerge from Speed, Glue & Shinki's entire canon of work, namely: 1) I'm taking too many drugs; 2) the Man is a Bitch so I'm taking too many drugs; and 3) my Bitch is a Man so I'm taking too many drugs. Moreover, Speed, Glue & Shinki's overall sound was the sloppiest and most unrestrained garage noise of its time, bringing forth an Ur-klang of extremely abrasive and repulsively degraded rock'n'roll riffs played in the grindingly trudgeful style of the Move's 'Brontosaurus' and 'When Alice Comes Back to the Farm' via the Beatles' 'I Want You (She's So Heavy)'. With the single exception of the almighty (and almightily underrated) Leigh Stephens-period Blue Cheer, heavy blues never lent itself much to free rock until Speed, Glue & Shinki came along three years later and reduced the blues' three chords to just one, snottily flouting all of the tense white boys' rules so painstakingly amassed by the likes of Mountain's Leslie West and Cream's Eric Clapton. Indeed, comparing Speed, Glue & Shinki to heavy contemporaries such as Mountain and Cream is pointless because, whereas those guys – even at their lowest ebb – at least always remembered to repeat their riffs the same every time, Speed, Glue & Shinki were far too wayward and, um, individual to muster up such consistencies. And seeing as they were powered by a Filipino singing drummer with a bad amphetamine habit and a propensity for setting his kit on fire with paraffin, inconsistency became the band's byword, their benchmark, their modus operandi, their *raison d'être*, as the ecstatically disjointed moves of their brilliant but erratic percussion powerhouse informed the rest of the band *and* everyone who worked for them. It was as though even the recording technicians involved with the band became temporarily zombified with that same inconsistency malaise, recovering only long after the session was over. A typical Speed, Glue & Shinki track would not only speed up and slow down radically during the same song, but it could also become extremely loud at points, tailing off just when you least needed such an effect. If ex-Iguanas drummer Iggy Pop had remained behind the drums when he became lead singer of the Stooges, you'd probably have already heard something close to Speed, Glue & Shinki. But then, even 5'1" Iggy would have fitted in with the Japanese rock'n'roll scene better than these barbarians. For, in a society where 5'7" is considered tall for a guy, these three rizla-thin loons were each well over six feet tall. Yup, these Joey Ramones wuz born to stand out. There's a town in southern Spain which shoulda been the home of Speed, Glue & Shinki. It's called Moron de la Frontera, and these guys were truly morons at the frontier of rock'n'roll.[1]

To reinforce their mystery, Speed, Glue & Shinki loved to portray themselves on record sleeves and posters as other people entirely. And while the front cover of their second album represented them with a sepia print of three bare-knuckle fighters of the Old West standing in a line, on their debut LP the band's alter egos are three late-

Victorian children in an absolute picture of innocence; three 'ickle kiddies with bad doper withdrawals. Curious, huh. However, it's for precisely these umpteen contradictions that the barbarian music of Speed, Glue & Shinki still sounds remarkably fresh to most twenty-first-century fans of underground rock'n'roll, our ears having long since been re-tuned, de-tuned and tweaked into submission by the punk movement of 1977, the post-punk and No Wave scenes of the late-'70s, and all of the other so-called lo-fi, no-fi and shoe-gazing noise-rock micro-phenomena that have been forced through our melted plastic brains since these three gentlemen first discharged their explosive ideas on to magnetic tape three-and-a-half decades ago.

With all of this in mind, it's easy to imagine that each member of Speed, Glue & Shinki was making his first-ever statement in the music business, that they'd spent their childhoods together sagging off school, hunched over a pool table or a jukebox for long periods of their adolescence. But that's where we'd be most mistaken. For, although still in their early twenties during their tenure in Speed, Glue & Shinki, each member was a seasoned veteran of the Japanese rock scene. Yes, two of the three had spent brief time together in their formative years of playing adolescent rock'n'roll. But the two had soon parted company in the quest for bigger things. Furthermore, and most peculiarly, this band was to a great extent a construct created as a useful vehicle for showcasing the talents of the new band's lead guitarist by his own biggest fan, record producer Ikuzo Orita, who also just happened to be in the process of leaving his previous position as head of Polydor Records to take up a similar role over at Warner Brothers' enormously successful Atlantic subsidiary. In other words, these three gentlemen dudes had money – and plenty of it – backing their miscreant muse. Kinda puts a different perspective on their howling, don't it? Bass player Masayoshi 'Glue' Kabe had enjoyed huge '60s chart success with Group Sounds heroes the Golden Cups. Lead guitarist Shinki Chen had even made his own Polydor Records solo LP before the formation of Speed, Glue & Shinki. Only singing drummer and chief songwriter Joey 'Speed' Smith of the Philippines was still an unknown at the time of this band's formation, and even he had long been a workaholic rock'n'roll singer, dutifully to-ing and fro-ing between Tokyo and Manila bringing money to his young family. Let us now go back and give some context to this bunch, shuffle through their medical records, leaf through their school reports, and do whatever we need to do in order to make sense of these three most intuitive of non-career movers.

Everybody's Courting Shinki Chen

The Speed, Glue & Shinki story centres around the aforementioned lead guitarist Shinki Chen, a six-foot-tall haystack-headed Chino-Japanese nutcase whose clamorous guitar style had, throughout the late '60s, eclipsed all comers save for future Flower Travellin' Band axe-wielder Hideki Ishima, and whose formidable height and dusky half-Chinese ancestry oozed Western rockstar charisma to the rest of the 'too short' Japanese. Coming on like Slash from Guns n' Roses twenty years too soon, a perpetual ciggie drooping from his sullen gob, a low-slung Gibson Les Paul around his neck, and even the occasional top hat rammed down upon his shoulder-length thatch, Shinki's effortless virtuosity drew countless bigwig admirers and mentors from within the Japanese music scene, all of whom believed him to be Japan's answer to Jimi Hendrix. Unfortunately for these legions of admirers, however, Shinki was a child of Yokohama City, a place where making an effort was considered uncool to the point of outright gaucheness. Indeed, by the time Speed, Glue & Shinki formed in the late summer of 1970, Shinki Chen's many and various patrons had been trying to help their boy make it to the top since 1966. But every time, Shinki would snatch defeat from the jaws of victory and move on to the next poor music-business sap, who, driven by an unquenchable belief that he alone could do what others had failed to, would pour yet more money and more time into just one more Shinki project, until the whole cycle would begin all over again.

182

And yet, by the time Speed, Glue & Shinki recorded their debut album in January 1970, Shinki Chen was still barely twenty-one years old. Born in May 1949, Shinki had begun life as a drummer in Yokohama's Midnight Express Blues Band, an outfit whose own bass guitarist was none other than the same Masayoshi Kabe who would join him in Speed, Glue & Shinki five long years hence. Of Franco-Japanese extraction and blessed with movie-star looks, Kabe was already famous in the city for his swooping descending bass runs performed on a futuristic Eko Rocket, and his capacity for inhaling vast amounts of paint thinners and thick purple Marusan Pro Bond, a notorious industrial glue with a reputation among teenagers for inducing comatose oblivion. Besides briefly sharing the same girlfriend, however, by late '66, Shinki and Kabe had parted company, as the latter's stylish Golden Cups stormed the burgeoning Group Sounds scene with 'Jizabel', the first of an uninterrupted run of hits.

Shinki's new band began to practise above a mod clothes shop called Bebe, run by a fey Malcolm McLaren-type clothes designer who promised to clothe and manage the band so long as they changed their name to the Bebes. But when the gigs offered to these too-cool Yokohama boys turned out to be at weddings, business functions and the like, the band split without recording a single session. By mid-1968, part of the band had re-formed as the heavy-blues outfit Powerhouse and signed to the

Golden Cups' management Towa Productions. It was during this period that Polydor Records' boss Ikuzo Orita attended a Powerhouse show, thereafter booking Shinki to lively-up one of the Tigers' recording sessions by adding some lead guitar. In late 1968, Towa Productions signed Powerhouse to Toshiba Records, who insisted that the band record the Beatles' dreadful 'Ob-la-di, Ob-la-da' for a Japanese tribute album dedicated to the fabulous four. Powerhouse freaked out at the very idea and nothing happened for months. Eventually, when they reluctantly acquiesced and recorded the song as a blues(!), Toshiba Records cynically released their version as a single and Shinki jumped ship in frustration. Solo pop singer Katsumi Kahashi then offered to buy the guitarist a full Marshall stack if he agreed to join Kahashi's group, but Shinki had been secretly approached by an anonymous manager, who was attempting to form a new Japanese supergroup comprised of Apryl Fool organist Hiro Yanagida, future Strawberry Path drummer Hiro Tsunoda and future Flower Travellin' Band singer Joe Yamanaka. With typical Yokohama disdain, the unbothered Shinki adopted a temporary *futen* lifestyle and hitched around Japan instead. However, when he arrived back at his parents' home in Yokohama City, Polydor Records boss Ikuzo Orita tracked him down and petitioned him, suggesting they work together on whatever Shinki wished to try. 'Let's form a loose aggregation of similarly minded virtuoso rock'n'rollers, Mr Ikuzo,' said Shinki (or words to that effect). 'We must name said ensemble Foodbrain.'

Foodbrain BC, Foodbrain AD

By this time, frustrated at the straitjacket that the Group Sounds scene had forced upon everyone, Masayoshi Kabe had quit the Golden Cups and was, after four years, back hanging out with the equally footloose Shinki Chen, who asked if Kabe wanted in on the Foodbrain deal. Natch, said Masayoshi Kabe. As the pair were most inspired by the ultra-loose so-called 'super session' albums that Mike Bloomfield and Al Kooper had been making in the USA, they suggested to Ikuzo Orita that a 'one day/ one album' Foodbrain 'super session' could best achieve their aims. Orita proposed they complete Foodbrain with former Apryl Fool organist Hiro Yanagida and jazz drummer Akira Ishikawa, both of whom were playing in the *Hair* musical ensemble, currently in production in Tokyo. But when Ishikawa proved too busy to make the date, Orita insisted that only a jazz guy could reach what they wished to achieve, and hired the Jacks' equally jazzy Hiro Tsunoda in Ishikawa's place. And thus Foodbrain's sole album release A SOCIAL GATHERING was born.

I've discussed the limited appeal of this record elsewhere in the book but, suffice to say, despite its curiously archaic Ten Years After organ stylings and lack of tear-arse Shinki Chen guitar mayhem, Foodbrain's sole album was still an essential baptism of fire, a break with the past, and a real step into the unknown that justified producer Ikuzo Orita's extravagant advertising claims: 'Finally in Japan a true heavy rock is born.' Just as Guy Stevens's brilliant but flawed Hapshash & the Coloured Coat freak-out project spawned Germany's Amon Düül, Italy's Le Stelle di Mario Schifano, America's Friendsound and others that easily transcended Stevens's original, so Foodbrain's A SOCIAL GATHERING wrote the road map for all subsequent Japanese experimental albums, opening the door to projects like Love Live Life +1's LOVE WILL MAKE A BETTER YOU, Masahiko Satoh's AMALGAMATION, Kimio Mizutani's A PATH THROUGH HAZE, Hiro Yanagida's MILK TIME, Kuni Kawachi's KIRIKYOGEN, People's BUDDHA MEETS ROCK and the many concept LPs released by Geino Yamashirogumi.

Not all of the post-Foodbrain projects worked out, though, and Shinki's Polydor solo album SHINKI CHEN & HIS FRIENDS proved to be yet another example of the guitarist's Yokohama lazyitis. With the nomadic Masayoshi Kabe temporarily out of the picture, Shinki delegated the arrangement and Clapton-alike vocal chores to former Powerhouse bassist George Yanagi and quickly became a passenger on his own record, which promptly lapsed into Foodbrain territory. Listeners awaiting guitar apocalypse and molten axe worship were confronted by a perplexingly eclectic hogwash of Delaney & Bonnie-period Eric Clapton, random experiments and backwards sound FX, Gustav Holst's 'Mars' by way of Zappa's 'Call Any Vegetable', all held together by further dutiful bursts of generic sub-sub-Gregg Allman gospel drivel. Shinki's mentor Ikuzo Orita decided that an entire rethink was necessary.

A Short Hop from Polydor to Atlantic ... Enter Joey Smith

During Christmas 1970, Ikuzo Orita called up all of his close friends and announced that he had left Polydor Records to take over at Atlantic. Determined to ape the 'heavy' success of the American parent company, Orita quickly offered his good mate Yuya Utchida a three-album deal for Flower Travellin' Band. Securing this contract, the new label boss was now on the lookout for something similar with which to create a twin-prong 'heavy sound' for his new label. Despite Orita's success with Kimio Mizutani's Polydor solo LP A PATH THROUGH HAZE, the ex-Out Cast leader had by now built up his reputation as an amazing session guitarist, and had no desire to pursue a solo career. The only other worthy guitar maestro was Blues Creation's Kazuo Takeda, who'd already set his sights on a career in the USA. Feeling somewhat marooned that Christmas, Orita was justifiably hesitant when Shinki called up to tell him: 'Hey Orita, we found a good one. His song and drums are superb.'[2]

The 'good one' in question was an itinerant singer/songwriter named Joseph 'Pepe' Smith, whom Shinki had noticed by chance playing R&B in Yokohama's local Astro shopping mall. Born and bred in the Philippines, but with an American soldier father, Joey had spent his childhood flitting between his dad's San Francisco home and his mother's place in the Filipino capital Manila. Right there at Christmas 1970, however, Joey was barely scraping by in Zero History, a gaggle of Filipino ex-pats blasting out R&B covers for uninterested bargain hunters in anonymous shopping malls. With a young family back in Manila, and a love of wine, women and drugs, Joey Smith was totally broke most of the time and slept on the floor of anyone who'd have him. In order to supplement his meagre vocalist wage, Smith had recently been taught to play drums by Eddie Fortuno of D'Swooners, the hot Filipino R&B band who'd become accepted as 'honorary members' of the GS scene. But Joey's wild performances caused so much damage to his hired drum kits that he seemed forever to be paying his wages back to his agents.[3] For Ikuzo Orita, however, Shinki's discovery of Joey Smith was a moment of destiny. Attending one of Zero History's daytime shows, Orita was mesmerised by the manner in which the singing drummer slowed the songs down in order to emphasise his vocal hooks, standing up during important passages, and even pretending to burn himself when pouring fuel over his cymbals and setting them alight. After years of struggling to find a Japanese drummer with a decent sound, Orita told Shinki that Joey Smith's drumming would 'make the band international'.

185

And so it came to pass that, less than one month after the release of Shinki's Polydor solo record, Orita was ensconced in Tokyo's Mouri Studio with Shinki Chen and Masayoshi Kabe, rehearsing the songs of Joey Smith with an Atlantic Records budget. The sound was deafening as Joey Smith took control of the sessions, performing each song as though he were playing at Budokan, exhibiting that same outrageous showmanship that he'd applied to rocking department stores. Urged on by Joey's pounding tom-toms, snarling punk bark, outta-control amphetamine habit and determination to tell everybody about it, Masayoshi Kabe's thunderous bass runs quickly returned to those heady days of the early Golden Cups – and then some – his bluesy bass licks often climbing right off the chart into chromatic free-bass territory, all of which conspired to goad Shinki Chen out of his too-cool Yokohama stasis and into Total Action. The recording session began with the hobbling proto-grunge of 'Mr Walking Drugstore Man', in which a horrible retarded sub-Standells blues riff introduces Joey Smith singing down a cassette-recorder mike with a truly Lou Reedian authenticity:

Hey, Mr Walking Drugstore Man,
What do you have for me today?
I've been feeling so ugly …
I'll just have to move around
Try to locate my brain alright.

But poor Joey's got that post-amphetamine withdrawal so bad that his 'brain is kinda tight' and he needs Mr Walking Drugstore Man to give him 'some of your special speed, yeah, special speed'. Whenever Joey Smith has a particular point to make, he does a very singularly excellent thing. He slows the song right down with his drums and crawls the lyrics along. It's as if to say: 'And … another … fucking … thing!' And it's in this strung-out state that the song pants to its conclusion and, in mute nostril agony, Joey calls out to no one in particular:

Hey, you wanna buy some speed
Uh no, I'm paranoid
No, peaceful.

That's what the libretto reads. It sure doesn't sound that way on record. I just hear the 'speed' reference. Next, please. Now it's obvious that someone like Joey Smith would attract the wrong kind of partner, and we discover this in a fairly big way on the second song 'Big Headed Woman'. The song starts off kind of hopefully and rocking, but soon gives itself to the sort of flaccid blues that causes dams to overflow. What a ghastly riff. What a woman you found for yourself, Joey. Get this for a lyric:

I gotta big-headed woman who talks about herself …
She drinks all my liquor
And she smokes all of my stuff.

What stuff is that, Joey? Could you qualify, perhaps?

Yeah, she smokes all my dope.

And as if this weren't enough for the poor sap, Joey then admits: 'at night she balls with another man.' Well, by this time Shinki Chen and Masayoshi Kabe are really delighted they don't speak English so good. They're happy to just play distended howling octopus rock and let Joey unleash his complain-o-thon. Next, Kabe takes the blues on a bass-run up the fretboard and just keeps on climbing like scales weren't never invented. Up and up like some steeplejack with a deathwish. Of course, Mr

Joey Smith is so empowered by this sonic overkill that he declares to his big-headed woman that suicide could be a very real option for her:

> I think you better do yourself in, do yourself in,
> Now take this, and … blow your mind.

After these first two very long and very druggy and very slow and very bluesy opening songs, Speed, Glue & Shinki obviously think it's about time to give their prospective audience a bit of a break. So they speed up the proceedings about one notch and hit us with a six-minute garage-rock crawl known as 'Stoned out of My Mind', wherein a 'lot of straight people' keep staring at Joey. Hey, these mother-fuckers are not only staring at his long *Hair*, but at his 'gear, too'. Whoa, looks like an excuse to get fucked up, baby, which Joey proceeds to do in a very big way. Joey's king of the snotty aside – 'Y'know, alright, hit it, hey!' – all those types of things pepper the recorded oeuvre of Speed, Glue & Shinki.

As song after obvious song cascaded from the drooling, bitten lips of Joey Smith, Ikuzo Orita and Shinki Chen knew that they had, at long last, discovered the secret combination. Space informed the new band's sound, space and a shattering slow-ness that only the ultra-confident can pull off. Cast to the four winds was the horribly rinky-dink Blackpool organ that Hiro Yanagida had foisted upon Foodbrain, replaced instead by … nothing. No keyboard sound, just pure glorious emptiness, into which Joey Smith, Masayoshi Kabe and Shinki Chen could empty the contents of their melt-ed plastic brains. During that first session, a lot of wine was drunk, a lot of Marusan Pro Bond was inhaled, a lot of amphetamine was snorted and a vast amount of pot was consumed. For this band was determined to make its mark not in spite of what they were, but because of it. On completion of their debut album EVE (and true to the supergroup mentality of those Emerson, Lake & Palmer times), the new trio announced to the media that their name would be – with supremely screwed and skewed logic – Speed, Glue & Shinki. Right on …

'Floats away Like a Stringless Kite'

If getting Speed, Glue & Shinki together in the first place had been a some-what protracted proposition, then keeping them together soon proved to be an insurmountable task. Throughout the spring, as Atlantic prepared for the summer release of the band's debut album, Speed, Glue & Shinki wrote songs for their second album and made their official concert debut on 20th May, performing alongside

Murahatchibu and Takehisa Kosugi's Taj Mahal Travellers at the second annual 'Mojo-west' festival at Kyoto's Daigaku Nishibu Koudou (University West Auditorium). But by 25th June 1971, the release date of the band's first LP EVE and debut single 'Mr Walking Drugstore Man', Masayoshi Kabe was already nowhere to be seen, disappearing mid-recording-session for a quick toke and last seen running down a river bank. As Ikuzo Orita commented later, keeping hold of Kabe was like being in charge of 'a stringless kite', and the Atlantic boss now opted to keep a close watch on his newest charge by having a bed set up in his Warner Brothers office for the itinerant Joey Smith.[4]

Seeing all this effort being expended on Speed, Glue & Shinki, Flower Travellin' Band's manager Yuya Utchida soon began to complain that Shinki Chen was Orita's pet project, but the truth was that Speed, Glue & Shinki had already begun to fall to pieces. Kabe returned briefly for a Beatles-inspired rooftop performance at Tokyo's prestigious Mitsukoshi department store, in Ginza, in which Speed, Glue & Shinki were joined by Fumio Miyashita's Far Out[5] and Atlantic label mates Too Much. But when Kabe disappeared yet again, Shinki bided his time by joining the 'super session' band that Yuya Utchida had got together to back former Flowers vocalist Remi Aso. Supporting Grand Funk Railroad at an arena show in Osaka, Remi was delighted to welcome Shinki to her all-star ensemble that contained Apryl Fool's organist Hiro Yanagida, Samurai's Yujin Harada and future free bassist Tetsu Yamauchi. Liberated from the pressures of their regular careers, this highly professional bunch enjoyed each other's company so much that they chose to continue backing Remi throughout the summer of '71.

In the meantime, Joey Smith had little time for Masayoshi Kabe's blasé ex-pop-star attitude. Indeed, the feisty Filipino made it crystal clear to Orita and Shinki that he intended to keep Speed, Glue & Shiki together with or without the ex-Golden Cup. He'd been starving too long to throw away this opportunity at stardom and was not about to go down without a fight. In September '71, Shinki and Joey drafted in bass player Mike Hanopol from Zero History, Joey's shopping-mall R&B band, and the three immediately commenced recording the band's second album with brand-new songs by Joey, and a couple of Mike Hanopol's equally brutal sludge trudges. On 28th October, Kabe deigned to return for a big Tokyo show with Flower Travellin' Band at the legendary Sankei Hall, both bands appearing together at the end for an encore rendition of 'Give Peace a Chance'. Kabe's unexpected return offered Orita and Shinki the opportunity to record with the original band line-up, and the producer opened Mouri Studios in the early hours after the show, facilitating the recording of Joey Smith's most sociopathic rant thus far, 'Sniffin' & Snortin''.

Coming on like Iguanas-period Iggy singing over Roky Erikson's pre-13th Floor Elevators band the Spades, Joey's 'Sniffin' & Snortin'' is garage rock's finest hour both musically and lyrically. Joey hips us to his quest over a tumultuous Texan riff, explaining how he's drinking wine and loading up his syringe on his way 'to a Sunday jam':

> Well, I'll shoot it, I'll shoot it nice and clean,
> By the time I pull it out of my veins I'm gonna feel so strange.

No shit, Sherlock! Next thing, some street scruff accosts Brother Joey with an even badder proposition. The scruff reaches into his pocket and shakes it in the singer's face:

> Let's snort it out of my hand,
> It'll make you feel like you've never been alive again.

Shrill as a motherfucker, Shinki kicks in an angular piercing solo and the band takes off like a Viet vet in a '69 Dodge Challenger. Joey's upside down hanging from the sky, determined to make this his everyday lifestyle:

> Well, I know for sure that I'd never come back home again,
> And we started sniffin' and snortin' until we turned into skin and bones,
> Yeah, we been snortin' and sniffin' our brains away.

189

Following this incredible tale, Joey, Shinki and Kabe laid down another classic within the hour, Joey's Utopian 'Run & Hide' being another seismic rollercoaster that lambasted the Man for his planetary dumping over an MC5-ian Cresta Run of truly exhilarating proportions. But when the three parted company in the early hours, Kabe was already history in the mind of Joey Smith.[6] Besides, Mike Hanopol's song-writing had already taken considerable pressure off the band, showing that he was more than capable of replacing their stringless kite. Indeed, the band increasingly turned to the songs of Hanopol, who soon found himself in the strange position of chief song-writer.

And yet, despite the 'heavy' brutal nature of Mike Hanopol's songs, Speed, Glue & Shinki's overall sound became just slightly straightened out without Masayoshi Kabe's ceaselessly strange and atonal riffing. From the near free rock of EVE, the second album began to take on some of the elements of Black Sabbath and Grand Funk that Speed, Glue & Shinki had previously avoided. In Hanopol's near-nine-minute epic 'Search for Love', the strung-out fuzz bass and analogue synthesiser brilliantly conjured up a kind of VOLUME 4-style Sabbath epic, something like 'Snowblind' if it had been played by Germany's ragged sub-sub-Kiss Tiger B. Smith.

Throughout the winter of 1971, as Mike Hanopol and Joey Smith's self-belief increased daily, the second album officially became a double-LP on Atlantic Records' 1972 schedule. But as the release date approached, Ikuzo Orita suspected that the two had run out of songs. When Hanopol proposed they record a new song of his entitled 'Wanna Take You Home', some in the studio convinced Orita that they'd heard the song somewhere else.[7] But as Hanopol was yet another six-foot Filipino addition to the band, the technical team diplomatically acquiesced. Besides, the finished song was a gloriously sludgy romp even if it was through somebody else's sewer, and 'Wanna Take You Home' made the list.

At this point, Japan's prestigious monthly magazine *Music Life* placed Speed, Glue & Shinki at number nine in their Top 50 International Artists of the Year, with Shinki gaining the number-five position in the Top 50 of International Guitarists. While Led Zeppelin, Yes and other international artists regularly topped the *Music Life* Top 50, Orita's Japanese acts had all, thus far, been ignored by the magazine. Delighted by the accolades and smelling a potential hit, Orita suggested they capitalise on this unexpected popularity and reduce the work to a single hard-hitting album. But Joey clearly had his heart set on a double-album and was having none of it. Feeling shut out of the creative process, Shinki invited his keyboard player mate Shigeki Watanabe from Wild Wand into Mouri Studios to record one of Shinki's own songs, a ridiculous flute-led instrumental that again undermined the guitarist's reputation. Worse still, Watanabe also recorded one of his own pieces, entitled 'Chuppy', a trite piece of pop fluff that Joey – without success – attempted to have banished from the album. Outraged by this interloper, Joey had a big Moog synthesiser installed in Mouri Studios, on which he began to 'write' his most outrageous work yet, a side-long experimental solo synthesiser medley entitled 'Sun, Planets, Life, Moon'. Coming on like Tangerine Dream's epic Moog album ZEIT, Joey's twenty-minute-long primitive weather-formation synth ramblings brought the protracted record sessions of this self-titled double-album to a conclusion.

Exit Speed, Pursued by Hanopol

Unfortunately, barely one month after the March '72 release of the band's double-LP masterpiece SPEED, GLUE & SHINKI, Joey Smith quit the band and headed for Manila, accompanied by bass player Mike Hanopol. The super-catchy second single 'Run & Hide' had failed to chart and the high price of the lavish album packaging had put people off the new record. Exasperated by Shinki's inability to supply his own heavy-rock riffage and frustrated by the slightness of the guitarist's few contributions, Joey Smith and Mike Hanopol formed their own Filipino power trio with former Zero History guitarist Wally Gonzales. Naming the band Juan De La Cruz, the new trio was brutal, sludgy, and somewhat inept. Gone was the bizarre free-rock of Speed, Glue & Shinki, replaced instead by almost humorous Hispanic twin vocals sung mostly in Spanish, accompanied by minor-chord heavy ballads and redundant guitar licks from the artless Wally Gonzales.

Back in Japan, Shinki revealed his lack of vision by forming Orange, an organ-dominated trio featuring ex-Tempters drummer Hiroshi Oguchi and led by Shigeki Watanabe, the perpetrator of the fetid 'Chuppy'. By now, even the ever benevolent Ikuzo Orita was ready to give up on Shinki's chronic underachievements, pulling the plug on the guitarist's free studio time soon after the split. Orange performed at a Mojo-west festival later that summer, but fell apart without a single record release. Thereafter, Shinki joined Remi Aso's backing band and eked out a living doing sessions for Yuya Utchida. With hindsight, it became clear to the Japanese rock scene that Shinki Chen's potential would remain unfulfilled, and he disappeared entirely from the scene for over twenty years, returning briefly in the late '90s in a part-time retro-styled act called the Mojos.

Down in the Philippines, on the other hand, the incorrigible Joey Smith went from strength to strength with his Juan De La Cruz workhorse, and was soon filling huge stadiums throughout the islands. Even more bizarre is the fact that he's sustained his meteoric success throughout these past decades. Recent documentary footage of Joey showed the six-foot-two singer still rizla thin, still in possession of his hair and his blazing stare, striding Kim Fowley-like around the teeming streets of Manila high-fiving every ecstatic punter who crossed his path, undermining every 'Just Say No' commercial with that same sheer Will-to-Live personality that first drew Shinki Chen to his inflammatory shopping-mall performances. Just as D'Swooners' Filipino lawlessness had injected an essential oomph into the often too-tame Group Sounds scene, so Joey Smith's gargantuan capacity for drugging and gigging infused Japan's early-'70s New Rock scene with a cavalier attitude all too often absent from their indigenous musicians. His heroic sensibilities, his mush-mouthed mike technique, his frankly outrageous lyric-writing and his Play Dumb clowning all conspired to make true legends of Speed, Glue & Shinki.

Footnotes:

1   Moron de la Frontera really means 'beginning of the moor'. Indeed, even in English, a moron was
    originally nothing more than a geographical description of one who lived on the moors. However, as
    most urbanites associated 'moor dwellers' with rural stupidity, 'moron' quickly became a disparaging
    term.

2   Interview with Ikuzo Orita, *Black Shapes of Doom* magazine, 2004.

3   In a 2004 interview with *Black Shapes of Doom* magazine, Masayoshi Kabe commented:
    'His drumming was amazing. There wasn't anyone like that … you know fuel oil? He'd squirt it and put
    fire to it … because he'd burn it while he's drumming, or banging the floor, drumming the
    microphone, while he bangs out he'd be squirting (laughs). And he'd act like he'd burned himself.'

4   Interview with Ikuzo Orita, *Black Shapes of Doom* magazine, 2004.

5   In a 2004 interview for *Black Shapes of Doom* magazine, Masayoshi Kabe commented:
    'We performed with Far Out … although they wouldn't share their [paint] thinner.'

6   According to the same interview with Masayoshi Kabe in *Black Shapes of Doom* magazine:
    'For Speed Glue's double LP I actually did only three or four songs. But then Orita called me and
    asked to use my name, so I complied.'

7   Despite Mike Hanopol's claims to be author of 'Wanna Take You Home', the song was based on a
    1969 UNI Records single, 'Take You Home', written by American guitarist and vocalist Richard
    Fortunato, and released by his late-psychedelic band Fields.

Discography
'Mr Walking Drugstore Man' (Atlantic 7" 1971)
EVE (Atlantic 1971)
'Run & Hide' b/w 'Calm Down' (Atlantic 7" 1972)
SPEED, GLUE & SHINKI (Atlantic 1972)

CHAPTER 9
TAJ MAHAL TRAVELLERS & TAKEHISA KOSUGI タージマハール旅行団
MUSIC AS SLOW AND UNFOLDING AS A LOVE AFFAIR IN REAL TIME

Taj Mahal Travellers played the music of the spheres, their sound reminiscent of the creaking rigging of the unmanned *Mary Celeste*, or a divine emanation of those moments we all have late at night when, exhausted after a hard day's work but too tired to crawl up to bed, our barely conscious minds – chronically searching out meaning as all humans are programmed to do – perceive the wind outside, the familiar whirr of the fridge's electric motor, and the awkward grind of the cranky and still-contracting central-heating pipes as they shut down for the night, but – from our low low point of consciousness – register the overall sound not as a collection of accidental noises but as something heavenly, something regal, something with intention behind it. Taj Mahal Travellers' music is psychedelic by its earliest and most Aldous Huxleyan definition, for their sound is truly 'mind manifesting', conjuring up the amplified inner workings of a world slowed down to 'Flower Petal Opening Speed', a collective sound so outside time to we Westerners, so achingly sedate that the word *mañana* appears vulgarly and treacherously urgent in comparison. Indeed, Taj Mahal Travellers' music reminds me of an acid trip I once took in South Wales, in 1981, throughout which I lay recumbent and immobile for six hours believing that I could hear the raindrops outside screaming as they hit the ground, each desperate to enjoy just one more millisecond of individuality before being subsumed into water's vast eternity.

Like John Cage's silent piece '4'33"', Taj Mahal Travellers' music is not merely silence but performed silence. But, unlike the aforementioned Cage composition, each Taj Mahal Travellers work is at least twenty minutes long. Inspired by Japan's traditional and mostly rhythmless *gagaku* percussion accompaniment to its day-long Buddhist rituals, seven long-haired outsider musicians came together in 1969 to challenge the precepts of the day by travelling to a wide array of geographical locations in order to perform music that accompanied the environmental sounds that were already present – on hilltops, on beaches, in quarries, beside roads, even in kindergartens. Deploying a wide range of mainly acoustic instruments, including tympani, bass tuba, mandolin, a multitude of hand percussion, harmonica, trumpet and *santur* (Iranian hammered dulcimer), plus electric violin, electric double bass, Mini Korg analogue synthesiser and an array of hand-made instruments, 'voices, stones, bamboo winds' and tree branches, Taj Mahal Travellers made a promise to themselves to play 'wherever a power supply was available'.[1]

For this ensemble, nothing was a given and everything was to be challenged. As if to symbolise Taj Mahal Travellers' collective refusal to follow the 'accepted way of doing things', double-bass player Ryo Koike even played his instrument horizontally by lying it on its side, like some funny farmer engaged in a highly private act of dubious animal husbandry. All around the recumbent electric double bass, which appeared as vulnerable as a gargantuan beached seal pup, numerous guitar leads stretched throughout the ensemble, leading to the bass itself, to Seiji Nagai's floor-level Mini Korg synthesiser, and to leader Takehisa Kosugi's electric violin, via the various percussion emplacements of Tokio Hasegawa, and the prayer mats of percussionist and occasional tuba player Yukio Tsuchiya, sound recordist Kinji Hayashi, and mandolinist and tree-branch shaker Michihiro Kimura. As a pop artist of considerable note, Michihiro Kimura it was whose striking animal prints decorated the front covers of LPs by Foodbrain, Hiro Yanagida and Speed, Glue & Shinki. But if the filmed evidence of the ensemble's sole TV documentary *Taj Mahal Travellers on Tour* is anything to go by, Kimura appears to have spent much of the early '70s shaking a tree branch in a wide variety of obscure locations around the world.

For travel was as much a part of this group's *raison d'être* as was the making of the music itself. Indeed, the Taj Mahal Travellers were formed by experimental violinist and former Group Ongaku founder Takehisa Kosugi in response to his somewhat accidentally self-enforced 'sabbatical' from the experimental music scene six years previously, when, in spring 1963, he'd accepted an invitation from electronic composer Matsuo Ohno to work on the musical score for the forthcoming 'space age' cartoon series 'Tetsuwan Atom' (Atom Boy). Unbeknownst to Kosugi, the unbelievable success of that first series foisted such pressure of work on to his hitherto freewheeling spirit that Kosugi's considerable energies were, to his utter chagrin, diverted away from the experimental scene into three consecutive series of TV theme music. Takehisa Kosugi, therefore, missed out on most of the mid-'60s' finest 'actions', even those instigated and realised by Kosugi's close friend and Group Ongaku co-founder Yasunao Tone, whose managerial and administrative skills helped to create so many of the high-profile (and to some 'infamous') actions by the Situationist trio Hi-Red Center (see Book One, Chapter Two). Incensed that his TV success had become such a self-inflicted 'Golden Handcuffs' award, Kosugi vowed to return to his former free-form lifestyle as soon as was possible. And so, sometime in the latter days of 1969, Kosugi invited six likeminded experimental musicians, or 'meta-music creators' as he portentously termed them, to enlist in his new ensemble.

197

Between Now and Now & Again

Taj Mahal Travellers' earliest performances were haphazard to say the least, their chaotic nature mainly brought on by the large age difference between leader Kosugi and the rest of the ensemble, most of whom were barely out of university. As the 32-year-old Kosugi struggled to free himself from all outside commitments, his six much younger cohorts were happy to indulge in the new freedoms available to them in Tokyo's burgeoning underground. By December '69, however, Taj Mahal Travellers had set up a week-long series of performances at Shibuya's Station 70 club, which were recorded by engineer, sound manipulator and seventh member Kinji Hayashi. But when the shows were taken over by street hippies all intent on contributing to the 'happening' on stage, Kosugi soon decided that Taj Mahal Travellers must separate themselves from such goings-on, or risk being mistaken for yet another commune band in the style of Jigen (Zero Dimension) and ○△□ aka Maru Sankaku Shikaku (Circle Triangle Square), action artist Kant Watanabe's clown-faced noise ensemble.

To this end, Kosugi proceeded to set up shows in art galleries and *kaikans* (culture halls) of the kind in which Group Ongaku had previously performed. Throughout spring '70, the ensemble played a series of shows in Shinjuku's prestigious New Jazz Hall, breaking briefly to allow Kosugi time to fulfil his musical commitments to the highly prestigious 'Expo '70' international exhibition, which took place in Osaka over the summer.

When Kosugi returned from 'Expo '70', however, his mind was blown from witnessing one of Karlheinz Stockhausen's long concerts at the West German 'Spherical Auditorium'. Like some Space Age twentieth-century psychedelic vision of Malta's subterranean prehistoric hypogeum at Hal Saflieni, the Spherical Auditorium was metallic blue and stood on the edge of a garden site. Visitors entered at ground level then descended into underground exhibition halls via the broad spiral staircase. On reaching the centre of the auditorium, they were there given ochre cushions on which to lounge. Stockhausen's extended group featured former Can founding member David Johnson on flute and Kosugi's friend, the German percussionist Michael Ranta. Bursting with inspiration and not a little envy, Kosugi returned to Tokyo to share the experience with his ensemble. By September, however, the younger musicians had once again pressured their leader into performing at a rock concert at the Tokyo University of the Arts. Unfortunately, Taj Mahal Travellers were forced to quit the stage barely an hour into their performance, so that Murahatchibu's road crew could set up their amplification. It was clearly time for a rethink.

Despite the wishes of Kosugi's young cohorts to pursue bookings at rock'n'roll venues, the violinist remained convinced that the best way forward was via art galleries and public halls, where more cultured audiences would at least remain open-minded towards the musical ideas taking place, never dreaming of drunkenly invading the stage to join in. Fortunately for all parties, a third option revealed itself that autumn when Taj Mahal Travellers were invited to play a day-long concert 'from pre-dawn to dusk' on Oiso Beach, that coming December. Situated on the southern Pacific coast in the Kanagawa prefecture, around one hour's drive southwest of Tokyo, Oiso is a place of mythical beauty to the Japanese, and is known to the local population as *shonan* (bright coast of sunlight). For the Taj Mahal Travellers themselves, the Oiso Beach show was a revelatory experience of possibilities, and thereafter no one wished to risk constrained performances at inhibitive coffee shops or small clubs. Henceforth, Taj Mahal Travellers were united in their collective aim to become a Gnostic ensemble whose music forever would conjure up spectacular images of strangely garbed hippies playing bizarre instruments in the lee of sacred snow-capped mountains, 'at windswept beaches at dawn', or at Shinto temples as cranes flew low across the horizon.

Exotic Outsiders Abroad in the Barbarian West

And so, between 1971 and '72, Taj Mahal Travellers hit the road in a rune-inscribed Volkswagen minibus, travelling from Japan to the Netherlands via Germany, Scandinavia and Great Britain, thence to Iran and back to Japan via the Taj Mahal itself. Indeed, the aforementioned 1972 documentary *Taj Mahal Travellers on Tour* explains more about the mindset of this wild ensemble than any book could hope to, revealing six inordinately hairy cosmic explorers hungry to make sounds in any possible situation. At one point, the documentary shows Michihiro Kimura holding one of his 'self-made instruments' (as the screen credits term it), which looks like one of those ritual folding chairs discovered in Danish Bronze Age mounds. Elsewhere in the film, Kimura is seen playing an acoustic guitar around the back of his head in a remarkably unconvincing Jimi Hendrix homage. Armed with two small spoon-shaped mallets, Yukio Tsuchiya batters his Japanese *shanai* and Iranian *santur* into submission. Trumpeter and percussionist Seiji Nagai is also seen violently shaking the (same?) tree branches almost continuously throughout the documentary. Of the sixth and final member, I still have no clear idea what vocalist and percussionist Tokio Hasegawa did. Credited in the documentary as having contributed 'voices, stones, bamboos, winds', Hasegawa's may be the most prominent Taj Mahal Traveller voice of all, but so subsumed is it into the general stew of sound that I've been unable to make a guess. What surprises the viewer most of all is the sheer exuberance of every Taj Mahal Traveller throughout the footage. Filmed in the back of a taxi, they even attempt a primitive harmonica and beer-bottle blues that shakes the listener with its underachievement.

Throughout this extended tour period, Taj Mahal Travellers gained mightily from leader Takehisa Kosugi's previous decade in the experimental field, as country after country welcomed the ensemble with open arms, directing them straight to the nearest arts festivals. At a time when most longhairs were experiencing the wider world via the threat of a police baton and a night in the cells should they put a foot wrong, even a cursory glance at Taj Mahal Travellers' 1971 itinerary reveals that, thanks to Kosugi's exemplary credentials, the ensemble always inhabited important cultural centres and corridors of power.

From several Swedish performances in the prestigious *moderna museets* (modern museums) of Stockholm[2] and Gothenburg, their Scandinavian progress took in Finland's Amos Anderson Konstmuseum, in Helsinki, and Copenhagen's St Nikola Church, before heading south for a Belgian radio concert in Brussels' Palais des Beaux-Arts, thence to London's New Vic Theatre. While 1972 opened with further concerts at Rotterdam's Art Akademie and Denmark's Musikonservatorium, in the northwest city of Aarhus, the whole of April and May was spent engaged in a series of 'travelling events' that took the ensemble from Western Europe to the Taj Mahal itself, via the Middle East. During this period, musical 'actions' were executed at various geographical points along the route and recorded for posterity in the manner of Fluxus's early-'60s operations.

The single down side to this highly attractive method of seeing the world was its sheer lack of confrontation, for the seven musicians were seen not as threatening frontiersmen out to challenge the social mores of the West, but as exotic aliens whose hefty art credentials should at all times be catered to. In this way, Taj Mahal Travellers' decision to opt out of the rock'n'roll circuit ensured that they would remain invisible and beyond judgement until decades later, by which time the Post-Everything rock'n'roll audience had had time to retune their ears to the ensemble's ambient, nay ambulant soundtracks.

The Recordings of Taj Mahal Travellers

From the Taj Mahal itself, the ensemble returned home in summer '72 in order to record their debut LP for Columbia Records. Captured in a single evening performance recorded in Tokyo at the Sogetsu Kaikan (culture hall) where so much
of Takehisa Kosugi's early Group Ongaku career had first flourished, JULY 15, 1972 was a monumental three-track brass'n'strings drone experience in the style of Tangerine Dream's ZEIT. Sounding more like three enormous weather formations or recordings of far-distant galaxies than any contemporary music, great care was taken by Kosugi to retain their sense of mystery by naming each track after the time period its performance occupied. Thus, the whole of side one's 26-minute epic took the simple title 'Taj Mahal Travellers Between 6.20 and 6.46pm'. With Takehisa Kosugi's harmonica to the fore, and the bugle-like single sustained notes of Seiji Nagai's lone trumpet, Sohgetsu Hall herein became a mile-deep cavern from whose deepest recesses various groups of hermit species gradually return blinkingly into the world of light. Similarly, side two was split between the comparatively brief 'Taj Mahal Travellers Between 7.03 and 7.15pm', which concluded with Michihiro Kimura's remarkably tangible and incongruously bluesy electric guitar, and the fifteen-minute-long deep-trance Henry Flyntisms of 'Taj Mahal Travellers Between 7.50 and 8.05pm'. But whilst the LP remains to this day a fabulously complete document, it's still to be wondered why Taj Mahal Travellers felt the need to return home in order to record their album debut, when so much of their oeuvre had already been captured during the previous two-year tour. Perhaps the staff of Nippon Columbia Records felt unable to trust the limitations of contemporary mobile recording studios, or perhaps – as evidenced from the sleevenotes – Tokio Hasegawa's

decision to replace his tree branch 'tour axe' for an echo-machine was their single concession to commercial palatability.

From AUGUST 1974 to CATCH-WAVE

Thereafter, Taj Mahal Travellers returned to the road and pretty much stayed there. Having honed down their modus operandi to its most streamlined components, the seven blazed through 1973–74 with concerts at Tokyo kindergartens, Hiroshima department stores, industrial designers' conferences (no shit!), educational TV shows, beach concerts on the southern island of Okinawa, snowy mountain villages, even turning up at the 'Oz Days' benefit festival for the owner of Tokyo's legendary Oz rock café, which had been shut down after one too many drug busts. (Ironically, while Takehisa Kosugi's refusal to court a rock'n'roll audience had ensured the invisibility of his ensemble, this single 'Oz Days' appearance alongside such underground legends as Les Rallizes Denudés, Miyako-ochi and Dr Acid Seven's own electric band would – simply because of the appearance of a double-vinyl bootleg of the show – contribute hugely to sustaining Taj Mahal Travellers' underground myth into the twenty-first century.)

A second album AUGUST 1974 was recorded in Tokyo, at Nippon Columbia's 201 enormous Studio Number One, and was released in double-LP form. Containing just four side-long tracks entitled 'I', 'II', 'III' and 'IV', this second release was a beautiful package but something of a sonic disappointment. Due to Taj Mahal Travellers' re-emphasis of the sound away from the vocals to fairly crummy acoustic everyday sounds, the huge resonances of the first album were simply not there. The closeness of all the sounds therein remind me somehow of an a-rhythmic take on the zoned-out music of AMM, Anima and Kluster (the pre-Cluster trio formed by Roedelius, Moebius and Conrad Schnitzler).

Just one month after the recording of AUGUST 1974, Takehisa Kosugi again entered Nippon Columbia's massive Studio One, but this time he was alone. Kosugi was here to record CATCH-WAVE, an all-time underground classic utterly bereft of tree branches, harmonicas and tubas. Propelled instead by Kosugi's magical blend of echoed violin, electronics and voice, this cool Martin-Rev-meets-Joji-Yuasa urban meditation was to become the 'Pushing Too Hard' of drone music, a Queasy Listening classic that sends the listener just like the Jaynettes' elliptical 'Sally Go round the Roses' sends you. The single-vinyl LP consisted of two enormous side-long pieces, the twenty-six minutes of 'Mano Daruma '74' (Mano Dharma) and side two's 'Ueibu Kodo e-1' (Wave Code #e-1), which the composer described as a 'triple performance by a solo vocalist' in which 'a vocal phrase is taken and electronically modified until it loses any meaning other than as part of the wave form'. But the strung-out mantras of side one's 'Mano Dharma '74' contained a secret ingredient that pitched it slightly ahead of its cohort. For Takehisa Kosugi had created the track by playing over several tape experiments that he had created back in 1967 while visiting Toshi Ichiyanagi in New York. And it was with the intention of shuttling between Tokyo and New York that he now focused many of his ideas.

Beyond the Valley of Taj Mahal Travellers ...

Takehisa Kosugi was almost forty by the time CATCH-WAVE was released, and he used its success as a springboard into the next phase of his career. After almost half a decade of travelling, Kosugi now took the opportunity to explore his on-the-road discoveries with a wide variety of different composers and musicians. A rare opportunity presented itself in September 1975 when the director of Tokyo's NHK-Broadcasting invited the composer to perform a collaborative improvisation with two old friends, Toshi Ichiyanagi and Stockhausen's percussionist Michael Ranta, to be broadcast on NHK-Radio. The excellent results, which were later released on the Iskra Records LP IMPROVISATION SEP. 1975, were a kind of stripped-down/punked-up version of Taj Mahal Travellers, in which Kosugi's violin was ring-modulated alongside Ichiyanagi's equally ring-modulated bass piano to present a kind of half-life music akin to the Residents' LP ESKIMO, the ring modulators conspiring to create an unearthly and hissing sibilance like the voices of many cartoon snakes.[3] However, with less than half the performers who had been involved in Taj Mahal Travellers' music, this improvisational trio revealed far more individuality; Michael Ranta's simple percussion often becoming particularly wild and Mo Tucker-like, akin to some singular shaman crazily exerting his authority.

By 1976, Kosugi's travel schedule had increased considerably as he took over the 'South-East Wave/East West Song' project for Merce Cunningham's New York dance company, and recorded another collaboration for Columbia Records with New York saxophonist Steve Lacy and experimental pianist Yuji Takahashi. However, Kosugi's most important project of the year was his involvement in the creation of the ten-piece Tokyo improvisational ensemble East Bionic Symphonia, whose instrumentation and attitude were to ensure that the musical legacy of the now-defunct Taj Mahal Travellers would continue along the same stratospheric trajectory. Formed by occasional Taj Mahal Travellers guest musician Kazuo Imai, the rest of the musicians were, once again, mainly young Tokyo music students, whose choice of instruments included double bass, piano, snake charmer, *viola da gamba* (upright descant viola) and *kokyu* (Chinese upright fiddle), combined with multiple percussion (water sticks, wands and the like), rudimentary electronics, and the inevitable 'found objects' and 'natural materials as thrown percussion'. With Kosugi at the helm, on the evening of 13th July 1976, East Bionic Symphonia entered Tokyo's Bigakko Jinbotyo Kanada studio, where they recorded their debut LP. It was an astounding work. Despite inevitable comparisons to Taj Mahal Travellers, the ensemble's overall sound was a transcendental combination of La Monte Young drone and Daevid Allen-style Gong glissando, ostensibly created by Chie Mukai's one-string upright fiddle and leader Kazuo Imai's baritone *viola da gamba*, but heavily modified by the potentiometers and FX pedals of electronics operators Tatuo Hattori, Tomonao Koshikawa and Masami Tada. Lacking Taj Mahal Travellers' brass players, Kazuo Imai further removed his ensemble's sound from its Ur-source by adding a brazen North African atmosphere with his reedy and abrasive snake charmer. East Bionic Symphonia would never achieve the status of Taj Mahal Travellers, but their brilliant debut ensured hefty solo musical careers for both Kazuo Imai and fiddle player Chie Mukai.

Beyond Japan ... & in Conclusion

In 1977, Takehisa Kosugi finally moved to New York full-time when he was invited to become resident composer/performer with the Merce Cunningham Dance Company. Thereafter, all emphasis shifted away from Japan as the composer worked flat-out to complete the heavy schedule required of him. However, Kosugi still found the time to perform in France in 1978, at Paris's Festival d'Automne, and at the festival at La Sainte-Baume in Provence. But Kosugi's rich artistic pedigree was best appreciated in New York, where he was constantly lauded and invited to provide sound installations. Indeed, the arrival in 1979 of Yasunao Tone, Kosugi's old friend and co-founder of Group Ongaku, provided the pair with a rare opportunity to collaborate on 'Geography & Music', a Tone composition specially commissioned by Merce Cunningham for his dance piece 'Roadrunners'. Featuring a line-up of true underground luminaries, the 21-minute work contained the piano of David Tudor, and the voices of John Cage and Kosugi himself, as Martin Kalve intoned sections of the I Ching like some Burroughsian cut-up.[4]

Moving into the '80s, Kosugi continued to release occasional albums, most of which I have no time for. However, as one of Japanese experimental music's founding fathers, nothing he does should be totally dismissed. By 1994, the Foundation for Contemporary Performance Arts had awarded the composer the John Cage Award for Music, and Sonic Youth invited him to contribute to their 1999 celebration of the avant-garde 'Good-bye 20th Century'. That same year, former Taj Mahal Traveller Seiji Nagai made a timely return with his superb album on Doppelganger Records, entitled ELECTRONIC NOISE IMPROVISATION 1999, which he described as 'the hypnotic throb and flux and the spirit of Taj Mahal Travellers ... recreated via dense electronic soundscapes'. Unlike most music made in reaction to an artist's past, the music was vast and wholly vital.

Strangest of all was the release in 1998 of Taj Mahal Travellers' best ever album LIVE STOCKHOLM JULY, 1971. Recorded at the Modernmuseet during their first tour, this double-CD easily eclipsed the ensemble's two Nippon Columbia albums, and made me hugely excited at what is still awaiting rediscovery out there in Europe. And as Taj Mahal Travellers made a special trip to Germany's Radio Bremen, whence so many classic and unique recordings from Guru Guru, Kraftwerk and Eno-period Roxy Music have sprung, we can only assume that Taj Mahal Travellers' Bremen performance is not far away from being set free into the public domain.[5] Finally, there is also the ninety-minute *Taj Mahal Travellers on Tour* documentary, which I showed at my 2003 festival Rome Wasn't Burned in a Day and which everyone should endeavour to search out. Again, it's to be hoped that the publication of this *Japrocksampler* will help to force the hand of whomsoever owns the rights, because the unique soundscapes of both Taj Mahal Travellers and Takehisa Kosugi need to be heard above the clamour of uniformity that permeates much of early-twenty-first-century culture.

204

Footnotes:

1   Yuji Takhashi, biographical sleevenotes written on the group's Columbia Records
    double-LP AUGUST 1974.

2   Recordings from the first Stockholm performance were eventually released in 2002, on the double-
    CD LIVE STOCKHOLM JULY, 1971, by Drone Syndicate Records.

3   IMPROVISATION was re-issued in 2002 as a limited edition of 300 on the Iskra imprint
    (catalogue 3004).

4   This evocative work was released together with another piece featuring Kosugi, Tone's 1961
    composition 'Anagram for Strings', on the LP YASUNAO TONE, on the Dutch Slowscan Editions label.
    I would have included it in my Top 50, were it not frustratingly difficult to find. Perhaps the publication
    of this *Japrocksampler* will motivate the tapes' owners to give it a more general release.

5   In December 1972, Taj Mahal Travellers also recorded a live BBC-TV show called *Music Fusion*,
    at the Cullompton studios. Preliminary investigations have yielded nothing, but it's still early days.

Taj Mahal Travellers Discography
JULY 15, 1972 (Nippon Columbia 1972)
OZ DAYS LIVE w/Rallizes (Oz 1973)
AUGUST 1974 (Nippon Columbia 1974)
LIVE STOCKHOLM JULY, 1971 (Drone Syndicate 1998)

Takehisa Kosugi Select Discography
MUSIC OF GROUP ONGAKU (1960)
CATCH-WAVE (CBS/Sony 1975)

CHAPTER 10
J.A. CAESAR & THE RADICAL THEATRE MUSIC OF JAPAN J·A·シーザー

The borderline between reality and illusion will be dissolving.
Voodoo rock that invokes blood and the memory of blood.
Original flyer announcing new J.A. Caesar music, 1971

The Era Comes in on the Back of a Circus Elephant

The clap of thunder deafens you from the start, as forked lightning zigzags across the stereo system and sound FX mystify. Is that rain on a tin roof or somebody frying an egg? A lone woman's voice screams. More lightning. You cling on as drums and percussion introduce a lone fuzzsaw guitar theme that interrupts then obliterates the weather and, as the rhythm picks up speed, a host of female voices ba-ba-ba along with the melody until suddenly ... blam. No sound. A single maraca s-s-shakes as an angry man's voice curses. He shouts some more then emits a braying laugh. No sound. A doomy organ chord far away heralds ugly stabbing piano in the near distance. Mr Angry resumes his rant, but a single woman's voice interrupts him. He answers incautiously and the other women gobble gobble gobble their sarcastic reply. A gunshot, a scream, a host of s-s-shaking percussion, and we're off again into the high-velocity fuzz-guitar theme ba-ba-ba'd back into existence by the garrulous gobbling of the female throng. Welcome to the World of J.A. Caesar. You're in the cheapest seats in the house.

Of all the great Japanese rock'n'roll music to emerge from the 1960s, it is most surely the musical soundtracks that Julius Arnest[1] Caesar produced for Shuji Terayama's Tenjo Sajiki Theatre Company that are the most instantly recognisable to any listener. Produced for and recorded during theatre performances, the records of J.A. Caesar ring with the clamorous tones of their age, the deafening refusal to let any tradition, any cultural given, any cliché pass by unexamined. Indeed, the Caesar soundtracks fail sometimes through their sheer commitment to creating 'astonish-ment overload', as Colin Wilson once described TV news. But their essential genius to the twenty-first-century listener lies in their usefulness as devices with which to break open the head, to steep the aching modern mind in an eye-bath of cool clear liquid, to swallow all misery whole and, temporarily at least, to kiss your ass goodbye and sink into the maelstrom of Caesar's who-knows-what-the-hell-is-going-on? Psyche-delic in its intent, psychedelic in its execution, the music of J.A. Caesar was created in the psychedelicised mind of one who understood intuitively that in order to recon-struct the damaged Japanese post-war collective psyche, it was essential first to go all the way and, only then, back off.

Between 1969 and 1983, Julius Arnest Caesar composed and produced dozens of original musical soundtracks for his mentor Shuji Terayama, Japan's foremost '60s dramatist, theatre director and 'avant-provocateur'. Through Terayama's fantastic satirical 'city plays', Caesar's work explored the most extreme cultural boundaries of the time, from the protest songs of SHO O SUTEYO, MACHI E DEYO (Throw Away the Books, We're Going Out in the Streets) to the glam rock-inspired BARAMON (Rose Gate), subtitled 'A Gay Sexual Liberation Record'; almost every work containing ex-amples of violent and challenging psychedelic music, disorientating chanting and mysterious narrative known as *sekkyobushi*. For extra inspiration, Caesar reached back into the confused memories of his rural childhood, bringing forth snatches of traditional folk melodies and rhymes that seemed alien and peculiar even to his own so-called liberated Japanese audience. The well-travelled Caesar intuitively recognised that much of this indigenous music could be lost to the post-war Japanese, so he consciously integrated such traditional instruments as the stringed *biwa* and the plucked *shamisen* into his songs. Added to this heady mix was a mind-manifesting dose of the strange Western rhythms emanating not only from Britain and the USA, but also from the hip Italian, French and Dutch progressive psychedelic musicians of the late '60s. Japanese commentators have been quick to note that Caesar, unlike the majority of his compatriots, showed no fear or revulsion towards psychedelic drugs; indeed, his liberated attitudes have been attributed to his traveller days as a *futen*, or wandering poet. In interviews, Caesar is nowadays coy about the size of his hallucinogenic intake in the late '60s, but associates remember his times in the Netherlands as having been particularly psychedelically informed. This vat of personal experience, buoyed up by the unrestrained attitudes of director Shuji Terayama, created in J.A. Caesar a psychedelic frontiersman spirit in which no subject could be considered taboo, however beyond the traditional boundaries of Japanese taste it appeared to be. In 1972's JASUMON (Heresy), there is a particularly harrowing scene that conjures up the Japanese army's infamous destruction of the Chinese city of Nanking, in 1937, as weeping Chinese women, recently raped, scream at their departing abusers: 'Come back, come back and violate us again, you heartless bastards!' Caesar's work was mostly commissioned by his mentor Terayama, the best example surely being SHIN TOKU MARU (Poison Body Circle), which included Terayama's cheerful sleevenote: 'When I was a young boy, I loved this book'. Not so cheerful is the Hitchcockian psychodrama contained within, about 209 an unhappy boy whose mother dies. Treated mercilessly, abused, imprisoned and eventually thrown out of the family home by his new stepmother, the boy steals then wears his dead mother's clothes and, in full make-up, returns to the house to murder his torturers. Goading his young charge ever onwards, Terayama played Andy Warhol to Caesar's Lou Reed.

J.A. Caesar was accompanied throughout all of these performances by his own rock ensemble Akuma no Ie,[2] which featured the brilliant lead guitarist Takeshi Mori, plus a whole host of percussionists as well as the aforementioned Japanese instrumentalists. Certain of Caesar's works required more specialised Western-styled rock'n'roll contributions, at which time Caesar would bring in auxiliary members to boost his musical arsenal. Such was the man's reputation in the early '70s that he could command the services of such well-known rock musicians as Foodbrain's organist Hiro Yanagida or the Happenings Four's Kuni Kawachi.

However, despite most of Caesar's LPs having consistently yielded large amounts of fascinating and wildly eventful music, I have included in my Top 50 section only those records that stand alone as coherent musical statements even when removed from the context of the play they were intended to illustrate. Otherwise, I am fearful that my own love of this artist's entire worldview will appear off-putting to those dipping their toes into his acid bath for the first time. Right now, however, we shall go back to J.A. Caesar's roots and deal with the historical content of his life story. For this singular artist has a story well worth telling ...

A Young Person's Guide to Desert Islands

J.A. Caesar's life began in 1948, on the sparsely populated southern island of Kyushu, over 600 miles southwest of Tokyo. Information about his early life is fragmented, for this natural self-mythologiser has always been reluctant to disclose details 'in order to retain my mystery',[3] but Caesar is happy enough to admit to having been born a Libran named Takaaki Terahara, and to have had his first vision down on the beach at Mimi Gawa, in 1952. Here, aged four, Caesar witnessed a lunar eclipse and was so transfixed by the event that he declared to his parents that he was 'jealous of God, because God had written the music of the tides moving the water back and forth'.[4] Although such displays of mysticism are rare in such young children, Kyushu islanders are well known throughout Japan for their independent spirits; indeed, it was a Kyushu man whose actions brought down the overly conservative government before World War I and instigated Japan's first policy of modernising the islands. Caesar, however, felt unhappy and too isolated on Kyushu's barren east coast. Mainly friendless, the lonely child steeped himself in Buddhist *prana* teachings and spent all of his spare time writing poetry or walking on the empty beaches staring at the horizon. Caesar became increasingly convinced that he could 'create his own world, his own original customs, civilisation or even nature',[5] and was, like the late-nineteenth-century American poet Vachel Lindsay, determined to experience life as a Gnostic odyssey through the land of his ancestors. And so, in late 1962, the fifteen-year-old Caesar packed up his belongings and headed northwards, taking with him a handwritten book of his own poetry and the first volume of *Hannya Shinkyo*, a Buddhist *prana* teaching written in Sanskrit.

In America, the early '60s was the era of the travelling beat poet, but the outer reaches of post-war Japan were still in such a chaotic state of repair that the wandering *futen* was an everyday sight, and it took the young Caesar several rides in the clapped-out cars of locals before he'd even left his own prefecture of Miyazuki. Thereafter, his journey took him up the northeast coast to Usuki, where he slept under the stars after visiting the famous Buddha statues on the road towards Notsu. The following day, with neither money nor food, Caesar was befriended by a young woman[6] on the outskirts of Oita prefecture's capital city. Eighteen long months older than Caesar, the girl told him that her name was Jiya (Freedom) and that she was a huge fan of Tokyo *eleki* band the Spiders. Entranced by Caesar's *futen* spirit and seemingly practical lifestyle, Jiya joined him on the road north formulating wild plans of travelling to Tokyo, where she would work for the Spiders. To further impress her, Caesar told Jiya that he too had taken a wanderer's name and was known to his friends as Jigen (Dimension). However, travelling together as a couple was far harder than either Jiya or Caesar had anticipated, and the pair took almost a week to reach Kita Kyushu passage, where their island met Japan's main island of Honshu. Heading east on the road to Hiroshima, the young couple were soon forced to take temporary cleaning jobs in the tiny town of Ajisu in order to earn enough money to eat, and, by the spring of 1963, they were still barely thirty miles from Kyushu's northernmost point. This was nothing like the romantic beat-poet lifestyle that Jigen Caesar had intended, and his self-belief plummeted. Indeed, the teenager found the situation so intolerable that he decided to get shit-faced drunk and commit himself to the ocean. Late the following evening, Jigen and Jiya walked drunkenly down on to the beach at Fushino Gawa, where Jiya suggested melodramatically that they should make a suicide pact. However, as the two walked out upon the shifting sands, neither knew that this particular stretch of shoreline contained some of the most vicious currents in the whole of Japan, and both found themselves in immediate difficulties. Drunk and exhausted, Caesar blacked out in the surf and woke up next morning to find Jiya gone. Her body was never retrieved from the sea.

Jigen Enters the Zero Dimension

Throughout 1963, Caesar struggled to rid himself of the guilt he felt over his companion's death, but his tortured mind veered between feelings of utter nihilism and a desperate desire to return to the safety of his family. His nihilistic feeling won the day, however, and the fifteen-year-old soon made connections with members of Hiroshima's *yakusa*, or criminal underworld. The *yakusa* set him to work as a Scout-man, a kind of pimp for their liquor industry, pressing young women to work for low wages as *hosutessu*, or hostesses. Caesar found this occupation easy and, between 1964 and late 1966, slowly worked his passage east towards his ultimate Tokyo destination, making an easy living as the *yakusa*'s Scoutman in the cities of Okayama, Osaka, Nagoya and finally Shizuoka, less than a hundred miles southwest of Tokyo. Here, Caesar met another Scoutman named Joji Abe, who claimed that he was off to Tokyo to make his fortune as an actor and writer. Around Christmas 1966, however, Caesar was enraged to discover that several of 'his' hostesses had been lured abroad by the *yakusa* to work as prostitutes. After a huge argument in which his *yakusa* boss drew a sword on him, Caesar was forced to flee. Swearing to break off all ties with the criminal underworld, he made for Tokyo.

Now comparatively wealthy from his illicit activities, Caesar decided to return to higher education in order to gain entrance to Tokyo University. For the next few months, he lived quietly in a small bedsit and attended one of the many cramming schools that are, even nowadays, still popular among students who have temporarily dropped out. Gaining the required passes for his intended university course, Caesar was happy to pay the huge 700,000 yen fee and set off one foggy morning to deposit the money with the university's entrance board. However, in a now-stereotypical J.A. Caesar moment, he lost his way in the thick fog and, in his own words:

> Unfamiliar with Tokyo, I ended up in front of Tokyo Designer Gakuin (Tokyo Design School). Suddenly, my instinct told me drawing and art was my destiny, and I felt a shiver pass through me. I immediately went in to sign up for the course and for a place in the boarding. Tokyo suddenly seemed very mysterious to me, almost spiritual. I felt as though I were an explorer just arrived in unknown territory, an astronaut who was on an unknown planet.[7]

Once ensconced in the design school's boarding house, however, Caesar's violent *yakusa* past almost got him expelled after he beat an older student to a bloody pulp for stealing the breakfast of one of his friends. Deciding to keep a low profile for once, Caesar worked hard throughout 1967 and began to grow his hair long after one of his female lecturers declared that long hair made one's sixth sense grow stronger. Modelling his hip new look on Scott Walker, Caesar was photographed at his college Christmas party singing 'House of the Rising Sun' in full Walker Brothers regalia. At the beginning of 1968, however, Caesar's *yakusa* past returned once more to haunt him. While playing a game of Mahjong in the college refectory, three of his new college friends returned from the local take-away empty-handed, their faces bloody and bruised. They had been robbed by the Tokyo *yakusa*, said his friends, who – from a safe distance – had cautiously followed their assailants to their home. A self-righteous fury descended upon Caesar, and he hastened to the *yakusa* hangout and beat several shades of shit out of two of the gangsters, returning with his friends' money. However, the following day, one of the three college friends who had suffered the attack encountered the same *yakusa* at the railway station. Caesar's college friend was informed that the *yakusa* knew who Caesar was, knew about his past, knew where he lived, and that there was now a price on his head.[8] In a panic, Caesar and his three friends left their college rooms and, in Caesar's own words:

> We took a train to Asagaya [another area of Tokyo]. At that time, there were no boarding houses there, it was all paddy fields and I can still picture the long shadows of the four of us running together. For a while,

we all rented a tiny room just four-and-a-half tatami long, but gradually each one departed until there was just me.[9]

Rebel without an Address

Caesar spent the summer of '68 in Tokyo's turbulent Shinjuku district, where the hippies of Japan had begun to gather around the Village Gate jazz club and two coffee shops, Ogi and the Go-Go-Café. With long straight black hair down to his waist, Caesar was now unrecognisable as the former underworld Scoutman; moreover, his canny ability to survive as a *futen* made him something of a blueprint to aspire to among the hordes of young refuseniks arriving from all over the islands, and many began to copy him. Three other particularly long-haired *futens* began to frequent Shinjuku, each gaining notoriety as uber-outsiders among the Japanese media. Unlike Caesar, they each acquired their nicknames from other hippies or media people, and were known as Kiristo (Christ), Gurriba (Gulliver the Traveller) and Barbara (the Barbarian). But Shinjuku was far too populated an area to accommodate the vast numbers of new hippie arrivals, and others began to set up communes in nearby Kokubunji, or in the ex-US Army camp at Fukuzumi. If the Group Sounds phenomenon had caused suspicion among Japan's conservative elders, this new lifestyle was about to send them through the roof; especially as the well-respected movie director Shuji Terayama was known to have gone into print encouraging young people to leave their parents' homes and embark on a life on the road.

But Caesar's disputes with the *yakusa* and his increasing media notoriety as '*Futen* Number One' were beginning to drive him to distraction, as his artistic life was now totally disrupted. The era of free love was giving way to the era of revolution, and a new breed of hippie had begun to appear on the streets. Known in America as Yippies and White Panthers, these were not peace freaks but activists determined to overthrow the present regime. And on the streets of Japan's biggest cities, these tough activists called themselves *Foku Gerira* (Folk Guerrilla) and, in Tokyo, they demanded of the four *futens* that they must declare on which side of the fence they stood. Paying no attention to the politics, Caesar regarded all the activists as just more of the same old threatening *yakusa* shit, and looked for a bolthole into which to escape.[10] Caesar was hanging out in Ogi one day, drinking coffee, when Christ walked up to him, proffering two tickets for the latest Shuji Terayama production *Hanafuda Denki*. But Caesar declined: 'Sorry, *Futen*, I'm never sure how to take actors. If they're prepared to parrot somebody else's lines, then I'm not sure I'm interested in them.'

Ms Saki, Ms Maki, Ms Emaki &
the Systemisation of Accidental Meetings

A couple of weeks later, Caesar was riding the bullet train back to Shinjuku, after a couple of days bumming around the beaches of Atami on the southeast coast an hour's ride away from Tokyo. He got talking to a pretty girl named Benten Emaki, who explained that she was an actress in the cast of Shuji Terayama's latest Tenjo Sajiki production *The Era Comes in on the Back of a Circus Elephant*. Caesar took an interest once he knew that his favourite singer Carmen Maki had become a Tenjo Sajiki member, but was disappointed to discover on the night of the performance that Maki was away making a TV performance. However, Caesar was mightily impressed by Maki's understudy Yoko Ran, and heard something in her song 'Dove' that resounded so deeply within him that he later described Ran's performance as having 'started my theatre music career'. Utterly convinced by this song alone, as well as with Tenjo Sajiki's whole production attitude, Caesar returned to the theatre next day, where he caught sight of Carmen Maki rehearsing. Entranced by Maki, Caesar had a romantic premonition and was unsurprised when she approached him after the rehearsal. He and Maki spent the evening in the Go-Go-Café and the following night together; thereafter they returned to Terayama's theatre, where Caesar ran into an old friend, Nigoshichi Shimouna, who was also member of Tenjo Sajiki. With Caesar still in shock from this discovery, who should walk in but Shuji Terayama himself. Taking one look at Caesar's outrageous appearance, Terayama asked: 'Do you do plays?' When Caesar replied in the negative, Terayama looked at Caesar's old friend and winked, then he caught Caesar's eye and said: 'Stay with us. You'll have some fun.' Caesar remarked later that after so many years of statelessness, Terayama's fatherly invitation to 'stay with us' was the most welcoming sound he could have imagined. Only much later did Caesar discover that Terayama's invitation had been motivated by one of the director's own major theories; a theory he had written about in a book entitled *The Systemisation of Accidental Meetings*, and which defined itself most succinctly in the manner in which J.A. Caesar had been 'delivered' to Shuji Terayama's door. The series of coincidences was completed, however, when Caesar developed an interest in Tenjo Sajiki actress and author Saki Takahashi,[11] only to discover that she was being courted by his old *yakuza* mate from Shizuoka, the former Scoutman Joji Abe, who was himself in the process of fulfilling his own ambition to become a writer and actor.

To celebrate Caesar's arrival, Terayama shoehorned a role for him into *The Era Comes in on the Back of a Circus Elephant*, casting him as a life-size rag doll who does nothing but play the drums. Despite having no lines at all, Caesar's appearance caused uproar and delighted approval among both audience and press. He moved into the apartment of his old school friend Nigoshichi Shimouna, inherited a kitten from singer Yoko Ran as a symbol of his new domesticity, and phoned his parents' home for the first time in four years. After a tearful reconciliation, they readily agreed to send all of the childhood songs and poems that had fuelled his days down on distant Kyushu. The time had come for Caesar to fulfil his longstanding dream of creating his 'own original customs, civilisation, or even nature' ...

The Scream That Wishes to Change the World

By early 1969, despite having zero experience in the field of theatre music, Caesar found himself thrown in at the deep end, writing and arranging songs for Tenjo Sajiki's highly experienced musical ensemble Kangokutai (Jail Team), who were unsurprisingly suspicious of the *futen*'s slight CV. However, the ultra-charming Caesar eventually won around the entire ensemble, with the exception of guitarist Shinichi Kurita, whose steady relationship with Carmen Maki had dissolved after her night with Caesar. But nothing could dissuade Caesar from the happiness he experienced in his new role, later commenting: 'I felt the purity of boyhood among the Tenjo Sajiki members, all of us completely absorbed, like children playing in a sandpit.'

By the middle of 1969, Caesar had completed his first wholly original theatre piece for Tenjo Sajiki. Entitled 'Odyssey '69', it utilised many of his teenage poems and some beat writings, but was unfortunately never recorded. However, the success of this first work allowed Caesar to increase considerably the pace at which he could compose, and the young ex-*futen* now took the opportunity to bring together his own musical ensemble, the aforementioned Akuma no Ie. First, the cuckolded Shinichi Kurita was replaced by Takeshi Mori, a beautiful young lead guitarist whose Whirling Dervish style shared an affinity with Flower Travellin' Band's Hideki Ishima, introducing a singularly Far Eastern and futuristic element into Tenjo Sajiki's soundtracks. With new boys Yuzo Kawata on bass and Shigeyuki Suzuki on drums, the 21-year-old Caesar now felt like the elder statesman, even confident enough to deliver new material written on *koto* as well as on piano and guitar. Sporting a Hendrix-style moustache to denote his new maturity and wearing his hair longer than ever, Caesar began the '70s with the chaotic rehearsals of *Sho o Suteyo, Machi e Deyo* (Throw Away the Books, We're Going Out in the Streets), Shuji Terayama's new 'city play' whose outsider ideas had first been published in the playwright's controversial book of the same name. Aimed at teenagers, and containing themes which espoused running away from home and rejecting traditional values, Terayama's book had helped instigate the entire *futen* movement of the late '60s and gained its author a high degree of notoriety throughout Japan's conservative society.

At this symbolic doorway between the vanishing idealism of the '60s and the decadence of the '70s, however, it's essential that we now step back for a moment in order to address Caesar's situation. For, despite our young culture hero's great trek across southern Japan and his subsequent warm welcome into the bosom of Terayama's 'family', this was in many ways the end of the J.A. Caesar story, as the young ex-*futen* surrounded himself with like minds and set about enriching Terayama's Tenjo Sajiki dreams by bringing forth songs and poems inspired by his time on the road. This was not to be a rock'n'roll tale of career-building in the traditional music-business sense. And no manager, visionary or otherwise, would ever be on hand to prepare Caesar's next strategy on the road to acclaim and riches, or to cause his downfall through excessive womanising or poor financial moves. Indeed, J.A. Caesar had no strategy of his own, being always at the beck-and-call of Shuji Terayama's enormous theatrical vision.

And so, for the next thirteen long years, Tenjo Sajiki's roller-coasting schedule and Terayama's extraordinary expectations of the young ex-*futen* pitched our hero into making the kind of artistic achievements that only gruellingly long hours and hard work can bring. Called upon daily to rewrite this and alter that, Caesar quickly became an adept at troubleshooting awkward situations in a manner that was both artistic and practical. Understanding how lucky he was to have been selected by such a cultural iconoclast as Terayama, Caesar shouldered as much responsibility as he could take and more, knowing that he had been granted an artistic platform like nobody else. For over a decade, songs and theatrical poems spewed out of him as though he were some minstrel at the court of a medieval king, one minute delivering some visionary elegy, the next involved in such thankless last-minute tasks as shoring up a play's dead moments with an invigorating 'ditty', sometimes pinched from an earlier work, or even eviscerating favourite songs so as to allow Terayama's folkie mate Kan Mikami more time for 'shouting'.

Throughout this fertile '70s period, Caesar was to write literally dozens of musical scores for Terayama. And yet Caesar's highest (known) artistic achievements – JASUMON, BARAMON, SHIN TOKU MARU, DENEN NI SHISU and AHOBUNE – were mostly barfed out in a fairly perfunctory manner wherever mobile recording facilities were easily accessible. Moreover, like many recordings of the classic jazz era, the Caesar albums that have passed down to us from this extremely plentiful period of his career (and whose superb contents have inspired me to write this short biography) were simply intended as live snapshots of certain shows. Who knows what works of psychedelicised genius await the future excavator of J.A. Caesar's work? Apart from those very few recordings that were deemed worthy of a full vinyl LP release, most were simply packaged 'musicassettes' available from Tenjo Sajiki's merchandise stall along with the posters and other memorabilia that concert goers like to spend money on as evidence of an enjoyable evening. Of course, it's to be hoped that the publication of this *Japrocksampler* will inspire those in control of Caesar's work to re-issue it all. But so little is available at the present time (December 2006) that I'm delighted to have had access to so much of it. When listening to Caesar's albums, it is also essential to remember that none were sequenced with any real thought about repeated listening in the manner of classic rock'n'roll LPs. Indeed, for this very reason, I have chosen to include in my Top 50 only those Caesar soundtracks that work coherently and cohesively as 'stand alone' pieces. As for cataloguing Caesar's enormous '70s work schedule and travel itinerary, suffice it to say that even during Tenjo Sajiki's annual travels to arts festivals in the Netherlands, France, Yugoslavia, Denmark and Iran, the composer appears always to have been at Terayama's right hand, just in case script adjustments meant the rewriting of a song, overture or poem.

The Death of Shuji Terayama & Afterwards ...

However, Caesar's world changed utterly on 4th May 1983, with the untimely death of Shuji Terayama at the age of forty-eight. Having spent all of his adult life in thrall to the master and even now only in his mid-thirties, Caesar yearned for the cloistered safety that his relationship with Terayama had brought. The feeling of empowerment he had derived from putting forward some particularly extreme concept was suddenly swept from under him, and Caesar spent much of the year engaged in composing a depressing eulogy to his mentor entitled 'Saraba Hakobune' (A Farewell to the Ark). Next Caesar instigated the Gravity theatre lab, but it was soon announced that Terayama had bequeathed Tenjo Sajiki to the middle-aged *futen*, and both Gravity and Tenjo Sajiki came to be run through the theatre company and publishing imprint Banryu Inryoku. With Terayama out of the picture, Caesar's star nevertheless began to fade. Unable to command the same attention without its figurehead, Tenjo Sajiki's 1984 production *Lemmings – Take Me to the End of the World* received only marginal publicity, and Caesar's soundtrack was deemed unworthy of a vinyl release, turning up instead as a cassette-only soundtrack available at shows.[12] For much of the '80s, Caesar and Tenjo Sajiki continued on this much-reduced level, so reduced indeed that my investigation of this period became tricky. Although Tenjo Sajiki's long-time international connections guaranteed the company's occasional return to the arts festivals in France, Belgrade, Amsterdam and Berlin, Caesar's career began to sink beneath the radar, and he bided his time by writing and arranging albums for singers Kauki Tomokawa, Morita Douji and his old flame Carmen Maki.

In 1991, Caesar's Banyru Inryoku group[13] was invited to perform Terayama's

Tokyo Kid Brothers

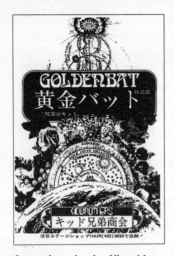

The story of the Tokyo Kid Brothers commenced in the summer of 1968, when Tenjo Sajiki's Yutaka Higashi left to form his own splinter underground/experimental theatre troupe with eight close friends from his former high school. Naming the troupe Kid Brothers in deference to his roots as an apprentice of Shuji Terayama, Higashi secured a residency at Shinjuku's Panic Disco, where the dancers performed *Kokyokyoku dai Hachi ban wa Mikansei Datta* (Symphony Number 8 Was Unfinished) from December '68 into the new year. In order to help finance themselves, leader Higashi opened a theatre shop named 'Hair', while the troupe's performance of their second musical *The Golden Bat*, written by singer Itsuro Shimoda, ran from December 1969 to April '70. In February 1970, a *Hair* producer B. Casteri came to see the Kid Brothers' performance, and was so impressed that he proposed helping to finance the troupe on a trip to New York. When negotiations with Casteri fell through, however, Yutaka Higashi decided to risk taking the troupe to New York at their own expense, at which time he changed their name to Tokyo Kid Brothers so as to resonate more strongly in the USA. From May to December 1970, the troupe performed The Golden Bat at an off-Broadway theatre named La Mama Experimental Theatre Club, where the play was advertised as a 'Voodoo Musical', declaring 'Golden Bat Is The 13th Emissary With A Universal Mission'; other poster comments included 'Noah's Ark Sailing Journal', 'The Paradise Of Tokyo In The Hell Of Japan', 'Japanese Pilgrimage Story' and 'Greek Tragedy: Tokyo Version'. Returning in January 1971, the company recorded the play as their debut LP for Polydor Records, with musical arrangements from Foodbrain's organist (and former *Hair* musician) Hiro Yanagida. After a triumphant Tokyo show entitled *Return of the Golden Bat* at the Korakuuen Hall, the troupe started work on their next show *Nanso Satomi Hakkende* (The Story of Eight Dogs), named after a very important Japanese mythical classic. In April 1971, the company left for Europe, first releasing a concert LP combining the best material from their three shows. However, it was not until Tokyo Kid Brothers rejected the work of Itsuro Shimoda in favour of their own

reading of Shuji Terayama's own 'Sho op Suteyo, Machi e Deyo' (Throw Away the Books, We're Going Out in the Streets) that this troupe really hit the mark. Gone was the pleasant singing and love'n'peace atmosphere, replaced instead by quarrelsome dialogue, hectic urgent guitar heavy rock, funereal dirges, ecstatic anthems and mawkish chorales in the vein of Tenjo Sajiki. Indeed, the album version released in 1971, on Victor Records, is an underground classic, said to have featured contributions from Flower Travellin' Band's guitarist Hideki Ishima and organ by J.A. Caesar himself. Unfortunately, this release proved to be the absolute zenith of Tokyo Kid Brothers' recordings, and future releases such as THE LOST COLOUR BLUE (Polydor Records), ONE & THE SAME DOOR (King Records), OCTOBER IS THE GOLDEN COUNTRY (Warner Pioneer) and the self-released EP LOVE & BANANA proved to be patchy affairs, with too many outside songwriters watering down their sound. In 2000, founder Yutaka Higashi died and P-Vine Records released a sumptuous 6CD commemorative box. However, despite the inclusion of song contributions by many Japrock legends, the overall standard of Tokyo Kid Brothers' performances was pale indeed, when compared to J.A. Caesar-period Tenjo Sajiki.

version of *King Lear* at London's Mermaid Theatre, as part of the Japan Festival. But thereafter work became sporadic and Caesar was reduced to supplementing his theatre work throughout the '90s by making cheaply recorded soundtracks for porn movies. It was in this manner that Caesar eked out the barest of livings until the arrival in the late '90s of a new animé superstar, the 'revolutionary girl Utena' of the series *Shojo Kakumei Utena*, written and produced by Kunihiro Ikuhara. As a former student activist himself, Ikuhara still held fond memories of Caesar's choral rock'n'roll, and was determined to evoke the spirit of the *futen*'s primary era in the musical accompaniment of his cartoon 'revolutionary girl Utena'. The Utena series propelled Caesar back into the spotlight with the release of seven soundtrack albums between 1998 and the end of the millennium, causing something of a J.A. Caesar revival. In 2002, the re-issue label P-Vine released a compilation of Caesar material OKAMI SHONEN (Wolf Boy), subtitled 'Pilgrimage of Blood'. Although the compilation contains music from as far back as the 1972 period, those seeking the wild orgasmic rock of Caesar's Akuma No Ie band should, however, proceed with caution. Nevertheless, as the music of Julius Arnest Caesar remains some of the greatest to have emerged from the late '60s and '70s rock dimension, we can only expect his *futen* phenomenon to grow and grow.

220

Footnotes:

1   Misunderstandings abound in the crazy world of J.A. Caesar, who admitted in later interviews
that his middle initial was intended to refer to one of his childhood heroes, actor Ernest Borgnine.
However, as the Japanese pronounce the name 'Arnest', so Caesar's middle initial became 'A' not 'E'.

2   In its most simplistic translation, Akuma no Ie means something like 'Devil's House'.
However, 'Akuma' does not really allude to anything approaching the Judaeo-Christian vision of the
Devil, and summons in the Japanese mind meanings closer to 'demon', 'deuce', 'diabolus', 'evil spirit',
'Old Nick', 'serpent', 'scratch', 'succubus' or 'unclean spirit'.

3   Takeo Udagawa, Shizumitsu Tsuchiya, Alex Mizuno, Toru Ueda, Tomisada Namura,
*The World of J. A. Caesar: Originator of Japanese Psychedelic Culture, the Living Legend of Tenjosajiki
& Banyuinyoko* (Byakuya Shobo 2002).

4   Ibid.

5   Ibid.

6   Caesar claims that he has never given out Freedom's real name for fear of reprisals from her family.
    But the more likely answer seems to be that he himself never knew it.

7   Udagawa et al., *The World of J.A. Caesar*.

8   When, in 2002, Caesar was asked to confirm this story by the journalist Seiko Tsuchiya, he replied
    simply: 'They were after a different person, a friend of mine.'

9   Udagawa et al., *The World of J.A. Caesar*. *Tatami* is a woven straw mat around 170 centimetres long
    by 90 centimetres wide. Its size is standardised and, therefore, is often used to describe the size of
    a room.

10 In 2002, Caesar told the journalist Seiko Tsuchiya: 'I was not a natural revolutionary, and believed
    that unless one liberated oneself, we could never be free. I always thought we ourselves should be
    the first area for liberation. Even when you chant revolution in a group, it tends to be one person
    chanting and the others getting together and sympathising with the word.'

11 Saki Takahashi later wrote a history of the early years of the Tenjo Sajiki Theatre Company,
    entitled '15 Sai: Tenjo Sajiki Monogatori' (Fifteen Years Old: The Tenjo Sajiki Story).

12 THE LEMMINGS cassette was re-issued on CD in 2000 on the Banyru Inryoku label.

13 There is much historical footage – posters, adverts, tickets and the like – on Caesar's current
    Banyru Inryoku homepage here: http://www2.ttcn.ne.jp/~banyuinryoku/index.html. More is available at:
    http://www.land-navi.com/backstage/tirasi/banyu2.htm

Select Discography

SHO O SUTEYO, MACHI E DEYO (Tenjo Sajiki 1970)
THROW AWAY THE BOOKS, WE'RE GOING OUT IN THE STREETS (Victor 1971)
JASUMON ('Heresy') (Victor 1972)
KOKKYOU JUNREIKA (Victor 1973)
BARAMON ('Rose Gate') (Victor 1973)
DENEN NI SHISU ('Death in the Country') (Sony 1974)
CACHE CACHE PASTORAL EP (Carrere 1974)
TENJO SAJIKI AHOUSEN (Columbia 1977)
SHIN TOKU MARU ('Poison Body Circle') (Victor 1978)
NUHIKUN ('Directions to Servants') (cassette only, 1979)
SEALBREAKING SONGS (Ain't Group Sounds, rec. 1980)
KUSA MEIKYU ('Grass labyrinth') (1983)
THE LEMMINGS (cassette only, 1984; Banyru Inryoku 2000)
SARABA HAKOBUNE ('Farewell to the Ark') (SMS 1984)
KING LEAR (cassette only, 1991)
OKAMI SHONEN aka PILGRIMAGE OF BLOOD (P-Vine compilation 2002)

CHAPTER 11
MASAHIKO SATOH & THE FREE-THINKERS' UNION

佐藤允彦と限りない可能性を模索した時代

Note: It's essential at this juncture in the narrative to labour the point that, as I made my discoveries of the records discussed in this chapter only through obsessive trawling and patient sifting, it has invariably been an arduously hit-and-miss affair. So, unless you have wads of cash and are not easily heartbroken, please don't leap aboard the same experiment and buy something just because it's by an artist mentioned here and it's from approximately the same period. I know that's a fair modus operandi with regard to most Western music. But I've spent a fortune buying Japanese stuff because it has a great jacket, and contains performances by my favourite musicians, and yet the record often still sucks. Without a guaranteed recommendation from one in the know, you are still On Your Own.

Only When Miles Gave the Go-Ahead

In order to better comprehend the Japanese rock scene of the late '60s and '70s, it's essential now for us to conduct a brief study of selected areas of the Japanese jazz scene. For a great deal of Japan's best progressive and experimental music came via jazz, and the avant-garde and free-jazz scenes especially. But first, it must be explained that, while jazz's roots as a night-club entertainment first became challenged in America by politicised black jazzmen playing free jazz – obviously with heavily loaded social symbolism – around the time of the 1964 civil-rights movement, no such challenge took place in Japan. Instead, the mid-'60s Japanese jazz scene continued to take its lead from Miles Davis, whose 'cool' they had long idolised, whose style and lifestyle they aped, and whose refusal to adopt the late-'50s/early-'60s free-jazz stylings of Albert Ayler, John Coltrane, Cecil Taylor and their ilk ensured that no Japanese jazz players could consider moving into a free-jazz area, at least until Miles himself had deemed such a move acceptable.

In the USA, Miles's refusal to embrace free jazz separated him temporarily from many of his black jazz brethren, to whom free jazz was, by the mid-'60s, inextricably linked to civil rights, Black Power and the rejection by black Americans of their slave owners' Christianity in favour of a new and radically Afrocentric worldview. And so, whilst Albert Ayler and John Coltrane's free blowing got them adopted by the 'Don't Trust Anyone Over 30' hippie white-rock scenes in the UK and USA, the still be-suited and none-more-debonair Miles Davis – already a grandfather and pushing forty – was labelled 'straight', 'stiff' and 'square' throughout that period, by a radicalised youth culture too young, too ignorant of the past, and too concerned with the Right Now to care that Miles it was whose constant and sustained forward-thinking attitudes had instigated umpteen new jazz forms from the so-called 'Cool Jazz' of the late '40s, via the Hard Bop of the mid-'50s, to the modal and orchestrated jazz of the late '50s.

In Japan, however, where none of the aforementioned black cultural concerns had any political or racial resonance, 1964 was marked not by civil-rights protests but by the storming debut of the Miles Davis Quintet, at the Tokyo-hosted World Jazz Festival. Then comprised of future jazz legends Herbie Hancock on piano, feisty teenage drummer Tony Williams and statuesque giant Ron Carter, Miles's stylish and urbane band systematically destroyed the audience at Tokyo's Kosenenkin Hall, reinforcing in the Japanese their long accepted view of what a true jazzman should be. Thereafter, Japanese jazz through the '60s remained a stylish late-night entertainment for a hard-working recently Westernised people whose weekends were seen by the majority as an opportunity to drink and dance excessively at the local jazz *kissa*, or night-club. To the majority of post-war Japanese, jazz was a symbol of 'cool' and of sharp dressing, but nothing more. Indeed, the concept of 'radicalized jazz' was something of an oxymoron, a contradiction in terms. Furthermore, the burgeoning Japanese rock scene was itself highly reliant on Japan's jazz musicians, who, having taken years to master this alien Western musical form, were those most readily equipped to provide the steady and sustained back-beat required by Japan's purveyors of commercially recorded rock'n'roll and pop music. And as so much of Japan's rock'n'roll and pop music was created with the aid of a highly professional jazz community in thrall to the Miles Davis 'cool school', much of the Davis orthodoxy – the sharp dressing, the outward displays of control – therefore filtered down to rock'n'roll and pop musicians via the Japanese jazz scene. This situation was by no means negative, for Miles's presence and enduring star qualities were such that almost all Japanese jazz players attempted to present themselves with the same élan as their charismatic icon, with the result that several Japanese jazz musicians – such as saxophonist Sadao Watanabe, trumpeter Terumasa Hino and guitarist Kazumi Watanabe – became huge stars, scoring major chart hits, and appearing regularly on TV, hosting quiz shows and endorsing international products. Indeed, most Japanese over-forties nowadays remember Sadao Watanabe less for his sax-playing than for his many commercials for Nissan cars, Bravas men's cosmetics and the Yamaha Townie motorbike.

By the late 1960s, however, Miles Davis's reluctance to join the neo-African bandwagon championed by his younger and more radicalised black colleagues had begun to affect his record sales dramatically, and the trumpeter found himself in the invidious position of supporting rock bands at the behest of his Columbia Records boss Clive Davis. Rejecting free jazz was one thing, but Miles had also been incredibly slow in joining in with the great Electric Experiment that had allowed jazz musicians to compete with rock'n'rollers by amplifying their acoustic instruments. Like many jazzers, Miles had initially dismissed electric guitars and electric keyboards as 'children's toys' unworthy of his time. But Miles's mind was changed in 1967, first by the guitar virtuosity of Jimi Hendrix and then by Joe Zawinul's electric piano performance on Julian 'Cannonball' Adderley's Top 20 R&B hit 'Mercy Mercy Mercy'.[1]

Taking their guru's lead, musicians of the Japanese jazz scene now jumped aboard the experimental, free-jazz and electronic bandwagon. But what made their experiments so pertinent to readers of this book is that, unlike those of many contemporary British and American jazzers, these experiments were undertaken by players who had long supplemented their incomes through pop, soul, R&B and rock'n'roll music. Lacking the snobbery of so many Western jazz musicians, the

Japanese now threw their considerable experience into creating a wild and unprovenanced hybrid music that, even today, sounds shockingly new. If there's any big problem with the music they created, however, it's mostly the hit-and-miss nature of the records they recorded with regard to our Western ears. Being jazz-based, the records are often far too traditionally 'jazz' and not enough experiment. Elsewhere, the jazz content is suppressed in favour of rock, soul or even pure experiment of the type found in jazz-based Krautrock such as Xhol Caravan, Et Cetera and their ilk. If you imagine a kind of *musique concrète* approach to jazz, or even a kind of Cosmic Couriers/Cosmic Jokers freewheeling take on John Coltrane-style free jazz then you are probably close to the pleasure centres that this music hits. If that description appals you, then it's probably best to bale out of this chapter right now. If not, however, please read on. Oh, and er … Look Out!

Hair Bequeaths Us ELECTRUM Which Disappoints, but UGANDA Nails It

As we have seen at several different points in this *Japrocksampler*, the great coming-together of musical styles that took place in 1969 reached its symbolic epicentre in the corridors of Shibuya's Toyoko Gekijo Theatre, during the rehearsals for *Hair*. When the infamous drug busts of February 1970 caused the show to be cancelled, however, drummer Akira Ishikawa and jazz guitarist Kiyoshi Sugimoto from the *Hair* musical ensemble, fearful of dissipating their vibe or having it evaporate altogether, decided to assemble a band from within the massed ranks of backstage conspirators with which to record an album. And so, billed as Akira Ishikawa & Count Buffaloes, a hastily assembled sextet entered the studio in the summer of 1970 to record their debut LP ELECTRUM. The Count Buffaloes were completed by sax player Ken Muraoka, bass player Masaaki Terakawa, and piano players Hiroaki Suzuki and Masahiko Satoh, the latter supplying all of the material for the recording session. Unfortunately for we fans of experimental rock'n'roll (and experimental music in general), there was nothing contained within the grooves of ELECTRUM to overly excite us. However, the jams had very definitely been kicked out at last, and Akira Ishikawa jumped aboard a plane to Uganda in the late summer of 1970 to fulfil his longstanding ambition to research African percussion music. Like many Japanese jazz musicians, Akira Ishikawa suffered from the terminal sickness of working too hard. Now, having believed that he'd have at least two years of guaranteed employment on the *Hair* musical, Ishikawa used this disruption to his life to break free of all constraints.

Landing in the Ugandan capital Kampala, in Baganda province, Ishikawa headed for the plains to the northwest, where the river Katu denotes the border. Having dreamed of visiting the country since he'd read Winston Churchill's description of it as 'The Pearl of Africa', the urban Ishikawa was initially overwhelmed by the endless plateaux. But once he'd got stoned (he later wrote of his surprise at being able to buy excellent grass for one penny per spliff), the drummer was next overwhelmed by the beauty of the Ugandan ladies, and later wrote of how he'd been unable to resist the advances of '3000 yen women with bad body odour'.[2] Ishikawa returned to Japan intoxicated by his Ugandan experiences and full of ideas for a new LP. He decided to retain bass player Masaaki Terakawa and sax player Ken Muraoka from the first Count Buffaloes album, but saw that ELECTRUM had failed on account of its jazz orthodoxy. Ishikawa now called *Hair* guitarist Kimio 'Foodbrain' Mizutani to replace Kiyoshi Sugimoto's bubbling, spangly solos with fuzzed-out feedback and pure noise. In the studio, the Ugandanised Ishikawa asked the jazz guys to forget their roots and 'to play with an African spirit', explaining that 'the most important thing was the music's poetic truth and that it was not influenced by American music'.[3] The results were remarkable for the emptiness and space that Ishikawa achieved on UGANDA. For, although credited once again to Akira Ishikawa & Count Buffaloes, the drummer had managed to compose an entirely non-jazz work that lapsed only rarely into clichéd 'Africana'. Most of the record was ritualistic, strung out, percussion-based and -led, but filled with epic and confrontationally noisy guitar mayhem.

How Masahiko Satoh Transcended Jazz through his German Influences

Perhaps the jazz musician whose career gained most from the cancellation of *Hair* was Akira Ishikawa's friend and cohort Masahiko Satoh, who had written the ELECTRUM LP for Count Buffaloes. For it was via *Hair* that Satoh came to work with fuzzed-out guitar freak Kimio Mizutani, whose errant muse was to steer Satoh's compositions temporarily out of jazz, via experimental rock, into some of the most remarkable and unclassifiable music of the early '70s. However, it's essential to understand that Masahiko Satoh also conducted a parallel and highly orthodox jazz career throughout this period, mainly with his trio. His early-'70s catalogue of hidden jewels can, therefore, be located only by traipsing through a minefield of disappointingly orthodox jazz statements. But even having added that caveat, it is still fair to state that Masahiko Satoh was one of those rare composers whose melted plastic brain allowed him to embrace and straddle successfully all and every new musical style without appearing to have merely jumped on the latest convenient bandwagon. As a jazz soloist, arranger, free player, or even as organist on the more extreme

Japanese rock LPs of the time, Masahiko Satoh successfully navigated his way through it all. Indeed, in this way, Satoh is probably the Japanese equivalent of German free spirit Wolfgang Dauner, with whom he played in the very early 1970s.

Born in Tokyo, in 1941, Masahiko Satoh's earliest influences came from Olivier Messiaen and Yuji Takahashi, although the pianist earned his living playing in various jazz combos in Japan, Europe and the USA throughout the late 1950s and early 1960s. Between 1966 and '68, the young Satoh studied at California's Berkeley Music School, after which his trio won the prestigious 1969 Swing Journal Award for their debut album PALLADIUM. Soon after, Satoh composed the ELECTRUM material for Ishikawa's Count Buffaloes, then arranged and played piano on the Columbia Records LP PERSPECTIVE by the ever experimental Toshiyuki Miyami & the New Herd Orchestra.[4] For his next trio LP DEFORMATION, recorded in concert at Tokyo's Sankei Hall, Satoh asked his musicians to respond to a reel-to-reel tape recorder playing segments of the New Herd's woodwind section, and things started to get interesting. A pure solo jazz LP HOLOGRAPHY came next, but the arrival of German jazz guitarist Attila Zoller, in summer 1970, brought an entirely fresh perspective to Satoh's work. In truth, the resulting Zoller/Satoh pure-jazz collaboration LP DUOLOGUE is outside the parameters of this book, but it was Zoller's tales of German musicians' determination to add uniquely German elements into their progressive jazz scene that opened Satoh's mind to the idea of incorporating purely Japanese elements in his music.

Masahiko Satoh and Stomu Yamashita's METEMPSYCHOSIS & Other Tales of Takehisa Kosugi-Informed Percussion Overload

Satoh's opportunity to create a 'uniquely Japanese' jazz came at the beginning of 1971, when he was commissioned by Columbia Records to write a futuristic work for the 24-year-old percussion prodigy Stomu Yamashita, then already over a decade into his career as a soloist. Yamashita had long been hailed as the 'world's greatest percussionist' by such esteemed figures as John Cage and Aram Khatchaturian; his early works were stunning fundamentalist broadsides of *gagaku* and other Japanese-based ritualistic percussion epics. His dynamic and extrovert showmanship, long hair waving and capes flaring, had brought such excitement to his performances that composers Toru Takemitsu, Hans Werner Henze and Peter Maxwell-Davies had already composed long percussion pieces especially for the young Japanese. Masahiko Satoh's piece for Stomu Yamashita took its cue from the orchestral arrangements composed the previous year for the New Herd Orchestra, and seventeen of those same New Herd musicians were invited to perform the epic work. Entitled METEMPSYCHOSIS, the composition was recorded in one single session on 27th January 1971, and was an avant-garde masterpiece of barely controlled cosmic chao, featuring an outrageous wind section comprised of four trumpeters, four trombonists, four sax players and a bassoonist. Stomu Yamashita and New Herd drummer Yoshisaburo Toyozumi rumbled and raged across Satoh's two side-long pieces, creating a music that was way beyond jazz and approached a kind of Godhead union between Sun Ra and the Cosmic Jokers. Its incredible artistic success so inspired Yamashita that he next asked Masahiko Satoh to create a similar work for a far-smaller ensemble. Hitting his stride, Satoh then enlisted the aid of Taj Mahal Travellers' leader and master improviser Takehisa Kosugi, over whose swaying and heavily FX'd violin, Satoh laid droning, atonal Yamaha organ. The ensemble was completed by percussionist Hideakira Sakurai, whose Japanese percussion, *shamisen* and *koto* united with Yamashita's own arsenal of percussion to create the massive hallucinatory piece later released as the London Records LP SUNRISE FROM WEST SEA LIVE and credited to Stomu Yamashita & the Horizon.

This was the uniquely Japanese music that Satoh had for so long been threatening, and he immediately set about the task of creating his own similar ensemble. Satoh contacted his producer friend and Polydor Records label boss Ikuzo Orita, who agreed to record and release whatever the composer wished. So inspired was Satoh 229 that, less than one week later, he was ensconced in Polydor Studio 1 with his trio drummer Masahiko Togashi and three percussionists, Joe Mizuki, Hozumi Tanaka and Isamu Harada, all of whom had backgrounds in *gagaku* ritual. Naming this scratch quintet Epos, Satoh recorded over the course of just one day a huge three-part quadraphonic percussion album entitled ETERNITY. Clearly inspired by Kosugi's own Taj Mahal Travellers, and subtitled '4Ch Niyoru Dagakki to Okesutora No Tameno Konpojishon' (Composition for Percussion & Orchestra in Quadraphonic), ETERNITY was an alienated and epic avant-garde wash of empty space music.

Polydor label boss Orita now believed that it was the turn of 'super session' guitar gunslinger Kimio Mizutani to make his own album, and so the producer sought the aid of both Masahiko Satoh's keyboard-playing and compositional skills, in order to create a Japanese equivalent of Frank Zappa's HOT RATS. Unfortunately, while the results were indeed charming, Mizutani's A PATH THROUGH HAZE suffered from an over-compressed mix and too many restrained performances from Mizutani himself, who clearly felt out of his depth surrounded by so many much older jazz heavyweights. Furthermore, the Satoh-composed title track was a meek affair that disappointed its composer so much that he decided to re-record it with his old German guitarist friend Attila Zoller. The resulting album, confusingly also entitled A PATH THROUGH HAZE, was once again comprised of orthodox jazz material that lies entirely outside the realms of this book save for its sublime title track, which was a quarter-of-an-hour-long tour de force.

Next came Satoh's most legendary album AMALGAMATION. Released in mid-1971, it seems most likely that Masahiko Satoh's primary inspiration for the album's recording was his Tokyo collaboration with German pianist Wolfgang Dauner on the duet LP PIANOLOGY. Dauner had long been experimenting with ring-modulated Hohner clavinets and pianos, the results of which were best seen on his albums FREE ACTION, FÜR and OUTPUT on Germany's ECM Records.

After the heavy drum-centred nirvana of AMALGAMATION, Masahiko Satoh decided to retain the same formula for his 1972 album YAMATAI-FU, on which he collaborated with bandleader Toshiyuki Miyami and his New Herd Orchestra. Unable to summon the return of Louis Hayes for the recording, but still demanding exhausting drum workouts to propel the new piece along, Satoh was forced to make huge demands of his own trio drummer Masaru Hiromi, around whom Satoh composed blasts of atonal yet euphoric brass sections to create a mighty work that was, arguably, even greater than its predecessor. Over three simply titled works of *kosmische* chaos, 'Ichi' (First), 'Ni' (Second) and 'San' (Third), drummer Togashi unleashed a fury worthy of John Coltrane's own Philly Joe Jones. By 1973, Satoh had established a new highly experimental trio named Garandoh, with former Epos percussionist Hozumi Tanaka and electric cellist Keiki Midorikawa. This trio performed at the 1973 jazz festival 'Inspiration & Power', and appeared on its wonderful accompanying double-LP of the same name. Unfortunately, Satoh's work thereafter drifted inexorably back into orthodox jazz, and his post-1973 records are of little appeal to non-jazz fans.

Stomu Yamashita & His Brilliantly Erratic Early Career

Next, we move swiftly on to a brief discussion of Masahiko Satoh's friend and sometime collaborator Stomu Yamashita. Unfortunately for this exceptional percussionist, rarely if ever has an artist's career been so derailed by outside influences and international possibilities. After spending his adolescence under the nurturing and watchful eye of his conductor father, who was leader of Kyoto Philharmonic Orchestra, the international success of Yamashita's early recordings brought umpteen invitations to work in Europe, most especially in Paris and London. In late 1971, Yamashita's fabulous percussion-only LP RED BUDDHA was prepared for release by the French Barclay label and Britain's own London Records, but only with the caveat that he change the final element of his name which, he was told, sounded too much like 'shitter'. Substituting an apostrophe for the offending 'i', the renamed Yamash'ta soon found himself drawn to the burgeoning English jazz-rock scene, and signed to Island Records with his new all-English jazz-rock ensemble Come to the Edge, led by percussionist Morris Pert. Thereafter, it was all downhill for Yamash'ta, his band and record label opting to showcase him as 'The Man from the East', an exotic freak whose proto-Rick Wakeman garb and dervish-like agility became entirely secondary to the worthy chuntering of his unremarkable band. Gone were the twenty-minute *gagaku* epics, the radical percussion assaults punctuated by Masahiko Satoh's visionary atonal brass arrangements, and the bewitching Takehisa Kosugi-informed drone-a-thons of his early career. All this was deemed to be too monolithic for British ears, and each subsequent LP release served further to integrate the boy wonder into UK jazz rock. And so, by 1975, Yamash'ta's genius had been diluted into the multi-media spectaculars RAIN DOG and GO, featuring such unlikely guests as Steve Winwood, jazz-guitar star Al Di Meola and Santana percussionist Michael Shrieve. Eventually, repelled by his overly modified public persona, the re-re-named Yamashita retired temporarily to a Buddhist temple in 1980, eventually re-emerging to create the kind of meditative music that fans of his Ur-muse should have been able to expect all along.

Masayuki Takayanagi's New Direction for the Arts

Our brief excavation of Japan's free-jazz underworld concludes with the splattered oblivion of electric guitarist Masayuki Takayanagi, one of those extreme mavericks who combined virtuosity and extensive grasp of musical theory with radically atonal free-rock amp destruction, inspiring and pissing off contemporaries throughout the entirety of his forty-year career. Nicknamed 'Jojo' and infamous for his wantonly outcast broadsides, he was notably excommunicated without trial by the jazz community of the late '60s for having described them as 'a bunch of losers' in the press. Plotting a musical trajectory somewhere between the free rock of the MC5's 'Gold' and Albert Ayler's 'Music Is the Healing Force of the Universe', Jojo's incredible power quartet New Directions for the Arts whipped up an a-rhythmical hurricane so frenzied that it became positively peaceful right there in the eye of the storm. In place of a bass player, Jojo substituted cellist Ino Nobuyoshi, and deployed percussionists Joe Mizuki and Hiroshi Yamazaki so as to provide an accompaniment more akin to organic aero-engines than to anything human. Some say his greatest work was 1970's MASS PROJECTION, others cite 1972's FREE FORM SUITE, or even 1982's LONELY WOMAN, while my mind's just a blur from the sonic soup that Jojo tips over my melted plastic brain every time I whip his records out. His guitar-playing rings the turkey necks of every other free-guitar wailer I've listened to, and his most obliterated music exerts such G-force that it's difficult to stay awake in the presence of his records. Despite these wild guitar manglings, Jojo's career began comparatively conventionally in the early '50s as a staff writer on Japan's prestigious jazz magazine *Swing Journal*, and he was playing in his own late-'60s bossanova outfit when he made the momentous decision to play free jazz. Some cite Terry Kath's 'Free Form Guitar' on Chicago's debut LP CHICAGO TRANSIT AUTHORITY as his unlikely source of inspiration, but where Takayanagi took it was far beyond the valley of 'If You Leave Me Now'. When Takayanagi died of liver failure in June 1991, his audiences had steadily reduced with each new out-there-a-minute move he'd made. But every shrill, distended, shrieking note I've ever heard this guy play screamed 'Jojo was a man'.

In Conclusive

In a book such as *Japrocksampler*, there can be no end to this chapter, for it's barely a scratch, a superficial graze of an unfathomably deep and atonal world awaiting excavation. For the Japanese are so faithful to music that moves them that I could write an entire book of a similar size to this *Japrocksampler* just on a discussion of the music that Japanese jazz musicians made in response to Miles Davis's funkathon experiments of 1975, a music so extreme that only Nippon Columbia agreed to release such material. When others lose the faith, so to speak, the Japanese do not. They just keep on excavating and digging deeper. Unfortunately, for our purposes we must yet again move on …

Footnotes:

1 Paul Tingen, *Miles Beyond* (Billboard 2001).

2 Akira Ishikawa's own sleevenotes, printed on the back cover of the
   Toshiba Records LP UGANDA.

3 Ibid.

4 Toshiyuki Miyami & His New Herd Orchestra was an orchestral big band
   whose material covered all bases from late-'40s swing to pure atonal avant-garde. Miyami was a
   bizarre combination of Gil Evans, Duke Ellington and Teo Macero, who appears to have been equally
   at home in all settings. His band provided the extraordinary brass and strings for some of my
   favourite experimental Japanese percussion LPs, but I've still to discover where Miyami fitted into all
   this, or whether he 'fitted in' at all.

Masahiko Satoh Select Discography
AMALGAMATION (Liberty/Toshiba 1971)
YAMATAI-FU (Toshiba 1972)
METEMPSYCHOSIS (Columbia 1971) with Stomu Yamashita

Stomu Yamashita Select Discography
GAGAKU ENSEMBLE OF TAKEMITSU & ISHII (EMI 1971)
RED BUDDHA (Barclay 1971)
MUSIC OF HANS WERNER HENZE, TORU TAKEMITSU &
PETER MAXWELL DAVIES (Decca 1972)

Masayuki Takayanagi Select Discography
MASS PROJECTION – A JAZZY PROFILE OF JOJO (Victor 1970)
FREE FORM SUITE – NEW DIRECTION FOR THE ARTS (Three Blind Mice 1972)
INSPIRATION & POWER 14 – FREE JAZZ FESTIVAL 1 (Trio Records 1973)
LONELY WOMAN (Trio 1982)
CALL IN QUESTION (PSF 1991)

CHAPTER 12
FAR EAST FAMILY BAND
ファー　イースト　ファミリー　バンド

Join Our Mental Phase Sound

If there is one single band whose tale concludes most righteously this little history of post-war Japanese music, then it has to be that of Far East Family Band. For, among all of the artists described herein, Far East Family Band's was the most thorough tale of searching and researching, of aspirations both artistic and altruistic, of dreams unfulfilled and of journeys that reached right around the globe only to return at last to their founder's first place of motivation right down in the foothills of Mt Fuji. During their five-year career, the music of Far East Family Band spanned almost all of the cosmic rock'n'roll genres, from epic twenty-minute-long funereal acoustic mantras in the style of Krautrockers Sand, Kalackakra and PARADIESWARTS DÜÜL-period Amon Düül to their Ash Ra Tempel-informed percussion-heavy power drives, via saccharine-sweet harmony-laden ballads through euphoric 'Careful with That Axe, Eugene' Pink

Floydian guitar epics to rigorously arranged West Coast psychedelic rock songs. From sniffing paint thinners alongside Too Much and Speed, Glue & Shinki in department-store record-company showcases to transcendental meditation, via marijuana, LSD, Krautrock, the Moody Blues and New Age healing techniques, the members of Far East Family Band did it all, and often in the most clichéd manner possible. Inspired by the then-fashionable late-'60s theories of lost Golden Ages and humanity as the progeny of ancient space travellers, the band sung of discovering new lost lands high to the north of Japan. On signing to Columbia Records, their first major-label LP embraced the so-called 'Hollow Earth Theory' that New Age theorists espoused, and the band's obsessive and capricious leader insisted on their own in-house vanity label Mu Land, named after that most ultimate of mythical lost lands.

Furthermore, the members of Far East Family Band were seekers. Hailing from a land whose people were more used to importing exotica than leaving their own landscape, nevertheless, Far East Family Band searched for the ultimate *kosmische* sound by travelling to England, where they worked with Krautrock legend Klaus Schultze, and appeared to recognise no irony in travelling to the USA explicitly in order to search for the wisdom of the Far East. On album covers, they depicted themselves in meditative poses, as Zen warriors, as romantic time travellers aboard an open boat adrift in space. And yet they were no more of a gang than Dexy's

Midnight Runners purported to be, forever in thrall to their capricious yet highly charismatic leader Fumio Miyashita. But if Miyashita was a New Age dreamer whose band spawned the blandly ambient million-selling artist Kitaro, then at least this singer/songwriter was never anything less than a highly achieving dreamer. Between 1973 and '76, Fumio delivered us a hefty sequence of four certified classic esoteric rock LPs by the names of NIHONJIN, CHIKYU KUDO SETSU – THE CAVE DOWN TO EARTH, NIPPONJIN and PARALLEL WORLD. And yet, when Miyashita died in 2004, it's clear from his published memories, dreams and remarkably few reflections upon this 'rock' period of his life, that he considered Far East Family Band to have been a gigantic failure. That this was really the case will not be shown in the following story, for Miyashita had high expectations that never approached the reality on offer to him. No visionary of the same calibre as Ikuzo Orita or Yuya Utchida ever stopped by to help facilitate his great ambitions. However, Miyashita did in later years achieve major success in his chosen field of healing. Perhaps that success made him judge his comparatively unsuccessful days in Far East Family Band overly harshly. For, in truth, brothers and sisters, the music didn't half sound good.

Let the Sunshine In ...

The story of Far East Family Band begins with the birth of Fumio Miyashita, in 1949, on a large farm near Nishifunabashi, in the green mountainous area of Nagano prefecture, northwest of Tokyo. Here, Miyashita was brought up by a newly impoverished but still highly resourceful family, whose fierce national pride had led them to name their son after the Japanese general in charge of the 1941 invasion of China. The Miyashita family's farm buildings had avoided the near-total destruction suffered by the conurbation to the southeast, and their remote location kept them removed from the daily brushes with immediate Westernisation and the US military. Unlike those of the city children, Miyashita's home was surrounded by woodland, this abundant fuel supply enabling the family both to keep warm enough and to slow-cook ropey vegetables on the point of rotting where they lay. However, many of the postwar privations that the Japanese were suffering could not be avoided, and much of Fumio's childhood was spent defending his honour against the rough children whose parents had been allowed by the new socialist government to occupy smallholdings across the family farm. Nevertheless, much to his ultra-conservative parents' dismay, the presence in the living room of a large radio set enabled Miyashita to catch all of the new sounds blasting out of the occupying force's Far East Network.

In 1965, the sixteen-year-old Miyashita joined local *eleki* band the Glories, ostensibly as rhythm guitarist. But he slowly insinuated his way into the band, adding songs into their act that he himself would sing. When the Beatles arrived in July '66, the Glories drove in to Tokyo in Miyashita's parents' old estate wagon to bask in the excitement. However, by the end of that mythical day, Fumio himself was less intoxicated by the arrival of the fabulous four than by the lines of Japanese refusenik students who had barred their way. For, in a land where acceptance of authority was all, this public show of outrage seemed more exotic than the four mysterious *gaijin* that his band had travelled so far to welcome.

Over the coming years, the Glories found that they were in a poor geographical location to score many prestigious gigs, although they did manage to support Yuzo Kayama's *eleki* sensation the Launchers. Miyashita was beside himself at the prospect of meeting Kayama, whose role as 'The Young General' had made such an impact in forging his identity. Sharing his name with a famous World War II major-general had always been a double-edged sword for the teenager. Outwardly, his refusenik tendencies and those of his cohorts encouraged him to disparage the military connection. But secretly Fumio had always been delighted to hold such a name, with all of the cachet of valour and honour that it held for the older Japanese people he would meet.

However, when the day of the Glories' support gig arrived, the Launchers were no longer led by the debonair Kayama, but by his younger first cousin, the brilliant guitar technician Osamu Kitajima. Nevertheless, the show was a revelation for Miyashita, as he watched Kitajima perform classic after *eleki* classic on his Californian Mosrite guitar, before turning his attentions to the Japanese *biwa*, a round full-bellied acoustic lute-styled instrument. Kitajima conjured up such beauty from the *biwa* that Miyashita was smitten, and returned to his parents' farm full of praise for Japanese musicians who refused to be dominated by Western culture.

The Glories' moments of glory were sporadic, however, and it was many months before their next thrill, supporting Terry Terauchi's Group Sounds prodigies 491. Backstage, the personable Miyashita struck up a relationship with 491's vocalist Joe Yamanaka, who declared his belief that the GS sound was a phenomenon on the way out. Yamanaka praised Miyashita's vocal styling and suggested that he audition for the part of Wolf in Tokyo's forthcoming production of the controversial rock musical *Hair* (see end of Book One, Chapter Two and Book Two, Chapter Five). Miyashita's audition went so well that the singer was shocked not to win the part of Wolf. However, when he realised that the show's cast of twenty-nine had been selected from a list of almost 4,000 candidates, Miyashita contented himself with a place in the 'Boy Tribe' chorus, alongside other ex-Groups Sounds musicians from the Carnabeats, the Fingers, the Dimensions, Apryl Fool and Miyashita's old acquaintance from 491, singer Joe Yamanaka, now sporting a wild rainbow-dyed Afro that made him look like the foxy love child of Jimi Hendrix and Marsha Hunt.

238

Despite their relatively low-ranking roles, Joe and Fumio's position in the controversial production of *Hair* quickly turned them into far more exotic rebellious figures than their equivalents on Broadway or London's Shaftesbury Avenue. Indeed, the heavyweight figures of the Tokyo underground scene all still held the traditional Japanese belief that theatre should be a gateway into normal regular consciousness, regarding *Hair* as an opportunity for total mass cultural change because the songs were all so insidiously catchy. And both Joe and Miyashita found themselves increasingly intrigued and stimulated to write their own protests songs when surrounded by members of nihilistic street bands Zuno Keisatsu (Brain Police), Yellow, Kant Watanabe's street freak-out band O △ □ (Maru Sankaku Shikaku) and the nihilistic Murahatchibu.

Leap Before You Look ...
or 'There Goes Justin Heathcliff'

Miyashita's brief tenure in the Tokyo cast of *Hair* ground to an unexpected conclusion in the spring of 1970, however, when several members of the production were busted for possession of marijuana, causing the authorities to shut down the entire show. Here at the crossroads of the '60s and '70s, Miyashita watched as his cohort Joe Yamanaka was whisked away to become the glamorous figurehead of Yuya Utchida's naked highwaymen Flower Travellin' Band. Determined that he too should capitalise on his days in *Hair*, Miyashita searched around for a likely musical partner. With few GS contacts of his own, the singer had sensibly kept in touch with Launchers guitarist Osamu Kitajima, who – after Yuzo Kayama's return to movie acting – had taken the Launchers into weird and unlikely realms in the late '60s with two bizarre concept LPs FREE ASSOCIATION and OASY KINGDOM. Kitajima was still enthusiastic about the electric guitar, but had, like Miyashita, become increasingly interested in reawakening Japanese ears to their own traditional instruments, and had recently abandoned the long-obsolete Launchers in favour of something more current. When Miyashita invited the guitarist over to jam at his apartment, the singer explained that his new songs had all arisen from long stoned jams with his new Shinjuku *futen* mates, his chord structures inevitably becoming more and more simple over the months in order to accommodate the large groups of freaks who'd regularly descend on the Toyoko Gekijo Theatre clutching percussion and such exotic Japanese stringed instruments as the *shamisen* and the *biwa*. To Osamu Kitajima, still struggling to rid himself of the *eleki* associations of the Launchers, this all sounded highly exotic and futuristic, so the two set about putting together an album of traditional Japanese music at a studio run by Kitajima's music publishers.

In autumn 1970, the duo's album NEW CHINA was released to absolutely no acclaim and promptly disappeared without trace. Ominously subtitling the record 'Leap Before You Look', the two – billed as 'Fumio & Osamu' – had become so obsessed with authenticity that Miyashita's songs were entirely lost, submerged under a crushing weight of Japanese and Far Eastern instruments. It was a salutary lesson to them both, and Osamu Kitajima's response was somewhat hysterical, as the guitarist immediately quit Tokyo and flew to London, where he formed the English-styled studio psychedelic band Justin Heathcliff.[1] Back in Tokyo, Miyashita attempted to follow Joe Yamanaka's 'New Rock' route by recording a ham-fisted version of Grand Funk Railroad's already brutal ballad 'Sin's a Good Man's Brother'. But the singer's heart remained bound to the Utopian songs composed during his *Hair* period and Miyashita decided to search out some of his erstwhile accomplices on the Shinjuku *futen* scene.

Precious & Precocious:
Here's Magical Power Mako

Possessed by an almost Blakean vision of the world, this self-styled
visionary has been releasing albums since the mid-70s, continuing to
do so up to the present day. Unfortunately, the extraordinarily varied
quality of Magical Power Mako's output during the '90s has contributed
dramatically to compromising the public's long-term perception of this
charming artist, whose first recordings were influenced by the studio
experiments of Faust, John Cale and Todd Rundgren. Viewed in equal
measures as both a legend and a chancer, there's no doubt that the here-
there-and-everywhere approach of Magical Power Mako's attitude to
releases has made it difficult to grasp what he's about. Mako's chequered
career began auspiciously enough with thunderous applause for his first
three Polydor LPs MAGICAL POWER MAKO, SUPER RECORD and JUMP.
However, like other single-minded '70s contemporaries such as Mike
Oldfield and Franco Battiato, the excruciatingly slow process of Mako's
recording techniques contributed to record company impatience, and
Polydor dropped him in 1980. Mako thereafter sunk beneath the radar of
public opinion, surfacing only occasionally on independent labels throughout the '80s and '90s.

Mako was born Makoto Kurita in 1955, growing up in the seaside resort of Izu Shuzenji, a coastal town similar to Brighton or Torquay. Throughout his childhood, he was an outsider who constantly wrote music, playing piano and guitar while still at primary school. At junior high school, Mako decided to make a more concerted effort to realise his musical visions, returning home every day to write at the family house, which was situated high in the mountains, overlooking the town's hot springs. From his bedroom window, Mako had a clear view of an octagonal-shaped hotel built close to the springs, from which, he believed, he was being observed by someone who lived on its third floor. This sense of being observed obsessed and inspired the teenager, spurring him on into the creation of music. During the summer of 1970, Mako began the arduous process of constructing his first solo LP on a reel-to-reel tape machine, ping-ponging the tracks back and forth in order to build up sound. When it was finished, Mako wrote on the reel-to-reel tape box: 'Summer 1970, things a 14-year-old boy thinks about'. In spring 1971, Mako moved to Tokyo, where he found a job in a steel factory and formed his first band Genge, who took up a residency at Shibuya's Jan Jan Theatre. A performance at the music festival 'Jiyu Kukan' (Freedom Space) impressed Lost Aaraaff's singer Keiji Heino, and the two became fast friends. From May 1972, Mako was employed as a writer of documentary soundtracks for NHK-TV, but gained his first real break in February 1973, when a duet with Keiji Heino on the daytime chat show *Hiru no Purezento* (Lunchtime Present) caused viewers to complain. The following month, Mako performed on NHK-TV's programme *Ongaku to Watashi* (Music and I), where he struck up a friendship with the experimental composer Toru Takemitsu, then already in his forties. Takemitsu invited the teenager to perform on some of his own new compositions, thereafter securing Mako a place on NHK-TV's prestigious *Heritage for the Future* series. Next, Takemitsu personally recommended Mako to the A&R team at Polydor Records, who promptly set him up in a home studio located in a rented house on the US Army's base at Fussa, on the outskirts of Tokyo. The resulting self-titled debut LP was something of a masterpiece, revealing Mako as a composer of extraordinary range, one minute bombarding them with *musique concrète*, the next dueting with himself on blissed-out ballads. Unfortunately for Mako, however, the agonisingly slow recording process that had achieved such a spectacular sound was so out-of-whack with the commercial necessities of the day that the artist would, thereafter, be forever chasing deadlines in an effort to make a career in such a demanding business world.

Far Out in the Foothills of Mt Fuji

Throughout 1971, Fumio Miyashita slowly assembled his dream band from the few high-quality street musicians that remained on the Tokyo scene. In the aftermath of the Yodo-go hijacking, many had fled to the far corners of Japan pursued by the authorities, while the few that remained on the streets of Shinjuku were mainly Johnny-come-lately types from rural areas. Miyashita's agricultural upbringing had instilled in him an innate sense of the need for patience, however, and he picked his musicians thoughtfully. His conservative parents offered the singer the use of their Nishifunabashi farmhouse as a rehearsal space and crash pad out of sight of the overly vigilant Tokyo drug squad. And it was here to the foothills of Mt Fuji that Miyashita brought Zuno Keisatsu's former lead guitarist Eiichi Sayu, with promises of a rent-free existence, clean air and loud music. Next came bass player and sitarist Keiju Ishikawa, formerly with the backing band of ex-Dynamites guitarist Fujio Yamagauchi. Ishikawa had first met Miyashita through producer Ikuzo Orita, while playing session bass on MILK TIME, the Polydor Records 'super session' by former Apryl Fool organist Hiro Yanagida. But the bass player had quit the ex-Dynamites' band after the chaos of the airliner hijacking had brought American CIA men round to his flat. Unfortunately for Miyashita's parents, the free-living Ishikawa also brought several young *futen* women with him, and the farm took on the look of a commune. Over the next few months, as the farm's population grew to over twenty, the still-drummerless ensemble rehearsed the singer's long unfolding acoustic songs in preparation for playing live. The line-up was finally completed by the arrival of Tomio Maeda, who'd played drums in the final incarnation of Group Sounds giants the Spiders. In the late summer of 1971, the band took the name Far Out and began playing small shows with festival bands Zuno Keisatsu, the M, Slash and former Blues Creation singer Fumio Nunoya's lumbering proto-metal behemoth Dew, whom Eiichi Sayu had left to join Far Out. Onstage, Miyashita was determined to let his band rip through his longest and most strung-out compositions, always remembering the massive jam sessions during the *Hair* rehearsals as musical high points of his life.

By the spring of '72, however, just as Miyashita finally believed that he had rehearsed Far Out enough to commence recording their first album, drummer Tomio Maeda announced that he was quitting. The band was devastated. Only through long months of rehearsals had the band learned all of the nuances, gear changes and guitar licks of Miyashita's twenty-minute songs, and now the unit had disintegrated. For several months, chaos reigned at the Nishifunabashi commune as the band held arduous drum auditions. None was deemed worthy, however, until bassist Ishikawa arrived one evening with the skinny and bespectacled longhair Manami Arai, who looked like a cross between Noel Redding and Budgie's Burke Shelley. Arai's drumming was incredibly dynamic and the ensemble knitted together within weeks. And by early autumn '72, the re-ignited Miyashita had secured a record deal with the small independent Denon label and set about recording their debut LP, to be titled NIHONJIN (Japanese).

A Child's Mitten Hangs by a Single Peg

Like the greatest '70s Krautrock bands, Far Out's debut LP offered a devastating combination of easily graspable chords and sentiments, all set into a highly unlikely ambient frame. With Miyashita's old *Hair* associate Joe Yamanaka temporarily AWOL from Flower Travellin' Band to provide his own inimitable banshee vocals, and the recently returned Osamu Kitajima playing an assortment of Japanese stringed instruments, Miyashita himself hired in a big Moog synthesiser from jazz pianist Masahiko Satoh and a Hammond organ for lead guitarist Eiichi Sayu. For the obsessive Miyashita, this was to be a recording of ritual precision, uniting Japanese thoroughness with Western modernity. And Miyashita was not about to fail …

Released in spring 1973, everything about the NIHONJIN LP was perfectly conceived and executed, comprised solely of two supremely confident side-long Miyashita songs delivered to its audience in an LP sleeve as iconically pop art as Faust copping Andy Warhol. A child's mitten hangs by a single peg from a washing line on an expansive and borderless cyan-blue background. Think of such classics as the Velvets' Banana LP, or the traffic cone on the sleeve of Kraftwerk's debut album, or La Düsseldorf's spray-painted VIVA.

The musical introduction of side one's eighteen-minute beauty 'Too Many People' emerges from its primordial synthesized soup on slow-picked acoustic guitars that plot a chord sequence straight out of the universal songwriter's handbook, whence emerged Funkadelic's 'I'll Stay', Led Zeppelin's 'Babe, I'm Gonna Leave You' and Tim Buckley's 'Pleasant Street'. Four sketchy and brittle and exquisite chords repeat over and over, as Miyashita hesitates and stutters and dwells longingly over each phrase. It's all so simple on the printed page but so desperately meaningful within its rock'n'roll that you only can feel compassion for all those self-absorbed singer/songwriters whose lyrics fly so wide of the mark. Perhaps, in order to have delivered the true depth of their alienation, they should have simply translated their songs into some foreign language and then back again.

Round and around goes the song, like that optical-illusion staircase that keeps returning us to the same point. Single low bass-guitar notes punctuate the rhythm, as leaden pumping drums introduce a lyrical and slightly out-of-tune lead guitar, which starts weak and slowly gains authority before pushing clear out of the fog into crystal blue. Then a riffing menace envelops the song that drags the whole band into a strange loping Japanese boogie raga. This featureless grind soon takes hold of the song – a slow single-note skank driven by the tom-toms of Manami Arai and the Coral electric sitar of bass player Kei Ishikawa.[2] And here on the NIHONJIN LP, Ishikawa turned into a kind of Samurai Tony Iommi, grinding and wailing his Coral axe into some whirlpool of meditative metal, as a cymbal-less leaden tom-tom rhythm free of any sonic top end drives us relentlessly onwards and inwards and never upwards. Two-thirds of the way into the piece, it comes to a dramatic and abrupt stop. The sitar picks up the descending rhythm again and an extra-unbalanced lead guitar screams from the speakers, before the song caravan trails off again across the desert, along the way picking up a following of beautiful harmony vocalists, another lead guitarist, and Joe Yamanaka's astral castrato worthy of the Moody Blues' John Lodge during IN SEARCH OF THE LOST CHORD. On side two's side-long epic title track, Eiichi Sayu reveals himself to be a lead guitarist of such confidence that he can inhabit the hoary territory of a J.J. Cale or even Hank B. Marvin without ever burning up in a conflagration of clichés. Indeed, the Far Out muse soars so unrestrainedly that we are even reminded of how exultant and beautiful that desert-guitar sound was before London's pub rock scene Hope'n'Anchored it to the ocean floor.[3] And here, Eiichi Sayu straps it back with a soaring wild rip-it-out which pushes this epic into a supremely dazed-and-confused autobahn ride. From this point, Far Out take us off into the wild blue yonder with a rumbling vocal chant and steaming guitar ride from the other side of the sky, before terminating with the glorious sound of some wading piper knee-deep in the paddy fields below Mount Fuji.

Turbulence … Personnel Differences … Far Out Family Band

Unfortunately, despite the artistic success of NIHONJIN, its considerable commercial failure once again caused Far Out to go into meltdown. Shows were cancelled when Manami Arai quit, replaced eventually by drummer Tetsuya Nishi, formerly of festival band the M. The obsessive rehearsal methods of Fumio Miyashita soon caused even this new drummer to walk, replaced by Osamu Takeda. In a sensible effort to shore up the vibe and deflect band members' somewhat justified accusations of being an overbearing leader, Miyashita renamed the ensemble Far Out Family Band, and invited organist Akira Ito to join. Unfortunately, peace and calm reigned only briefly, as Miyashita's endless reading pitched him into the world of occult theorists, conspiracy theories and the lost worlds of Atlantis and Mu. For the rest of the band – city dwellers all, and stranded miles from anywhere – this rural idyll was anything but. The singer's beliefs in lost Golden Ages, the seemingly endless rehearsals at the farm commune, all of this coupled with the chronic presence of Miyashita's parents, became too much for new drummer Osamu Takeda, who disappeared one night, taking long-time bass player Kei Ishikawa with him. When the commune members discovered, one month later, that the rhythm section had flown to Los Angeles to form their own band Kuronikuru (Chronicle),[4] the exasperated lead guitarist Eiichi Sayu also quit Far Out, leaving Miyashita entirely alone at Nishifunabashi, save for his parents, new organist Akira Ito and a few remaining *futen* women.

Jagged Time Lapse ... Name Changes ... Far East Family Band

Surveying the devastation of his parents' farm and his musical career thus far, Fumio Miyashita decided to follow a course of concentrated action. No more could he rely on Shinjuku hippies for his musical backing, the next bunch had to be professionals; no longer could he impose on his parents' goodwill, Miyashita must now re-enter the city and pursue his career with vigour and thoroughness. And no more could he simply put himself in the hands of the wider cosmos, he must demand that it accept him by thinking in vast terms. This latter course the singer implemented immediately by altering two of the Chinese characters in his name to read 'wealth' and 'substance'. Take that, ye Gods!

Throughout 1974, Miyashita and organist Akira Ito recorded high-quality demos of the singer's new songs and touted them around the Tokyo music business. Even without a band, Miyashita's determination was such that he soon found a deal with the enormous Columbia Records, whose head of A&R Teruaki Kuroda agreed to front the money for new equipment and to give Miyashita his own vanity label within the corporation. For Miyashita, this latter element was essential to the mystery that he insisted the new band must project. The singer had become infatuated with the Moody Blues' main sequence of Utopian concept LPs: IN SEARCH OF THE LOST CHORD, ON THE THRESHOLD OF A DREAM, TO OUR CHILDREN'S CHILDREN'S CHILDREN, A QUESTION OF BALANCE and EVERY GOOD BOY DESERVES FAVOUR. Released after a collective acid trip in an avalanche of visionary ideas between 1968 and '72, the Moodies had adopted their own Threshold vanity label, which Miyashita now wished to ape. He called his new label Mu Land, after the greatest mythical lost land of them all.

Slowly, Miyashita and Akira Ito assembled a highly skilled new band, now renamed Far *East* Family Band to symbolise their uniquely Japocentric worldview.

The long strung-out songs had all been ejected in favour of highly crafted melodic and cosmic ballads, chock-full of lyrical double meanings. Many of the new songs had two or even three titles, and all were inspired by the Moody Blues' Mellotron-heavy sound. The ensemble was an extraordinary sight, every one of them super-long-haired and exquisitely dressed, and seven in number. With his abrupt fringe and crimped perm, new bass player Akira Fukukusa looked for all the world like PARANOID-period Geezer Butler, while bearded lead guitarist Hirohito Fukushima had the look of a Russian mystic. On drums was Shizu Takahashi, who played with a huge Japanese Horai Dora gong behind his head, while most unique to the new band was the inclusion of the wonderfully monikered Joe USA, a Yankee flautist who doubled on sax. And helping out organist Akira Ito was another young keyboardist, Masaaki Takahashi, who went by the nickname 'Kitaro'. Born and raised in the industrial city of Nagoya, Kitaro had been a guitarist in Albatros, a failed New Rock band from his home town. Thereafter, he had bought a synthesiser and formed his own band, Zero. But now, with the financial support of Columbia, Kitaro and Akira Ito were able to summon all kinds of new and unearthly sounds from their enormous arsenal comprised of Minimoog, Mellotron 400, Korg organ, Hammond organ, Fender electric piano, and multiple analogue synthesisers.

Undiscovered Northern Lands & CHIKYU KUDO SETSU

In March 1975, Far East Family Band entered Columbia's main studio and commenced the recording of their first album. Entitled CHIKYU KUDO SETSU (Hollow Earth Theory), the record was conceived as a series of interlocking concepts, all driven by wonderful melodies and fantastic sounds from the Mellotrons, synthesisers and Joe USA's exotic Japanese flutes, *biwas*, *shamisens*, etc. Moreover, Miyashita had decided that most of the songs should bear an English title that bore little resem-blance to its Japanese equivalent, creating an ambivalent art statement that was so multi-layered as to be almost opaque. For example, the album's opening song 'Michi no Tairiku' (Unknown Landmass) was given the English title 'Undiscovered Northern Land'. Track two, 'Jidai Kara' (From the Era), was also called 'Birds Flying to the Cave Down to Earth'. Track six, 'Enshinkoku' (Country of the Smoking God), became in English 'Moving, Looking, Trying, Jumping in a Maze', while the album's sole clunker – the mawkishly sentimental 'Kidoairaku' (Delight, Anger, Sorrow, Pleasure) – became known simply as 'Four Minds'. Even the album's title CHIKYU KUDO SETSU (Hollow Earth Theory) bore an entirely different English title THE CAVE DOWN TO EARTH on its exquisitely printed and tooled sleeve. Inside the jacket, a full-colour inner depicted a magnificent sunset, whilst a separate gatefold lyric sheet showed the new ensemble standing – Pink Floyd-like – surrounded by masses of state-of-the-art instruments and amplification. On the red vertical Obi-strip used to advertise the contents, a portentous message proclaimed: 'The eternal word woven into creation with eleven keyboards. At last the road of the 21st Century is open. The eastern spirit has touched people all over the world.' On the gatefold inner, A&R director Teruaki Kuroda caught the (nowadays absurdly clichéd) Zeitgeist with sleevenotes that ran:

> There's an entrance at the North and South Pole where you can enter the earth, and there's a highly civilised society deep within this hollow earth. These are the old ones who invented UFOs. In an old document called *Takeuchi*, a vehicle called Amenoukifune (floating ships) is mentioned a number of times. This floating ship is like a sophisticated zeppelin, able to go 8,000–10,000 miles per day …

Besides the colossal sound of 'eleven keyboards' and wind accompaniment by Joe USA, Miyashita had invigorated his new shorter songs by adopting an entirely new lead-vocal method. Aping the singing style of Moody Blues keyboardist Mike Pinder on certain songs, whilst copping Moody Blues drummer Graeme Edge's spoken-word ideas on others, Miyashita also employed a call-and-answer soul-revue technique in which the band members were each given key words to sing one after the other. So thorough and so complete was Miyashita's dedication to his muse that, despite its shameless Moody Blues influences, the whole album sounded like the brand-new band that it claimed to be.

All Aboard the Klaus Schultze Express!

With considerable money now invested in Far East Family Band, Columbia Records sent the seven musicians out on a Japanese tour throughout summer 1975. In August, however, A&R director Teruaki Kuroda called Miyashita to inform him that Germany's Vertigo Records was interested in the band. Apparently, German synthesiser genius Klaus Schultze had discovered the original Far Out LP and, wishing to produce the band, had alerted friends at the label. Schultze was on tour for most of the year, but Vertigo now asked the German synthesist if he could help Miyashita to create an interim German-only album[5] by radically re-mixing most of the new record CHIKYU KUDO SETSU/THE CAVE DOWN TO EARTH (removing the laborious Easy Listening of 'Four Minds' in the process), and adding to it a re-working of the huge cosmic epic title track from Far Out's NIHONJIN. Barely one week later, Klaus Schultze and various members of the seven-piece ensemble were ensconced in Tokyo's Onkyo House Studios adding synthesisers to the re-mixed tracks and laying down the new version of 'Nihonjin' as requested. For Miyashita, this was a joyous return to his underestimated past, while recording for the rest of the band was entirely painless, as they had been performing the song nightly during the Japanese tour. In Germany, Vertigo's art director conflated together the many exotic front-cover images from CHIKYU KUDO SETSU/THE CAVE DOWN TO EARTH, and added the agreed new title NIPPONJIN, a Westernised version of the original Far Out title. Added below, for extra mystery, was the intriguing tag line 'Join Our Mental Phase Sound', for Klaus had added a whole slew of Dieter Derks-ian dub mixing to their Moody Blues sound, making NIPPONJIN sound like an epic Cosmic Jokers re-mix.

If Fumio Miyashita had found that the first ten years of his career moved at an inconceivably slow pace, the singer was sure to soon be yearning for the past when, in late '75, he found himself aboard Klaus Schultze's chain-smoking Teutonic juggernaut of one of '70s rock'n'roll's most iconoclastic hard-workers this side of Frank Zappa and Todd Rundgren. For, in the work schedule of Miyashita's new producer, every Japanese would have met their match. On a promotional tour for the NIPPONJIN Germany-only album with his new wife Linda and A&R man Teruaki Kuroda, Miyashita caught up with Klaus in Frankfurt, where the German was in the middle of a concert tour promoting his latest LP TIMEWIND. Under the impression that Far East Family Band were all in town just waiting to record, Klaus casually announced that he wouldn't be ready until the end of the month, but could they all please fly to England, where he'd already booked time in the Manor Studios, owned by Virgin Records, with whom Klaus had just struck his own deal. Looking green around the gills, Miyashita smiled dryly and confided in his A&R man that they needed another four months to get the songs ready. Grinning and chain-smoking, the effusive German let it be known that by that time he'd have encircled the world several times, orchestrated a double-LP and invented three new synthesisers. But he'd see them in Good Old Blighty in six weeks if they could get it together ... Er, Look Out!

The Recording of PARALLEL WORLD

And thus, on a pissy 14th November 1975, buoyed up by incredibly high expectations, six members of Far East Family Band and their partners entered Virgin Records' already legendary studios, at Shipton-on-Cherwell Manor, just east of Woodstock, in the verdant Oxfordshire countryside. Unfortunately, due to the ludicrously strict regulations enforced by Britain's Musicians' Union, poor Joe USA had been unable to secure a work permit in time. For the six Japanese band members, however, the recording could only be a thrill ride of epic proportions. For, although barely three years into its existence, 'The Manor' had already entered Japan's progressive rock folklore as the birthplace of Mike Oldfield's TUBULAR BELLS, and Fumio was almost overwhelmed to be following in the footsteps of personal favourites such as Faust, Gong and Slapp Happy. With almost thirty rooms to choose from, Far East Family Band's entourage spread out around the main house and got stoned down at the lake while Fumio and Linda Miyashita scanned the new material to see if enough had been prepared. Feeling under pressure from the Frankfurt encounter, Miyashita had asked his wife to contribute lyrics to the new record. Downstairs, Klaus Schultze, accompanied by guitar maestro Gunther Schickert,[6] decided where to set up Shizu Takahashi's drums. Thereafter, Klaus, Kitaro and Akira Ito set up their huge arsenal of analogue synthesisers in an antechamber next to the control room, including a VCS3 and two ARP 2600s that the producer had shipped over from Berlin.

Throughout the first week, the band worked exclusively on Fumio and Linda Miyashita's new songs, laying down tracks long into the early hours and surfacing only in the late morning. By the second week, however, the musicians were feeling so confident around Klaus Schultze that they readily agreed to his suggestions of creating music out of the moment, and Miyashita felt considerable pressure lifting off him as the band followed their German producer's directions taking them into genuinely unknown territory.

Klaus grew particularly close to drummer Shizu Takahashi and synthesists Akira Ito and Kitaro, both of whom were now encouraged by their German producer to dump chords in favour of a more *kosmische* approach. Indeed, by the second week, Far East Family Band were approaching the kind of thunderous percussion and synthesiser meltdown rarely achieved outside Germany, and in particular by music informed by Klaus Schultze! Like a melding-together of the Cosmic Jokers, the first Funkadelic album, Agitation Free's LAST-period 26-minute 'Looping' and much of Klaus Schultze's own work of the same period, the Japanese ensemble had – with the help of their German mentor – deployed their electronic arsenal with such effortless aplomb that each new track eclipsed their previous work, conspiring to create a wholly original work. Virtually without vocals, PARALLEL WORLD occupied the kind of vast and eternal *kosmische* space that only the greatest Krautrock albums had thus far commanded. Whatever crazy titles Miyashita would at a later date decide to impose on these tracks, Klaus had created one seamless and ever unfolding earth-shaking, occasionally skanking masterpiece. Indeed, by the end of the third week, both band and producer were convinced that they had a classic double-album on their hands. Moreover, staff at the Manor Studios had alerted Virgin Records' company people, who were considering signing the band for the UK. With just one typical Miyashita composition on the whole album, the rest of the band – especially the drummer and synthesists – considered PARALLEL WORLD to be their own work, and understandably now expected writing credits as the staff at Tokyo's Columbia offices anticipated that the record could go stellar.

Disaster ... Haemorrhages ... Kitaro Goes Stellar Alone

Unfortunately for Far East Family Band, nothing but chaos ensued. Sensing that Klaus Schultze would insist on PARALLEL WORLD's being a double-LP, Virgin Records pulled out of the deal entirely, sending such negative vibes to the Japanese company that they too got cold feet. In order to fit on to one vinyl disc, Klaus was now forced to edit twenty minutes from the final album, reducing it to sixty minutes in length – still as long as the Rolling Stones' double-LP EXILE ON MAIN STREET. In Tokyo, the LP was released in a magnificent sleeve, with a massive two-sided poster that depicted the band aboard a Viking ship, Fumio Miyashita straddling the prow. Unfortunately, after the previously ecstatic songs and sounds of CHIKYU KUDO SETSU/THE CAVE DOWN TO EARTH, the band's move into such a heavy underground sound almost totally free of melodies or even of guitars was too much for Japanese fans, who rejected it completely. What had sounded complete and righteous in the English landscape meant nothing to the people who'd expected more Moody Blues and Pink Floyd. And so, right after delivering their most astonishing and forward-thinking work, Far East Family Band were dropped altogether by Columbia.

For those three musicians most involved in the recording, the rejection was too much. Drummer Shizu Takahashi and synthesists Akira Ito and Kitaro immediately quit, causing the Miyashitas and their two remaining shell-shocked cohorts – bass player Akira Fukukusa and guitarist Hirohito Fukushima – to flee to America with Mickey Curtis's drummer Yujin Harada. In Los Angeles, the shattered quartet attempted to carry on without record-company support, as synthesist Kitaro returned to Japan, where he was invited by Dr Acid Seven to move into a commune run by the guru in the village of Asaka in the mountainous region of Shinshu, near Tokyo. Urged on by Acid Seven and inspired by Klaus Schultze's solo success, Kitaro recorded his own music with the financial help of the local director of NHK Shinshu. Soon after, Kitaro commenced a Grammy Award-winning solo career that would see his bland New Age music embraced by millions.

The Final Ignominy ... the Craft Descends ... Disintegrates

In Los Angeles, however, all was gloom and despondency. No major label was interested in the band, and the musicians were forced to make a deal with a wealthy English progressive rock fan named Anthony Harrington, who ran his own independent record label and idolised Genesis. Harrington had styled his company All Ears after the English band's progressive label Charisma, even the company logo being a poor Charisma copy featuring a cartoon white rabbit from Lewis Carroll's *Alice's Adventures in Wonderland*. Pumping money into the band was no problem for Harrington, but Miyashita's muse had entirely evaporated. And so, over the coming months, the depleted Far East Family Band slowly recorded a new album of limp material co-written by the band with lyrics mainly by Linda Miyashita. In the summer of 1977, the band released their final record TENKUJIN (Heavenly Being) on the All Ears label, complete with cover art by Genesis artist Paul Whitehead, whom Anthony Harrington had commissioned at great expense. Despite opening with the ultra-brief Krautrock-styled 'Descension', which sounded like Neu's Michael Rother in his Harmonia incarnation, the rest of this appallingly sentimental record saw Miyashita return to the safety of his Moody Blues sound, Mike Pinder vocals'n'all. Moreover, as the record cover looked like the natural follow-up to Genesis' NURSERY CRYME and 251 FOXTROT albums, the confusing TENKUJIN simply slipped beneath everyone's radar and the band promptly disintegrated.

Remaining in Los Angeles for the next few years, Fumio Miyashita studied acupuncture, Eastern medicine, philosophy and esoteric theory, even recording a funk-styled solo LP DIGITAL CITY in June 1981. After its inevitable failure, however, Fumio and Linda Miyashita returned to the Iizuna Highlands of Japan, where the songwriter embarked on a hugely successful career making 'Healing Music', a New Age ambient-style pulse music for sleep and meditation. His book *The Healing Life* was accompanied by ambient concerts at Shinto shrines, and Miyashita remained highly successful until his death from respiratory failure in August 2004. Inevitably, Miyashita's failure discoloured his memories of Far East Family Band's achievements, especially in the light of his subsequent success. From sniffing paint thinner to creating Shinto temple meditations is not such a great jump for those truly seeking transformation. And it can only be hoped that, in the coming years, Far East Family Band – and PARALLEL WORLD particularly – begin to gain the plaudits they so clearly deserve.

Footnotes:

1   The Justin Heathcliff project released one LP and was Kitajima's successful attempt to cop the kind of English post-REVOLVER psychedelia that such London bands as the Syn, Mike Stuart Span, and the Flies were recording in 1967–68. Considering the record was recorded in London by a former GS guitarist with a fixation for traditional Japanese instruments, its sound is highly believable.

2   I pay particular attention to the make of the sitar because this was no gourd-shaped acoustic Indian instrument, but a fully fledged solid-bodied rock axe fashioned out of Burgundy vinyl-covered masonite aka hardboard by the American Danelectro company. Found on many of the greatest '60s pop-psychedelic raga moments, it's impossible to play this thing like Ravi Shankar and cohorts.

3   Praise must be inserted here for the current so-called 'desert generator' bands Yawning Man and Ten East, whose epic re-assessment of Hank B. Marvin and his ilk has created a new stoner-rock-meets-post-punk take on the surf instrumental. Slowing the rhythms down considerably and throwing in dark bass notes has resulted in classic current LPs such as Yawning Man's ROCK FORMATIONS (Alone 2005) and POT HEAD (Alone 2005).

4   Although based in Los Angeles, Chronicle was comprised entirely of Japanese members, guitarist Nobuo Hatchi and organist Kenji Mishiro completing the line-up. After limited success in the USA, including 1975's LIVE AT WHISKY A GO-GO, Keiju Ishikawa returned to a Japanese career of songwriting and cartoon theme tunes.

5   The re-recording of Far Out's epic 'Nihonjin' for the German-only LP meant that two songs, 'Four Minds' and 'Rebirth' (Transmigration), from THE CAVE DOWN TO EARTH had to be omitted. Although created specifically for the German market, NIPPONJIN also gained release in Italy and New Zealand.

6   Although credited only as engineer on PARALLEL WORLD, Gunther Schickert's echoed guitar work with the experimental power trio GAM was incredible, as was his 1975 Brain Records solo LP SAMTVOGEL.

Discography
NIHONJIN (Denon 1973)
THE CAVE DOWN TO EARTH (Columbia/Mu Land 1975)
NIPPONJIN (Vertigo 1975)
PARALLEL WORLD (Columbia/Mu Land 1976)
TENKUJIN (All Ears 1977)

AUTHOR'S TOP 50

The music contained within this Top 50 consists of hard rock, proto-metal, purely psychedelic free-rock, experimental theatre works, choral and orchestral music, experimental percussion works, improvised ambient wipe-outs, progressive rock, and unadulterated guitar mayhem. However, I have chosen to place the albums in order of personal preference because certain readers of my *Krautrocksampler* pointed out that this would be an easier way into the trip. That said, it's essential to read more than just these reviews so as to gain a genuine perspective. Almost every artist mentioned in these reviews receives attention somewhere in the main text, so this Top 50 is included as an at-a-glance reference section.

Ta, mein hairies, JULIAN.

ベスト **TOP 50** 50

=1	**Flower Travellin' Band**	SATORI
=1	**Speed, Glue & Shinki**	EVE
3	**Les Rallizes Denudés**	HEAVIER THAN A DEATH IN THE FAMILY
4	**Far East Family Band**	PARALLEL WORLD
5	**J.A. Caesar**	KOKKYOU JUNREIKA
6	**Love Live Life +1**	LOVE WILL MAKE A BETTER YOU
7	**Masahiko Satoh & Soundbreakers**	AMALGAMATION
8	**Geino Yamashirogumi**	OSOREZAN
9	**Takehisa Kosugi**	CATCH-WAVE
10	**J.A. Caesar**	JASUMON
11	**Far Out**	NIHONJIN
12	**Les Rallizes Denudés**	BLIND BABY HAS ITS MOTHERS EYES
13	**Tokyo Kid Brothers**	THROW AWAY THE BOOKS, WE'RE GOING OUT IN THE STREETS
14	**Far East Family Band**	NIPPONJIN
15	**Speed, Glue & Shinki**	SPEED, GLUE & SHINKI
16	**People**	CEREMONY – BUDDHA MEETS ROCK
17	**Blues Creation**	DEMON & ELEVEN CHILDREN
18	**Flower Travellin' Band**	MADE IN JAPAN
19	**Karuna Khyal**	ALOMONI 1985
20	**Les Rallizes Denudés**	FLIGHTLESS BIRD (YODO-GO-A-GO-GO)
21	**Masahiko Satoh & New Herd Orchestra**	YAMATAI-FU
22	**Magical Power Mako**	MAGICAL POWER MAKO
23	**Taj Mahal Travellers**	LIVE STOCKHOLM JULY, 1971
24	**Magical Power Mako**	JUMP
25	**Kuni Kawachi & Friends**	KIRIKYOGEN

=1
Flower Travellin' Band
SATORI
(Atlantic 1971)

In which Yuya Utchida's naked biker boys came of age and then some. For SATORI is one of the all-time great hard-rock rages to have been unleashed upon the world, a festival of guitar worship led by axe-wielding maniac Hideki Ishima, who Jeff Becked and Jimmy Paged a number of archetypal Tony Iommisms, interlacing each Satanic riff with a more dazzling stellar lick, and invigorating every troll-like subbasement grunt with a bazillion squirly Hindu sitar figures. The magical results were regally exultant and wantonly barbaric simultaneously, yet so musically complete that they rendered vocalist Joe all but obsolete for the entire duration of the album and did away with the need for song titles entirely. So, following occult heavy rocker J.D. Blackfoot's 1970 LP THE ULTIMATE PROPHECY, which named its tracks 'Song I', 'Song II', etc., Flower also opted for this futuristic approach, naming each track 'Satori I' through to 'Satori V'. During the record's early-twenty-first-century re-evaluation, this apparently experimental and avant-garde 'nameless songs' approach has only lent further authority to SATORI's kudos and mystery, for it has added a gloss of intellectual mystique to this already highly authoritative record. Although this was Flower's second album, it was the first with Atlantic Records visionary Ikuzo Orita's money and production skills behind it. The sound was sensational and the playing superb, high above the Japanese standard of the day and infinitely beyond Flower's feet-of-clay label-mates Speed, Glue & Shinki. Indeed, so out on a limb was SATORI that it still defies true comparison with other records. They just haven't really been recorded yet.

=1
Speed, Glue & Shinki
EVE
(Atlantic 1971)

Blues-based funereal dirges about scoring amphetamines ('Mr Walking Drugstore Man'), paranoid sludge-trudge proto-metal anthems about taking drugs to avoid straight people ('Stoned out of My Mind'), cuckolded dead marches to cheating women with invitations to them to commit suicide ('Big Headed Woman'): welcome to the world of Speed, Glue & Shinki. Even before Atlantic had unleashed this astonishingly raw debut LP on to an unsuspecting public in 1971, guitarist Shinki Chen was already touted as Japan's answer to Jimi Hendrix (he wasn't) and the gorgeous Franco-Japanese heart-throb Masayoshi Kabe was adored by thousands of GS fans as Louis Louis of the Golden Cups. Bandleader, songwriter and singing drummer Joey 'Pepe' Smith was something else again, however, for this six-foot-two Filipino had an out-of-control amphetamine habit and a need to tell everybody about it. Imagine the Move's ultra-slow pre-glam single 'Brontosaurus' as a blueprint for an entire career, and you have this bunch of ne'er-do-wells in your sights. Add ominous atonal sub-sub-Tony Visconti basslines and sub-sub-Bill Ward bibles-thrown-at-the-sofa drumfills, and you've hit their pleasure centre head-on. Songs came courtesy of the singing drummer, and if his lyrics are killer, then his asides are even more masterfully snotty ('Do yourself in', 'she smokes all of my dope', 'You can get love if you want it, baby, but you can never get it from me'). Let's conclude this review with bass player Masayoshi 'Glue' Kabe's current thoughts on his old band: 'We were loose … Joey would break the drums and stuff … Even when I listen to it now, I think, "What a great band." Crude, too.'

257

3
Les Rallizes Denudés
HEAVIER
THAN A DEATH
IN THE FAMILY
(Ain't Group Sounds 1995)

Has a one-way trip into the Heart of Darkness ever been made on a more handsome jalopy? For those of you who love their rock'n'roll mayhem to be grounded in traditional chord sequences à la Electric Eels and the mid-'70s Cleveland bands, here Mizutani's channelling both Lou Reed *and* Leigh Stephens. Side one is just the massively hooky 'Strong out Deeper Than the Night', a fifteen-minute plod that slows down Booker T's 'Green Onions' to funeral pace. 'The Night Collectors' opens side two like eight minutes of La Düsseldorf in a wind tunnel, as Mizutani's axe envelops us in a sonic Niagara Falls. 'Night of the Assassins' is Little Peggy March's 'I Will Follow Him' surfing to Hell down a giant scree-slope. Side three commences with the slow drone of 'Enter the Mirror', two Velvets chords and the bass player still gets it wrong, eventually coming back to the root note by way of a detour through musical back gardens and alleys. Side three concludes with the breathtaking beauty of 'People Can Choose', an I-musta-heard-this-before ten minutes of splashy cymbals, climbing-the-walls basslines, and on-off torrential guitar torment. Side four's sixteen minutes of 'Ice Fire' is almost Flipper's epic 'Sex Bomb (My Baby Yeah)' – muscular as Joy Division's 'Wilderness', but scrawled over in thick permanent marker by Mizutani's festival of distortion. It's relentless to the point of becoming meditative, and cylindrical to the point of being useful … I wanna be *that* bass player and stand in *that* wind tunnel, anchoring *that* level of rage.

4
Far East Family Band
PARALLEL WORLD
(Columbia/Mu Land 1976)

This righteous *kosmische* union of Japanese commune band and legendary Krautrock producer yielded two sides of extraordinary meditative space rock, setting it apart from almost all other Japrock. Indeed, only Speed, Glue's side-long Moog suite and M. Satoh's YAMATAI-FU approach this unworldly beast. Recorded at the height of K. Schultze's powers, between his own TIMEWIND and MOONDAWN, and hot on the heels of BLACKDANCE, the LP sees the producer arrange the twin synthesisers of Akira Ito and Kitaro around Shizu Takahashi's drums, pushing guitars, bass and voices to the horizon. Like the so-called Keltic languages, Japanese often cloaks its meanings in ambiguity and none more so than in this work. Acting as a smokescreen for two seamless thirty-minute sides of music, the many titles contain multiple meanings and intentional ambiguities to further mystify listeners. The opening track 'Saisei' (Rebirth) takes the English title 'Metempsychosis', while 'Sei no Kakucho' (Expansion of Life) becomes simply 'Entering', and 'Jikukan no Kozui' (Flood of Time & Space) becomes 'Times'. Side one closes with the unambiguous 'Kokoro' (Heart). On side two, 'Tagenuchu eno Tabi' (The Trip to the Parallel World) becomes PARALLEL WORLD's title track, and 'Amanescan no Yoake' (The Dawn of Amanezcan) is rendered in English simply as 'Amanezcan'. Although the beautifully poetic 'Yomigaeru Kishiten' (The Point of Origin Reborn) is reduced simply to 'Origin', 'Zen' is a direct translation. Somehow, 'Muso no Shinri' (Reverie) migrates into 'Reality', while the two final tracks 'Kikosen' (New Lights) and 'Seireki 2000 Nen' (In the Year 2000) contain no ambiguities. By journey's end, so-called reality appears somewhat raw to the cushioned and cocooned listener.

5
J.A. Caesar
KOKKYOU JUNREIKA
(Victor 1973)

Anyone searching out a single J.A. Caesar record for their library should aim for this album, for its shrewd editing and powerful tracklisting put it head-and-shoulders above the rest. Caesar was forced by Victor Records to include only the most obvious excerpts, culled from the five-hour original play, in order to reduce the work to a single vinyl LP. In so doing, the composer unintentionally created a 'greatest hits' compilation for us, as classic track follows classic track. In 2002, the re-issue label P-Vine created an exact replica of the 1973 edition on Victor (even the orange label copied the original) and KOKKYOU JUNREIKA was officially re-issued in an edition of 500 copies with four pages of liner notes and Obi-strip. It's to be hoped that further editions will be forthcoming, for the album certainly works best on vinyl. While side one contains six excellent tracks in a kind of proto-metal/garage-rock style, the three hugely mysterious and long songs of side two are up there with any of the greatest *kosmische*-styled Krautrock – early Ash Ra Tempel, Cosmic Jokers, Agitation Free and ATEM-period Tangerine Dream, most especially. Throughout the proceedings, J.A. Caesar's droning electric organ hangs like a curtain of mist across a Welsh v-shaped valley, while the eerie female vocals of singers Yoko Ran, Keiko Shinko and Seigo Showa add a Norn-like mountain mystery even to the most brutal of side one's vicious hard-rock onslaughts. Behind the intentionally off-putting titles (eg: 'Jinriki-hikoki no Tame no Entetsu Soan' (Public Speech for the sake of pedal-powered aircraft), anyone?) is an all-time classic rock'n'roll album.

6
Love Live Life +1
LOVE WILL MAKE A BETTER YOU
(King 1971)

Commencing with singer Akira Fuse's goggle-eyed one-day-old-baby innocence, Love Live Life +1's album opener 'The Question Mark' escorts us through an eighteen-minute free-rock R&B adventure like nothing before or since. Clanking harsher than even the title track of Funkadelic's FREE YOUR MIND & YOUR ASS WILL FOLLOW, and twice as long; cosmic as the Cosmic Jokers' GALACTIC SUPERMARKET, and gnarly as John McLaughlin's out-there-a-minute axe excursions on Miles's 'Right Off' or his own DEVOTION solo LP, do these guys fight for their right to party! The mellower second side includes the insanely brilliant eight-minute epic 'Shadows of My Mind', in which Akira Fuse sings like some drunken Italian baritone, while atonal swooping strings and crazy brass support/undermine him; then it's off into a juggernaut bass-heavy clatterthon with duel-axe outrage of the highest level. And how about that title track whose catchy bastard licks unashamedly rip Sly's 'I Wanna Take You Higher', but still have you singing along with Fuse? The record closes brilliantly with the demented 'Facts about It All', which opens like Fuse laying a grunting 6/8 James Brown/Eric Burdon ballad on us. But no, this miniature R&B opera says in 2 minutes and 56 seconds what prog bands took a whole side to say. All hail visionary genius Ikuzo Orita for uniting his fave guitarist Kimio Mizutani with the errant free-jazz Gibson 335 of Takao Naoi, whose brittle spittle pops permanent wheelies around these slippery rhythm tracks. Also hail Orita for recognising the genius of these songs of sax player Kei Ichihara, for trusting Akira Fuse's professionalism and open-mindedness, and for seeing this 33-minute-long classic to its unlikely conclusion.

7
Masahiko Satoh & Soundbreakers
AMALGAMATION
(Liberty/Toshiba 1971)

This preposterous piece of psychedelic avant-jazz sounds like the work of aliens, each with only one foot in our universe. Propelled by cacophonous brassy blasts, volleys of machine-gunning, ecstatically 'Light Fantastic' rhythms and moments of Teo Macero-style 'Mixing Concrète' (during which the whole track becomes consumed by waves of new sound); the result is the most singular mash-up of inappropriate sounds any listener is ever likely to hear. Over two side-long tracks, shaman Masahiko Satoh sends us through a sonic mind-field, baffling our senses *and* our sense of gravity. Located at the centre of AMALGAMATION's giddy sessions was the frantic Detroit drumming of hard-bop legend Louis Hayes, whose role it was to play the bubbling ever unfolding fundament on which Masahiko Satoh's whole trip proceeded, as though the rhythm section were a magic carpet constantly being pulled out from under the feet of the other performers. Over this rhythmic shaking, Satoh scattered Hammond organ around and ring-modulated* his Fender Rhodes piano solos (*Roland built three especially for the record), added lead guitar from 'super session' legend Kimio Mizutani, trumpets and sax from Mototeru Takagi, scat singing from Kayoko Itoh, and strings from the Wehnne Strings Consort. As if to further disorientate us, the composer divided the single fifteen-minute track of side one into ten absurd titles (eg 'The Atomic Bomb Was Not Follen' [sic], 'All Quite on the Western Front' [sic]), and the single twenty-one minutes of side two similarly ('Hear Me Talking to Ya', 'Ancient Tales of Days to Come'), though both tracks are intended as single pieces, being encoded thus on CD re-issues. Essential stuff.

8
Geino Yamashirogumi
OSOREZAN
(Invitation 1976)

Commencing with the greatest scream of any rock'n'roll record ever, this transcendental debut by Geino Yamashirogumi (Yamashiro's Performing Arts Group) inhabits its own space like no other. Recorded in Tokyo, at Victor Records' enormous Studio Number One, the LP is comprised of two side-long pieces of ritual chanting and theatre music in the J.A. Caesar tradition. Side one's title track celebrates the sacred northern mountain Osorezan, said to be the haunt of ancient ancestors and historically infamous as the place where the old were left to die. 'Osorezan' was performed by seventy singers accompanied by a highly authoritative and psychedelic band (including two ex-Spiders), something like the Flowers' side-long epic 'I'm Dead'. There was in Japan no previous precedent for such transcendental music, and 'Osorezan''s unfathomable beauty should be compared to a highly extended Doors-influenced theatre piece, incorporating elements of Dr John during his Night Tripper phase, Carl Orff's ecstatic chorale *Carmina Burana* and Japan's own chanting oddities Karuna Khyal and Brast Burn. Side two's 'Do No Kenbai' (Copper Sword Dance) continues the intrigue but at much-reduced wattage, being performed entirely a cappella by only thirty performers. This piece occupies much the same space as the Residents' bizarre LP ESKIMO. However, being unaccompanied by electric instruments, it lacks that same 'Amphetamine up the psychic jacksie' that renders the title track so great. Unfortunately, as the 'Osorezan' title track is one of rock'n'roll's highest ever achievements, its greatness eclipsed all of the ensemble's future releases. The ensemble was assembled, named and led by arranger Shoji Yamashiro, who co-wrote both pieces with composer Chumei 'Light Universe' Watanabe.

9
Takehisa Kosugi
CATCH-WAVE
(CBS/Sony 1975)

Clad in a super-appropriate sub-Bridget Riley Op-art sleeve and comprised of two side-long compositions, 'Mano Dharma '74' and 'Wave Code #e-1', this is Kosugi's most immediate and essential work ever. An all-time *kosmische* drone classic, its stratospheric violin and wah-mouth explorations are guaranteed to make moonwalkers out of fans of Tony Conrad's OUTSIDE THE DREAM SYNDICATE, Klaus Schultze's IRRLICHT, CYBORG or BLACK-DANCE's 'Some Velvet Phasing', my own 73-minute-long 'Breath of Odin' or even Hi T. Moon-weed's 'A Sprinkling of Clouds' (yeah, I know). The twenty-six minutes of side one sound like primary-school Clangers making faces at commuter Clangers from out of the school-bus window in the traffic jam from Hell. Side two's 'triple performance by a solo vocalist' returns to the same territory as Joji Yuasa's very early '60s work, most especially his 1961 Noh Theatre epic 'Aoi No Ue'. However, instead of employing Noh actors like Yuasa chose to do, Kosugi here just turns the echo machine back on itself and becomes the Four Tops of the Underworld. As Iskra Records gave this a limited vinyl release a few years back, there's always hope that it's about to make a return to the shelves. If so, search out the vinyl if only to catch such back-sleeve proclamations as 'The Deaf Listen To Sounds Touching Watching ... The Blind Watch Sight Listening Smelling' and 'Sounds Speeding On Lights, Lights Speeding On Sounds, Music Between Riddles & Solutions'. Yowzah! Finally, be sure to avoid Kosugi's god-awful improvisational VIOLIN SOLO 1980 at any cost, because its epileptic bucking bronco-isms suck beyond the call of duty.

10
J.A. Caesar
JASUMON
(Victor 1972)

This mighty soundtrack for Shuji Terayama's nihilistic movie of the same name contains all of the elements necessary to reach J.A. Caesar's intended pleasure centres. Here, turmoil, mind-numbing repetition, abject misery and grisly patriarchs abound, and all orchestrated by Caesar's damaged proto-metal and choral-led psychedelic sound. Mind-manifesting in the truest sense, this soundtrack played in the dark is as certified a Gateway to the Underworld as any acknowledged classic by Faust, Magma, the Cosmic Jokers, Ash Ra Tempel or early Amon Düül. Playwright Terayama populates his play with crucified crazy women, enormous-nosed titans living in the foothills of legendary mountains, sparrow torturers and a Zorro-styled revenge-seeking Samurai named Kurama Tengu. However, his genius is equalled by Caesar's canny ability to access the Weird by all and any means; traditional song, easy listening, stupefying musical clumsiness, hoary rock cliché, everything is an ingredient here to be subsumed into the composer's end dish. And it's a concoction best served up hot, and with time on your hands. Nineteen songs with multiple meanings and such opaque titles such as 'Tsuru no Tema' (The Crane's Theme), 'Shishi no ko' (The Lion's Child) and 'Kanoke Buro' (Coughing Bath) (see Book Two, Chapter Ten for more) are split over seven equally strangely monikered phases. Twice, following particularly ecstatic musical broadsides, calm descends long enough for Kan Mikami's solo guitar and ragingly insulting mouth to throw us all into the nearest pond. Finally, the whole chaotic mess concludes with 'Wasan', a Buddhist hymn sung in Japanese to a modern trendy melody so that people can understand the teaching more easily. It figures.

11
Far Out
NIHONJIN
(Denon 1973)

Arriving in a flurry of analogue heartbeats and echo chambers, formless monophonic Moog synthesisers and microphone feedback, Far Out's 1973 album is an alien and exquisitely beautiful music embodying all the greatest aspects of rock'n'roll at once. Herein, there are rhythms with which to brain yourself, howling banshee vocals, melancholy tunes, dive-bombing seagull guitars, overly hopeful Utopian lyrics, and harmonies to live for. This, their sole LP before transforming into monstrous ensemble Far East Family Band, was a place where tradition and novelty sat together side by side; a place where cheesy melody and hoary chord sequences rubbed shoulders with shockingly unbalanced sonic gimmicks. Side one's 'Too Many People' is an acoustic ritual performed in a gargantuan Cretan antron, stopping, re-starting, lurching and s-s-shaking. The whole effect creates a sense of total mystery and awe, as though we've eavesdropped on some long-planned pilgrimage and found ourselves along for the ride. Although side two begins in another rhythm-less flurry – this time full of gongs and reverbed guitars, sitars and tom-toms – the music contains vibrant Krautrock power drives and intense guitar displays. This is the mighty twenty minutes of 'Nihonjin', which Far Out would later record for their first German Far East Family Band LP. There it was to evolve into a masterwork of layered Mellotrons, twin monosynths and mucho choirs. But here in 1973, that reverbed soup of an introduction soon evaporates to reveal a dry frame of melancholy minor chords and more lyrics of tragedy and loss. It's truly one of those rare pieces that confounds listeners with its musical obviousness yet sparklingly emotional freshness.

12
Les Rallizes Denudés
BLIND BABY
HAS ITS MOTHERS
EYES
(Japanese Rock 2003)

Massive slabs of distortion inhabit every seam of this monstrously linear album. The bass lines are uber-monolithic, in places dropping away in a dubby style that leaves the top end teetering like a tiny boat waiting to be swallowed by a whirlpool. The lead guitar seems even more extravagantly committed to tinnitus oblivion than ever, Mizutani having intentionally ditched the between rhythms played by hi-hats and chugging guitars in a desire to bring a post-apocalyptical featurelessness to his muse. Despite the horrendous amp buzz, there's just enough instrument separation to suggest these were studio takes and that the buzz was explicitly sought after. Mizutani is known to have played shorter live versions of these tracks during the early '80s, also at studio sessions during the mid-to-late '80s. The juggernaut opening title track is a heavily re-worked '80s version of their epic 'Flames of Ice', which appeared on several albums before this one. That this version is borne along by an entirely different bass line, and features different lyrics delivered with an entirely different melody and method of delivery, should come as no surprise to us. Track two is a suppressed monster called 'An Aweful Eternitie' aka 'Zankoko Na Ai' (Cruel Love) aka 'Koi Monogatari' (Tale of Love), a remote and mysterious thing without highs or lows, its rambling meditation in no hurry to reach its destination. This version first appeared on a 10CD box set STUDIO & SOUNDBOARD 1979–1986, and is said to have been recorded in April 1986. Typically, 'The Last One' concludes the record, here a taut-wired high-energy seventeen-minute version.

13
Tokyo Kid Brothers
THROW AWAY
THE BOOKS,
WE'RE GOING OUT
IN THE STREETS
(Victor 1971)

Sounding as thrilling and berserk as J.A. Caesar in full flight, this amazing interpretation of Shuji Terayama's 'city play' is by far and away this ensemble's finest hour. The psychedelic guitar riffs are said to be the work of Flower Travellin' Band's Hideki Ishima, the stock chatter, the screaming, and the chorale all supporting rumours that Caesar himself was involved. Only the movie version betters this ecstatic performance. Formed in 1968 by former Tenjo Sajiki member Yutaka Higashi, the company was initially known as Kiddo Kyodai Shokai ('Kid Brother Company'), as Higashi had chosen the eight other members from students at his old high school. In 1969, they opened a stage shop in Shibuya called 'Hair', and performed their next work 'Tokyo Kid' in July 1969. In early spring 1970, *Hair*'s producer was so impressed by their new *Golden Bat* production that he considered paying for them to perform in New York. When this fell through, they decided to pay their own way and became Tokyo Kid Brothers to clarify their background to the American market. Apart from this album, few Tokyo Kid Brothers works are essential, many being actual mainstream musicals. A 6CD box released by P-Vine Records a few years ago collected together material from Victor, Polydor, Warner Pioneer and Toshiba EMI Records. Originally released between 1971 and '77, this highly mixed bag was of variable quality; some of it was so downright bland that prospective buyers of this lot should ensure they hear albums before buying anything from the huge back catalogue.

14
Far East Family Band
NIPPONJIN
(Vertigo 1975)

Ey-up, it's the Cosmic Jokers … Oops, silly me, Klaus Schultze has been at the mix again and turned Far East Family Band's Moody Blues fixation into a *kosmische* classic. Always utterly devoid of any sense of proportion and sonic balance, Klaus transformed the band's merely excellent second album into an entirely new beast, replete with fangs, fiery tongue and sixty-metre tail. Not content with goading bandleader Fumio Miyashita into entirely re-recording Far Out's monstrous debut-LP title track from 1973, Klaus then commandeered the master tapes of their latest epic and barfed VCS3 and ARP 2600 synthesisers all over the already synthesiser-heavy sound. *Ja, mein* hairy! Next, he craftily sodded off the vocal-heavy songs and brought everything up louder than everything else. Mellotrons deliver warm choirs of angels and ice-rink orchestras throughout, while the immaculately named Joe USA provides just enough panpipes to stop Mike Pinder suing them, but not enough (mercifully) to get them played as background music in the local patchouli shop. Finally, Klaus smoked enough green to out-dub Dennis Bovelle and kicked Dieter Derks' dick into the dirt with this all-time phase-o-thon. Best of all, at the present time (December 2006), everybody thinks Far East Family Band does what it says on the tin: ie, too Eastern, too familiar, too prog to be worth taking a risk on. So, like NEU! '75 a decade ago, it's still possible to pick these vinyl gems up for a tenner. Race to eBay and make sure you don't fall for the late-night drunken 'Buy It Now' at over-inflated price. So, er … Look Out!

263

15
Speed, Glue & Shinki
SPEED, GLUE & SHINKI
(Atlantic 1972)

Sagging under the weight of Joey Smith's howling, lupine genius and loopy extended metaphors, it's hard to imagine this self-titled double-LP barrage was created by a disintegrating band just twelve months into their career, but it's true. Determined to kiss off this power trio in style, Brother Joey demanded his own EXILE … and brought in a Moog synthesiser and old friend Mike Hanopol to shore up the gaps left by departing itinerant bassist Masayoshi 'Glue' Kabe. Unlike self-doubting heavies such as Mountain, Bang, Dust, Warpig, Cactus, Bloodrock, Boomerang, Captain Beyond or even our beloved Sir Lord Baltimore, Joey was far too smart to feel the need to prove he had his own vocabulary. His art was the evidence; this double-LP high art. The excellent results included the finest cartoon drug lyric ever ('Sniffin' & Snortin'), the best non-MC5 Utopian battle-cry ever ('Run & Hide'), and the most presumptuous-yet-wholly-successful bit of metaphor-jumping ever (side four's Moog-only instrumental suite 'Sun, Planets, Life, Moon', which this power trio shamelessly performed in the style of T. Dream's ZEIT). Yowzah! Even better, guest bassist Mike Hanopol managed to cop as many song credits (nine!) as leader Joey. Good job, too, as Shinki Chen's two contributions were pitiful sub-Peter Criss twaddle. The album package, created by Taj Mahal Travellers' Michihiro Kimura, arrived in two highly glossy single yellow jackets screen-printed with tigers, enfolded in heavy printed brown paper outers, and replete with three lyric sheets. What a way to go, ay? Thereafter, Joey and friend Hanopol flew south to Manila, where they became Filipino superstars and remain so to this day.

16
People
CEREMONY –
BUDDHA MEETS ROCK
(Teichiku 1971)

Released in answer to Ikuzo Orita's superb 'Polydor Super Session' series of LPs, this riposte/rip-off, written by Buddhist poet/songwriter Naoki Tachikawa and organised by Teichiku Records' A&R director Hideki Sakamoto, challenged every one of Orita's projects and beat most of them cold simply by working through Orita's own blueprint line by line. People even deployed the arsenal of Orita's own guitar star, ex-Out Cast hired gun Kimio Mizutani, whose subtle licks inform the entire work. Mizutani shines brightest on side one's twelve-minute drone chant 'Shomyo Part One', but the bluesy bell tone of 'Shomyo Part Two' is pure and exquisite cosmic monotony, as is that employed on 'Flower Strewing', which elevates the track right out of authentic religious bore into a Funkadelic Deadmarch. On the five-minute wa-funk of 'Gatha', the apparently egoless Mizutani conjures up a typical Hideki Ishema-style axe scrawl, giving the track a sound just like Kuni Kawachi's KIRIKYOGEN. By the middle of side two, the tension has broken and the record starts to sound like Tim Leary's 7UP collaboration with Ash Ra Tempel, as orgasmic Gille Lettmann/Rosi Muller-style female shrieks overwhelm 'Prayer'. Director Sakamoto kept it all spacey and minimal, then added plenty more LUMPY GRAVY-period Frank Zappa and mucho David Axelrod (whence came many of the original concepts) to the stew. As if to prove People's pragmatism, 'Epilogue' concludes with two minutes of jamming over Axelrod's immaculate 'Holy Thursday' from SONGS OF INNOCENCE. People's success is in their tenacity in holding on both to the drone and, therefore, to the metaphor, which permeates the entire recording and lays serious meditative usefulness on to the listener.

17
Blues Creation
DEMON & ELEVEN CHILDREN
(Columbia 1971)

Opening with the super-stoner anthem 'Atomic. Bombs Away', this brilliant second Blues Creation LP is a proto-metal classic. Its eight songs were both complex and supremely individual, despite showing clear influences from fellow countrymen and free-thinkers Flower Travellin' Band. Indeed, guitarist Kazuo Takeda's own 'Mississippi Mountain Blues' mirrors the heaviness located within the grooves of Flower Travellin' Band's juggernaut 'Louisiana Blues', as sent through a Yardbirds filter. This LP featured a brand-new version of Blues Creation after superstar guitarist Kazuo Takeda, on hearing the new, strung-out music of Led Zeppelin, Black Sabbath and Eric Clapton's solo LP CLAPTON, decided he should take the opportunity to start again from scratch. New conscripts bassist Masashi Saeki and drummer Akiyoshi Higuchi add massive balls, giving Takeda the confidence to eschew his previous covers style in favour of his own excellent compositions, which come on like the Yardbirds meets Black Sabbath's debut. But if this scorching collection of proto-metal kacks logs on the band's debut, it's mostly because of the arrival of singer Hiromi Osawa, whose mighty larynx eclipsed that of founder Fumio Nunoya. At the end of 1971, another essential gem was released in the form of BLUES CREATION LIVE. However, Takeda was by now a famous Japanese guitar hero and split the band before splitting for London in 1972. In 1973, when he returned to Japan to support Lesley West's Mountain, it was as the lead singer/guitarist of a new power trio called simply Creation. The debut Creation album cover featured a crowd of naked pre-teen boys pissing on the floor.

18
Flower Travellin' Band
MADE IN JAPAN
(Atlantic 1972)

Recorded in Canada by a jazz keyboard player who didn't understand them, Flower's SATORI follow-up was confused, disorientated, depressed, self-deprecating and a wonderful album. The raging experimental near-instrumental jet fighters of SATORI here gave way to Middle European proto-metal of the Amon Düül 2 variety, replete with acoustic Tony Iommisms and mucho Satanic raga. The depressing album opener 'Unaware' comes on like Arthur Lee's electro-acoustic OUT THERE version of 'Signed DC' rewritten by Amon Düül 2's Chris Karrer into some over-reaching ballad. Joe repeats verse one an octave higher each time until it sheers off into coyote cackle, the bizarrely off-kilter un-rock refrain then kicking in: 'Determined am I now to live all in flame till nature snuffs it out to rest'. 'Aw, Give Me Air' still retains the proto-metal Devilish chord changes of SATORI, but it's more Asian than demonic, as is the tense demonic riffing and a banshee vocal of 'Kamikaze'. All descends into Yardbirds-ian gothic choir, Joe asking have we lived in Sodom and Gomorrah? Then, building inexorably, the song ejects us into more YETI-period Amon Düül 2 via the proto-metal guitar freak-out. 'Hiroshima' is the finest song here, utilising the 'Satori Part 3' music combined with chilling, confrontational lyrics all mightily un-nerving to any Westerner. The scything guitar of 'Spasms' cuts across the staccato rhythm, its melody's mounting insanities conjuring demons out of nowhere. The lyrically facile 'Heaven and Hell' is musically pure Hendrix, while album closer 'That's All' – possessed of gymnastically atonal vocals – brings the record to a close via one of the longest '70s fades I can remember.

19
Karuna Khyal
ALOMONI 1985
(Voice 1974)

Imagine the Jehovah's Witnesses were right and the world had ended in 1975. Imagine a tribe of Louisiana backwoodsmen who'd been reared on a diet of freak-out albums such as Amon Düül's, Hapshash & the Coloured Coat's, Friendsound's JOYRIDE, Kalakackra's CRAWLING TO LHASA, voodoo rituals and re-runs of *Bewitched*. Yup, Karuna Khyal is *that* kind of paganism. Their line-up is thought to have been similar to that of Brast Burn, but as the Japanese *futen* scene was so genuinely itinerant, people came and went with the same cavalier attitude as Amon Düül's Berliner Eins. Some have speculated that this outfit was comprised of members of Tokyo's Jigen re-located to Kyoto; others believe its provenance had nothing at all to do with the main *futen* scene, hatching its plans far to the north of Sapporo. Whatever the truth, Karuna Khyal clearly bears the same relationship to Brast Burn as East Bionic Symphonia shared with Taj Mahal Travellers, ie: Karuna Khyal is a far smaller ensemble with better equipment (the recording techniques betray an engineer more at ease with his technology, employing mike distortion intelligently on the drums without letting it destroy the rest of the track). 'First time musette' of the Captain Beefheart/Pere Ubu variety adds variety to their Faustian muse, plus a fondness for deploying their own field recordings. Imagine Acid Mothers Temple come not from the Brum of Japan (Nagoya), but instead hailed from a little hamlet outside Melksham or one of those equally scary Wiltshire 'towns'. *That* is Karuna Khyal. Like Brast Burn's DEBON, this was re-issued in 1998 on the Paradigm label.

20
Les Rallizes Denudés
FLIGHTLESS BIRD
(YODO-GO-A-GO-GO)
(10th Avenue Freeze-out 2006)

Come Doomsday, when all of us line up to be judged for what we did or didn't do, there'll surely be a big queue of artists such as Scott Walker and Half Man/Half Biscuit's N. Blackwell awkwardly harrumphing under an 'Intuitive Non-Career Movers' neon sign. Right at the head, of course, will be Rallizes's own Takeshi Mizutani, who'll still be blaming his bass player for the hijack and the recording engineer for making his studio debut such a nightmare. Which is why this particular Rallizes release is so refreshing, because some deluded soul has clearly attempted – on CD and double vinyl, no less – to create a 'retrospective/best of' to sit in HMV's racks alongside all the Sony/EMI corporate compilations. YODO-GO-A-GO-GO even opens with a track from Mizutani's aborted first studio mission, 'Otherwise My Conviction' sounding pretty damn fine in a post-PEBBLES kind of way. Two minutes of unprovenanced 'I'll Be Your Mirror'-style querulous balladry follows with 'Vallé de L'Eau', while the thirteen minutes of 'Enter the Mirror' is a tinnitus-inducing Dronefest Maximus. It's the full Wakabayashi version of 'Smokin' Cigarette Blues' that opens side two, while the nineteen-minutes-long BLIND BABY … mid-'80s version of 'Flames of Ice' extends right across side three. The final side lashes the ten-minute wipe-out of 'Field of Artificial Flowers' to a startlingly brief brain-crushing 'Deeper Than Night' that sounds remarkably like the HEAVIER THAN A DEATH … version, but concludes naturally rather than fading. Unfortunately, a second (and vastly inferior) version of 'Otherwise My Conviction' brings this double-LP to a stumbling halt. But, then, 7-out-of-8 classics ain't half bad, especially on the coloured vinyl versh!

21
Masahiko Satoh & New Herd Orchestra
YAMATAI-FU
(Toshiba/Far East 1972)

The greatest cosmic jazz album ever made? The pursuit of Krautrock's highest accolades armed only with an acoustic jazz orchestra and a single ring-modulator? The Dawning of Humanity's earliest ages as filtered through the ultimate urban musical filter? YAMATAI-FU is all of these things and more, a spell-binding and iconoclastic work the like of which has never before been encountered. Hot on the heels of the hard-bop drum-fuelled *kosmische* classic AMALGAMATION, and once again highly inspired by his collaborations with experimental pianist Wolfgang Dauner, Masahiko Satoh next delivered this huge three-part score for Toshiyuki Miyama & New Herd Orchestra, in which drummer Masaru Hiromi became the lynchpin for its entire monumental groove. Indeed, it's difficult to image how much weight the drummer would have lost over the course of this mighty session. Around Togashi's flailing Philly Joe Jones-meets-Klaus Schultze drum insanity, the composer built a series of highly arranged and ever unfolding brass pieces (sometimes cacophonous/sometimes sweet) that united more cosmic jazz in the style of his own AMALGAMATION together with elements of full-flight Archie Shepp on the title track of his YAS-MINA, A BLACK WOMAN. Over this bizarre mix, Satoh added his own heavily ring-modulated electric piano, sending out Ur-sparks and shards of sonic light into the heavens with this primitive electronic device, kicking Christian Vander's underachieving butt and creating a proto-Cosmic Jokers work in the process. Side one contained the single epic 'Ichi' (First), while side two was split into 'Ni' (Second) and 'San' (Third). The whole album is a righteous ducking for those who believe the Japanese never get anywhere first.

22
Magical Power Mako
MAGICAL POWER MAKO
(Polydor 1974)

Five years in preparation and at-home recording, this extraordinary debut album, released by a precocious and still-adolescent nineteen-year-old, was a highly strange mixture of pop art and Krautrock (its cover, inspired by the Faust and Neu! debuts, simply enlarged the Polydor label and price to cover the entire front and back sleeves). Opening with Mako's fake radio announcement of impending apocalypse, slightly undermined by a background of cats miaowing and D. Duck impersonations, the shamanic vocal chanting of 'Cha Cha' follows, thence to the biwa'n'guru declarations of 'Tsugaru', and the field records of 'In a Stalactite Cavern, Astoronaus' (Mako beating drums in an ancient cave) and 'Town' (solo street-corner singing). 'Flying' evokes a sub-Flower Travellin' Band 'Stairway to Heaven' ballad, replete with Mellotron 400 flutes, before ascending skywards on a psychedelic trajectory similar to early Tractor. Side one concludes with the psychedelic post-commune shriek of 'Restraint, Freedom', Mako here accompanied by cohort Keiji Heino (credited as 'Kei-chan'). Side two commences with the perfect kindergarten piano ballad 'Open the Morning Window, the Sunshine Comes in, the Hope of Today Is Small Bird Singing'. Imagine the third Velvets album as an X-Mass number one. Mako sings this in a Yoko Ono-as-infant voice, until gently accompanied by an earnest tiny boy, singing tunelessly. Mellotron 400 eventually buries everything in luxurious strings, until abruptly cut down by the Cossack yelping of 'Ruding Piano', after which the LP devolves into sound FX, chanting and mucho Mellotron. The twelve-minute closer 'Look up at the Sky' is a devotional hymn halfway between J. Cale, Colin Blunstone and E. Frankenstein. Essential.

23
Taj Mahal Travellers
LIVE STOCKHOLM
JULY, 1971
(Drone Syndicate 1998)

This album is a discorporated, cerebral dance whose rhythm sounds like six weather Gods emulating the cover of Deep Purple's FIREBALL by zooming around Silverstone circuit just inches above the track, each urging himself on by making engine noises: 'Eee-oww-urghh-ow!!!!!!' Opening with Ryo Koike's horizontally played bowed double bass, it's my fave of Taj Mahal Travellers' three releases, better even than the obstinate medication of the first official LP JULY 15, 1972, because there's twice as much of it. Meditatively, it's extremely useful too: at the entrance portals of this live record, Ryo Koike uses his bass to invoke phlegm phantoms and cranny demons from the butt walls of Cronosian caverns; conjuring a sound as Biblical as Conrad Schnitzler's bizarre bowed cello on T. Dream's ELECTRONIC MEDITATION. Gradually, hesitatingly, almost imperceptibly, a violin theme installs itself, establishing over the next quarter of an hour clop-clopping hooves of hollow rhythm that conjure up the image of frustrated pastoralists driving their reluctant donkeys around the highest and most precipitous cliff edges, as their valuable cargoes sway and shudder and threaten to come untied at any moment. Recorded a full year before their first official LP, I think this In Concert album is a far better and more confident shamanic statement, for this Stockholm recording melded together all six group members in such a way that no single musician rises from the primal soup long enough to establish his singular muse. The vocal effects are truly stunning, evoking everything from comb-and-paper voices playing Zeus in the sixty-metre deep Dhikhtean Antron to braying cartoon coyotes laughing to their deaths.

24
Magical Power Mako
JUMP
(Polydor 1977)

After the impish precociousness of his debut, Mako got caught up in the post-TUBULAR BELLS fallout that afflicted much music of 1974–75, so his second release, SUPER RECORD, was unlistenable New Age twaddle of the World Music variety, with sleevenotes comparing it to 'folk music of India, Turkey and Russia … expressing fully the odour of the soil'. Where the cattle pissed, mate. Sheesh! A good slapping from occasional cohort Keiji Heino got him back on track, as evidenced from the massively crunchy Kraut-funk of JUMP. Bye-bye panpipes; back comes the RIOT-period Sly Stone mind-numbing bass, plus madly catchy glampop hooks, phased twin-lead guitars and ridiculous catchy hooklines. A glam racket clothed in a jacket that, simultaneously, harked back to Jobriath and anticipated the '80s. Imagine Franco Battiato's FETUS meets John Cale's THE ACADEMY IN PERIL meets Moebius & Plank's RASTAKRAUTPASTA three years early, all mashed up with Eno's 'Third Uncle' and bits of Slapp Happy's Anthony Moore during his FLYING DOESN'T HELP underground pop phase. Sometimes cantankerous, mostly essential, very Krautrock in attitude and occasionally lapsing into L. Voag's THE WAY OUT territory. 'Jump to You' is Faust on a NYC funk trip, 'The Story of Our Master' is instant composition at its catchiest, 'Give Me Present' is ecstatic gypsy Battiato, 'Rest Light Down' is Charlie Brown theme music for Peter Hammill, 'So' is FAUST IV as is 'Blue Wind', 'Elephant's Jungle' is avant-crap, the brilliant eight-minute title track is early VISITATION-period Chrome meets DELUXE-period Harmonia being a hard-rock band, and '21st Ocean' is Curved Air's 'Rob One'. Specific enough for ya?

25
Kuni Kawachi & Friends
KIRIKYOGEN
(Capitol 1970)

Flower Travellin' Band obsessives or any fans with a predilection for Joe Yamanaka's mutant cakehole and Hideki Ishima's mighty axe should direct their hard-earned at this classic forthwith, for its contents are all shot through with precisely the yawp you're requiring. Despite being former organist and leader of Group Sounds underachievers Happenings Four, Kuni Kawachi nailed this sucker to the floor with an entire album of classic songs, featuring the aforementioned Flower Gods in pole positions throughout. Moreover, an early version of Flower's non-LP single 'Map' lurks within, hiding behind the title 'Music Composed Mainly by Humans'. While dry, spaced-out and highly original hard-rocking ballads occupy side one, side two is possessed of a hitherto unseen acoustic side of Hideki Ishima's playing in the highly catchy 'Graveyard of Love', 'Classroom for Women' and the late Velvets-styled 'Scientific Investigation'. And while Joe's tonsils never get the same rigorous overhauling that his Flower cohorts demand, even his most gentle contributions herein showcase 'that' voice to perfection. That KIRIKYOGEN runs with the big boys shouldn't be such a surprise, as Kawachi was a talent who contributed to such LPs as Tokyo Kid Brothers' amazing version of THROW AWAY THE BOOKS, WE'RE GOING OUT IN THE STREETS and Kimio Mizutani's flawed-but-excellent A PATH THROUGH HAZE, as well as contributing the inner-sleeve artwork for the latter. In his later years, Kawachi moved north to become a farmer in Hokkaido, keeping his musical hand in by writing TV commercials. A couple of years ago, his crap old Group Sounds band reformed, but are said to have played KIRIKYOGEN in its entirety.

26
Brast Burn
DEBON
(Voice 1974)

Emerging from the woodland murk of a single pulsing analogue synthesiser, Brast Burn's glorious chaos was a vital and catchy hogwash of Cajun chanting and slide guitar, massed sleighbells, Amon Düül I-style single-note piano, recorders and tin whistles, rudimentary electronics, highly reverb'd hand drums played by people trying to convince us they possess a full kit, and gnarly repetitious lead vocals in the style of the Race Marbles' 'Like A Dribbling Fram' off PEBBLES VOLUME 3, or maybe Exuma the Obeah Man. 'Sewer mind, sewer mind, sewer mind Sue' sings the head shaman over and over. Hey, this guy thinks he's singing an Everly Brothers hit, and Sewermind Sue is Runaround Sue's errant kid sister. Unknown in Japan except for their loose association with the equally catchy and bizarre Karuna Khyal, Brast Burn's sole LP DEBON is an unconditional classic. Released on the private Voice Records label in 1974, the LP is split into two epic side-long tracks simply entitled 'Debon Part One' and 'Debon Part Two'. It all takes place in a proper studio and sounds pretty damned stereo, but it's the interface between the electronics, sound FX and fastidious Noggin the Nog jamming that sets this lot apart from other similar efforts. This ain't just another crackle-and-pop fest like some stuff Japanese hippies laid at our door. Nevertheless, even though the sleeve states 'Produced by Tokiyushi Nemoto and available from Nakano Record Shop', no one knows who they were, what town they came from or even what prefecture. Quite a feat considering the obsessive Japanese quest to learn the provenance of everything.

27
Akira Ishikawa &
Count Buffaloes
UGANDA
(Toshiba 1972)

This rampant album of four enormous fuzz'n'
percussion wipe-outs almost fulfils its ambition
to avoid American musical influence and achieve
'its poetic truth', tromping through long grass
with Ikuzo Orita's 'super session' guitar star
Kimio Mizutani in tow. The enormous twelve-
minute opener 'Wanyama Na Mapambazuko'
(Animals and Dawn) heralds the sunrise with
lone farting sub-bass guitar (filtered through a
Moog synthesiser) as tribal drums respond,
hestitantly at first, before whipping the track
into life with a 6/4 proto-metal riff courtesy of
axe mangler Kimio Mizutani. African voices call-
and-answer awhile until crude power-trio riff-
ology opens out making way for yet more patent
Mizutani soloing. Side one concludes with the
nine minutes of 'Na Tu Penda Sana' (Asking for
Love), whose African 'Sympathy for the Devil'-
style introduction collapses into a tribal guitar
chant of Sammy Hagar Montrose-period simplicity (!). The riffing subsides into lone wooden
hand drums, before increasing pace into a formidable crescendo of utter Mizutani fuzz-axe
destruction. Side two begins with a brief angular early Zappa-style theme, which introduces
the epic clock-ticking eight-minute grooves of
'Vita (battle, fighting, war)', complete with field
recordings of animal noises and chanting. Echoes of Magical Power Mako's 'Tsugaru' or even
Nihilist Spasm Band are conjured up in Mizutani's frenzied Japanese banjo freak-out, before
the eight-minute concluding grooves of 'Pygmy'
devolve into a repetitive Afro-Funkadelic groove
similar to the longer People grooves on their
Mizutani-propelled 'super session' CEREMONY –
BUDDHA MEETS ROCK. This excellent experimental LP parallels the tradition of Can's Ethno-
logical Forgery Series.

28
Flower Travellin' Band
ANYWHERE
(Philips 1970)

It's a dead cert that those who dismiss this
Flower debut as a covers album have never
heard it, only heard about it. For its grooves
contain such monstrous modifications that each
track leaves the starting block a full metre lower
than the hoary jalopy originals, a Ferrari where
once was a Ford. For a start, Flower Travellin'
Band do not cover the song 'Black Sabbath'.
Instead, they let its tyres down and ride it across
a ploughed field. They do to it what no British
band could ever have done, dissolving the 4/4
rhythm into an ambient metal assault over which
Joe sings the lyrics when he feels like it.
Flower's version of '21st Century Schizoid
Man' ejects all the nasty sax flourishes and
prissy jazz snare drums of the original and gets
down to the real power-trio business that riff
always demanded. In this mood, you even begin
to believe they could have taken Yes's
proto-metal epic 'Heart of the Sunrise' and
turned it into the Troggs' 'Feels Like a Woman'.
And if you shudder at the thought of Flower
approaching an archaic standard such as
'House of the Rising Sun', open up your mind
to receive the proto-'Stairway to Heaven' shock-
of-a-lifetime. For Flower have taken away those
chords and, lo, the arrangement hath been
lifted up umpteen cosmic notches. By the end
of it, the 'House ...' has been displaced by
the 'Land of the Rising Sun' and Joe's sense
of loss has us all blarting like babbies. Moreover, sole original 'Louisiana Blues' is nearly
sixteen minutes of 1970 Dodge Challenger
highway grind. Epic.

29
J.A. Caesar & Shirubu
SHIN TOKU MARU
(Victor 1978)

Music that evokes the Khanate Golden Horde invading eastern Turkey, anyone? Yes, please. This album is full of Cossack knees-ups played by prog-punks with a Magma fixation, its strident bass guitars echoed by Klaus Blasquiz'n'Stella Vanderesque banshee themes, as though Caesar had sent Carl Orff's *Carmina Burana* through a MEKANÏK DESTRUKTÏW KOMMANÖH filter. Kan Mikami gets to do lots of shouting, while the main themes are held together by charming, stumbling solo piano pieces from Caesar himself, fascinatingly reminiscent of Bryan Ferry's contributions to the first Roxy Music LP. 'When I was a young boy I loved this book ...' writes playwright Shuji Terayama cheerfully, in the sleevenotes; then tells us that it's the unhappy story of a boy who, after his mother's death, is brought up by his father and a stepmother who can't stand him, treats him mercilessly and drives him out of the family home. Eventually, the boy dresses as his mother and, in full make-up, returns home to off the offenders. Unfortunately, this album does feature rather more dialogue than I'd have liked to offer you. But its unfathomable plot holds listeners spellbound through the sheer exotic nature of the sounds and vocal delivery. In 2002, P-Vine Records put out a perfect facsimile of this LP, complete with gatefold inner lyric sheet and original cover art. Those in need of more music delivered in this archly stentorian manner should search out Caesar's 1980 album SEALBREAKING. Although lo-fi in quality and mainly available through bootlegs, it nevertheless contains much of my favourite Caesar music – ten headlong tracks of Magma-meets-early Stranglers/Music Machine riffothons.

30
Gedo
GEDO
(Showboat 1974)

Kings of the biker scene, Gedo is what I'd imagined Murahatchibu would've sounded like. If only! Indeed, Gedo's only disappointment is that, like their Western festival equivalents the Pink Fairies, they had a fondness for old-fashioned rock'n'roll from time to time. Still, this LP is an absolute must-have, scorching with manic hard rock. GEDO opens with 'Kaori' (Scent), a proto-High Rise monster, while 'Nigeruna' (Don't Run Away) is an empty 'Hey Joe' driven by the staccato drums and elastic bass. 'Gedo' is the Pistols' 'Liar' years too early, but 'Rock'n'roll Baka' (Rock'n'roll Stupid) is just shit 'Johnny B. Goode'. However, side one closes with the fabulous 'Dance Dance Dance', whose hybrid of the Velvets' 'Rock'n'roll' and the Byrds' 'So You Wanna Be a Rock'n'roll Star' tails out in a drum solos, in-jokes, high jinx and chants of 'Gedo' (Believe me, this is typical of every Gedo record I've ever encountered). Side-two opener 'Byoon Byoon' is a more coherent version of High Rise's 'Outside Gentiles'. And although 'Itsumo No Tokoro De' (At the Usual Place) is a useless 6/8 '50s re-tread, it's followed by the nihilistic riffery of 'Kusatta Inochi' (Rotten Life), full of lyrics about rotting pigs and fool's paradises. The Stooges finally rear their heads in 'Kanryo' (Completed), which features amazingly slithery axe from Hideto Kano in a truly full-on juggernaut white-lightning tailout. Dunno why but the record ends with Hideto Kano's unnecessary Latino acoustic ballad 'Yasashii Uragirio' (Tender Betrayal), followed by the sound FX of 'Sutato', as the band exit on massive Honda hogs, gaining them instant cult rock'n'roll status.

31

Les Rallizes Denudés
DECEMBER'S BLACK
CHILDREN
(No label 1989)

Taking its name from the US-only Rolling Stones album DECEMBER'S CHILDREN, this mighty double-CD is essential to the Rallizes story as one of the few available recordings of the band with former Murahatchibu/Dynamites guitarist Fujio Yamacauchi. Recorded in Tokyo's Yaneura district on 13th December 1980, the album opens with an eight-minutes twin-axe spectacular version of 'Kori no Hono'o' (Flames of Ice), vastly different to the version that opens BLIND BABY … before opening out into the thirteen-minute distorto-soul of 'Yoru Yori Fukaku' (Deeper Than the Night), Fujio's mournful wailing adding a ZUMA-like quality. The hiccupping quarter-of-an-hour version of 'A Distant Memory' included herein is a loping and inverted funeral karaoke, returning to a twenty-minute brain-basting 'Deeper Than the Night', the two guitars possessed by stellar feedback and total chordal indifference. Disc one concludes with a romping Frankie Laine *eleki* posse-in-a-blender version of 'The Night Assassins' that tumbles over itself until everyone is playing the chord sequence according to their own calendar. Note: disc two claims to commence with another 'Yoru, Ansatsusha no Yoru' (Night of the Assassins), but on this version substitutes the original Wakabayashi-period 1969 line-up playing the full nineteen minutes of 'Smokin' Cigarette Blues'. An amazing bonus. Then, 'Shiro'i Mezame' (White Awakening) is sixteen minutes of pure Velvets' LIVE 1969, Mizutani dragging his axe through rudimentary melody into bagpipe hell'n'back. Then commence the drones of 'Enter the Mirror', herein being the finest 'Heroin'-style version I've ever heard. In true Rallizes fashion, this epic double concludes with yet another cinematic carouse through 'The Last One'.

32

Datetenryu
UNTO 1971
(Dragon Freek 1996)

Included here as representatives of the early '70s festival scene, Datetenryu was an obscure cousin to Communist agitator bands Zuno Keisatsu (Brain Police), Yellow, Les Rallizes Denudés and Murahatchibu. Led by organist Masao Tonari, the band on UNTO played a frantic hogwash of soul-based progressive space rock that inhabited the same territory as the Soft Machine's debut-LP period (imagine 'Why Are We Sleeping?' or 'Hope for Happiness' by way of '21st Century Schizoid Man'). Mainly instrumental, their music is a space trek through endless R&B riffs and classic soul moments, like some ever unfolding medley. UNTO purports to be what the band members would have chosen had they had the opportunity to release an official debut album at the time, ie: a total barrage of lo-fi progressive garage rock. The twenty-minute epic 'Doromamire' (Covered All Over in Mud) is the killer, but really it's all one insane 47-minute-long rush. Formed in May 1971, at Kyoto Sangyo ('Industrial') University, Datetenryu was a right bunch of refusenik longhairs. Masao Tonari set up sideways on to the rest of the band, while drummer Shogo Ueda played, head down, facing away from the stage pointing towards Tonari's Yamaha organ. Indeed, guitarist Kei Yamashita appears to have been permanently out of proceedings in the same way that Yes's Pete Banks and the Nice's Davy O'List were forever being sidelined. Datetenryu's biggest claim to fame, however, was the presence of bassist/singer Hiroshi Narazaki, who later became Hiroshi Nar and joined Les Rallizes Denudés, thereafter forming his own very excellent band the Niplets, who continue to perform right up to the present time.

33
East Bionic Symphonia
EAST BIONIC
SYMPHONIA
(L.A.M. Records 1976)

Tripped-out vocal drones, ominous bowed glissandos courtesy of an upright bowed viola and a one-string Chinese fiddle, deep meditations undermined by reedy snake charmer and scattered bamboo rods bouncing across the polished floor; this direct descendant of Taj Mahal Travellers is a certified classic of improvisation, occupying the same general space as that incredible ensemble. Formed by occasional Taj Mahal Traveller guest Kazuo Imai and featuring ten members as opposed to the Travellers' seven, East Bionic Symphonia had very much their own sound. Side one's '7.30 pm–7.47 pm' is less satisfying simply because it's too short, whereas side two's '8.15pm – 8.43pm' is highly repeatable. Mentor Takehisa Kosugi edited both of the tracks. On 18th October 1997, six of the ten original members re-united for a hugely successful four-hour-long concert in Tokyo's Asahi Square, recording the results for a future album. The continued presence of Chie Mukai's bowed *kokyu*, Kazuo Imai's *viola da gamba* and Yasushi Ozawa's bowed bass guitar ensured that the reunion lacked only certain percussive elements from the original dectet, though beaten tambourine, orchestral samples and electronics heaped new exotic elements of static interference into the stew, contributing to an overall sound reminiscent of a Shuji Terayama soundtrack. Unlike most cynical reunions, however, the six musicians felt it dishonourable to capitalise on their original name without the presence of Kaoru Okabe, Tatuo Hattori, Kazuaki Hamada and Masaharu Minegishi, choosing instead to release the resulting album COLLECTIVE IMPROVISTION on PSF Records under the new name Marginal Consort.

34
Stomu Yamashita &
Masahiko Satoh
METEMPSYCHOSIS
(Columbia 1971)

Although billed by Columbia's marketing team as Masahiko Satoh's latest 'Composition for Percussion & Jazz Orchestra', this monumental sonic slab, played by New Herd Orchestra and conducted by leader Toshiyuki Miyami, sounds more like a bizarre hybrid of T. Dream's ELECTRONIC MEDITATION and John Coltrane's ASCENSION. Split into two single tracks, the music drifts in over several minutes under a foggy blanket of low-grade funereal brass, a cold clammy cosmic conductor's hand of doom controlling the atmosphere, the huge brass section anonymously aping Edgar Froese's Mellotron 400 brass samples, before bursting forth suddenly with the shamanic paroxysms of Yamashita's percussion and cloudbursts of spectacular atonal brass and wind sections. Indeed, the line-up of New Herd musicians here is in itself so monumental that it creates a unique Middle European sound, like the movie soundtrack from some imaginary Hungarian Creation Myth. The music then slowly fades out like some death ship passing in the stillness of night. Suddenly, every instrument tears into life with peals of wanton sax sections, urban blues trumpets, and Yamashita's berserk percussive freakouts. Besides the standard drums, piano, bass and guitar, a brass section of four trumpets, four trombones, four saxophones and a bassoon tear the soul apart with their vicious combinations of meditative low-church drones and uplifting Zoroastrian fire fights. At times, the music becomes a drums-and-percussion tantrum between Yamashita and drummer Yoshisaburo Toyozumi, the percussionist's close-miked and high-tuned drums boggling the senses as the seething and sibilant rush of cymbals leaves the brain feeling like a tiny ship caught in the eye of a hurricane.

35
Taj Mahal Travellers
JULY 15, 1972
(Nippon Columbia 1972)

Drifting in on Takehisa Kosugi's radio receivers and frequency oscillators, the stillness of the performers during the opening moments of this debut is such that even the slamming doors of embarrassed late arrivals at Tokyo's Sogetsu Kaikan Hall make major contributions to the music. Seiji Nagai's lone trumpet and Kosugi's bowed violin occupy most of the space until heavily treated harmonica oozes through the murk, and the four echo machines of electronics operators Michihiro Kimura, Tokio Hasegawa, Yuki Tsuchiya and Kinji Hayashi fuse together to render any evaluation of the original sound sources quite impossible. The twenty-six minutes of 'Taj Mahal Travellers between 6.20pm and 6.46pm' covers the whole first side of this album, the electric contrabass and tuba occasionally calling out to each other like rival walruses vying for possession of the same stretch of iceberg. Side two is split into two twelve-minute and fifteen-minute pieces, the first catching them adrift in a chorale of Buddhist chanting from within some ancient cave of the dead. Unusually, the first track, 'Taj Mahal Travellers between 7.03pm and 7.15pm', concludes with Michihiro Kimura's devolved bluesy electric guitar and Kosugi's strummed violin à la mandolin. 'Taj Mahal Travellers between 7.50pm and 8.05pm' ploughs an entirely rural violin furrow within the realms of Henry Flynt's BACK PORCH HILLBILLY BLUES. Fans of this recording may wish to search out Taj Mahal Travellers' performance on the OZ DAYS LIVE vinyl bootleg, where – sandwiched between Les Rallizes Denudés and Acid Seven's group – they kicked up a veritable shitstorm whilst playing (on one of their rare occasions) in front of a rock crowd. Those showboaters!

36
Toshi Ichiyanagi
OPERA INSPIRED BY THE WORKS OF TADANORI YOKO'O
(The End 1969)

More of a musical tribute to a cultural hero than a genuine opera, Toshi Ichiyanagi's massive project nevertheless united almost every essential musical genre in this impressively packaged homage to Japan's own Andy Warhol/Roy Lichtenstein modern-art titan Tadanori Yoko'o. Delivered in a magnificent presentation box over four sides of 12" vinyl, side one of the opera opens with a lone female voice singing a cappella, the work continuing into Ichiyanagi's synthesiser drone, under which rousing traditional Japanese military songs play, thence to a rehearsal session for the gentle ballad 'Man's Pure Heart', and the side's closing track of sound FX and boxing audience. The Flowers' magnificent instrumental 'I'm Dead' occupies all of side two and seven minutes of side three, followed by the spoken-word soundtrack 'Song of New York', and the evocative orchestral cut-ups of 'Kayo Musicale'. The final side commences with the disorientating 'Love Blinded Ballad', a bizarre combination of mawkish *enka* and *musique concrète*, thence to the full-on experimental blast of *musique concrète* and analogue synthesiser that is 'Spite Song'. The opera concludes ironically with a bossanova homage to Tadanori Yoko'o sung by hardman actor Ken Takakura, star of multiple gangster movies. It was the composer's intention that listeners should play the picture discs while scanning the sumptuous box art and flicking through an accompanying set of Yoko'o-designed playing cards. In 2005, Bridge Records re-released the entire package as four CDs in a 12" box, complete with playing cards.

37
Taj Mahal Travellers
AUGUST 1974
(Nippon Columbia 1974)

Taj Mahal Travellers had a dedication to capturing the moment that ran far deeper than even T. Dream during ZEIT or Popol Vuh's brief AFFENSTUNDE period. Hail, these guys made so much of even their non-moments that the real moments seemed like declarations of war in comparison. But if the music of those aforementioned Krautrockers was a ship adrift on an ocean, then the music of Taj Mahal Travellers was Noah's Ark encircling the eye of the storm itself. For this double-LP, their final album, the ensemble opted for a more acoustically pure approach, even naming their four side-long epics simply 'I', 'II', 'III' and 'IV'. Underplaying the deep theta meditations of the first record, here the Taj Mahal Travellers fuss with their primitive electronic gadgetry and Ur-babble like endangered species seeking collective closure, this album's refusal to dwell in deep ponds of reverb ensuring that the first clawing steps towards the individual are forever approaching, and all achieved with such a remarkable sense of orchestration that a strangely syncopated universal funk develops between the six. Their deployment of primitive electronic delays, in which certain sounds they had made were played back, just milliseconds later through speakers, created for each musician a 'wyrd', or shadow figure who is soon working almost in tandem with his sacred twin. For hour upon hour, Taj Mahal Travellers heap more and more ingredients – mainly voices and percussion – into their dronality, until the sound source is as mysterious as the roots of monotheism. Despite being the weakest of their albums, AUGUST 1974 remains deeply out-there music for deeply out-there circumstances.

38
Seishokki
ORGANS OF BLUE ECLIPSE (1975–77)
(Siwa 2005)

Standing midway between early Faust and Michel Bulteau's Mahogany Brain, this sextet of teenage ne'er-do-wells tears the walls apart throughout this mid-'70s avant-garde retrospective, battering down the doors of pre-conception with an array of melodicas, shaken piggy-banks, primitive electric-guitar blitzes, percussion wipe-outs and all-purpose mung worship. Over nine aimless (endless/nameless) tracks of avant-chaos, acid-campfire and post-apocalyptical freefölk, Seishokki also conjure up the ghosts of the Red Crayola, Taj Mahal Travellers, Amon Düül, and Yo Ha Wa 13. Seishokki was formed while its members – Hitoshi Matsumoto, Yuji Nakamura, Masanori Komatsu, Yasuaki Harabuchi, Tetsuya Takashio and Ikuro Takahashi – were still at school in the far-northern island of Hokkaido during 1975. Most of the musicians became future underground movers and shakers, especially drummer Takahashi, who went on to perform with a variety of '90s bands, including Maher Shalal Hash Baz, Keiji Heino's Fushitsusha, Asahito Nanjo's High Rise, and LSD March. ORGANS OF BLUE ECLIPSE was Seishokki's sole album and is mostly a collection of home freak-outs taken from the period 1975–77, recorded in an outbuilding on the banks of the river Chubetsu Gawa, on the outskirts of their home town Asahikawa. However, the final (and most 'rock') piece on the LP, the nine-and-a-half-minutes of 'Abashiri Blues', was recorded live at a local club. Apparently, one track was excluded from the record because its lyrics were too excruciatingly ridden with teenage angst for its now-middle-aged protagonists to bear listening to! The album received a limited vinyl release in 2005 on the Siwa label.

39
Joji Yuasa
MUSIC FOR THEATRICAL DRAMA
(Omega Point 2004)

40
Group Ongaku
MUSIC OF GROUP ONGAKU
(Hear Sound Art 2000)

Two vast pieces of highly evocative theatre music, one recorded in 1959 using orchestral scores and tape manipulation, the other a piece of *musique concrète* that surfaced in 1963, and both as current as anything emanating from the twenty-first-century underground scene. With my own *Krautrocksampler* now twelve years old, and the re-issue programme of so many highly rare experimental works now proceeding apace, it's not so very difficult to understand why this early experimental minimalist music remains so listenable to twenty-first-century ears. Indeed, we have this past decade expanded our melted plastic brains to such an extent that no one in their right mind would dare anticipate where next our musical pleasure centres will take us. Joji Yuasa's music, created over a period of months (rather than the long hours in which digital technology allows us to achieve such material), conjures up the sound of ancestor spirits deep within the caves of the dead, Yuasa's highly manipulated sounds still close enough to their original source to tweak at our amphibian selves, not so far submerged below our everyday. While the real joy of this pre-synthesiser music is in the detail contained within each sound, the labour involved must have been excruciating. Those in need of more such music should search out Yuasa's AOI NO UE, also on the same 'Obscure Tape Music of Japan' series. Comprised of 1961's half-hour-long title track and the sixteen minutes of 'My Blue Sky', recorded fourteen years later in 1975, these amazing works are also available on the Omega Point label (Arxchive Series OPA-001).

Although it sounds more like the result of some '70s drugged-out post-HYMNEN Krautrock experiment, the 26-minute-long opening track of this sole Group Ongaku album was recorded on 8th May 1960, less than a month after Eddie Cochran's fatal accident. The other tracks are just as psychotic. As I wrote in my Head Heritage Album of the Month for September 2003: 'Group Ongaku's brutal muse was more *sonique-concrète* than *musique-concrète*. Opening with kitchen sounds, bottles clinked together, wild spaced-out women's voices, hoovers, insane pianos, shortwave radio, tannoy voices, etc., it was the *performances* of the musicians of the ensemble itself that set MUSIC OF GROUP ONGAKU apart from every other bunch … Assaults on the microphones are particularly violent on this album, as are … well, let's call it natter pure and simple. Employing the principle that foreign voices sound more exotic because we don't know what they're on about, Group Ongaku included all of these already standard experimental elements and devices in their record and still came out of it sounding like rock stars – proof that it's "who-does-it" not "what-notes-get-played".' Strangest of all is the forward-thinking manner in which this music was achieved. For, despite employing such standard and stylish early-'60s accessories as a guitarist (by the name of Genichi Tsuge), at least half of the music herein was generated through tape playback, over which the ensemble spewed further venomous offences. Gargling, surprised exclamations, irritating hoovering, a too-early garbage collection, clarinet rehearsals, cut-up tapes of all the aforementioned tells us it's THE FAUST TAPES thirteen years ahead of its time.

41
Far East Family Band
THE CAVE DOWN
TO EARTH
(Columbia Mu Land 1975)

Delivered to the public in a mysterious cover whose bright red Obi-strip screamed: 'The eternal word woven into creation with eleven keyboards,' Far East Family Band's monumental debut played every progressive rock trick in the book and then some, its interior awash with lyrics sheets, Floydian pix of the band surrounded by mountains of equipment, inner sleeves depicting amazing sunsets visible through an outer decorated with a modified Sri Yantra, and sleevenotes à la Moody Blues' Tony Clarke that discussed the music as part of an impending new age. Like the Moody Blues' LPs that spawned its mystical gush, the record itself sits midway between the late-'60s kid-in-a-sweet-shop mentality that wished to gorge itself on the stunning new sounds available through Mellotron, Moog and the like, and the post-war mindset that yearned for Everly Brothers innocence. Mostly, like the Moodies' IN SEARCH OF THE LOST CHORD, this record is essential if only for the enriching sounds pouring forth. And although its lowest artistic moments scrape the sub-Graham Gouldman wellspring of twee, it's always buoyed up by the onslaught of the aforementioned eleven keyboards. Even hidden under their massive sonic arsenal, however, guitarist Hirohito Fukushima was a weak link whose rote solos may have sufficed once Klaus Schultze had embedded them within dollops of *kosmische* goo, but herein are too insubstantial to carry such a Spanish Armada of sound. This album's real genius belongs to leader Fumio Miyashita's clever subsuming of all five Moody Blues members into his own psyche, barfing out Mike Pinderisms with such aplomb that their provenance can never be immediately located.

42
The Jacks
VACANT WORLD
(Toshiba 1968)

Nihilist doom folk in advance of the third Velvet Underground album, anyone? Welcome to the debut with the most astonishingly original opening track ever. Imagine Love's 'Signed DC' played by a free-jazz ensemble intent on uniting the Communist Bloc rage of 'European Sun' with a shed-building competition. Over this, a Jacques Brel with an inner child-of-five tells us it's okay to be possessed by the siren Marianne, as she cops a feel of his inner psyche and drags him into the sea. Inevitably, the impact of the rest of the LP is somewhat lessened by this beginning. 'Stop the Clock' is a quiet seashore 'Candy Says' with vibraphone, while 'Vacant World' is more proto-Emo self-pity ('Am I indulging myself? I feel as if I were dead, Am I dead?'), flute-driven existential angst from too many Gitanes, but great 'loud' quiet guitar solo. 'In the Broken Mirror' is what GS should have been, replete with fuzz guitars and ELECTRIC MUSIC-period Country Joe W. Coast groove, while side two closes with the storming epic fuzz 6/8 minor blues weepy 'Gloomy Flower'. 'Love Generation' opens side two with more minor-key Country Joe, while 'Bara-Manji' (Swastika Rose) has the singer being 'flagellated with a chain of roses' over a crazy country backing track like Tim Hardin's debut played 'Marianne' style. Although 'Where?' is smooth, generic and forgettably out-of-character (these guys sound like they're enjoying themselves!), 'Love' is more excellent sobbing seashore Velvets Euro-tragedy. The album closes with the appropriately churchy '500 Miles from the Sky', an organ-only minor-key hymn with earnest spoken word from singer Yoshio Hayakawa.

43
3/3
SANBUN NO SAN
(LLX 1975)

Lo-fi 1975 studio recordings from one of only five surviving acetates, released in 2005 on red vinyl, these seven long generic sub-Stooges, proto-Friction jams sum up the late commune scene even better than Dr Acid Seven's own UNDERGROUND '70s CD series (which you still need, by the way). 3/3 was three ex- ○△□ members: Chiko Hige on drums, Hiroshi Higo on bass, and future No Waver/Friction leader Reck on guitar and vocals. With a sound akin to the Stooges' own RUBBER LEGS boot, y'all knows what you're in for, and it's right up there with the Notting Hill jams of Shagrat and the Fairies, occupying the kind of space you either need or don't give a damn about. 'Machine Song' opens the album somewhat dutifully, but 'Jump' deploys astral workouts of the highest Sir Lord Baltimore's 'Hard Rain Fallin'' calibre. Side one's concluder 'Always' appropriates the tail-riff of Focus's 'Hocus Pocus', over which Reck heaps mucho excellent ernie-ernie licks. Side two's 'In a Cloud' is relentless Stones-meets-Stooge trudge sparked up by Reck's catchy proto-Fiction gob and defiantly R. Blackmore axe worship. Another 'Hard Rain Fallin'' rip kicks off 'Fly', fuelled by yet more Friction-style vocals ('Automatic-Fru'?), plus double-tracked guitar solos. 'Open a Window' is 'Raw Power', with Friction vocals and a classic wah-wah solo. The album closes with the downbeat Velvets-third-album-styled ballad 'Let It Flow'. Final comment: the back sleeve photos cannot be 3/3 as Reck's playing a Fender Musicmaster bass in one and looks well Richard Helled up. Born yesterday? They sure think we wuz! Definitely one for the X-Mass prezzie list, though.

44
Blues Creation
LIVE
(Toshiba 1971)

Brutally apocalyptic Sabbath-informed post-Altamont blues hot on the heels of Flower Travellin' Band, this is a fantastic album of industrial strength played with all the artistic finesse of Olympic weightlifters. Containing just six monstrous workouts over fifty-three minutes, Kazuo Takeda & Co shamelessly tear off Hendrix's 'Voodoo Chile', Tony Iommi's 'Sleeping Village' solo and all kinds of classical moments, as the rhythm section of drummer Masayuki Higuchi and bassist Masashi Saeki thunder through each track leaving vocalist Hiromi Osawa as isolated as Flower Travellin' Band's Joe Yamanaka was on that band's first two LPs (hey, this kind of tear-arse music is just as killer without a singer). LIVE opens with a near-quarter-of-an-hour version of Muddy Water's 'Rolling Stone', here reduced to one chord like Flower's equally long juggernaut drone 'Louisiana Blues'. The seven minutes of 'Nightmare' that follow are more of the same bile, suffused with that same incandescent glow that Takeda burned into every groove on DEMON ... 'Drinkin' Blues' closes side one with seven-and-a-half minutes of minor blues played like Neil Young, singer Osawa rendering the whole track truly tragic with the querulous ON THE BEACH-like tones of his fragile vocals. 'Demon & Eleven Children' here is even better than the excellent original, but still lacks the incredible dynamism of the GENYA CONCERT version. Takeda drags boring Carmen Maki out for five minutes of 'Understand', her strained larynx herein actually taking on a wonderfully strident early Siouxsie timbre. LIVE concludes with the band's radically empty eleven-minute version of 'Tobacco Road', and you wonder what made Takeda tick breaking up such a brilliant band right after this release.

45
Various Artists
GENYA CONCERT
(Solid Records 1971)

This festival recording is one of the most important social documents of Japan's early-'70s underground scene, so it's good to learn that the contents are also highly listenable. The original LP (re-issued as a facsimile edition two years ago) featured an essential version of Blues Creation's 'Atomic Bombs Away', the ten-minute dementia of Lost Aaraaff's 'Kyokan Jigoku' (Screaming Hell), three of Zuno Keisatsu's most crucial protest songs ('World Revolutionary War Declaration', 'Pick up Your Gun' and 'Sect Boogie-Oogie'), plus rare recordings of Dew, the short-lived heavy outfit led by former Blues Creation singer Fumio Nunoya. Recorded at the legendary Sanrizuka three-day protest festival on 14th–16th August 1971 (see Book Two, Chapter Five), the recordings were initially released in single-LP form, with great emphasis being placed upon the scene-makers of the time: Zuno Keisatsu (Brain Police), Blues Creation, Keiji Heino's Lost Aaraaff and the aforementioned Dew. Although no other record had better showcased the multifarious talents plying their trade during this portal between the '60s and '70s, this LP soon disappeared. However, an unexpurgated box set (3CD/DVD plus 28-page booklet) manufactured by Hayabusa Landings (FLPB-001) has recently hit the streets, tripling the length of the original release by adding much Super-8 *cinema verité* alongside previously lost music by Toshi Ochiai Trio, free bassist Mototeru Takagi's trio, and the incredible six-minute-long free-rock guitar onslaught of 'Lagrima' (Tears) by Masayuki Takayanagi's New Direction for the Arts. Also included is eleven minutes of the traditional *Bon-odori* festival's *Takeda-bushi* singing performed by the local farmers' wives. Indispensable.

46
Toshi Ichiyanagi/Michael Ranta/Takehisa Kosugi
IMPROVISATION SEP. 1975
(Iskra 1975)

In response to the excesses achieved by such massive improvisational ensembles as Group Ongaku and Taj Mahal Travellers, this improvised battle of the heavyweights successfully reduced everything to its punked-out power-trio *summum bonum*; Stockhausen percussionist Michael Ranta taking on a Mo Tucker-style driving role, as Ichiyanagi and Kosugi threaded vocals, melodicas, pianos, violins, gongs and Japanese instruments (*biwas, shamisens*) through their beloved ring modulators. Indeed, it's the extreme use of ring modulators that so successfully transforms this improvisational music into the region of Krautrock and such Stockhausen-informed progressive rock as Peter Leopold's enormous drum clatter for Amon Düül 2's 'Marylin Monroe Memorial Church'. This distilled power-trio approach certainly focused the attentions of the listener, doing for this minimalist music what removing a rhythm guitar or organ does for rock music, ie: weeding out the extraneous and shining the spotlight entirely on individual elements. With nowhere to run and no one to hide behind, each sound made by each performer takes on a huge sense of the moment, and even renders the gaps interesting. Recorded for broadcasting at NHK-Radio's enormous Tokyo studio, these performances in places even achieve the sonic meltdown of Takehisa Kosugi's own CATCH-WAVE. Iskra re-issued this album recently as a vinyl facsimile (Iskra 3004), so first check out eBay. Fans of this recording will probably enjoy the similar ambulant sounds of Out to Lunch's 1999 experiment SPEAKERS. Led by Overhang Party drummer Iwao Yamazaki, the CD was released on Captain Trip Records (Out TL-7000).

47

Itsutsu no Akai Fusen
FLIGHT 1&2
(URC 1970–71)

Imagine an LP half full of songs such as Erika Eigen's 'I Wanna Marry a Lighthouse Keeper' from the A CLOCKWORK ORANGE soundtrack, Mo Tucker's Velvet Underground ballads 'After-hours' and 'I'm Sticking with You', and that uber-cute ditty 'Tonight You Belong to Me' that Steve Martin and Bernadette Peters sang together in *The Jerk*. Imagine that same album also contains a few euphorically strung-out cosmic folk ballads somewhere in the style of Tim Buckley's Straight Records LP BLUE AFTERNOON united with Culture's super-sweet TWO SEVENS CLASH, but sung by a man and a woman in the manner of Emtidi's SAAT. Then imagine that some of that material was extended to cover a whole side of 12" vinyl, Rolf-Ulrich Kaiser-stylee. Okay, now imagine there were two such LPs and that they were released one year apart on a cult label called Underground Record Club, and you've hit exactly where Itsutsu no Akai Fusen is coming from. It's a weird combination of urban torch songs, rural lovey-dovey indoor campfire, and transcendental tripped out meditative space folk. Both LPs were packaged in cosmic spacious gatefold sleeves, and the records were mainly sung by female singer Hideko Fujiwara and written by songwriter Takashi Nishioka, the man responsible for a fairly legendary Japanese album, MELTING GLASS BOX, that I've never really found much time for. These two records I like very much indeed, however, so they're hidden away at number 47 because I listen to them all the time, despite having never had much time for the Japanese early-'70s folk scene. So please excuse this review hyping two LPs simultaneously, but by 2012, you'll most likely have found time to investigate these records and, hopefully, are by now digging them.

○△□
(Maru Sankaku Shikaku)
COMPLETE WORKS
(1970–73)
(Captain Trip 2003 re-release)

Emanating from the late '60s Shinjuku *futen* scene that hung around Ogi and the Go-Go-Cafe, ○△□ was a painted bunch of commune rockers and percussion tribe second to none, whose random bells, flute, and remedial tea-tray flay-lings (though horribly more-ish in a rent-a-freak Noggin the Nog meets Towser manner) were still way more like the Godz or Nihilist Spasm Band than the deep theta-space obliterations of Taj Mahal Travellers. Indoor stoned parrot-torture cutlery & crockery grooves, anyone? Then check out this 2003 compendium of ○△□ 's three original self-financed, self-pressed, hand-painted and hand-sleeved early LPs, released on Tokyo's Captain Trip Records, complete with enough crackles'n'hiss to remind you constantly that this was mastered from the kind of ancient vinyl that makes Robert Johnson sound digital. Tracks burst in then stop … then re-start. It's a punky meditation. Led by future Murahatchibu drummer 'Kant' Watanabe, ○△□ are part of an elite bunch of Shinjuku *futen* bands who actually made it on to record. By the mid-'70s, members Reck, Chiko Hige and Tôhchan had formed the Stooge-alike power trio 3/3. Thereafter, Reck formed the excellent No Wave band Friction, and even played bass for Lydia Lunch at the tail-end of Teenage Jesus & the Jerks. ○△□ 're-formed' in the early twenty-first century for a collaboration album with psychedelic oldies Marble Sheep. But like many so-called re-formations, the ○△□ line-up was a fudge, based around 'Kant' Watanabe and containing fifteen members where once there were only five. As the Shinjuku *futen* scene was such a 'you had to be there' thing anyway, I wish they'd left it alone.

49

Yonin Bayashi
ISHOKU-SOKUHATSU
(Tam 1974)

Somewhere between the Doors and Santana, the fuzzy soul of 3+3-period Isley Brothers, and the poppy English prog rock of Pete Banks-period early Yes and THE LEAST WE CAN DO IS WAVE TO EACH OTHER-period Van der Graaf Generator is this romantic, soul-influenced album ISHOKU-SOKUHATSU ('Dangerous Situation'). Occasionally detestable but frequently exquisite, the record's component parts are always righteous so long as these gentlemen get them in the correct order. From mock-Italian harmonies and bossanova rhythms, they'll thrust straight into pure Van der Graaf Generator as played by the first Alice Cooper band, then off into some American guitar-epic treks, perhaps with a 13/8 moment thrown in for good measure. This album is progressive pop music in a similar manner to that of solo Todd Rundgren or even the Zombies' experimental LP ODESSY & ORACLE [sic]. Okay, if your maiden aunt were to have designed a generic rock soundtrack for a movie about '70s prog youth, it most likely would have sounded just like this does. Nevertheless, side two's epic title track is killer once you get acclimatised to their cultural kleptomania. Moreover, they pull every trick in the book to lure you in there, mainly through keyboard player Hidemi Sakashita's wanton use of 'Riders on the Storm' electric-piano licks … oh, and his extravagant deployment of Mellotrons, Hammond organs and Minimoogs. Considerate bass player Shinichi Nakamura contributes only the most uber-obvious Ray Manzarek bass lines, while guitarist Katsutoshi Morizono's exhilaratingly generic rock axe certainly contributes masses to easing our egression into their sound. Hey, who's to say every band has to break barriers?

50

The Helpful Soul
FIRST ALBUM
(Victor 1969)

We're not here to praise this Helpful Soul album, it's shit. Who wants another quarter-of-an-hour of 'Spoonful'? No one. Who wants inept renditions of Hendrix's 'Fire'? Exactly. Which makes side one's closing song – the 10-minutes-and-33-seconds of 'Peace for Fools' – all the more remarkable; it's a strung-out slab of monolithic genius down there with anything on Blue Cheer's VINCEBUS ERUPTUM, or the Guess Who's appallingly gauche Doors rip-offs 'Friends of Mine' and 'Trucking off across the Sky'. 'Peace for Fools' is the kind of nihilistic tragedy that kicks Lost Aaraaff's black-clad dick into the dust, and makes Keiji Heino sound like he secretly cares! Junio Nakahara is the Fall's Mark Smith before he became a professional Northerner, you know that innocent time around 'Bingo Master's Breakout' before he became more cynical than Zappa? Yup, Nakahara is that guy, and his band are Luddites armed with pitchforks and sharpened shovels, punks from the American school at Kobe who grab anything to hand, even appropriating Kim Fowley's OUTRAGEOUS vocal delivery from the 'California Hayride' freak-out, propelling it along with the bass riff from 'In-a-Gadda-Da-Vida'; shameless errant genius on the slug-trail of the Doors' 'Five to One', the Chambers Brothers' 'Time Has Come Today', Funkadelic's 'I'll Bet You', anticipating Alice Cooper's LOVE IT TO DEATH-period proto-Jimbo doggerel by twenty-four months. Like some Too Perfect retro scam conjured up by latterday pranksters to cane our melted plastic brains, you expect to hear Burton Cumming's 'cocaine'n'morphine too, lots of shit to get you high'-rap oozing out. That this clod-plod is all the real deal is … unreal.

CLUNKERS, WHITE ELEPHANTS, ANOTHER MAN'S SAC: ALBUMS TO AVOID

In the cloistered world of record collectors and vinyl junkies, deadly rare foreign albums often become classed as classics merely because no one outside an elite few has even heard what goes on within the grooves let alone owns their own copy. For this reason, certain Japanese records of the late '60s and '70s have become collectable purely on account of the artist's past or future associations, or because of the desirable sleeve in which the record is housed. Here's an at-a-glance list of purported classics that are, in truth, anything but.

SHINKI CHEN & HIS FRIENDS (Polydor): Bloated boring sub-Clapton yawnothon touted as psychedelia by people who shelled out too much money on an original and need to feel better about having been ripped off.

Foodbrain's A SOCIAL GATHERING: Anti-social gathering, more like; this crock trawls the same depths as Ten Years After, with sub-Chick Churchill early-'60s keyboards and never a peep from Shinki Chen. Disastrous.

Kimio Mizutani's A PATH THROUGH HAZE: Sub-HOT RATS perfunctory solo LP from otherwise genius muso guitar God.

Jun Kamikubo's NOTHINGNESS: If this mid-tempo boozy blues is psychedelic, as some collectors claim, then gimme any late-period Robin Trower yawnothon with which to secure nirvana. Nothingness indeed.

BRUSH: This self-titled LP is so eclectic and wide-ranging in its styles that it manages to provide absolutely nothing for absolutely every-one. Worthless.

BIBLIOGRAPHY

Hans H. Baerwald
'Postwar Japan – A Reminiscence'
(Japan Policy Research Institute 2002)

Barry Bergstein
'Miles Davis and Karlheinz Stockhausen: a reciprocal relationship'
in *Musical Quarterly* 76, Number 4 (1992)

Peter Brown and Steven Gaines
The Love You Make
(Pan 1983)

Kelly Burnette
'Mikami Kan and the Language of the Japanese Blues'
(*Perfect Sound Forever* magazine 2002)

Ian Buruma
Inventing Japan: From Empire to Economic Miracle
(Weidenfeld & Nicolson 2003)

Amy Dempsey
Art in the Modern Era: A Guide to Styles, Schools & Movements
(Abrams 2002)

John Dower
Embracing Defeat: Japan in the Aftermath of World War II
(Norton 1999)

Yumi Goto
Those Days in Muramatsu
(Publication of the Center for East Asian Studies, University of Kansas)

Paul Griffiths
A Guide to Electronic Music
(Thames & Hudson 1979)

H. Wiley Hitchcock
Music in the United States: A Historical Introduction
(Englewood Cliffs 1974)

J. Hopkins
Yoko Ono
(Sidgwick & Jackson 1987)

Toshi Ichiyanagi
'Japanese Experimental Music of the 1960s: "Where Are We Going? And What Are We Doing?"'
(1997)

Marius Jansen
The Making of Modern Japan
(Harvard University Press 2000)

Toreno Kobayashi
'Shinki Chen Interview'
in *Black Shapes of Doom* magazine (2004)

Toreno Kobayashi
'Ikuzo Orita Interview'
in *Black Shapes of Doom* magazine (2004)

Yukiko Koshiro
Trans-Pacific Racisms and the US Occupation of Japan
(Columbia University Press 1999)

Yukiko Koshiro
Beyond an Alliance of Colour: The African American Impact on Modern Japan
(Duke University Press 2003)

Shigeku Kubota
'Hi Red Center' (information poster)
(Fluxus Publishing 1965)

Michael Kurtz
Stockhausen: A Biography
(Faber & Faber 1988)

Peter Manning
Electronic and Computer Music
(Oxford Press 1985)

Chris McLean,
**'Japanese psychedelic,
progressive, experimental
& heavy rock'**
(unpublished manuscript 2005)

Jonas Mekas
Film Culture (Expanded Arts issue)
No. 43 (NYC 1966)

Alexandra Monroe
Tadanori Yokoo: Be It All
(Heibonsha 1996)

Hideo Namba
Breaking out of the Prison of the Ego
(Heibonsha 1996)

Masahiro Nogami
Happy Snapshot Diary: Tokyo
(Blues Interactions 2000)

Yoko Ono
Onobox (notes)
(Rykodisc 1992)

Frank Popper
Art – Action & Participation
(New York University 1975)

Donald Ritchie
The Japan Journals 1947–2004
(Stone Bridge Press 2005)

Herbert Ruscol
*The Liberation of Sound:
An Introduction to Electronic Music*
(Englewood Cliffs 1972)

Glenn Sadin
'Made in Japan: Eleki & Group Sounds'
(Internet essay 2003)

Thomas Schultz
**'A Biographical Sketch
and Appreciation of Yuji Takahashi'**
(Internet essay 2003)

Yuji Takahashi
'The Life of the Composer'
(Internet essay 1996)

Paul Tingen
*Miles Beyond: The Electric Explorations of
Miles Davis 1967–1991*
(Billboard Books 2003)

Takeo Udagawa, Shizumitsu Tsuchiya,
Alex Mizuno, Toru Ueda, Tomisada Namura
*The World of J. A. Caesar:
Originator of Japanese Psychedelic
Culture, the Living Legend of
Tenjosajiki & Banyuinyoko*
(Byakuya Shobo 2002)

Balint Andras Varga
Conversations with Iannis Xenakis
(Faber & Faber 1996)

Jonathan Watts
**'Japanese Hijackers Go Home
After 32 Years on the Run'**
in the *Guardian*, 9th September 2002

INDEX

301

302

X

Y

Z

JULIAN COPE was born in Deri, South Glamorgan, and grew up in Tamworth. After forming a succession of half-groups and writing songs with Ian McCulloch (later of Echo & the Bunnymen), he eventually formed Teardrop Explodes with Gary Dwyer in 1978. He is the author of *Krautrocksampler*, *The Megalithic European*, *The Modern Antiquarian*, *Head-On* and *Repossessed*.

His website, www.headheritage.co.uk, contains some of the most entertaining and insightful album reviews on the web.

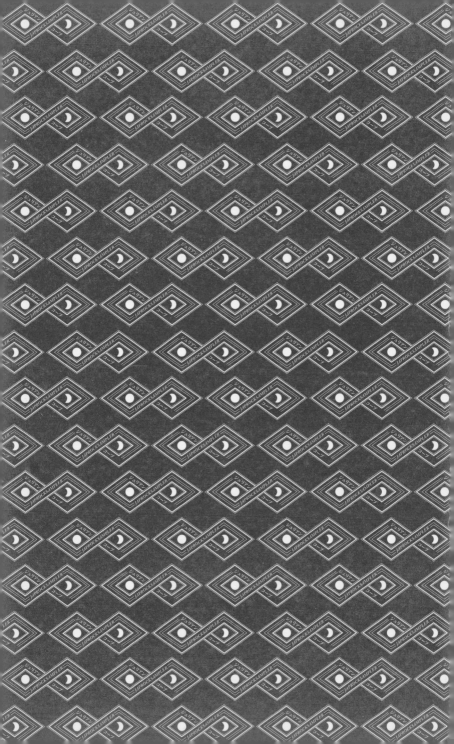